W9-BDN-319

To the Memory of
Dr. Martin Luther King, Jr.

THE AFRO-AMERICAN IN UNITED STATES HISTORY

Benjamin DaSilva
Principal
Danbury School System

Milton Finkelstein
Assistant Principal
New York City School System

Arlene Loshin
Teacher
Danbury School System

GENERAL EDITOR
Hon. Jawn A. Sandifer
Justice, Supreme Court of the State of
New York

THE AFRO-AMERICAN IN UNITED STATES HISTORY

Globe Book Company • New York, New York 10010

SECOND EDITION, 1972. This edition may be used
in the same classrooms with previous editions, without conflict
of any substantive kind.

Copyright © 1969 by Globe Book Company, Inc.
50 West 23rd Street, New York, N.Y. 10010

Published simultaneously in Canada by Globe/Modern Curriculum Press.

ISBN: 0-87065-520-5

Photographs in this text appear courtesy of the following:
American Museum of Natural History: page 18 top and bottom.
Judy Binder: page 338.
Chicago Historical Society: page 168.
Cincinnati Art Museum: page 128.
F.D.R. Library, Hyde Park, N.Y.: page 271.
The Granger Collection: pages 60, 62, 154, 187 top, middle and bottom, 189, 211.
Historical Picture Service—Chicago: page 103.
Library of Congress: pages 101, 199, 275, 366.
John W. Mott, City of Cleveland: page 446.
New York Public Library, Lincoln Center: page 373; Schomburg Collection: pages
    20, 31, 47, 59, 71, 78, 86, 114, 117, 125, 131, 142, 152, 157, 164, 165, 176,
    179, 201, 232, 234 left and right, 235, 245, 258, 260, 267, 296 top and bottom,
    298, 360, 362, 363, 365, 367, 375 top, 376, 377, 378 top, 391, 409, 410, 447,
    452, 453 top.
OEO: page 411.
Sidney W. Turner, Colonial Williamsburg: page 58.
UNATIONS: page 301.
UPI: pages 257, 436.
Wide World Photos: pages 27, 213, 214, 278, 282, 283, 295, 297, 311 top and bot-
    tom, 322, 326, 327, 334, 335, 340 left, middle and right, 350, 374, 375 bottom,
    378 bottom, 379 left and right, 384, 386, 387, 389 top and bottom, 397, 398,
    401, 402, 414, 421, 425, 426, 437, 449, 453 bottom.
Yale University Art Gallery, Mabel Brady Garven Collection: page 50.

Edited by Marilyn Z. Wilkes
Design by Mel Williamson
Illustrations by George Ford
Cartography by Milton Venezky

PRINTED IN THE UNITED STATES OF AMERICA   11 12 13 14 15

About The Authors

BENJAMIN DaSILVA brings to this book a broad background in both elementary and junior high school education. He is a specialist in social sciences, has published in the field of education and has extensive experience in teaching history and related subjects to students with learning difficulties. His long-standing involvement in the civil-rights movement includes an active role in improving the education of minority group children in Connecticut.

MILTON FINKELSTEIN is that rare historian who is equally at home engaged in scholarly research or dealing with the needs of the disadvantaged student. Dr. Finkelstein has spent more than twenty years teaching and supervising the instruction of disadvantaged students and is coauthor of two New York City curricula in social studies. He was a member of the Joint Committee on Common Learnings of the National Council of Social Studies and National Council of Teachers of English and has published more than two hundred works, including articles in leading educational magazines and several textbooks.

ARLENE LOSHIN is a reading and social studies teacher whose commitment to writing black history first bore fruit in a master's thesis on civil rights. An experienced educator who has taught special studies on the junior high school level, Mrs. Loshin has also worked in all areas of reading difficulties. She has been a leader in organized efforts to improve instruction for disadvantaged children in Danbury—one of the nation's most successful programs. Mrs. Loshin also served as a member of both the (Connecticut) Governor's Conference and (Danbury) Mayor's Conference on Human Rights and Opportunities.

JAWN A. SANDIFER is a Justice of the Supreme Court of the State of New York and has been a judge of the Civil Court of the City of New York. He is a former member of the Advisory Council of the New York State Department of Education. In a long career devoted to the rights of minority groups, he was New York State Legal Redress Chairman of the NAACP, Secretary of the HARYOU Poverty Program and a leading attorney appearing in civil rights cases before the courts of many states and before the United States Supreme Court.

ELFREDA S. WRIGHT, who reviewed the entire manuscript and tested chapters with pupils and teachers, is an Assistant Principal in the New York City School System. She has taught children on all grade levels and recently served as instructor in a course on human relations conducted by the New York City Board of Education.

This book could not have been completed without the invaluable assistance rendered by GEORGE BUNDY SMITH, who reviewed the entire manuscript and enriched it by his wide background in the civil rights movement. He is a former staff attorney for the NAACP Legal Defense and Educational Fund and is a member of the legal staff of the New York State Supreme Court.

The authors' thanks are also extended to MARILYN B. FINKELSTEIN for the countless hours she contributed as editorial secretary during the development of the manuscript.

Introduction

The part of our history of which Americans can be least proud is that dealing with the black American. For two and a half centuries, the great mass of black people in this country were victims of a brutal slavery. For over a hundred years since, black men have faced discrimination and segregation. Yet black Americans have struggled continuously to progress and have made countless major contributions to American civilization.

History books have not dealt honestly with the black man's situation in America. Often they have hidden or ignored the harsh treatment that was his lot. And, too often, Americans have accepted without challenge the story that the black man was well treated and satisfied. The contributions of black Americans have not been recognized. Many history books just never spoke of them. Others stated that blacks made no significant contributions. Few individuals took the trouble to find out what black Americans really have given our society.

This book was written for several important reasons. The time has come when the history, achievements and problems of black Americans must find their proper place in America's history. This is so not only because we want our history to be correct, but also because it is right. Moreover, all Americans, black and white, are seeking to learn what the past has done to our nation and what we must do in the future to remedy that past. Further, there is a need for accurate materials for the ever-growing number of "black studies" courses given in our schools.

The Afro-American in United States History is a historically accurate account of the black man's existence in America. Beginning with some of the great African civilizations of the past, it traces his history to the present day. Thus the book deals with slavery—its origins, growth, characteristics and eventual elimination. The book deals with contributions made by blacks in every war in which America has fought, including the War for Independence. It tells of the many contributions—scientific, cultural, political and economic—that black men and women have made. It describes the post-slavery period, during which a series of laws and prejudices hindered the progress of the black man. Finally, it deals with present-day problems, the efforts to find solutions to them and the different approaches to those solutions.

The book is divided into short chapters that can be easily read and understood. All important factors of the black American's existence are treated, so that the book can serve as a starting point for further effort if desired. The facts in the book have been gathered from long and painstaking research. Both the best available sources and considerable original research have been used to insure accuracy. The authors have cut through the historical errors and journalistic exaggerations that have characterized so much writing about black Americans. Also, they have distinguished fact from myth.

This editor has attempted in several ways to make the book a sound portrayal of the black man in our society. He has guided the selection of content and checked the accuracy of facts. He has assisted the authors in their search for sources and individuals to make the text more meaningful. And he has suggested and reviewed activities to bring the text alive for young people and encourage their participation in discussion.

This book attempts to correct certain inaccuracies in our history texts: that black people arrived here from Africa with no civilization, that they have contributed little or nothing to American society, that black Americans have been entirely satisfied with their status. The book seeks to face squarely the problems of the black man's existence in the United States. It seeks to stimulate open debate with the hope that out of such debate will come constructive attitudes and actions for the future. Although written primarily for young men and women, it has value for parents and other adults as well. They, too, need to know and appreciate the history of the black American.

Finally, this book is a lesson in building a democracy. To some it will set the record straight and demonstrate that they have had a hand in building our nation, have a stake in it and can make meaningful contributions. To others it will expose realities of which no nation can be proud. In so doing it will show how a nation failed to attain true equality and perhaps give students an idea of how to reverse that failure. To all it will give a sense of urgency to the black man's quest for justice and a recognition that democracy, if it is to prevail, must be assured by a struggle that must continue day by day.

JAWN A. SANDIFER

CONTENTS

Unit One

ROOTS IN AFRICA

Introduction

The long history of Africa has largely been forgotten by the rest of the world. Yet Africa may have been the first home of man. In it were found great civilizations and cultures. Its many kingdoms and tribes remained important in the history of the world for thousands of years. This unit tells about some of those kingdoms. It reviews the stories of Egypt, Kush and Ethiopia. It presents the history of the kingdoms of Ghana, Mali and Songhai. It describes the life of the tribes of Africa and gives the history of the powerful group called the Bantu.

Black people in the United States—and every other country in the Americas—can be called Afro-Americans. They had their roots in Africa. This unit describes the way they lived there. It tells about their ways of making a living, their many skills and some of the problems they faced. It also shows how West Africa became the center of a giant slave trade. This trade in time destroyed most of the tribes and kingdoms of Africa.

The slave trade became the largest business in the world. Tens of millions of men, women and children were taken from West Africa and brought to other lands. The greatest number of them came to the Americas. This unit tells of the terrible voyage slaves had to make across the Atlantic. You will see how they lived and worked in the New World. You will learn also that much of the wealth of the settlements in the Americas came from the work of slaves.

This unit raises the question of right and wrong. It shows how white Europeans refused to face that question as they built their fortunes from the evil slave trade. Over the years Africa was drained of its young people. The continent grew weaker and fell largely under foreign control.

Chapter 1

BEGINNINGS IN AFRICA

Let's Discover

1. How early Africans settled and used their land.
2. How life was lived in ancient Egypt.

Words to Know

ancient	The time in history from the beginning of written records until about 1,400 years ago.
	The king ruled with complete power in ancient times.
climate	The average weather in any place over a long period of time.
	The climate in the desert was hot and dry.
ancestor	A person who lived before others in a family line.
	My great-great-grandfather is one of my ancestors.
continent	One of the seven main land areas in the world.
	Africa is a continent.
irrigation	Bringing water to land through ditches.
	The people of Egypt used irrigation on their farms.
shadoof	A machine used to lift water to high ground.
	Egyptians were the first to use the shadoof.
conquer	To take control by force, as through war.
	The Egyptians were able to conquer other lands.
civilization	The stage in the life of a people when they have developed arts, science and government.
	Egyptian civilization was one of the greatest.
dynasty	A family of kings.
	King Menes began the first dynasty of Egypt.
pharaoh	The name used for the kings of ancient Egypt.
	Ikhnaton was a pharaoh.

1 / *A Beginning in Africa.* Where did man first appear? When? We do not have exact answers to such questions. The first men did not keep records. They did draw pictures on cave walls, and some of these have been found. They often buried their dead, and some graves have been found. They made some stone tools; a number of these have also been found. The oldest findings have been made in Africa and Asia. These places were the home of early man. Africa may have been the first home of men living in groups. We cannot be sure how long ago this was. It may have been as much as half a million years ago—perhaps even before then. One writer has said that Africa was "the father and mother of the whole world."

2 / *The Climate of Africa Changed.* Your ancestors are those who came before you in your family—parents, grandparents, great-grandparents and so on back into time. The ancestors of the people of Africa spread through that continent for thousands of years. They learned to make and use tools. They learned to plant crops. They settled in one place after another. Then, about eight thousand years ago, they saw the climate begin to change. The northern part of the continent became a green prairie—flat grasslands and farmland. Many trees grew in and near the mountains. There was plenty of water. Men could fish and hunt. They could raise herds of animals for food. But about three thousand years after that, the climate changed again. People saw their green land going dry. Less rain fell, and rivers began to dry up. The forests died. Much of the land turned into desert. Only

A hunter of early Africa.

a thin strip near the coast remained good farmland. People had to leave. They settled where water could help them keep on living as farmers.

3 / *The Nile River Valley*. Look at the map of Africa on page 7. Find the Nile River, which flows north from east central Africa to the Mediterranean Sea. When northern Africa began to turn into desert, this large river did not dry up. It began in a great lake to the south. This was an area that had much rain. Therefore the Nile River continued to flow. Large numbers of Africans settled along this river about six or seven thousand years ago. The river gave them a safe home, for there was little danger of attack along its banks. Any enemy would have to cross great deserts to get to the Nile Valley. The people in the valley farmed, raised animals and developed lasting forms of government. Some of these Nile Valley people had black skins; some had light skins. They lived together. They built towns. They set up temples to their gods; they made pottery and other goods that were needed. In such ways, they built one of the world's first great civilizations. A civilization is that stage in the life of a people when they have worked out ways of living together, governing themselves and passing on these ways of living and thinking to their children.

4 / *Early Egyptian Paintings*. The Nile Valley was the home of millions of people. They soon formed a country—the land we call Egypt. Its people were called Egyptians. They left many records of their life. Among these are the pictures they painted on rocks and cave walls. They mixed colors well, colors that have lasted in the dry desert air. Their pictures show that they saw themselves as black, white, reddish-brown and yellow. They left many records of their hunting of animals for food. We see that they had bows, arrows and spears, and that they used them well.

5 / *Egypt—Gift of the Nile*. Most of Egypt's people lived along the Nile, and for ten or twenty miles to each side of it. They depended on the river. Their land would have died without it. Each spring and summer, rains fell in the south for months. The river would begin to rise, and then it would flood. The people would move to the hills or desert until the flood passed. When they returned, there were new deposits of rich black soil on their land. This happened every year. The land was always good. Cotton, vegetables and wheat grew well. Fruit trees grew all year long. It was in Egypt that the first sailboats we know of were built—probably by fishermen. They trailed large nets to catch the fish so easily found in the river. Nearby, other men cared for great herds of cattle. Egypt, often called the "Gift of the Nile," was a rich land.

6 / *Irrigation in Egypt*. The people of Egypt worked out a new way to bring water to land that was some distance away from the river. We call such watering of land irrigation. The Egyptians made little dams along the edge of the flowing river. These dams pushed water into pools they prepared farther inland. From these pools they dug ditches into which the water would flow.

AFRICA

★ National capital

Miles
0   500   1000   1500

These ditches went deep into nearby farmland. There the farmers used a machine called a shadoof to lift water from a ditch to the farmland above it. The shadoof had a bucket attached to the end of a pole. The bucket would be dipped into the water. When it was raised, the water could be poured on the higher ground. The shadoof, or a machine like it, is still being used today. Irrigation was of great help in growing the crops in ancient Egypt.

7 / Egypt Became a United Kingdom. The people of Egypt made good use of their land. They used the plow to turn their soil. They used irrigation wisely. They made many of the same tools we use today. They began to use metals. They also developed into a single country. At first a different chief had been in charge of each of the many sections along the river. Then some of these chiefs grew more powerful than others. Finally two such rulers came to control the parts of the land called Upper Egypt (the south) and Lower Egypt (the north). About 5,000 years ago (most dates of things that happened so long ago cannot be exact), Menes became the ruler of both parts of Egypt. First he became the ruler of Upper Egypt. Then he was able to conquer Lower Egypt. From that time on, Egypt was a single kingdom. Menes made the city of

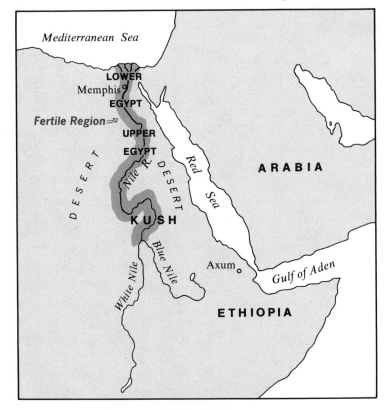

Lands of the Nile

Farmers used a shadoof to water their crops.

Memphis his capital. This city was near Cairo, the capital of Egypt today.

8 / *Government in the Ancient World.* Students of history divide the thousands of years they study into time periods. They call the years until about 1,400 years ago Ancient Times. In most of the world during these years, people were ruled by kings who had complete power. These kings gained power in one of two ways. Sometimes they were soldiers who took control of their country. More often, they were the sons of men who had been kings before them. A family would gain power in a country and would keep it for perhaps hundreds of years. We call such a family of kings a dynasty. Egypt had thirty dynasties in the 2,700 years after Menes. The Egyptian king ruled from a great palace in the capital city. He was called pharaoh (which means "great house"). In Egypt the king was the head of the country and also the head of its religion. To most of the people, the pharaoh was also a god. With his priests and soldiers, he ruled in any way he wished. At his orders, men became slaves or could be killed. The people of Egypt never had the kind of rights people work for today.

9 / *The Kingdom of Kush.* About 4,000 years ago the rulers of Egypt began to spread their power. They conquered nearby lands to the south. One of the countries south of them in the Nile Valley was called Kush. Its people lived in the area we now call the Sudan. These were dark-skinned people who had an advanced civilization. Egypt conquered Kush and made some of its people slaves. Still, the people of Kush were able to keep some of their self-rule by paying large taxes and giving the pharaoh men for his armies. After about 500 years, Egypt lost some of its power. The Kushites again took full control of their kingdom. Later Egypt grew even weaker. The Kushites then conquered much of Egypt for a time. The ancient Greeks, who wrote the

first histories, spoke about Kush. They called its people "Aithiops," which means dark-skinned people.

10 / Ikhnaton and Nefertiti. Throughout the history of Egypt its dark-skinned people were important. From Kush came the soldiers called Nubians. Ikhnaton, the pharaoh about 3,300 years ago, married one of his black subjects, the famous Queen Nefertiti. She and her husband tried to make a great change in the life of their country. Ikhnaton ordered his people to worship only one god —Aton, the sun. This was the first time any people had turned to the worship of one god. The attempt failed, and Egypt returned to its worship of many gods. Nefertiti is today one of the best known of all Egyptian queens because of her beauty. Copies of a limestone sculpture of her head are in museums all over the world.

11 / The End of Egypt's Power. Egypt was conquered several times by people from Asia who used horses to cross the desert and iron weapons to win their battles. The pharoahs lost their great power about 2,500 years ago. Yet they had done much to build the world that was to follow them. Their country brought the world the sail and the plow, irrigation and organized government, and the beginnings of science. In all this, black Africa played an important role. One Greek historian, describing the Egyptians, called them "black and curly-haired." The many peoples of ancient Egypt, both black and white, made it for over two thousand years the most powerful land in Africa.

Ikhnaton and Queen Nefertiti.

Understanding What You Have Read

I. REVIEWING WORD MEANINGS

Write the letter of the choice that best explains the meaning of each word.

1. A shadoof is a (a) chief, (b) place, (c) machine.
2. When you irrigate land, you bring it (a) water, (b) buildings, (c) money.
3. Of the following, the person who is one of your ancestors is your (a) father, (b) sister, (c) child.
4. A dynasty is (a) any family, (b) a family of kings, (c) a family that knows its ancestors.
5. The only one of the following that is a continent is (a) Egypt, (b) Kush, (c) Africa.
6. A pharaoh was a (a) king, (b) farmer, (c) house.
7. A country that has been conquered has lost its (a) people, (b) freedom, (c) farmland.
8. The climate of Egypt in ancient times was (a) hot and rainy, (b) cold and windy, (c) hot and dry.
9. The more ancient a thing is, (a) the newer it is, (b) the older it is, (c) the better it is.
10. A civilized country always has a (a) king, (b) government, (c) good climate.

II. UNDERSTANDING MAIN IDEAS

Write the letter of the choice that best completes each statement.

1. Of these continents, the one in which man probably lived first is (a) North America, (b) Africa, (c) Europe.
2. The part of Africa in which the climate changed from wet to dry was (a) the south, (b) the north, (c) the west.
3. The one of these who had the *least* power in ancient Egypt was the (a) farmer, (b) chief, (c) pharaoh.

4. We know that early Egypt contained many black-skinned people from the (a) cave paintings, (b) stories written by travelers from Kush, (c) letters left by Queen Nefertiti.

5. The Nile River gave the people of Egypt (a) water and food, (b) protection from other countries, (c) an easy route to Asia.

6. The man who would most need a shadoof would be a (a) tax collector, (b) soldier, (c) farmer.

7. Most rulers in the ancient world (a) had little power, (b) had as much power as their people allowed, (c) had complete power.

8. An army of Nubians was made up of (a) Egyptians, (b) black-skinned soldiers from south of Egypt, (c) Asian fighters.

9. Ikhnaton and Nefertiti are best remembered for the changes they tried to bring in (a) religion, (b) marriage laws, (c) army rules.

10. Egypt lost its power chiefly because (a) it did not use its farmland wisely, (b) its armies were defeated, (c) its pharaohs did not have enough power within Egypt.

III. REMEMBERING IMPORTANT FACTS

Write the number of the paragraph in which each of these facts is found. You can look back to find your answers.

1. Shadoofs were used to lift water.
2. There was once plenty of water in the parts of northern Africa that are desert today.
3. Kush was a black kingdom in the area now called the Sudan.
4. One of the queens of Egypt, Nefertiti, was a black African.
5. Africa has been called "the father and mother of the whole world."
6. The Nile River begins in a lake south of Egypt.
7. Egypt had thirty dynasties in about 2,700 years.
8. Menes united Upper and Lower Egypt.
9. The Egyptians were the first to use the sail.

10. Egyptian cave paintings tell us that some of the people of that country were black.

IV. ANSWER EACH OF THE FOLLOWING QUESTIONS WITH A COMPLETE SENTENCE.

1. How do we know that men lived in Africa about half a million years ago or earlier?
2. Why did people living in northern Africa about five thousand years ago have to move away?
3. How do we know that the early Egyptians used bows and arrows?
4. Why is Egypt called the "Gift of the Nile"?
5. How was Menes important in the history of Egypt?
6. How much power did the pharaohs of Egypt have?
7. How did Ikhnaton try to change Egypt's religion?

V. THINGS TO DO

1. Use an encyclopedia to find the answer to one of these questions. Report your findings to your class.
   a. How did the Egyptians dress?
   b. What kinds of weapons did the Egyptians make and use?
   c. Describe one of the battles in which Nubian troops were important.
   d. What is archaeology? How is it important in our study of Egypt and other ancient countries?
2. Work alone or with a committee to do one of the following art projects.
   a. Draw a group of pictures showing life on a Nile Valley farm.
   b. Draw pictures of an Egyptian temple; an Egyptian chariot; a Nubian soldier in battle dress; an ancient sailboat; a group of Egyptian slaves building a road.

c. Use a large project map of Africa. On it color and label
the following places: Egypt, the Nile River, Kush, the city of
Memphis, the Sahara Desert, the Red Sea, the Gulf of Aden,
the Mediterranean Sea, the Atlantic Ocean and the Indian
Ocean.

Chapter 2 / TRIBAL AFRICA

Let's Discover

1. How tribes lived in Africa about 1,000 years ago.
2. How the Bantu tribe lived in southern Africa.
3. What the way of life called feudalism was like.

Words to Know

chief	The person chosen to lead a group of people.
	The chief of the tribe had great control over his subjects.
Bantu	The name of a tribe of people who settled in southern Africa.
	The Bantu were a large and powerful tribe.
Rhodesia	A country in southern Africa.
	The Bantu tribe lived in Rhodesia.
feudalism	A way of life in which men gave service to other men in return for protection.
	Under feudalism, some men had few rights.
vassal	Under feudalism, a person who was given land by a more powerful person and in return did service for that person.
	The village chief was a vassal to the king.
serfs	The lowest group under feudalism—farm workers or herdsmen who had to stay in the village in which they worked.
	The serfs were bound to the land.
craftsman	A skilled worker.
	The shoemaker was a fine craftsman.
Rozwi	The ruling group of the Bantu tribe.
	The Rozwi were the lords of each Bantu village.

1 / *Kingdoms and Tribes*. We have seen that Egypt was a great kingdom. There were many kingdoms in ancient times. Each had a large number of people living under a single government. But not all of the people of Africa lived in kingdoms. Africa is large —much larger than North America. Huge parts of this continent held only small numbers of people. There might be only a few thousand living in a forest or jungle, or near a desert. These people might live in one village or in a group of them. They would not travel much, or have much contact with other groups living many miles away. Such small groups are called tribes.

2 / *How Tribes Developed*. Students of the history of man have learned a great deal about how men organized their lives in groups. There are some parts of the world where people live in very small groups of fifty or fewer, all related to one another. These small groups may remain in the forest where they hunt and gather fruits and nuts. Or they may have learned how to plant crops and raise herds of animals. Many more people can live in one place when farming gives them a steady food supply. Such a group, which might have thousands of people, develops its own rules. It sets up a government, usually under a chief. All of the people in the group or tribe speak the same language. They follow the same religion. They share their tribe's name and follow the same ways of living.

3 / *Life in a Tribe*. There were many tribes in the lands south of ancient Egypt. How did the people of a tribe live? There were many differences from one tribe to another, but certain things were usually the same. Some of the people of the tribe took care of the fields and raised the crops. Others cared for the animals. At first these Africans made their tools and weapons of stone, bone and wood. Then, about two thousand years ago, they learned how to take metals from the earth. From that time on, they made their tools and weapons out of these metals. Clay was used to make pottery and many kinds of containers. Each tribe tried to make all that it needed. However, just as no modern country can get along without trade with

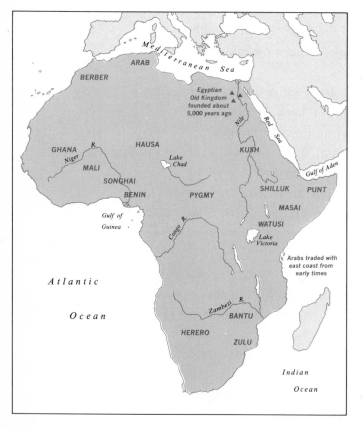

Tribes of Africa

other countries, the tribes of ancient Africa also had to trade to get some of the things they needed.

4 / *The Bantu Tribe*. One of the African tribes that grew large and important about 1,000 years ago was called the Bantu. Their skins were black. In time there were so many of the Bantu people that they split into many tribes, all related. Most of the Bantu lived in the region of southern Africa now known as Rhodesia. There had been too many people living in the north and northwest, so the Bantu left and went south to find fresh land and room in which to live. For about six hundred years the Bantu lived in and ruled the new lands they had found.

5 / *Life Among the Bantu*. There were a few very rich and powerful people among the Bantu. They held most of the power. They also held most of the wealth. The herds of animals belonged to them. Other people worked their land. One of these rich and powerful people was chosen to be chief of the tribe, usually for life. He and the other

important men of the tribe promised to protect the rest of the people from any enemy who might attack them. In return for this protection, the poorer people had to agree to fight for their chief. The Bantu may be divided into three groups. First were the rich and powerful. They led the people, became the rulers and religious leaders and controlled the armies. Only this rich group had time for study, poetry and "fine manners." The second group were the farmers and soldiers. They were closest to the ruling

Cattle meant wealth to the Bantu.

group, and worked with and for them. The third group was the lowest and poorest. These were the workers who did whatever the higher groups ordered them to do. They were not really free, but had to do what they were told in return for the right to remain safe within the tribe.

6 / *The Way of Life Called Feudalism*. We call this way of life the feudal system. Most people in Europe and Asia, as well as those in most of Africa, lived under this system about 1,000 years ago. A small group ruled. Those who were next in power, and who had to obey the small ruling group, were called vassals. Some of them owned land; some were only soldiers. They all knew they had to fight for the chief or lord who ruled over them. The vassals in turn held power over the common people. These lowest members of the group were called serfs or

These "kitchen" knives have carved bone handles and metal blades.

Bronze sculpture shows a chief attended by musicians and members of his court.

servants in Europe. They were bound to the land they farmed. This meant that they were not allowed to leave it. If they tried to leave, they were caught and punished by their lords. Each person's place was fixed by law or custom. No man or woman could make any great change in the way he or she lived. Feudalism was the way of life among the tribes of Africa and among the peoples of most of the rest of the world.

7 / *Differences in African Feudalism*. The kind of feudalism found among the Bantus was a little freer than that found in Europe and Asia. There was a greater chance for a person to improve himself. If he could fight well, he might become a leading soldier instead of remaining a serf. If he became a good ironworker or some other kind of craftsman, he might be honored for that ability and gain greater wealth. In much of Europe it was not permitted to marry some-

In a Bantu marketplace.

one of a higher class. The Bantu allowed this. In their kind of feudalism, although a person had to follow the rules set by the chief and lords, he always knew that there were ways in which he could better himself if he tried.

8 / *The Rise and Fall of the Bantu.* The Bantu settled in southern Rhodesia and soon gained control of it. Their rulers were called the Rozwi. These men were the lords and chiefs. The Bantu thought of themselves as one great tribe, but each village had its own chief. Some of the chiefs had enough

men and enough ability to rule over several villages. The Rozwi found much wealth in Rhodesia. The farmland was good. Villages were well able to feed themselves. Some even had enough food to trade with other villages. There was gold in southern Rhodesia. The leaders of the Bantu learned how to mine it. Soon traders from other lands learned of this gold and were ready to trade for it. Trade routes to and across the Indian Ocean were developed. Perhaps it was this trade in gold that in the end destroyed the Bantu. They had become very powerful, but they were still a people who used simple

A typical tribal village.

weapons—bows, arrows and spears. In time some chiefs became kings who ruled over tens of thousands of people in hundreds of villages. A Bantu kingdom had come into being. Then, in 1628, at the same time that English Pilgrims and others were building their settlements in America, the Portuguese came to Africa with their great ships and armies and guns. They soon conquered the Bantu lands. After 600 years of power, the tribes fell under European control.

Understanding What You Have Read

I. UNDERSTANDING WORD MEANINGS

Write the letter of the choice that best completes each statement.

1. No man should be a chief unless he is a good (a) leader, (b) farmer, (c) hunter.
2. The members of the Bantu tribe moved to (a) Egypt, (b) Kush, (c) southern Africa.
3. The farthest south of the following places is (a) Kush, (b) Rhodesia, (c) Egypt.
4. A craftsman might be able to (a) carve jewelry out of ivory, (b) sail a fishing boat, (c) care for a herd of animals.

5. A serf was not allowed to (a) farm land, (b) leave his village to live somewhere else, (c) get married.

6. In a Bantu village, a member of the Rozwi would be most likely to (a) own land, (b) work for other villagers, (c) care for animals.

7. The king might give land to his (a) vassals, (b) serfs, (c) tribes.

8. Under feudalism, each person (a) had equal rights, (b) held power over some serfs, (c) knew his position in the tribe.

II. UNDERSTANDING MAIN IDEAS

Write the letter of the choice that best completes each statement.

1. People had few rights in ancient times. This helps us understand why (a) tribes were organized, (b) life did not change much from year to year, (c) kings had armies.

2. Early Africa was divided among the tribes. This gave each member of the tribe greater (a) safety, (b) wealth, (c) land to farm.

3. Each tribe tried to make all the things it needed. This meant that trade was (a) very important, (b) not very important, (c) not allowed.

4. The Bantu was one of many tribes in Africa. This means that (a) all of Africa was ruled by tribes and their chiefs, (b) there were other important tribes in Africa, (c) the Bantu ruled over thousands of villages.

5. Life among the Bantu followed the system we call feudalism. This means that (a) a small group of people held most of the power, (b) kings were chosen each year by the people, (c) each village made whatever rules it wanted.

6. Each Bantu village had its soldiers or warriors. These men were needed to (a) punish the people who did not farm well, (b) protect the village from its enemies, (c) fight against the Rozwi.

7. Each person's place in the Bantu tribe was fixed by law or

custom. This meant that a serf was expected to (a) try to become a Rozwi, (b) become a wealthy man by hard work, (c) remain a serf.

8. Suppose a certain Bantu village found deposits of iron nearby. You would expect that village to (a) trade more than other villages, (b) build an army to conquer the rest of the Bantu tribe, (c) share its wealth among all its people.

9. In its later years, the Bantu tribe became a kingdom. This shows that (a) feudalism had failed to control the people, (b) one feudal lord had become stronger than others, (c) the Rozwi had lost their power in the villages.

10. The Bantu were conquered by the Portuguese in 1628. This was about the same time as the (a) American Revolution, (b) invention of gunpowder, (c) first settlements in what is now the United States.

III. REMEMBERING IMPORTANT FACTS

Write the numbers 1 through 10 on your paper. After each number, write the letter A if the statement tells you how the Bantu made a living. Write the letter B if the statement tells you how the Bantu were governed. Write the letter C if the statement tells you about daily life in the Bantu villages.

1. After hundreds of years as a tribe, the Bantu became a kingdom.
2. Bantu farmers made use of the plow.
3. The black-skinned Bantu followed the ideas of feudalism.
4. The Rozwi controlled the Bantu villages.
5. Each Bantu family lived in its own grass or wooden house.
6. In most Bantu villages, the chief held his power for life.
7. Herdsmen were important in each Bantu village.
8. Each Bantu was able to marry any other Bantu.
9. Pottery makers gave the Bantu the containers they needed.
10. Each member of the Bantu tribe was ordered to remain part of his village.

IV. ANSWER EACH OF THE FOLLOWING QUESTIONS WITH
A COMPLETE SENTENCE.

1. Why was trade necessary among the Bantu villages?
2. Why can more people live in a farm village than in a village
that lives only by hunting and gathering fruits and nuts?
3. How did the finding of gold by the Bantu help destroy their
kingdom?
4. How did the use of metal for tools improve farming for the
Bantu?
5. In what area of Africa did the Bantu settle and grow powerful?
6. Why had the Bantu moved from the north to the south?
7. Why did the serfs make up the largest part of the Bantu people?
8. Why is there little change in the way people live under a feudal
system?
9. Why do we say that a people with fine craftsmen has a more
advanced civilization than a people without such craftsmen?
10. How is a vassal different from a serf?

V. THINGS TO DO

1. Use each of the following questions as the beginning of a class
discussion:
a. How does a tribe become a nation?
b. What is the difference between a nation and an empire?
c. How does foreign trade help a nation? How did it help or
harm the Bantu?
d. Why did most African nations make slaves of those they
captured in war?
2. Understanding Currents in History:
a. We have few records of Bantu life. But we have detailed
records of life in Europe during the 600 years of the Bantu
period discussed in this chapter. Explain possible reasons
for this.
b. Portugal, a small country, was able to defeat the great

armies of the Bantu empire. Explain how this was possible.

3. **Special Activities:**

    a. Fill in the facts to complete this chart.

GROUP	NUMBER OF PEOPLE IT PROBABLY CONTAINED
1. Forest Family	1. _____
2. Tribe	2. _____
3. Bantu Nation	3. _____

    b. Ask your school librarian to help you find a book about life in the Middle Ages, the time of feudalism in Europe. Then prepare a one-page report on a day in the life of a serf.

    c. Here is an activity that can continue for all the time that you work with this book. Prepare a set of index cards. On one side of each, write one of the vocabulary words at the beginning of a chapter. Write the meaning of the word on the other side of the card. Use these cards to review word meanings.

    d. Arrange the five sentences listed below in proper order. The one that happened first should be first; the one that happened last should be last. Look back at the chapter to check your listing.

        1. The Portuguese conquered the Bantus in 1628.
        2. The Bantu tribes became a kingdom.
        3. Gold was found in the Bantu lands.
        4. The Bantu traded with other peoples across the Indian Ocean.
        5. The Rozwi gained power in each Bantu village.

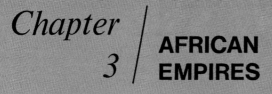

Chapter 3 | AFRICAN EMPIRES

Let's Discover

1. How four great African empires developed.
2. How people lived in these empires.
3 What happened to each of these empires.

Words to Know

empire
Several countries ruled over by one country, and whose ruler calls himself emperor.
The rulers of Mali conquered other lands and built an empire.

culture
The way of life of a people.
Interest in art and music is part of our culture.

Axum
The capital of ancient Ethiopia.
The city of Axum was in the northern part of Ethiopia.

The ancient city of Timbuktu.

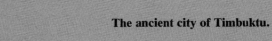

Ghana	A country in West Africa.
	One thousand years ago Ghana was the most powerful nation in West Africa.
Sahara	The name of the great desert across much of North Africa.
	Trade routes crossed the sands of the Sahara Desert.
Mandingo	A group of tribes in West Africa.
	The Mandingo people formed a powerful empire.
Muslim	The religion, believing in one god, begun by Mohammed in Arabia after 622 and today followed by almost 500 million people.
	Many Africans, black and white, follow the Muslim religion.
Mali	An ancient empire in West Africa, and the name of an African country today.
	Mali defeated Ghana.
Songhai	An ancient empire in West Africa.
	Songhai defeated Mali.
Timbuktu	A city in ancient Africa best known for its wealth and schools.
	Timbuktu had a fine university.

---

1 / *The Oldest Black Kingdom.* The story of the eastern African land called Ethiopia goes back to the early days of Egypt. This is more than five thousand years ago. Some of Ethiopia's people had come from Kush. Others came from Arabia. About three thousand years ago all its tribes fell under the rule of Menelik—the first of a long line of kings. Since that time Ethiopia has been an independent land ruled by an emperor. It is still so today. Ethiopia's many tribes have had to follow the rules of their kings.

Sometimes they fought against this strict rule. As time passed they grew to accept their kings. Yet the people of Ethiopia have remained proud. They are still a tribal people, except for those living in the country's few towns and cities.

2 / *Ethiopia Grew Rich.* The word *culture* describes the way of life of any people. It includes their thoughts and their skills. It includes their arts and their tools. The people of Ethiopia had an advanced culture.

This was true even two thousand years ago. Axum was their capital city. It was so rich that the people of the country were often called Axumites. From this city they sent traders to other parts of East Africa. They sent their goods north to Egypt too. They built ships for travel and trade across the Indian Ocean to India, Persia and Arabia. From Axum came gold, ivory and animal hides. To it came cloth and other goods. The tribe that settled in and near Axum was very successful. It grew into a powerful country—Ethiopia.

3 / *The Power of the King.* Ethiopia was one of the first countries in the world to become Christian. This happened about the year 300. This was before most of Europe had accepted the new religion. However, the king of Ethiopia held complete power over his people. They had to become Christians when he did. In 531 a visitor told of the great wealth of the Ethiopian king. He saw "the King . . . dressed in a linen garment woven with gold and set with pearls." The king's throne was a chariot covered with gold paint. It was drawn by four elephants. Such wealth and power continued, even though there were times when kings were weakened by war or problems with other countries. Ethiopia was a feudal land. The king held full power over his vassals. These men, proud nobles, ruled in each district. They kept the people under tight control. In these ways life was much the same as it was in the kingdoms of Europe.

4 / *Black Empires in West Africa.* Look at the map on page 29. It shows you where

Emperor Haile Selassie of Ethiopia.

three great African kingdoms were found. The first of these grew important about 1,200 years ago. It was named Ghana. The second, Mali, came to power about 800 years ago. The third was Songhai, or Songhay. It took Mali's place as the strongest West African nation 600 years ago. The coming of Europeans 200 years later, about 1600, meant the end of this last great West African power. Yet the story of these three kingdoms, all ruled and peopled by black men, has almost been lost in history. Most of the records we have of Ghana, Mali and Songhai were left by Arabs who traded or lived in these lands.

5 / *The People of Ghana and Their Government.* We know much of what happened in Ghana back to about the year 200. Its people were at first a weak tribe. We know that they found iron. They soon learned how to work with it. This meant that they had swords and spears made of iron. This

An Ethiopian caravan.

made them stronger than their neighbors. The number of people in their tribe grew. The tribe slowly became a country. A king was chosen to rule. He and his vassals built up a strong army. Laws were passed and courts were set up. After hundreds of years, Ghana became a large, strong kingdom. Its king ruled over thousands of villages in West Africa.

6 / Ghana—Center of Trade and Power. Ghana lived largely by trade. Its people needed salt. They could trade for it with people living near the Sahara Desert. The kings of Ghana began to work gold mines in their land. They soon had plenty of gold. They traded this gold for the salt they needed. The men who carried on this trade had to pay high taxes. Wealth from such taxes, and from the sale of gold, helped keep the king and his vassals in power. Gold made Ghana strong. It also made other

peoples want its wealth. By 1060 Ghana was under attack by powerful neighbors. It is said that a king of Ghana once raised an army of 200,000 men—then the largest army in the world. But by 1180 the kings of Ghana no longer had such power. The armies of the country were destroyed in battle. Koumbi, the capital, lay in ruins. The Mandingo were a group of tribes who had set up a nation called Mali. The armies of Mali swept through Ghana and took its lands and wealth. The empire of Ghana came to its end.

7 / Mali Rules in West Africa. The kings of Ghana and their vassals had many slaves. Most of these men, women and children had been captured in war. Then Ghana was conquered. Many of its own people were made slaves by the new masters of the land, the Mandingo tribes. Mali, the new nation, was even larger than Ghana had been. It reached from the Atlantic Ocean to the Niger River. It went north to the Sahara Desert. The rulers of Mali were Muslims. They followed the new religion that had swept out of Arabia and across Africa. Sundiata had been their first great ruler. Their most important king, Mansa Musa, gained world fame when he made the journey to Mecca in Arabia. Each Muslim is expected to make it at least once in his lifetime. Mansa Musa is said to have taken sixty thousand people with him, as well as five hundred slaves! He spent more than a hundred camel-loads of gold on this holy trip. Perhaps such wild spending by its kings was one reason for the fall of Mali. It was, for a while, one of the world's great trading nations. It was in turn conquered by one of its neighbors, the kingdom of Songhai.

8 / *Songhai Rules in West Africa.* Songhai had been a small kingdom along the Niger River east of Ghana and Mali. This river was much like the Nile. It flooded each year. It left the soil rich when the flood ended. The people who lived along the Niger had plenty of food. Farming was good. Hunting and fishing were easy. The number of people grew. They moved up the Niger Valley. Soon they reached the lands of Mali. By 1300 Mali had grown weaker. Its kings did not rule well; each chief tried to make his own part of the country into a tiny kingdom. The people of Songhai were more united. They pushed into Mali's lands. Wars followed. The Sunni dynasty of Songhai, from their capital city of Gao, planned and won battle after battle. The Songhai conquered Mali. By the 1470's, at the time when

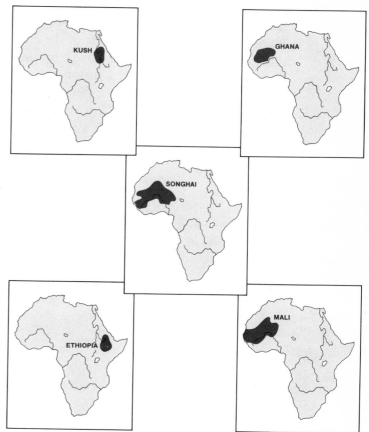

African Empires

Christopher Columbus was a young sailor in Italy, Songhai had become the largest and richest country in Africa. Among its great cities was Timbuktu, center of learning and trade for much of the Muslim world.

9 / *Life in Timbuktu.* This city was best known for its many schools. Men and boys lived and studied in these schools and in

the great university there. Writers have left many records of Timbuktu. They tell of large stone palaces. They describe the busy trade to West Africa and the rest of the continent. They speak of many active libraries. Here men studied books on history, medicine, astronomy and poetry. Sunni Ali, the Songhai king who first took Timbuktu, had destroyed much of the city. A king named Askia gained power after Sunni Ali died. He did much to rebuild the city of learning. Askia ruled strongly and well for more than forty years. After his death the Songhai Empire began to weaken. Countries to the north attacked with guns. They soon cut Songhai to pieces. Timbuktu became a little desert town, important only in memory. The days of the great black kingdoms of West Africa were over.

10 / *The Black Empires of West Africa in History.* Each of the kingdoms we have studied began as a small tribe. In each case, the tribe grew. It gained control of the lands near it. It came under the rule of a strong king. This king then led his people to greater power. All of these were black kingdoms ruled by black men. These kingdoms had advanced cultures. They traded with other lands just as countries do today. In each of these lands, people with many skills worked to keep their country strong. Fine craftsmen helped the people meet their daily needs. They worked in stone and clay. They made and worked metals. But the picture had its sad parts too. These African peoples were like most of the world around them. They were often cruel to one another. They lived in a feudal world, made more cruel by widespread slavery. When the last of these African empires had ended, a terrible new time faced the people of that part of the world. The men with chains were coming.

African craftsmen made metals.

Understanding What You Have Read

I. REVIEWING WORD MEANINGS

Write the letter of the choice that best completes each statement.

1. If a man calls himself an emperor he probably rules over (a) a single city, (b) a single country, (c) more than one country.
2. If you were a student of culture you would be most interested in a country's (a) trade, (b) writings, (c) size.
3. A trader from Axum would be a citizen of (a) Ghana, (b) Ethiopia, (c) Mali.
4. The country farthest west was (a) Egypt, (b) Ghana, (c) Ethiopia.
5. If you traveled north from Ghana you would come to (a) Egypt, (b) the Sahara Desert, (c) the Niger River.
6. The word Mandingo describes a (a) river, (b) country, (c) group of tribes.
7. If a person is a Muslim leader then we know his (a) country, (b) language, (c) religion.
8. The story of Mali is part of the story of (a) South Africa, (b) West Africa, (c) East Africa.
9. If you were a member of a tribe that began on the Niger River, and then pushed west toward the Atlantic, you would most probably be from (a) Songhai, (b) Ethiopia, (c) Ghana.
10. A person traveling to Timbuktu would be going to a (a) city, (b) large lake, (c) mountain.

An ancient mosque, or temple, at Timbuktu.

II. UNDERSTANDING IMPORTANT IDEAS

Write the name of the country that is described in each of the sentences below. You can list a country more than once.

1. The people of this land began as a tribe that settled near Axum.
2. Sunni Ali and Askia made this country strong.
3. This was the first country in West Africa to develop gold mines.
4. Rulers like Mansa Musa spent the wealth of this country.
5. Timbuktu, in its last days as a great city, was part of this country.
6. This is the oldest black kingdom in the world today.
7. The ruler of this country once took 60,000 people with him on a holy voyage to Arabia.
8. This was one of the first countries in the world to become Christian.
9. This country became known to the rest of Africa as one ready to trade gold for salt.
10. This country was destroyed by countries to the north who used guns.

III. WHICH CAME FIRST?

Write the letter of the event in each pair that happened first. Look back in the chapter to check your answers.

1. a. Sunni Ali destroyed Timbuktu.
   b. Menelik made himself emperor of Ethiopia.
2. a. Ghana was defeated by Mali.
   b. Songhai gained control of West Africa.
3. a. The city of Koumbi was ruined in a war.
   b. The Songhai Empire ended.
4. a. Askia became ruler of Songhai.
   b. Ethiopians built ships to trade with India.
5. a. Mali was attacked by Songhai.
   b. A West African tribe began the country called Ghana.

IV. UNDERSTANDING OTHER PEOPLES

Write the letter of the choice that best completes each statement.

1. The people of Ethiopia today (a) accept their king's power, (b) demand the same rights people want in the United States, (c) have moved to large cities where they have fuller rights.

2. The people of Ghana had to turn to trade because (a) they could not grow the food they needed, (b) they did not have enough salt, (c) their king sold their crops for gold.

3. Each of the empires we have studied in this chapter (a) allowed slavery, (b) gave freedom to those it conquered, (c) did not believe in war.

4. The story of the black empires in this chapter shows us that the people of Africa (a) follow the same religion, (b) follow different religions, (c) follow no religion.

5. All of the peoples studied in this chapter lived under the system we call (a) democracy, (b) independent tribes, (c) feudalism.

V. ANSWER EACH OF THE FOLLOWING QUESTIONS IN A COMPLETE SENTENCE.

1. What products did the traders of Ethiopia take to other lands?

2. How did the use of iron help make Ghana powerful?

3. Why was Timbuktu an important city?

4. How did one country replace another as the most powerful nation in West Africa?

5. Why were the people of Ethiopia once called Axumites?

6. How did the need for salt change the history of Ghana?

7. What was the usual way in which a person became a slave in the empires of West Africa?

8. How do we know the story of life in Timbuktu?

9. How was the Niger Valley similar to the Nile Valley?

10. Why did the people of Ethiopia become Christians?

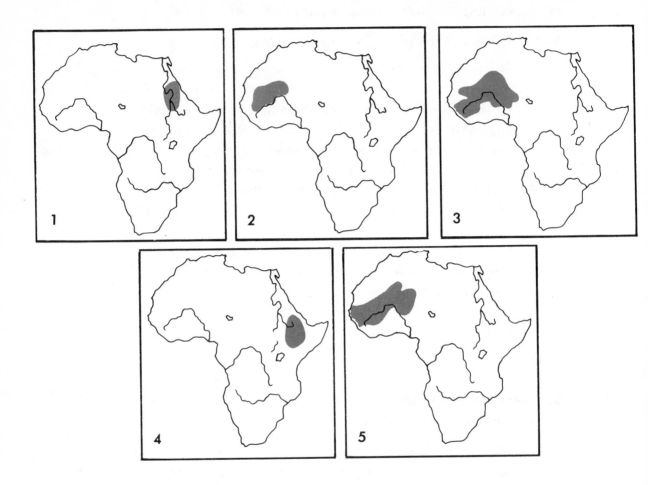

VI. THINGS TO DO

1. Here are five small maps of Africa. One country is shown on
    each map. Write the name of that country on your paper.

2. Working alone or in a committee, show each of these places on
    an outline map of Africa: Ghana, the Niger River, Ethiopia,
    Egypt, the Nile Valley, the Sahara Desert.

3. Read one of the three chapters of the book *A Glorious Age in
    Africa* by Daniel Chu and Elliot Skinner, published by Double-
    day and Company. Report to your class on life in Ghana, Mali
    or Songhai as presented in this book.

Chapter 4 / THE AFRICAN SLAVE TRADE

Let's Discover

1. What it meant to be a slave.
2. How people became slaves.
3. How the slave trade became a European business.
4. How the slave trade harmed Africa and its people.

Words to Know

chattel
Something that is owned and can be moved from place to place.
African slaves were chattel to their masters.

pirate
Someone who attacks and robs ships on the ocean.
The pirate captain ordered his men to fire at the approaching ship.

kidnap
To carry off a person against his will.
The pirate decided to kidnap the people on the captured ship.

slave trader
A person in the business of buying and selling slaves.
The slave trader brought his slaves to the market.

Arab
Any of the people living in or near Arabia or in northern Africa.
The people of Egypt today call themselves Arabs.

profit
The amount of money a person makes in business after all his expenses have been subtracted.
He bought the slave for ten dollars and sold him for fifty dollars, making a profit of forty dollars.

New World
North and South America and their neighboring islands.
The people of Europe called the Americas the "New World."

captive   A person who has become a prisoner.

The soldier turned his captive into a slave.

revolt   To use force to try to gain freedom or to change a government.

Life had become so bad that the slaves decided to revolt.

runaway   A person who runs away.

The Spanish soldiers searched for the runaway slave.

---

1 / *Slavery in Ancient Times.* A slave was a person who belonged to another person, called his master. A slave was property; he or she could be bought and sold. We use the word *chattel* to describe any piece of property that can be moved. Slaves were chattel. They could be taken from one place to another and would still be slaves. There were slaves in Europe, Asia and Africa thousands of years ago. Most countries had them. There were also slaves in tribal Africa. Herdsmen might keep a few slaves to help care for the animals. Slaves might be used to do the work in some rich man's home. Other slaves worked as farmers. Many slaves had fine skills and worked as craftsmen. The Egyptians made slaves of the people they captured in war. Other African empires did the same. The idea that all men have the right to be free and equal under law did not yet exist. Instead, there were masters and slaves. And the slaves had to do whatever their masters ordered them to do.

2 / *How a Person Became a Slave.* There were five chief ways in which people became slaves. 1) Some children were born into slavery because their parents were slaves. 2) Sometimes the head of a family sold his wife, son or daughter as a slave. 3) Any man, woman or child captured in a war could be made a slave. 4) A person could be kidnaped and made a slave. This often happened when pirates attacked ships and captured them. All the people on the ship might then be sold as slaves. 5) Many people became slaves because they were forced to by slave traders. These men ran an evil business. They bought or captured people and then sold them for a profit. Most of the Africans who came to the Americas were brought by slave traders.

3 / *The Slave Trade to North Africa and Asia.* Muslims who ruled in North Africa and Arabia owned many slaves, black and white. Many black Africans had been made slaves; some of them had been taken deep into Asia by their Arab masters. Bands of Arabs might make a raid into some tribal area. There they would attack a village and take as many men, women and children as they could. Other slave traders would buy the slaves already held by an African chief

or rich man. Much of Muslim civilization was based on the wide use of slaves.

4 / *The European Slave Trade Begins.* Portugal was the first country in Europe to enter the slave trade. We have a good record of some slave activity in 1441. Prince Henry, son of the king of Portugal, sent a sea captain named Antam Goncalvez to Africa. Henry had ordered his captain to bring back animal skins and palm oil. Goncalvez thought his prince would be pleased if the ship also brought back some people from the African coast. He returned to Portugal with twelve Africans. One of the captured men said that he was a member of the ruling family of his tribe. He asked for his freedom and promised to send back five or six other black men in his place. Goncalvez sailed back to Africa with the prisoner. He came home with "ten blacks, male and female." They became slaves in Portugal.

5 / *African Rulers Traded Their People.* These were not the first slaves taken by Portugal. Prince Henry had ordered his sea captains not to raid African villages for slaves. But the slave trade brought great profits. Henry's orders were not followed. More and more slaves were brought into Portugal. At first they were captured by direct attacks on villages by the Portuguese. Then, by the year 1457, an easier way to get slaves was worked out. The chiefs who ruled in West Africa wanted horses. The horse became the mark of power. A sea captain from Portugal found that he could get ten to fifteen slaves for one horse! The rulers

An Arab band tries to capture a slave.

of the Mali and Songhai empires seemed to have the greatest need for horses. They became active slave traders. Prince Henry died in 1469. For the next forty years the slave trade grew and grew. One Portuguese record tells us that "when the trade of the country was well ordered, it [brought] 3,500 slaves and more, many tusks of ivory, gold, fine cotton cloth and much [more]. . . ." Some of these slaves were sold to Spain by the Portuguese. (The Spaniards used their word for black, *negro,* to describe the black slaves. Since then Europeans have called black people Negroes.) Meanwhile, the chief goal of Portugal in its trade with Africa was to get goods wanted in Europe. There was a busy trade in gold, ivory, pepper and palm oil. Yet the slave trade had also grown important, and would become ever larger.

6 / *Slavery Grew with the Discovery of the Americas.* The people of Europe called the two continents discovered by Christopher Columbus the "New World." They used these new lands for one main purpose—to bring wealth back to Europe. For more than a hundred years after Columbus, Spain and Portugal were the most important powers in the New World. The rulers of these countries cared little about what happened to the people of the Americas. All they wanted was gold. They made slaves of the Indians. But Indians died quickly under slavery. So, eleven years after Columbus' first voyage, "Negro" slaves were brought across the Atlantic. During the next 350 years, one country after another joined in the slave trade. An English writer named Davidson tells us what happened: ". . . millions upon

millions of captives [were brought across] in the ships of Portugal and Spain, and afterwards in those of England, France, Holland, Prussia, Denmark, Sweden, Brazil and the United States of America." From the beginning this was a cruel trade. Tens of thousands died on the way across the ocean. Negro slaves were property. They were bought and sold like any other chattels. It seemed that there was no end to the need for slaves. And there was no feeling on the part of the slave traders that what they were doing was wrong.

7 / *Negroes Fought Against Slavery.* The people who were made slaves tried to become free. They tried to escape. They rose against their masters again and again, even when they knew this might cost them their lives. They were fighting for life itself, for the harsh conditions of slavery meant a shorter life for any slave. The first Negro slave revolt in the New World was in the year 1522 in the West Indies. Five years later there was another in Puerto Rico, to which thousands of slaves had been brought from Africa. Then, in the next few years, other slave revolts followed. They failed. More and more slaves tried to escape. The men who ruled the New World for Spain became frightened. They set up a police group to catch runaway slaves.

8 / *How Slavery Made Money for Europe.* How could any man own slaves without feeling that he was doing something wrong? The New World saw police and masters bringing suffering and even death to slaves

in chains. Slavery grew because people made money from it. The kings of Europe helped slavery grow because they made large profits. They taxed their slave traders. This meant that the king made money every time a slave was bought or sold. All kinds of businesses also made money from slavery. Blacksmiths made chains. Shipbuilders had to fit out ships to carry slaves. A large farm worked by slaves gave business to many people in the nearest town. For this was the chief use of slaves—to work the land. Some slaves might be servants; some might be craftsmen. But the largest number of men, women and children who became slaves worked on the land. The crops they grew made their masters rich. Owning slaves meant making money. No other thought disturbed the men from Europe who had come to the New World to become rich.

Horses were often traded for men.

9 / *How the Slave Trade Changed Africa.*
The slave trade did great harm to the people of Africa. Millions of them were dragged away, never to return. Some parts of West Africa have few people even today. For hundreds of years, Africans could not build up their countries. They did less trading and selling of goods. There was so much more profit in selling people! These people were needed at home if Africa was to grow as the rest of the world was growing. There is great wealth in Africa, but it could not be developed without people. There was a great need for improving the life of the African; this need was forgotten. African countries could have built industries, improved their farming and become the equals of other countries. But slavery and the slave trade made such growth impossible. The men who ruled over the tribes and the African kingdoms kept their power while making money from the busy slave trade. They came to depend on European countries. Portugal, for example, sent its armies to assist African kings who helped in the slave trade. These armies remained to rule. They had guns and cannon. With such weapons Europe became the master of Africa.

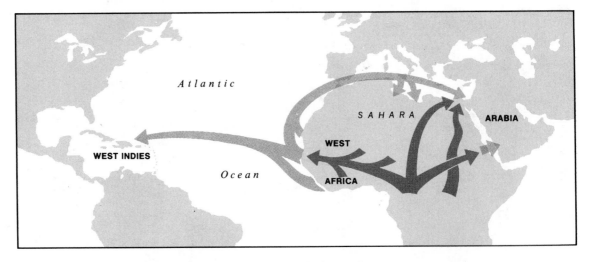

Routes of the Slave Trade

Understanding What You Have Read

I. REVIEWING WORD MEANINGS

Write the letter of the choice that best completes each statement.

1. A slave was a chattel because he was (a) not free, (b) something owned that could be moved from place to place, (c) able to become free.
2. A pirate was most likely to steal something from a (a) house, (b) bank, (c) ship.
3. When you kidnap someone you make him your (a) helper, (b) prisoner, (c) son.
4. Slavery was spread to the Americas with the help of (a) freed slaves from Africa, (b) slave traders, (c) Prince Henry of Portugal.
5. A person living in North Africa is most probably (a) an Egyptian, (b) a slave, (c) an Arab.
6. The amount of money left over after all business expenses is called the (a) loss, (b) profit, (c) expense.
7. A European sailing to South America about 1500 would have said he was going to the (a) West Indies, (b) western world, (c) New World.
8. Once you are captured you become (a) a captain, (b) an officer, (c) a captive.
9. An uprising against a government is called (a) a war, (b) an escape, (c) a revolt.
10. A runaway slave is one who has (a) escaped, (b) been freed, (c) learned how to run.

II. UNDERSTANDING MAIN IDEAS

Write the letter of the choice that best explains the main idea in the paragraph. You may look back at that paragraph to work out your answer.

1. In Paragraph 1:
   a. we see what it meant to be a slave.
   b. we compare the life of a slave and a free person.
   c. we learn how a person became a master.
2. Paragraph 2 explains:
   a. how much money slave traders made.
   b. why slaves could not become free.
   c. the ways in which people became slaves.
3. Paragraph 3 tells about:
   a. slavery in Asia.
   b. the work of Arab slave traders.
   c. the Muslim religion.
4. Paragraph 4 tells about:
   a. the life of Antam Goncalvez.
   b. how Portugal entered the slave trade.
   c. Prince Henry's orders to his captains.
5. Paragraph 5 explains how:
   a. Prince Henry kept the slave trade out of Portugal.
   b. African rulers helped build the slave trade.
   c. horses were first brought to Africa.
6. Paragraph 6 describes:
   a. the work of Christopher Columbus.
   b. the power of Spain and Portugal.
   c. the spread of slavery to the New World.
7. A good title for Paragraph 7 would be:
   a. Slave Revolts in the Americas.
   b. Life and Death of Slaves.
   c. Growth of Police Power.
8. Paragraph 8 helps you understand:
   a. why white people in Europe and the Americas like money.
   b. why white people in Europe and the Americas sold slaves.
   c. how people made money because of slavery.
9. Paragraph 9 explains how slavery:
   a. made Portugal the master of Africa.

    b. kept Africa from developing.

    c. ended all trade in Africa.

10. The chapter helps you understand that slavery:

    a. was first brought to Africa by Europeans.

    b. began to weaken Africa after Europeans entered the slave trade.

    c. began to end because most slaves were able to run away.

III. REMEMBERING IMPORTANT FACTS

Match the letter of the fact in column B with the place in column A it describes.

A	B
_____1. Ancient Egypt	A. Country that first brought black slaves to Europe.
_____2. Portugal	B. Country whose rulers sold slaves to European slave traders.
_____3. West Indies	C. Country that first made slaves of people captured in war.
_____4. Songhai	D. Country whose slave traders sent slaves into Asia.
_____5. Arabia	E. Place at which the first slave revolt in the New World happened.

IV. WHICH CAME FIRST?

For each pair of events below, write the letter of the one that happened first.

1. a. Prince Henry of Portugal died.
    b. Slavery came to the New World.
2. a. Black slaves were brought to Europe.
    b. Black slaves were brought to Asia.
3. a. The ships of the United States of America carried slaves.
    b. The ships of Spain carried slaves.

4. a. Portuguese raids on African villages began.
   b. Slave revolts frightened Spain and Portugal.
5. a. European kings taxed the slave trade.
   b. West Africa lost millions of people to slavery.

V. ANSWER EACH OF THE FOLLOWING QUESTIONS. LOOK BACK IN THE CHAPTER FOR YOUR ANSWERS.

1. In what five ways could a person become a slave?
2. In what five ways did the slave trade harm Africa?
3. Why didn't the African tribes fight to end slavery in Africa? Give two reasons.
4. In what four ways did Europeans in the Americas profit from slavery?
5. How did Negroes fight against slavery? List two ways.

VI. THINGS TO DO

1. Prepare and give for the class a short play about a slave market in an African seaport town. A slave trader has four slaves for sale. He describes them to a European buyer who in the end buys them for four small barrels of rum.
2. What was life like aboard a slave ship? Read an encyclopedia article about the slave trade and then report to the class. Be sure to explain why there were few slave revolts aboard these ships. Explain as well why so many slaves died on the voyage across the Atlantic.
3. Prepare a panel discussion on slavery. One person acts as the discussion leader. The discussion leader explains how slavery changed life in Africa. Two speakers give excuses for continuing the slave trade. Two other speakers explain why the slave trade was evil and should be ended.

Chapter 5 | SLAVERY COMES TO THE NEW WORLD

Let's Discover

1. How European colonies in the Americas got and used slaves.
2. How Europe profited from the slave trade.
3. How many African nations lost their freedom because of the slave trade.

Words to Know

colony	A land ruled by another country. *New York was once an English colony.*
mother country	The country that rules a colony, and whose citizens have settled in the colony. *Englishmen who settled in New York often spoke of their mother country.*
historian	A person who writes histories or is an expert in history. *The historian wrote about the slave trade.*
Afro-American	A person born in Africa or whose ancestors were African, and who then lived or lives in the United States. *The Negroes who landed in Jamestown were the first Afro-Americans.*
legal	Something allowed by law. *He has a legal right to travel where he wishes.*
Triangular Trade	A trade route shaped like a triangle. *A ship in the Triangular Trade went from Boston to Cuba to West Africa.*
rum	A liquor made from sugar. *Rum was one of the things used to pay for slaves in West Africa.*
merchant	A person who buys and sells goods, hoping to make a profit. *The merchant sold supplies to the captain of the slave ship.*
harvest	To gather in a crop, such as wheat, sugar or corn. *Many men were needed to harvest the crops.*
bondage	Slavery. *A slave was a person kept in bondage.*

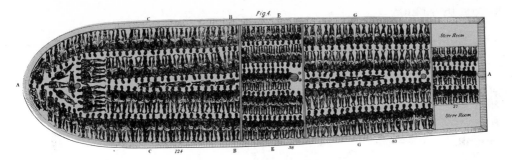

An actual diagram of a slave ship.

1 / *Why Did the Kings of Europe Want Colonies?* A colony is a place that is ruled by another country. Settlers may come from the ruling country to live in the colony. These people then speak of the ruling country as their mother country. England was the mother country of Virginia and other colonies in North America. Some countries, like Spain and Portugal, did not use their colonies as a place to settle people. Instead, they took control of other lands in order to make money. This happened as far back as 1500; it went on for hundreds of years. The kings wanted wealth and power for themselves and for their countries. They could get these things by gaining colonies. For those who did rule land in the Americas— chiefly Spain, Portugal and England—colonies meant wealth.

2 / *Slavery in the New World.* Spain, Portugal and England were most successful in setting up and keeping colonies in the Americas. Look at the lands shown on the map. In most of them, slavery came soon after the first people from Europe had settled. We will never know how many black Africans were forced to leave their homes and, almost always in chains, dragged off to slavery in the New World. In the hundred years after 1580, it is believed, the Portuguese carried one million slaves to their colony in Brazil. Spanish slave ships were several times as active. The English colonies in the New World received between a million and two million slaves in the 1700's. Most of the records kept by slave traders have been lost. However, historians agree that at least fifteen million Africans were brought to the Americas. Some have placed the number as high as fifty million.

3 / *Death on the Way.* We cannot even guess how many slaves died on the terrible trip to the New World. Many sailors and captains wrote of what they had done and seen in the slave trade. From their stories, and from the records gathered from slaves who lived through the voyage, we know what the passage was like. The people were crowded together under the deck. They were handcuffed to one another, and their legs were chained. The men who ran these ships packed their black passengers together so closely that often there wasn't enough room to sit down. The trip across the Atlantic might take six weeks. For most of that time the slaves were kept below. Some

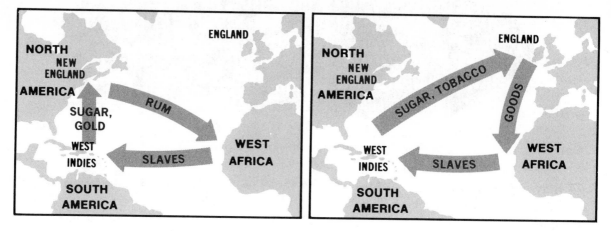

The Triangular Trade

ship captains did not even allow them to come up for exercise. They did not get enough food or water. Proper food supplies would have taken space that could better be used for more slaves! Men, women and children fell ill; the horrible conditions aboard the slave ships meant their quick death. Millions may have died in this way.

4 / Slavery Spreads Through the Americas. The men from Spain, with their guns, armor and horses, had defeated the Indians. They had made the Indians their slaves. They soon found that Indians died quickly as slaves. They turned to the use of black Africans instead. They first brought African slaves to Peru and Mexico and the other lands held by Spain. The Portuguese did the same in their great colony of Brazil. When the English began to settle in North America, they too soon made use of slaves. In 1619 a ship from Holland stopped at Jamestown, Virginia. Its captain had twenty Africans on board. He sold them as servants who were promised freedom after several years of

work for their new masters. Today American Negroes who are proud of their African past speak of these black ancestors as the first Afro-Americans—people from Africa who were to spend their lives in what would later become the United States of America. In later years many more ships carrying slaves came to Virginia and other English colonies. The Negroes they carried were sold as true slaves. The first "sale" in Jamestown is considered to be the start of slavery in the United States.

5 / Most Slaves Worked on the Land. The kings of Europe set up their colonies in the New World to gain riches. There was not very much gold or silver in the New World. But there was rich farmland. There was a climate good for raising products people in Europe wanted. They could grow sugar in the Caribbean islands. They could grow rice in some of the English colonies. Tobacco, a new crop found in the New World, quickly became a favorite in Europe. These were crops that could bring cash. But they could not be grown without a great deal of hand labor. If a man hoped to make money growing sugar, rice or tobacco, he had to have lots of help. He got this help by buying slaves. The more land he farmed, the more slaves he needed. And there was so much land! The number of slaves grew and grew. In 1661, Virginia, with a rich trade in tobacco, passed a law to make slavery legal.

6 / *The Triangular Trade.* A certain pattern of trade developed because of slavery. Suppose we begin in Europe. A ship would pick up supplies and trade goods. Businessmen in Europe made money by selling to these ships. The ship would then sail to West Africa. There the captain sold his goods or traded them for slaves. He then brought the slaves to the New World. There he sold or traded them for sugar, tobacco or other products. Again profits were made. Then the crops were sailed back to Europe and sold. This part of the voyage made the most money of all! When the English colonies of New England were settled, a similar trade appeared. New England merchants sold rum to Africa. They bought slaves there. They took the slaves to the West Indies and sold them for gold and for sugar. They then took the sugar back to New England to make into rum.

7 / *Much of Europe's Wealth Came from the Slave Trade.* There seemed no end to the money that could be made from the triangular trade. Merchants and the men who owned ships grew rich. They invested some of their wealth in the factories that began to appear after 1700. The first great

industry in England was the making of cloth and clothing. New machines were built that made it possible to produce more cloth. Much of this cloth went into the slave trade. Much of the money that factory owners raised came from people whose wealth was from the slave trade. Many cities grew rich as they too became part of the triangular trade. Liverpool, England, is one example. By 1792 its yearly shipments of goods had risen to fourteen times what they were in 1719! The people of this English city owed their living in large part to the slave trade.

8 / *The Cheap Labor of Slaves.* The real beginning of much of Europe's wealth in the 1600's and 1700's was slavery. A country became richer because of the crops it received from its colonies. How were these crops grown? Slaves did most of the work of clearing new land. They planted the crops and cared for them. Later, they harvested them. They loaded them into the ships that then sailed to Europe. On the great farms, or plantations, that developed in the col-

Money from the slave trade built industry.

onies, slaves put up the buildings and repaired them. In all the growing and building, slaves made no profits. Their masters made the profits. In return their masters gave them the simplest kind of shelter, their food and no more clothing or other goods than a person has to have to remain alive. Why spend more on a slave than you had to? Slaves were cheap, and you could always buy more of them. This seems to have been the thinking of the colonists. They did not think about how evil it was to hold a human being in bondage.

9 / *Africa Weakens.* Where did the millions of slaves come from? Most of them came from the west coast of Africa. The seacoast kings and chiefs were in business. They bought and sold other Africans. This part of Africa sent the rest of the world nothing but slaves. African states went to war again and again. Prisoners taken in these wars were sold as slaves. Each stronger tribe raided the weaker tribes nearby. The strength of the continent was drawn away as its young and healthy people were dragged off to become slaves. Africa was finally too weak to fight back. The nations of Europe moved in. They took control of most of Africa. Millions of Africans had lost their freedom and had become slaves. Those who remained in Africa saw their countries, one after another, lose their freedom too.

Understanding What You Have Read

I. REVIEWING WORD MEANINGS

Write the letter of the statement in Column B that matches each word in Column A.

	A		B
1.	colony	a.	Spain was the ruler of other lands.
2.	mother country	b.	It is allowed by law.
3.	triangular	c.	Being a slave is a terrible life.
4.	legal	d.	America was long ruled by another country.
5.	bondage	e.	The ship followed a three-cornered route.
6.	historian	f.	It is made from sugar cane.
7.	Afro-American	g.	Let's gather up the crops.
8.	rum	h.	I buy and sell to make profits.
9.	merchant	i.	He knows a lot about the past.
10.	harvest	j.	His ancestors might have lived in Ghana.

II. UNDERSTANDING MAIN IDEAS

Write the letter of the choice that best completes each statement.

1. Europe's kings wanted colonies so that they could (a) give their people better land, (b) gain riches and power, (c) help the people of the colonies.
2. The first two countries to bring slaves to the New World were (a) England and Spain, (b) Spain and Portugal, (c) Sweden and Spain.
3. The best title for Paragraph 3 is (a) Life in Chains, (b) Crossing the Atlantic on a Slave Ship, (c) A Sailor's Story.
4. The first African slaves in the New World were brought to (a) the West Indies, (b) Portugal, (c) Virginia.
5. Most of the slaves in the New World worked (a) as house servants, (b) on farms, (c) repairing buildings.
6. The West Indies are a group of (a) islands, (b) Indian tribes, (c) slave traders.
7. The slave trade gave the countries of Europe (a) gold mines, (b) business profits, (c) equal shares in the New World.
8. The story of the triangular trade shows that (a) ships went only

to West Africa and the West Indies, (b) merchants made all of their money from the slave trade, (c) the slave trade was an important part of the world's business growth.

9. The owners of plantations in the New World wanted slaves because (a) slave labor cost less than paid labor, (b) only slaves could do the work on their farms, (c) slaves did not mind how hard they had to work.

10. Because of the slave trade (a) African wars continued, (b) African wars ended, (c) African nations fought harder for their freedom.

III. REMEMBERING WHEN THINGS HAPPENED

One of the ways in which we remember when things happened in history is to place them next to some easy date to remember. Dates like 1500, 1600, 1700 and 1800 are easy to remember. Each of the events listed below happened in a year that is closest to 1500, 1600, 1700 or 1800. Which one was it for each event? After you have answered these questions, look at the paragraph listed at the end of each question to check your answers.

1. The first black African slaves were brought to the New World. (Paragraph 2)

2. The first Negroes were sold in Jamestown, Virginia. (Paragraph 4)

3. English factories using machines to make cloth began to develop. (Paragraph 7)

4. Liverpool, England, had grown to be one of the country's largest trading cities. (Paragraph 7)

5. Slavery was made legal in Virginia. (Paragraph 5)

IV. ANSWER EACH OF THE FOLLOWING QUESTIONS WITH A COMPLETE SENTENCE.

1. Why was it easy for European nations to set up colonies in the New World?

2. Why did many Africans die on the voyage to the New World?

3. What crops became important in the New World?

4. How did the slave trade help cause wars in Africa?

5. Why did the men who owned plantations want more and more slaves?

V. QUESTIONS TO DISCUSS

1. Why didn't the men who owned slaves think about how evil it was to hold another human being in bondage?

2. Why didn't the African nations, with their many skilled workers, develop industries as the English did?

3. Why were sailors and ship captains willing to be part of the slave trade?

4. What happens to the people of a country when another country takes control of their government?

VI. THINGS TO DO

1. Use an outline map of the world. Draw the route that a ship might take from England to West Africa to the West Indies, and then home again to England. How many miles would each part of this voyage cover? How many weeks would each part of it take? Remember that a sailing ship, with good winds, can sail about 100 to 200 miles a day, and only half that without good winds. Show these distances and times on your map.

2. Pretend you were aboard a slave ship sailing from Africa to the West Indies. Use a tape recorder to tell the class some of the things you saw and felt during the voyage.

3. Imagine that you were an African soldier who had been captured in a war and then sold to a slave trader. You have arrived in the New World and have been sold as a farm slave. Explain why you might plan with others to revolt.

Unit Two

AFRO-AMERICANS IN THE YOUNG NATION

Introduction

England's thirteen colonies in North America were soon settled. Much of the work on the land was done by the growing numbers of slaves. This unit describes how the slaves lived. It tells how they tried to escape from their terrible life. Some were able to buy their freedom. Others ran away to join Indians. Still others escaped to lands ruled by other countries. Not all white settlers wanted to keep slaves. Many of them, such as the Quakers, worked to bring freedom to all.

The slaves lived very unhappy lives. There seemed no reason for them to help their masters. Yet, when war with England came, thousands of Afro-Americans joined in the fight for "freedom." This unit tells about some of the black heroes of the American Revolution. It shows how important their help was in gaining victory. You will also see that freedom for the colonies did not mean freedom for the slaves. Slavery went on. It was even protected by the Constitution of the new country!

The unit describes how black Americans began to be important in the new country's life. It tells of some who were poets and writers. Phillis Wheatley wrote poems that were read and loved here and in England. Benjamin Banneker became one of the world's best-known men of science. Other black people became well known in business, medicine and community life. In the early years of the new nation, large numbers of white people kept up their work to end slavery.

As the country grew, many Americans moved west. Here again black Americans played an important part in developing the new lands. Unit 2 tells how the spread of slavery to the West became a national question. Would the new lands become "free" states or "slave" states? The future of the whole country depended on the answer.

Chapter 6 / SLAVERY IN COLONIAL AMERICA

Let's Discover

1. How slavery began in the American colonies.
2. How slaves and indentured servants were different.
3. How Quakers and others tried to end slavery.

Words to Know

permanent	Meant to last for good.
	He decided to make his permanent home in the New World.
indenture	An agreement in which one person agrees to work for another person for a certain number of years.
	He signed an indenture in order to get free passage to the New World.
indentured servant	A person who has signed an indenture agreeing to be someone's servant for a certain number of years.
	An indentured servant's service could be sold.
plantation	A very large farm on which crops are grown by people who live on the farm.
	There were more than fifty slaves working on the plantation.
indigo	A plant of the pea family from which a deep blue dye can be made.
	Indigo was an important crop in the days before men had chemical dyes.
savage	A person who is not civilized and has no culture.

56

The pirate acted like a savage, destroying and killing without mercy.

Quakers — Members of a Christian group called the Society of Friends, who believe in living simply and are against violence.

The Quakers wanted to see an end to slavery.

slaveholder — A person who owns slaves.

Every slaveowner was called a slaveholder.

hatred — The strongest possible dislike of something or someone.

Men who believed in human rights often showed their hatred of slavery.

settlement — A place where people have gone to settle, or the group of buildings and people who have come to live in that place.

The people in the settlement fought the attacking Indians.

The uprising of 1723.

1 / *England and Its Empire.* Great Britain is the country made up of England, Scotland, Wales and, until 1922, all of Ireland. The people of England have long ruled over the rest of Great Britain. For that reason, we often call the whole country England. The English people also call themselves the British. The two words—English and British —are often used to have the same meaning. In this book, we use the word *English* when we speak of the people or the government of Great Britain. The English call their country and its colonies the British Empire. England has had colonies all over the world. In this chapter, we mean the colonies in North America when we speak of the English colonies. These are the thirteen colonies that later became the United States.

2 / *The English Come to Stay.* Most of the men from Spain and Portugal who came to the New World did not plan to remain there. They came to make their fortunes; then they would return to Europe. They hoped to take all they could out of the lands their countries had conquered. The English followed a different plan. Their first North American colony, Virginia, was begun in 1607. Their last one, Georgia, was set up in 1733. In all of their thirteen colonies, the people who came from England planned to make permanent homes in the New World. They had come to stay. For most of them, farming was the way they hoped to make a better living than they had known in England.

3 / *Getting Farm Workers.* The real wealth of the colonies was in its land. There was so much of it! A man could own a farm much larger than he had ever had in England. But a large farm needs many farm workers. Indians could not be used for this work. They were too used to their freedom. If one was made a slave, he soon escaped to his tribe. The colonists tried another way. They found poor people in England who wanted to begin a new life in America. They paid the cost of bringing these people over. In exchange, the people brought over signed an agreement called an indenture. In it, they agreed to work as servants for five or more years. After that time they were free of their service and could look for their own land.

4 / *Negroes Come to Jamestown.* The first English settlement in North America was begun at Jamestown, Virginia, in 1607. For a few years it seemed that the people who had come there would not succeed. They

The first Africans came to Jamestown, Va.

Most slaves were used on the big plantations of the South.

had to clear the forests. They had to plow fields for planting. They never seemed to have enough help to do all the work that was needed. They began to bring in indentured servants; this helped for a while. Then, in 1619, the first Negroes were landed. They were not slaves, but were sold as indentured servants. They joined the many white indentured servants who were also working in Jamestown.

5 / Being an Indentured Servant. Indentured servants worked without pay for their years of service. At the end they might receive some cash, some land or whatever had been agreed. Many of these servants were later very successful. They became landowners and farmers. They opened shops.

Sometimes they made enough money to become the masters of indentured servants themselves. But not all of them waited until the end of their agreed service. Many of them escaped. They went to other colonies where workers were so badly needed that they could get a job without answering too many questions. This was easier for white servants than for black ones. A black person could be found more easily because of his color. Still, many tried to escape. This may be one reason for the change that soon came. Before long Negroes were brought in as slaves, not as indentured servants.

6 / How Slaves Were Used. The colonies grew rapidly. More and more land was opened to settlers. Slaves were brought into each colony to do the work. These Africans were usually brought to the West Indies first. There they were sold in slave markets the way cattle or food might be sold. Slave traders from the English colonies then brought groups of slaves to the larger towns on the Atlantic coast. There people bought them. Many were bought to be house servants or workers in some shop or business. Most of the slaves, however, were bought to be used on the plantations, or large farms, in the southern colonies. There were few large farms in the northern colonies. Slaves were less useful there. In New England, for example, there were always about fifty times as many free people as slaves. In the South there were many places where there were more slaves than free people.

7 / *Slavery Grew in the Southern Colonies.* The land in New England was often rocky. Farms were small. Most of them could be worked by a farmer and his own family. In the South there was better farmland with richer soil. Many plantations, some as large as a square mile, were set up. Good cash crops could be grown on such land. Southern slaves were soon working on the plantations. They raised rice and sugar first. They began growing indigo, a plant used in making dyes. Tobacco brought very large profits. The growers wanted more and more slaves so that they could grow more tobacco. It soon became clear that owning slaves in the South was a way to become rich and powerful. Some men owned several hundred slaves! These men were not going to give up slavery. The people of Georgia did not allow slavery when they began their colony.

The Quakers wanted to end slavery.

They soon permitted it when they saw how slaves made slaveowners wealthy.

8 / *How Slaves Were Treated in the South.* Most slaves worked in the fields. Many of them became skilled workers and craftsmen. Some of them became sailors. Others helped defend settlements against attacking Indians. In some places slaves worked alongside white indentured servants and free workers. In some parts of the South there were so many slaves that their white masters began to worry. Suppose these slaves tried to take their freedom by force! Strict rules were made to keep this from happening. In many places slaves could not leave their homes at night. They were not allowed to walk with canes, or even to meet their friends in large groups.

9 / *Slaves in the North.* The life of a slave was better in the North. Perhaps this was because there were fewer slaves there. Black people could go to many white hospitals

when they were sick. There were some Negro schools. Slaves were sometimes excused from work on Sunday. In New England a slave might hope to gain his freedom. Many masters freed their slaves when they realized that keeping slaves was wrong. A large part of the people in the North soon came to agree that slavery was evil. However, the chief reason why there was less slavery in the North than in the South was that a man made less money in the North from the work of a slave. The long winters in the North meant that any man who owned a slave on his farm would have to feed and care for that slave while there was no work for the slave to do.

10 / *Afro-Americans Fought Against Slavery.* The slaves who had been brought to the English colonies hated slavery. Many of them took action that showed their feelings. Some escaped and joined nearby Indian tribes. We know that as early as 1657 Negroes and Indians, both suffering from the acts of white settlers, joined in an attack on Hartford, Connecticut, where they burned many homes. Slaves in Boston, Massachusetts, were believed to have set many fires in that city in April, 1723. Indians and Negroes attacked Virginia towns in 1727. There were many more events of this kind. Afro-Americans were showing their desire

to be free and their hatred of those who would keep them slaves.

11 / *Negroes Defend the Colonies.* The settlements lived in daily fear of Indian attacks. In many of them, Afro-Americans joined their white masters in the defense against the Indians. Again and again a town was saved by the strong defense made possible by whites and blacks fighting on the same side. Some slaves were given their freedom for fighting bravely. Slaves and free Negroes fought in all of the Indian wars. They were sailors on the ships owned by colonists. On these ships they were given the same pay, goods and duties that white sailors received.

12 / *The Quakers Wanted to End Slavery.* Many white people in the colonies wanted to see an end to slavery. Thomas Paine, one of the leading thinkers, wrote against the evils of slavery. Colonial leaders like Roger Williams, Samuel Sewall, James Otis and John Woolman spoke out against it. Many church leaders tried to stop it. The religious group that tried hardest to free slaves was the Quakers. This group has always been against war and violence. Pennsylvania had been settled by the Quakers. Quaker ideas remained important there. Men like Benjamin Franklin who had once owned slaves freed them when they realized how evil slavery

Peter Kalm was a Swede who visited America in 1748 and then wrote about what he had seen. He noted that even some Quakers in Pennsylvania owned slaves. But, he wrote, ". . . many people cannot conquer the idea of its being contrary to the laws of Christianity to keep slaves. There are . . . several free Negroes in town, who have been lucky enough to get a . . . Quaker for their master, who gave them their liberty. . . ."

Benjamin Franklin freed his slaves.

was. Franklin and those who agreed with him then tried to get others to free their slaves too.

13 / *An Excuse for Slavery.* Very early in the history of England's thirteen colonies, men who owned slaves began to find reasons for keeping them. If men like Roger Williams and Benjamin Franklin could speak out against slavery, then perhaps it was wrong. If it was wrong, then every slaveholder was doing wrong. Yet men made their living from the work of their slaves. They began to say that they were really helping the black people they owned. Slaveholders claimed that slavery was a way to bring civilization to "black savages." We know that they were only fooling themselves by this argument. The black African had come from a continent that had many advanced civilizations. The real reason for keeping slaves was that people were gaining wealth from them.

Understanding What You Have Read

I. REVIEWING WORD MEANINGS

Write the letter of the choice that best explains the meaning of each word.

1. **permanent** (a) It's going to last. (b) It's just for today. (c) It happened long ago.
2. **settlement** (a) Jamestown was one. (b) The Atlantic Ocean was one. (c) Sailors lived in them.
3. **indenture** (a) A slave order. (b) A legal work agreement. (c) A secret plan.

4. **plantation** (a) Any farm with slaves on it. (b) Any farm in the South. (c) A very large farm whose workers live on it.
5. **slaveholder** (a) I trade slaves. (b) I capture slaves. (c) I own slaves.
6. **indentured servant** (a) I'm a slave. (b) I've agreed to work at this job for several years. (c) I can quit my job whenever I wish.
7. **indigo** (a) A plant used to make a blue dye. (b) An important food crop. (c) A crop grown only by slaves.
8. **savage** (a) I have many skills. (b) I act like a beast. (c) I am weak.
9. **Quakers** (a) Fight to the death to get what you want! (b) Peace should be our chief goal! (c) Control your slaves with strict rules!
10. **hatred** (a) Any strong feeling. (b) Lack of feeling. (c) A very strong dislike.

II. UNDERSTANDING IMPORTANT IDEAS

Look back in the chapter to find the best title among those listed for each paragraph.

1. The best title for Paragraph 1 is:
   a. The English People.
   b. The British Empire.
   c. The Thirteen Colonies.
2. The best title for Paragraph 2 is:
   a. Permanent English Settlements.
   b. Spain's Plan of Conquest.
   c. English Farmers.
3. The best title for Paragraph 3 is:
   a. Indian Slavery.
   b. Indentured Servants.
   c. Filling the Need for Farm Help.
4. The best title for Paragraph 5 is:
   a. How Slavery Began in the Colonies.
   b. A Servant's Success.

      c. Life as an Indentured Servant.

5. The best title for Paragraph 6 is:
   a. How the Colonies Grew.
   b. Slaves in the Colonies.
   c. Slaves and Free People.

6. The best title for Paragraph 8 is:
   a. Being a Southern Slave.
   b. The Success of Southern Slaves.
   c. Planning for Freedom.

7. The best title for Paragraph 9 is:
   a. Why Slaves Liked Northern Slavery.
   b. Slave Life in the North.
   c. The Battle to End Slavery.

8. The best title for Paragraph 10 is:
   a. Hatred for White Settlers.
   b. Indians and Afro-Americans.
   c. Early Fights for Freedom.

9. The best title for Paragraph 11 is:
   a. How Negroes Helped the Settlements.
   b. How Negroes Received Equal Treatment.
   c. How the Indians Fought Slavery.

10. The best title for Paragraph 12 is:
   a. An End to Slavery.
   b. Working for Freedom.
   c. The Quaker Religion.

III. REMEMBERING IMPORTANT FACTS

Write the letter of the choice that best completes each statement.

1. The reason why men held slaves was to (a) help the slaves, (b) learn from the slaves, (c) make money from slave labor.

2. Scotland is part of (a) England's colonies, (b) Great Britain, (c) England.

3. The country whose citizens came to the New World to begin

permanent settlements was (a) Germany, (b) Italy, (c) England.

4. Jamestown, Virginia, was first settled in (a) 1600, (b) 1607, (c) 1619.
5. The first to arrive in Virginia were (a) free men, (b) slaves, (c) indentured servants.
6. Strict rules were made for slaves in the South because white slaveowners feared slaves (a) would grow lazy, (b) might revolt, (c) might get lost.
7. Afro-Americans soon proved that they could (a) fight well, (b) run a government, (c) make Indians their slaves.
8. The Quakers were most important in (a) New England, (b) Pennsylvania, (c) Virginia.
9. The English colony that at first did not allow slavery and later did allow it was (a) Massachusetts, (b) Virginia, (c) Georgia.
10. The group that joined many runaway slaves in attacks against white settlements was the (a) Quakers, (b) Indians, (c) English army.

IV. WRITE A SHORT PARAGRAPH TO ANSWER EACH OF THE FOLLOWING QUESTIONS.

1. How was slavery in the North different from slavery in the South?
2. What kinds of work did slaves do in the English colonies?
3. Explain why slaveholders used slaves instead of indentured servants or free workers.
4. Why didn't Quakers own slaves?
5. Why did plantation owners seek more and more slaves?

V. THINGS TO DO

1. Use an encyclopedia to find out why each of these men was important in the development of freedom in the United States. Report your findings to your class.

Thomas Paine   Roger Williams   Samuel Sewall
James Otis   John Woolman   Benjamin Franklin

2. Prepare a one-page report on the Quakers in which you answer each of these questions:
   a. What are the chief ideas in the Quaker religion?
   b. What happened to the Quakers in England?
   c. Who was William Penn? How did he help the Quakers?
   d. How did the Quakers treat the Indians in Pennsylvania?
   e. How did the Quakers try to end slavery?

3. Ask your school librarian to help you find a book about the early settlements. Draw a plan for such a settlement in which you show homes, defenses and other buildings.

4. Work with a committee and a tape recorder to present a short play that tells this story: A settlement in the South is being attacked by Indians. The settlement has forty whites and ten black slaves. The whites decide they need the help of their slaves to defend the settlement. The slaves load guns and use them. One slave fights off an Indian who has climbed to the top of the settlement wall. The Indians retreat. Then write your own finish. There are several ways in which you could end this story.

5. Here is a special research job. The man who began tobacco farming in Virginia is believed to be John Rolfe, who married the famous Indian princess Pocahontas. How was John Rolfe important in the history of Virginia?

Chapter 7 | NEGROES IN THE AMERICAN REVOLUTION

Let's Discover

1. How American Negroes helped our country gain freedom from England.
2. How many black Americans became war heroes.

The first to die for freedom.

Words to Know

revolution	A complete change in the way something is done.
	The American Revolution ended English rule.
economic	Having to do with the way people make a living.
	The economic condition of free Negroes was often poor.
political	Having to do with government.
	Few freed Negroes had full political rights.
social	Having to do with the ways people live together in groups.
	The English believed in upper and lower social classes.
talent	A special skill.
	He has great talent in music.
massacre	The murder of a large number of people.
	Samuel Adams called the death of five citizens of Boston a massacre.
Haiti	A country in the West Indies, found in the western part of the island of Hispaniola.
	Free Negroes from Haiti helped fight against England.
Congress	The group in our government chosen to make the laws.
	Congress passed a law to tax the people.
Continental	The word used to describe all the colonists together during the American Revolution.
	The Continental armies were under the control of the Continental Congress.
Northwest Territory	The land ruled by Congress in 1787 from which the separate states of Ohio, Illinois,

Michigan, Indiana and Wisconsin were later made.
Slavery was not allowed in the Northwest Territory.

---

1 / *The American Revolution.* The colonies broke away from English control in the fight we call the American Revolution. It had three different kinds of causes. We should try to understand each of them.

2 / *Economic, Political and Social Causes.* The word *economic* describes those things that affect the way people make a living. Such causes were a major part of the break with England. New tax laws and rules about trade were used to keep the colonies from growing. The people of the colonies thought they should be allowed to run their own businesses in their own ways. The word *political* describes those things that affect the way people are governed. The people of the colonies wanted to govern themselves. The English who ruled them wanted to keep close control. The word *social* describes the way people live together in groups. The English had ideas about the upper and lower classes—nobles, rich people and common people. The people of the colonies could no longer accept these ideas. In the colonies, a man could grow rich or important through his own work and talent. This, of course, was true for white people, not for slaves.

3 / *Afro-Americans in the War.* A revolution is a complete change in the way something is done. It can mean a complete change in the way a country is governed. The war with England was such a revolution. The people of the colonies fought for the right to rule themselves. They won this fight. One reason for their success was the aid they received from Afro-Americans. This is a part of our history that has almost. been lost. Negroes were in the fight from the first day. They fought in the army. They served in the navy. Some of them were with George Washington at Valley Forge. They were with him when he crossed the Delaware River to defeat an English army. They were among his best spies. In fact, the first American killed in the fight for freedom from England was a Negro!

4 / *Trouble in Boston.* Boston was the busiest port in New England. Its people depended on the city's trade and the business of its merchants. When the English raised taxes, the people of Boston became upset. Led by men like Samuel Adams and John Hancock, they tried to get people to refuse to pay the taxes. The men who ran England's government felt that they had to keep real control of places like Boston. If not, they might lose control of all their lands in North America. They sent more soldiers to Boston. The people there, full of thoughts of freedom from England, hated these soldiers. There were many arguments. At times, fights broke out between the people of the town and the soldiers. One of these fights took place in

Peter Salem shot the English leader, Major Pitcairn.

March, 1770. Some soldiers had been frightened by boys who threw snowballs at them. They fired into a crowd. Five people were killed. A massacre is the murder of a large number of people. This shooting became known as the Boston Massacre.

5 / *Crispus Attucks, Hero of Boston.* The man who led the crowd in Boston was a Negro sailor named Crispus Attucks. He was one of those who agreed with Samuel Adams. He too wanted an end to rule by England. Crispus Attucks led a group of men and boys who wanted the soldiers to leave Boston. Carrying a piece of wood, he moved to the front of the crowd that had gathered around some soldiers. He was the first to be shot and killed. Crispus Attucks was well known in Boston. He had been a slave. Twenty years before, he had run away from his master and had become a seaman. In Boston today a monument honors Crispus Attucks and the four others who died in the Boston Massacre. Like many black Americans, then as now, he felt strongly about the need to be free.

6 / *Negroes Were Good Soldiers.* Five years later the people of the colonies and the English were at war. The Revolution had begun. Many Afro-Americans fought bravely at the Battle of Bunker Hill on June 17, 1775. A freed slave named Peter Salem is believed to have shot Major Pitcairn, leader of the English troops. This was the second brave act for Peter Salem. Two months before, he had fought at Lexington and Concord. Salem Poor was another black hero of the Battle of Bunker Hill. He did so well that fourteen of his officers asked that he be given a special honor for fighting "like an experienced officer, as well as an excellent soldier."

7 / *White People Were Afraid to Arm Negroes.* Few black Americans were allowed to fight in the first years of the war. Some white people thought black men could not be good soldiers. They had forgotten the long history of Negro success in defending settlements against Indian attacks. Other white people were simply afraid to put guns into the hands of black men. They feared that an armed free Negro might use the gun to set other black men free. They feared that an armed slave might use his gun to set himself free. The English promised to free any slave who would join their armies. The colonists then used black men in their army rather than see them run away to the English side. More and more Afro-Americans became soldiers and sailors. This was true in all the states except South Carolina and Georgia. The white people there remained afraid to arm the Negroes.

8 / *Afro-Americans Helped Win the War.* Negroes entered the army in several ways. Some were brought in by the officers who set up companies of soldiers in their towns. Some ran away from places held by the English. Colonial leaders who had a great need for men would sometimes accept slaves. They might promise them their freedom in return for fighting in the war. Free Negroes were most ready to fight against the English. A group of about 500 free Negroes from Haiti fought in some important battles. It is believed that about 5,000 Afro-Americans, free and slave, served in the Continental armies. They served well. When the war ended, Baron von Closen, one of Washing-

The discharge of a black soldier.

BY HIS EXCELLENCY
GEORGE WASHINGTON, ESQ;
General and Commander in Chief of the Forces of the United States of America.

THESE are to CERTIFY that the Bearer hereof *Brister Baker Soldier* in the *Second Connecticut* Regiment, having faithfully Served the United States *from April 8th 1777 to June 8th 1783* —— and being inlisted for the War only, is hereby DISCHARGED from the American Army.

GIVEN at HEAD-QUARTERS the *8th June 1783*

G Washington

BY HIS EXCELLENCY'S
Command,
J Trumbull Jun Sy

REGISTERED in the Books
of the Regiment,

G Curtiss Adjutant,

THE above *Baker* has been honored with the BADGE of MERIT for *Six* Years faithful Service. *H Swift Col*

HEAD-QUARTERS, June 10th 1783.

THE within CERTIFICATE shall not avail the Bearer as a Discharge, until the Ratification of the definitive Treaty of Peace; previous to which Time, and until Proclamation thereof shall be made, He is to be considered as being on Furlough.

GEORGE WASHINGTON.

The Northwest Territory

the heavy work needed in any army. This freed many English soldiers to fight. At the end of the war, hundreds of Negroes went to Canada or Europe with the English. Others found a less happy ending. They found themselves slaves again in the West Indies! The English promises had not been kept for them!

10 / *Some Americans Tried to End Slavery.* The government during the war was made up of men sent from each of the colonies, or states. It was called the Continental Congress. Some of its leaders tried to end slavery while the war was still being fought. Benjamin Franklin and Thomas Jefferson were among these men. They and others tried to get the Congress to agree to some plan that would in time free all slaves. This, they believed, had to be part of the fight for freedom for all of the states and their people. Most of the men in Congress did not agree with them.

11 / *Groups Were Set Up to Fight Slavery.* Still, the work of men like Jefferson and Franklin did have some good results. More white people came to feel that the slaves should be freed. Benjamin Franklin led one group that worked to free the slaves. Alexander Hamilton led another group in New York. Such groups were set up all over the country. They had one great success in 1787. In that year Congress passed a law that made rules for the government of the lands then called the Northwest Territory. There was to be no slavery in the five states to be made from these lands! The country had taken a first step toward ending slavery.

ton's officers, spoke highly of some of these brave men. He said that a Rhode Island regiment of soldiers, three-fourths of whom were black, were "the best under arms" in the army!

9 / *Afro-Americans in the English Armies.* Some slaves did gain freedom by joining the English. Thousands may have found freedom in this way. The English needed men to fight and men to work. They used slaves for both these tasks. Some were spies. Some were craftsmen. But most were used to do

The 5,000 Afro-Americans who helped Washington win the war were a very large number for that time. During most of the war Washington had only a few thousand men at any one time. When the English armies under Lord Cornwallis surrendered to Washington, the winning army had only about 15,000 men. And more than one-third of these were French allies!

Understanding What You Have Read

I. REVIEWING WORD MEANINGS

Write the letter of the choice that best explains the meaning of each word.

1. **revolution** (a) Keep things as they are. (b) Make a complete change. (c) Make as few changes as possible.

2. **economic** (a) Making a living. (b) Ruling a country. (c) Living together in groups.

3. **political** (a) Passing laws. (b) Improving business. (c) Letting everyone come to a meeting.

4. **social** (a) Changing the government. (b) Setting up a neighborhood club. (c) Making a profit.

5. **talent** (a) Being richer than others. (b) Being able to live longer than others. (c) Being able to do something better than others.

6. **massacre** (a) Jailing someone. (b) Killing many at the same time. (c) Going to church.

7. **Haiti** (a) An island country. (b) A small country in South America. (c) A country that borders the United States.

8. **Congress** (a) Chooses the President. (b) Runs the courts. (c) Passes the laws.

9. **Continental** (a) Any one of the colonies. (b) None of the colonies. (c) All of the colonies working together.

10. **territory** (a) Land becoming a state. (b) Land already a state. (c) Any place that does not allow slavery.

II. UNDERSTANDING MAIN IDEAS

Write the word *social* if the sentence describes a social problem or development. Write the word *economic* if the sentence describes an economic problem or development. Write the word *political* if the sentence describes a political problem or development. If you think the sentence can be more than one of these, choose the one that fits best.

1. High taxes make it harder to make a living.

2. The colonies set up their own congress, which tried to run the war.

3. Each man should be considered as good as the next man.

4. White people ruled strictly in the South.

5. Five states were made from the Northwest Territory.

6. Salem Poor was well liked by the other soldiers.

7. Crispus Attucks worked as a seaman.

8. Franklin and Jefferson tried to change the laws.

9. The English returned many black soldiers to slavery.

10. Southern whites lived in fear of a slave revolt.

III. REMEMBERING IMPORTANT FACTS

Write the letter of the choice that best completes each statement.

1. The fighting of the American Revolution began in (a) 1770, (b) 1775, (c) 1787.

2. The desire of the colonists to be free from English rule was represented in Boston by (a) Samuel Adams, (b) George Washington, (c) Thomas Jefferson.

3. The social ideas of the English were (a) accepted by the colonists, (b) disliked by the colonists, (c) not important to the colonists.

4. George Washington used some of his Negro soldiers as (a) slaves, (b) spies, (c) high officers.

5. Crispus Attucks was killed in (a) New York, (b) the Northwest Territory, (c) Boston.

6. Peter Salem and Salem Poor each gained fame at (a) the Boston Massacre, (b) Washington's crossing of the Delaware, (c) the Battle of Bunker Hill.

7. At the end of the war, groups to fight slavery were set up by (a) George Washington, (b) Benjamin Franklin, (c) Baron von Closen.

8. The number of Afro-Americans in the Continental forces was about (a) 500, (b) 5,000, (c) 50,000.

9. The smallest number of these black Americans came from (a) Georgia, (b) Massachusetts, (c) Virginia.

10. Many Negroes joined the English armies because they had been promised (a) free land, (b) a trip to Europe, (c) freedom.

11. Alexander Hamilton worked against slavery in (a) Pennsylvania, (b) South Carolina, (c) New York.

12. Crispus Attucks had been a (a) slave, (b) soldier, (c) businessman.

13. Southern whites did not want to arm black men because they (a) were winning the war without them, (b) feared they might use the guns to seek freedom, (c) thought they could not learn how to use guns.

14. The Negroes who fought in the American Revolution were (a) slaves only, (b) free men only, (c) both free men and slaves.

15. Slavery was not allowed in (a) Massachusetts, (b) New York, (c) the Northwest Territory.

IV. ANSWER EACH OF THE FOLLOWING QUESTIONS WITH A COMPLETE SENTENCE.

1. Describe one economic reason for the American Revolution.
2. Describe one political reason for the American Revolution.
3. Describe one social reason for the American Revolution.
4. Why have the people of Boston honored the memory of Crispus Attucks?
5. Why did the English armies offer freedom to slaves who came over to their side?
6. How much change does a revolution bring?
7. What work did Negroes do in the English armies?
8. How did Afro-Americans help win the Battle of Bunker Hill?
9. Why would you expect a man like Benjamin Franklin to want to see an end to slavery?
10. Why was it important that slavery was not allowed in the Northwest Territory?

V. THINGS TO DO

1. Prepare a short play about the Boston Massacre. Three or four classmates act the part of English soldiers. The rest of the class are the crowd of boys and men who scream at the soldiers ("Go back to England! We don't want Englishmen ruling us!"), throw snowballs and threaten the soldiers. Crispus Attucks, with a piece of firewood, leads the crowd. The soldiers become nervous and finally fire.
2. The soldiers who shot Crispus Attucks and the others were tried in court and found not guilty. They were defended by John Adams, who was later a President of the United States. Discuss the reasons he might have given to the jury. Did the jury do wrong? Why or why not?
3. It was the English who settled in the colonies and first allowed slavery here. Take sides on the question: Were the slaves who helped the English right in doing so?

Chapter 8

FAMOUS AFRO-AMERICANS OF THE 1770'S

Let's Discover

1. How Afro-Americans were part of the many new developments in our country's early years.
2. What some leading Negroes did that made them well known in America and Europe.

Words to Know

treaty	A peace agreement between two groups or countries. *The colonists made a treaty with the Indians.*
inoculation	Giving a person a mild form of a disease so that his body will build up defenses against the disease. *People in Africa used inoculation to control smallpox.*
smallpox	A very serious disease causing a high fever and sores on the skin that can leave deep scars. *People in the colonies feared smallpox.*
Mason	A member of a world-wide secret society called the Freemasons. *Prince Hall began the Afro-American Masons.*
poetess	A woman poet. *Phillis Wheatley was a fine poetess.*
astronomy	The science that studies the stars, planets and other bodies in space. *Benjamin Banneker became expert in astronomy.*
predict	To tell about something before it happens. *He was able to predict the weather.*
eclipse	A hiding of the sun by the moon when it passes between the earth and the sun. *The sky turned dark during the eclipse.*

77

almanac   A kind of calendar that contains information about the weather, the tides and whatever else its author chooses to include.

Benjamin Banneker's almanacs were full of wise sayings.

brethren   Brothers.

Members of the same group call themselves brethren.

---

1 / *A Time of Many Firsts.* When the men and women who settled in the New World came to this land, almost all that they did was being done for the first time. They built the first colony. They set up the first town. They finished the first road. They made the first treaty with the Indians. They wrote the first plan of government. Hundreds of other firsts followed. The Afro-Americans who had been brought here as slaves also had their long list of firsts. Let's look at some of them.

2 / *Helping in Medicine.* John Derham was a slave in New Orleans who was made assistant to a doctor. At that time a man could become a doctor by learning from another doctor. Before long John Derham knew enough to be a doctor. He was freed and set up in business for himself. He was the first Negro doctor in America. But he was not the first Afro-American to be wise in medical matters. Onesimus was the slave of Cotton Mather, a minister in Massachusetts. Onesimus had been born in Africa. There men had learned how smallpox could be prevented by inoculation. In 1716, Cotton Mather wrote about this method he had learned from his slave. In five years it was being used by doctors.

3 / *First in Print.* Some of the slaves had much to say to the rest of the world. Even though they were slaves, they learned to read and write. Some taught themselves.

Prince Hall founded the Negro Masons.

Some were taught by their masters. Often their true powers of thought became clear to all. One such man was Jupiter Hammon. He turned to poetry and was well known for his skill. His poem "An Evening Thought" was the first work by a Negro to be printed in the colonies. It appeared in 1761. This New York slave became well known for his religious poems. Gustavus Vasa (or Vassa) was a slave who bought his own freedom. He then went to England. There he wrote a book about his life. This was the first book about slave life by a man who had suffered as a slave. In his book he tried to show people all over the world that slavery was wrong and should be ended.

4 / *The First Negro Masons.* The Masons are a secret social group with a long history. George Washington was a member. The Masons did not accept black members. Prince Hall had been one of the free Negro soldiers in Washington's army. He thought Afro-Americans should have their own Mason groups. He set up the first and oldest Negro social organization. It was called the African Masonic Lodge. There are hundreds such lodges today. Prince Hall was later a minister. He bought land in Boston. He was a voter at a time when most white men had not yet won that right. He was truly a successful man. Prince Hall also worked to end

Paul Cuffe was a wealthy shipowner.

Phillis Wheatley.

slavery in Massachusetts and to educate Negro children.

5 / *The First Negro Shipowner.* Paul Cuffe was a free Negro and a Quaker. He lived in Westport, Massachusetts. There he became the first black ship captain. He later owned five ships and much land. Paul Cuffe found that Westport had no school. He had one built on his own land. In it black and white children studied together. Paul Cuffe hoped for equal treatment for all. He joined a group of Massachusetts Negroes who asked their state for the right to vote. After a three-year struggle, this right was won by those who paid taxes. When he was older, Cuffe came to feel that many freed slaves would be better off if they went back to Africa. At his own cost, he helped some of them make new homes there. Paul Cuffe died in 1817; the Westport Quakers buried him with honors.

6 / *Phillis Wheatley, World-Famous Poetess.* Phillis Wheatley had been a slave. She was given her name by the family who bought her when she was nine years old. Her masters were very proud of her. They taught her to read and write. They watched as she taught herself much more. She was about fifteen years old when she wrote her first poems. Three years later one of them was published. By the time she was twenty, a book of her poems appeared. It was called *Poems on Various Subjects.* That year, 1773, her master gave her her freedom. Phillis went to England. There she was greatly admired. When she died at the early age of thirty-one, Phillis Wheatley was one of the best-known American Negroes of her time. Many free

men and slaves must have thought deeply about one of her poems. In it she had said:

I, young in life, by seeming cruel fate
Was snatch'd from Afric's fancy'd
happy seat.

* * *

Steel'd was the soul and by no misery
mov'd
That from a father seiz'd his babe
belov'd.

7 / Benjamin Banneker, Man of Science.

The three best men of science in America in the 1700's were probably Benjamin Franklin, Thomas Jefferson and Benjamin Banneker. Banneker was a free Negro who had been born in Maryland. His father was a slave who became free before Benjamin was born. The Bannekers were farmers who grew tobacco and fruit. Benjamin went to a Quaker school until he was fifteen. Much of what he later learned about mathematics, astronomy and other sciences he taught himself. At the age of thirty he built a wooden clock. It was the first clock made entirely in America! People came from far away to see it. They also came to speak to this quiet black man, a man whose one true desire was to learn more about science.

8 / Benjamin Banneker's Many Firsts.

The clock was only a start. Benjamin Banneker continued to study. He soon mastered the few books on astronomy that a man could buy at that time. He even corrected some of the information in them! In 1789 he could predict, or tell about in advance, an eclipse of the sun. A few years later Benjamin Banneker was chosen one of the three men who were to plan the new capital city, Washington, D.C. Thomas Jefferson had picked him for this work. Jefferson had once said that he thought Negroes were not intelligent. He later said that the great success of Benjamin Banneker proved that ". . . nature has given to our black brethren talents equal to those of the other colors of men. . . ." As more proof of his talent, Banneker wrote a series of almanacs. These were books that gave weather and other information. They were the first scientific books written by an Afro-American.

Benjamin Banneker helped design Washington, D.C.

9 / *Banneker and the Rights of Man.* Benjamin Banneker worked hard in other fields besides science. Many of his ideas are found in his almanacs. He tried to show that black Americans, given the training, could do as well as other men. He offered the world ways to keep peace. He thought peace should be a chief aim of all governments. One of the world's great needs, he explained, was for all people to attend free schools. His own life did much to prove that any man of real ability could make the whole world better. After all, as Banneker had said in a letter he wrote to Jefferson, ". . . we are all of the same family." It was Jefferson who had written "all men are created equal" in the Declaration of Independence. The life of Benjamin Banneker proved that this black American was the equal of any man in the field of science.

Understanding What You Have Read

I. REVIEWING WORD MEANINGS

Write the letter of the choice that best completes each statement.

1. Every treaty is a kind of (a) attack, (b) agreement, (c) ending of a war.
2. If a person is inoculated, he has been given (a) medicine to cure a disease, (b) drugs to prevent a disease, (c) a mild form of a disease.
3. A person with smallpox will have (a) a high fever, (b) no fever at all, (c) a bad cough.
4. It is not easy to find out what the Masons are doing because they (a) no longer exist, (b) are a secret society, (c) are a group of spies.
5. Every poetess is a (a) slave, (b) man, (c) woman.
6. A student of astronomy is most interested in (a) weather, (b) writing almanacs, (c) understanding the stars.
7. If you predict something correctly, you tell (a) why it will happen, (b) when it will happen, (c) the last time it happened.
8. When the sun is in eclipse, we see (a) it become brighter, (b) the stars disappear, (c) the sky grow dark.
9. You would use an almanac to check the (a) time, (b) weather, (c) lives of great men.

10. If all men are brethren, then they are all of the same (a) age, (b) size, (c) family.

II. REVIEWING IMPORTANT IDEAS

Write the field of activity in which each of these people was important. A listing of the possible fields appears below the questions. They may be used more than once.

1. John Derham was important in ————————.
2. Benjamin Banneker was most important in ————————.
3. Prince Hall was the first black ————————.
4. Jupiter Hammon was known for his ————————.
5. Paul Cuffe made his living through ————————.
6. Phillis Wheatley became world famous for her ———————— ————————.
7. Onesimus helped improve the field of ————————.
8. Gustavus Vasa wrote the first book about ————————.

medicine   shipowning   poetry   Mason   science   slave life

III. REVIEWING IMPORTANT FACTS

In each group below, match the letter of each item in Column B with the person it describes in Column A.

A	B
1. Benjamin Banneker	a. Built a school for white and black children.
2. Phillis Wheatley	
3. Paul Cuffe	b. Master of the slave Onesimus.
4. John Derham	c. Planned the city of Washington, D.C.
5. Cotton Mather	d. Became world famous for poetry.
	e. First Negro doctor in America.
6. Prince Hall	f. Wrote the first scientific works by an Afro-American.
7. Jupiter Hammon	

8. Paul Cuffe
9. Benjamin Banneker
10. Gustavus Vasa

g. Helped some freed slaves return to Africa.
h. Began the oldest Negro social group.
i. Wrote about his life as a slave.
j. Wrote poems on religious subjects.

IV. WHO AM I?

Write the name of the person described by each of the statements below.

1. People first began to understand that I had a good scientific mind when I built a wooden clock that really worked!
2. I began to write poetry when I was a girl in my teens.
3. It was not easy for a man who began as a slave to become one of the best-known doctors in America!
4. I became so well known as a minister and voter in Boston that people began to listen when I spoke out against slavery and in favor of better schools for all children.
5. I was a Quaker in Westport, Massachusetts, where I built the town school on my own land.

V. WRITE AT LEAST TWO SENTENCES ON EACH OF THESE TOPICS.

1. Why Thomas Jefferson changed his mind.
2. How Paul Cuffe tried to help poor free Negroes.
3. How a Negro slave taught Boston's doctors something new.
4. The meaning of the lines by Phillis Wheatley in Paragraph 6.

VI. THINGS TO DO

1. Read the book *Pioneers and Patriots* by Lavinia Dobler and Edgar A. Toppin (Zenith Books, Doubleday and Company). It tells the stories of Benjamin Banneker, Paul Cuffe, Phillis

Wheatley and three other Afro-Americans important in our country's early history. Report to the class on the life of one of these six.

2. Lucy Terry was another Negro poetess who lived about the same time as Phillis Wheatley. She was the first Negro poet in America. Find out about her poem "Bars Fight." Why was this poem important?

3. Plan a debate in class. Your topic should be: "Was Paul Cuffe's Plan to Help Negroes Return to Africa a Wise One?"

4. Explain what Prince Hall meant by these words, part of a speech he made to the African Lodge of Masons in 1797: "My brethren, let us not be cast down under these and many abuses we at present labor under: for the darkest is before the break of day . . . give the right hand of affection and fellowship to whom it justly belongs . . . let their color and complexion be what it will . . . for they are your brethren."

Chapter 9 / BLACK AMERICANS MOVE WEST

Let's Discover

1. Why Negroes and other Americans moved west.
2. What some black Americans did in the West.
3. How the question of slavery in the West became a national problem.

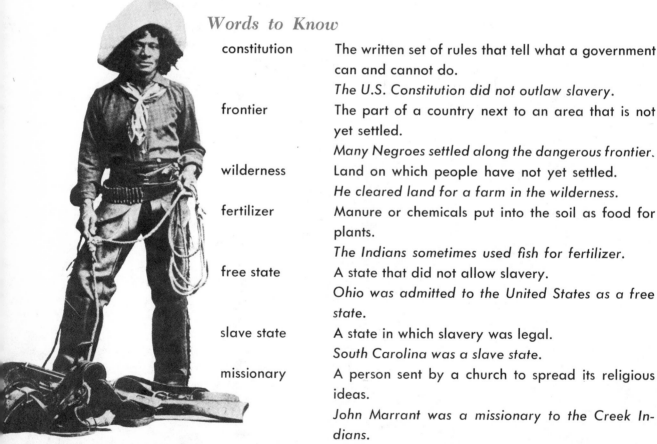

Words to Know

constitution	The written set of rules that tell what a government can and cannot do. *The U.S. Constitution did not outlaw slavery.*
frontier	The part of a country next to an area that is not yet settled. *Many Negroes settled along the dangerous frontier.*
wilderness	Land on which people have not yet settled. *He cleared land for a farm in the wilderness.*
fertilizer	Manure or chemicals put into the soil as food for plants. *The Indians sometimes used fish for fertilizer.*
free state	A state that did not allow slavery. *Ohio was admitted to the United States as a free state.*
slave state	A state in which slavery was legal. *South Carolina was a slave state.*
missionary	A person sent by a church to spread its religious ideas. *John Marrant was a missionary to the Creek Indians.*

Deadwood Dick.

86

trapper
A person who traps wild animals to get their furs. *James Beckwourth spent some winters as a trapper.*

Mountain Men
Hunters and trappers who went into the wilderness years before other men came to settle there. *Some Negroes became Mountain Men and explored parts of the Rocky Mountains.*

Sierra Nevada
A mountain range in eastern California. *Beckwourth Pass led through the Sierra Nevada Mountains.*

---

1 / *A Growing Country.* The American Revolution ended in 1783. Six years later the people of the United States were being governed under a new Constitution. Then, for a hundred years, our country grew— mostly toward the west. The American people moved west. The Indians were pushed aside. A war with Mexico was followed by our taking a large part of that country's land. The story of the drive toward the Pacific Ocean has been told many times. Let's see what part Afro-Americans played in it.

2 / *The Moving Frontier.* Our country had a frontier until 1890. A frontier is the make-believe line that marks the edge of settlement. Beyond it is wilderness or unsettled land. The frontier kept moving west. It was at the borders of the thirteen states when freedom was won from England. After the war, large numbers of people moved to the West. Some soldiers who had fought in the war were paid in western land instead of money. They went west to take their property. Other people moved west because the land was cheap. There was little unused land left in the thirteen states near the Atlantic.

A man had to go west if he wanted to farm his own land.

3 / *Searching for a Better Life.* Who were the people who moved west? Some of them were men hoping for adventure. Others were farmers whose old lands in the East were wearing out. A man had to have money to buy land and build his first home. He knew he had to wait for a full growing season before his new lands could feed him and his family. Most free Negroes did not have enough money to buy land. Yet many of them still moved west. They found jobs working on farms and as craftsmen in the new towns. They saved their money, and many did in time become farmers or go into business. They too were searching for a better life.

4 / *The Northwest Territory Was Free Land.* Most people, when they read the words "free land," think of farm land that a man can just move into. Afro-Americans had a different meaning for these words. When the United States set up its government under the Constitution in 1789, most of the states

still allowed slavery. The Constitution had failed to end it. The new government was ready to pass laws to catch and return runaway slaves. There was still a slave trade. Slavery was not allowed in the new lands of the Northwest Territory. Negroes who could moved there. They knew this was really "free land."

5 / *Slavery Moved West Too.* In the early 1800's cotton became the most important crop in the South. Men did not know much about fertilizers then. They did not know how to keep their land from wearing out after a few years of cotton growing. They had to find new land if they hoped to continue to grow cotton. Many of these cotton farmers owned large numbers of slaves. When they moved west to find new land, they took their slaves with them. Before long the whole country was faced with a problem. As the frontier moved west, would we allow slavery to move too? Would the new territories become free states or slave states?

6 / *Building the West.* The new lands of the West needed lots of work. Fields had to be cleared. Homes had to be built. Roads had to be started. Crops had to be planted and cared for. Cowboys had to work with the large herds of cattle to be raised on the plains. Negroes were part of the movement west; they worked hard too as the West was won. They fought the Indians, worked the mines, became famous cowboys and did all the jobs we have come to think of as part of the history of the West. The growth of the country toward the West was the work of millions of people. Negroes were an important part of these millions.

7 / *Spreading the Christian Religion.* Not many people know the story of two important Negro ministers. The Indians were not Christians. They followed their own gods in their own ways. A missionary is a person

Negroes also farmed the frontier.

who tries to spread his religion. John Marrant, a New York Negro, was one of the successful missionaries to the Indians. The Cherokees, the Creeks and other tribes allowed him to travel among their people to teach. Many of them accepted the religious ideas he offered. John Stewart, another black minister, came to the Northwest Territory. There he was the first Christian minister to have success with the large Wyandot tribe. These men are remembered too because they worked at a time when it was becoming hard for any Afro-American to be a minister. Slaveowners had learned that a man who became a minister would think and speak about freedom. In much of the South, black men were not allowed to be ministers at all!

8 / *Exploring Louisiana Territory.* The United States doubled its size in 1803. In that year it bought the Louisiana Territory from France. The new land had to be explored. President Jefferson sent a group led by two men, Lewis and Clark, to find out what the new lands contained. William Clark

brought his Negro slave York with him. York could speak English and a little French. A Frenchman named Charbonneau and his Indian wife Sacajawea led the explorers west. Each time they met new groups of Indians, York became the voice through which Lewis and Clark spoke to the Frenchman. Charbonneau then spoke to his wife. She spoke to the Indians. York was well liked by the Indians. He was a big man. His skin was dark. His manner was friendly. The Indians seemed to trust him. For his good work, his master set him free after the two and a half years of the trip.

9 / *Black Men Joined Red Men.* How did any new part of the frontier become settled? Someone had to go in first to see what the land was like. Fur trappers and Indian traders moved in long before the settlers arrived. Many Negroes were active trappers. They were among the Mountain Men, those brave people who went into strange Indian country to hunt and trade. Afro-Americans were very successful in fur trading with the

The Route of Lewis and Clark

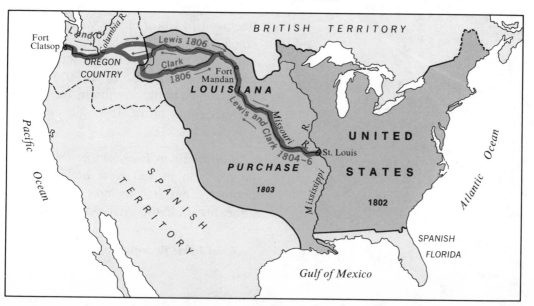

Indians. Many of these men married into Indian tribes. Indians and Negroes seemed to get along well. Often black men were allowed to join Indian tribes. Tribes like the Shawnees and the Cherokees accepted and helped runaway slaves, hiding them in their villages. Some later tried to reach the free states in the North.

10 / *James Beckwourth, Chief of the Crow Nation.* James Beckwourth was the most successful of those Negroes who joined the Indians. He had been a slave in St. Louis, Missouri. He escaped and moved west when he was nineteen years old. He was taken into the Crow Indian tribe after an old Indian woman said he was her long lost son. James Beckwourth was brave and fearless. He became the fighting chief of the Crows. He led them in many battles and was soon known as one of the West's leading Indian fighters. When the United States went to war with Mexico, General Stephen Kearney, a commander of troops in the West, asked for and received Beckwourth's help.

11 / *Finding Beckwourth Pass.* It was James Beckwourth who found a way for settlers to reach California. The Sierra Nevada Mountains were a high wall that settlers did not know how to cross. In 1850 Beckwourth found a pass in the mountains through which wagons could move. It is still called Beckwourth Pass.

12 / *A Limit to Freedom in the West.* The people who moved west had to help one another. They had to fight together against attacking Indians. Afro-Americans worked

Chief James Beckwourth.

to help others in the West. They too fought against the Indians. Yet they did not gain all of the freedom that the West is supposed to have given to settlers. The people in most of the West did not like slavery. But they did not like giving equal rights to black men either. Free Negroes could not enter Iowa unless they had five hundred dollars. Texas did not allow its free Negroes to vote at all. Not one state on the frontier before 1860 allowed Afro-Americans to hold public office.

13 / *Free or Slave in the West?* Slavery was ended in one northern state after another in the years after 1800. The country was being divided into "free" and "slave" sections. From 1801 to 1825, men from the South held the office of President, while other men from the South held control of Congress. These men did not try to end slavery. Most of them wanted it to spread into the new states to be made from the lands in the West. As cotton became more important in the South, slavery grew with it. Rice, tobacco and cotton—all were crops grown by slaves. Southern planters wanted more land. They moved west. Then, again and again, Congress had to decide whether each new state was to be "free" or "slave."

14 / *Power in Congress.* The men in Congress defended the feelings of the people of their states. By 1819 the number of slave states and the number of free states was equal. Neither side had control of Congress. Still, if a question came up in the Senate, where each state had two votes, men from the South could vote together and prevent any weakening of slavery. But the West was being settled. New states were being formed. Were they to be "free" or "slave"? If they were "free," then the South would lose its power in Congress. The question of slavery in the West divided the United States more and more. The Civil War answered that question for all time.

Understanding What You Have Read

I.   CHECK YOUR UNDERSTANDING

Write the letter of the choice that best completes each statement.

1.   If a written document contains the list of things that a government is allowed to do, then it is most probably a (a) treaty, (b) law, (c) constitution.

2.   You would have the smallest number of neighbors if you lived (a) on a farm, (b) on the frontier, (c) in a settlement town.

3.   Of these words, the one that is most closely connected to the idea of a frontier is (a) slavery, (b) freedom, (c) wilderness.

4. A farmer whose land cannot grow cotton as well as it used to could be helped most by (a) using fertilizer, (b) planting better cotton seeds, (c) planting more cotton seeds than before.

5. If you were a slaveowner, you would want the lands in the West to become (a) free states, (b) slave states, (c) either slave or free states.

6. A runaway slave would try to get to a (a) slave state, (b) free state, (c) better master.

7. The work of a missionary has to do with (a) religion, (b) the spread of slavery, (c) the ending of slavery.

8. A trapper is most interested in (a) exploring, (b) eating wild animal meat, (c) getting animal furs.

9. The Mountain Men were important chiefly in (a) exploring the West, (b) feeding the rest of the country, (c) making peace with the Indians.

10. A person speaking about the "sierra" is speaking about (a) mountains, (b) people, (c) cities.

II. BUILDING YOUR VOCABULARY

These words are related to the new words you found in this chapter. Use a dictionary to find the meaning of each. Then write a sentence in which you use the word.

1. constitute
2. constitutional
3. frontiersman
4. frontierswoman
5. fertilize
6. fertilization
7. mission
8. trap line

III. UNDERSTANDING MAIN IDEAS

1. Which of these ideas is found in Paragraph 5?
   a. Slavery ended at the frontier.
   b. Slavery moved west with the settlers.
   c. Cotton could not be grown without slaves.

2. Paragraph 2 tells about:
   a. People moving west.
   b. The cost of western land.
   c. Land in the thirteen states.

3. For which of these reasons did Afro-Americans go to the North-west Territory? (See Paragraph 4.)
   a. The Constitution ordered them to go.
   b. There was no slavery in the Northwest Territory.
   c. The land was free.

4. Paragraph 6 explains that:
   a. Negroes were important in the growth of the West.
   b. All cowboys were Negroes.
   c. Only Negroes worked to build the West.

5. Paragraph 10 tells about:
   a. A black Indian chief who fought against General Kearney.
   b. A black Indian chief who fought for Mexico.
   c. A black Indian chief who helped defeat Mexico.

IV. KNOWING WHY

Choose the item that best completes the statement.

1. Most Americans moved west because they:
   a. Hoped to build better lives for themselves and their families.
   b. Liked to fight Indians.
   c. Wanted to spread slavery.

2. Slaveowners wanted land in the West because:
   a. There was very little land in the slave states near the Atlantic.
   b. Land in the West was closer to the markets in Europe.
   c. Land in the East was being worn out by years of growing cotton.

3. The frontier kept moving west because:
   a. The best land was always a little farther west.
   b. Indians forced the settlers to keep moving.

   c. The line of settlement kept filling in as people moved into one new area after another.

4. York was important to Lewis and Clark because he:
   a. Helped them speak to the Indians.
   b. Knew the way through the Louisiana Territory.
   c. Was an Indian himself.

5. The finding of Beckwourth Pass was important to the settlers heading for California because:
   a. It was the only way to reach Nevada.
   b. It helped them become Mountain Men.
   c. It allowed them to cross the Sierra Nevada.

V. ANSWER EACH OF THESE QUESTIONS IN A SHORT SENTENCE.

1. In what year did the United States begin its government under the Constitution? (See Paragraph 1.)

2. What new part of the United States did not allow slavery in 1789? (See Paragraph 4.)

3. For what work did John Stewart become known? (See paragraph 7.)

4. What Indian tribe was led by James Beckwourth? (See Paragraph 10.)

5. How many states on the frontier allowed Afro-Americans to hold public office in 1860? (See Paragraph 12.)

6. In what year did the frontier end? (See Paragraph 2.)

7. State three ways in which Negroes earned a living in the West. (See Paragraph 6.)

8. What reward did York receive after the explorations of Lewis and Clark had ended? (See Paragraph 8.)

9. In what state is Beckwourth Pass? (See Paragraph 11.)

10. Name three Indian tribes in which Christian missionaries worked. (See Paragraph 7.)

VI. DO YOU AGREE OR DISAGREE?

Give the reasons why you agree or disagree with each of these statements.

1. The people of the West believed in democracy.
2. Afro-Americans had a better chance to improve their lives in the West.
3. Afro-Americans were not given a chance to help build the West.
4. Slaveholders had a right to take their slaves west.
5. In 1789 the Northwest Territory was the best place in the United States for a black man.

VII. THINGS TO DO

1. Choose one of the states west of the Mississippi River. Use an encyclopedia to find out when it became a state, what Indian tribes lived in it and what happened to those Indian tribes.
2. The Seminole Indians allowed many runaway slaves to remain with them. Report to your class on the Seminole Wars. What finally happened to the Seminoles?
3. Find out more about the life of James Beckwourth, including the answers to these questions:
   a. How did he become the fighting chief of the Crows?
   b. What did he do in Beckwourth Valley?
   c. How is he supposed to have died?
4. Some states in the North took steps to end slavery. Vermont ended it in its constitution. Rhode Island freed all slaves brought into it. A court decision ended slavery in Massachusetts. Other states passed laws freeing the children of slaves. Discuss the reasons why all slaves in the United States didn't simply rush to these free states to gain their freedom.

Unit Three

THE EVILS OF BONDAGE

Introduction

The invention of the cotton gin made cotton the most important crop in the South. This unit describes how the money that men could make from cotton led to a steady growth in the number of slaves. Most of these slaves lived poorly on large and small plantations. They lived, worked and died with little hope of freedom. Day and night they were kept under tight control.

The slaves would not always accept such a life. Again and again groups of them revolted. You will learn why they did this, and whether they succeeded. You will read about men like Gabriel Prosser, Denmark Vesey and Nat Turner. The fear of revolts such as the ones led by these men made white men in the South ever harsher toward their slaves. At the same time, states outside the South ended slavery.

What, then, was a slave to do when revolts had failed so many times? Slaves all over the South decided to run away. They tried to move north to a free state and then on to Canada and lasting freedom. They were helped by tens of thousands of men and women, blacks and whites. These people had set up an organization called the Underground Railroad. You will learn in this unit how the "railroad" was run. You will also find out about some of its leaders. Some of them, like Harriet Tubman, "never lost a passenger."

Unit 3 also describes what life was like for Negroes who escaped to freedom in the cities of the North. There they found problems facing them as they tried to find homes, jobs and schools. Yet, as you will see, some black people in the North did become successful in the years before 1860. Among them were Ira Aldridge, the actor; Martin Delany, a man of many talents; and James Forten, a leading man of business.

Chapter 10 / PLANTATION LIFE FOR SLAVES

Let's Discover

1. How the invention of the cotton gin made cotton the most important crop of the South.
2. How the profits to be made from cotton caused slaveowners to build the way of living we call plantation life.
3. How slaves lived and worked on cotton plantations.
4. How the slave codes helped make slaves obey their masters.

Some slaves were carpenters and craftsmen.

Words to Know

smuggle	To bring something not allowed by law into a country, usually in some secret way.
	The slave trader smuggled slaves into the United States through small ports in the South.
planter	The owner of a plantation.
	The planter had more than one hundred slaves.
fibers	The threads that are part of some plants.
	Cotton fibers are usually short.
cotton gin	A machine that separates cotton fibers from the seeds.
	Eli Whitney invented the cotton gin in 1793.
King Cotton	The name given to the cotton crop, the most important crop grown in the South.
	The planters believed King Cotton would make them rich and powerful.
overseer	A person who watches over and directs the work of other people.
	The overseer made sure the slaves worked hard.
labor	Workers as a group, or the work they do.
	Negro slave labor was used on the plantations.
system	A plan or method to get things done.
	Slaves worked under the gang system on some farms.
code	A set of laws on a single subject.
	A slave code was a group of rules about what slaves could and could not do.
troublesome	Causing trouble or bothering others.
	He was a troublesome person who caused many fights.

---

1 / *The African Slave Trade Ended.* The United States government passed a law in 1808 ending the African slave trade. The slave trade continued for a while anyway. In 1820 another law made the trade piracy. The punishment for piracy is death. From then on the new slaves brought to the United States were smuggled in—landed secretly in the South at towns along the ocean. The men in the South who owned slaves were

largely in favor of these laws. They did not want to end slavery. But they did hope to keep the price of their slaves high. With fewer new slaves coming in, this was possible.

2 / *Slavery Seemed to Be Weakening.* By 1800 most of the states in the North had taken steps to end or weaken slavery. In some states it was simply ended by law. In others, laws were passed that would end it slowly. One such law was to allow no new slaves. That meant that the children of slaves would be free. When the slaves in the state had died, all slavery would be ended. Thinking men and women felt that slavery was wrong and should be ended. Men like George Washington and Thomas Jefferson had offered another way. When these slaveowners died, they left orders to free their slaves. Still, by 1810 there were more than a million slaves in the southern states. Until this time, most of them were busy growing tobacco, rice and indigo.

3 / *Problems of the Cotton Farmer.* For a while it seemed that slavery did not pay. There weren't enough good crops a man could grow. How much rice or tobacco could be sold to Europe? There were years when too much had been grown, and the prices received by planters were low. Cotton was a good cash crop. The new machines in England and New England had built up a new clothing industry. This industry needed cotton—all it could get! But most of the cotton grown in the world had short fibers. When the fibers were long, a man could get his cotton cleaned and ready for sale without much trouble. When the fibers were short, it was very slow, hard work to clean out the seeds found in the fibers. It might take a slave most of a working day to prepare just one pound of cotton for market. At first cotton-growing did not make a good living for a slaveowning farmer.

4 / *The Cotton Gin Made Slavery Pay.* Many slaves found the work of cleaning cotton hard. They had worked out tools to help them get the job done. Then, in 1793, a man named Eli Whitney invented a new machine. He called it the cotton engine; it was soon known as the "cotton gin." His machine removed cotton seeds quickly. One slave using a cotton gin could clean fifty or more pounds of cotton a day! Better machines were soon built, and before long one man could clean hundreds of pounds of cotton a day. Suddenly a cotton farmer could make money from his crop! Suddenly slavery, when used to grow cotton, did pay.

5 / *King Cotton.* The cotton gin quickly made cotton the most important crop in the South. How could slavery end now? The men who grew cotton began to speak of "King Cotton," the crop that would help them rule the economic life of the country. They began to look for more land on which to grow more and more cotton. Plantation owners sent their sons west to the rich lands of Mississippi and Alabama, and beyond to Louisiana and Arkansas. There they set up new plantations. They also looked for more slaves to work these great farms. By 1830 they had convinced themselves that slavery

was good for the slaves. Each year the number of slaves, most working at cotton growing, was greater. By 1860 it reached four million! Most of these slaves lived on cotton plantations on which there were twenty or more slaves.

6 / A Cotton Plantation. Each plantation was a little different from every other. Yet they were enough the same so that we can describe what most were like. Let's choose a large one, with a hundred or more slaves. On it was the grand home in which the owner and his family lived. There might be a smaller home for the overseer. An overseer ran the farm for the owner. It was his job to see to it that the slaves did the work well. The slaves lived in cabins near the main houses. Their cabins were poorly made, sometimes of logs. They were small, and few had windows. Most of them had dirt floors. All around the living area were acres and acres of fields. George Washington, one of Virginia's great landowners, had almost six square miles of land for his crops alone. There were many other planters in the South with farms just as large.

7 / Slaves Were Cheap Labor. Why did cotton planters use slaves instead of paid workers? They could make a greater profit from the work of slaves. It is hard work to grow cotton. Slaveowners could work their slaves as hard as they wished. They did this in any way possible, using the whip when they wanted to get more out of a slave. Most of the slaves worked in the fields, tending the plants, picking the cotton and preparing it for market. Sometimes a slave

Cleaning cotton with a cotton gin.

was used to help the overseer. A few slaves were house servants in the master's home. Some slaves were carpenters and craftsmen. Some were more highly trained, serving even as doctors and nurses. But the fields were the chief place of work. When the cotton had to be picked, every slave, even the children, went into the fields from sunrise to sundown.

8 / Two Ways of Getting Work from Slaves. Planters managed their slave workers in one of two ways. Some used the "gang system." Others used the "task system." A system is a way of getting things done. In the gang system the field workers were put into groups or gangs. Each gang was under the charge of a leader called a driver. It was his job to make his gang work quickly, and keep working until sundown. In the task system each slave was given a certain amount of work to do each day. He might be ordered to pick 200 pounds of cotton. He could work slowly or quickly, but he had to finish his work or task. It was the driver's job to see to it that each slave finished his task before he left the fields for the day.

9 / *The Slave Family*. We have learned that slaves were the chattel of their masters. No slave could really have a life of his own, in which he made the important decisions. A man or woman could choose a wife or husband only from among the slaves on the same plantation. The marriage itself was not even legal. The master could break it up whenever he wished. He was in business to make money. If he wanted to sell a slave, then he would do so. If this meant breaking up a family, then he could still do it. He could sell a mother away from her children or a child away from its parents. Once sold,

A few slaves even served as doctors.

the slave might never be seen again. Slave families often were broken up in such ways. We know that boys and girls learn most of what they know as children from their parents. How hard it must have been for these slave children to grow up knowing that they and their families might be cut apart at any time! Even when this didn't happen, the fear that it would made every day that much harder.

10 / *How Much Could a Slave Learn?* A slave could not have a real family life. He could not receive an education. Most slave-owners were afraid to let their slaves learn. They tried to teach them only what was needed to do the job assigned. A slave who knew how to read and write and work with numbers might become a problem.

He might even run away and use these skills to make a living somewhere far away. From the beginning of slavery in the New World, slaves had followed the religious ideas of their masters. They were Christians, but they were not even given a Bible. The slave masters knew that if slaves had even one book, many of them would learn to read it—even without the help of a teacher. A slaveholder did all he could to make his slaves feel that they were not as good as their white master. He did this so that his slaves would obey every order given to them. Slaves had little free time in which to try to learn more than they knew. They worked every day but Sunday, when they went to church.

11 / *The Slave Codes.* Slaves hoped for

A typical plantation.

Slaves were often punished by whipping.

freedom above anything else. Their masters wanted slavery to continue. In every state in the South, strict laws were passed to help control the slaves. These were called "slave codes." A code is a set of laws. Here are some of the special rules found in these slave codes. A slave could not raise his hand against a white man. He could not raise his voice in anger against a white man. One slave code even said that "a look, the pointing of a finger or refusing to step out of the way for a white man, when passing each other on the street," were against the law for black slaves. There were other rules to limit the things a slave might do. He could not beat a drum or blow a horn. He could never own a gun. If he met with five or more of his friends away from home, he was breaking a law. These acts were made crimes. A slave could be punished for

Slave life was ruled by the overseer.

such crimes. The usual punishment was a public whipping. In states like Louisiana, a slave could be put into prison for breaking rules in the slave code. White men, of course, could do any of these things without fear.

12 / Slaves Fought Back. Slaves did not take this terrible treatment without fighting against it. In the next chapter we will learn about the many slave revolts. Let's look now at some of the other defenses they found. All slaves knew that some Afro-Americans were free men. They knew that they might be able to buy their freedom if they had enough money. Many slaves worked nights and Sundays to earn money. With it they bought freedom. Frederick Douglass, who had escaped from slavery himself, wrote how every slave felt. "Give him a *bad* master and he (hopes for) a good master; give him a good master, and he wishes to become his *own* master." Yet most slaves knew they could not win their freedom. They showed their anger against bondage in other ways.

13 / *Troublesome Property.* A person is called "troublesome" when the things he does bother other people. The slaves learned many ways to be troublesome to their masters. Often they pretended not to know how to do things. One Virginia slave owner complained that "many slaves pretended to be stupid to fool their masters." Sometimes, when carrying cleaned cotton from the cotton gin, a slave would put rocks and dirt in with the cotton. This made it weigh more. It also made trouble for the master when he tried to sell his cotton. Slaves enjoyed causing trouble between a master and his overseer. They might do their work poorly. They often damaged the crops. They cut through sacks and weakened buildings. They often pretended to be sick. If they could not be free, at least they would make it harder for those who kept them in slavery to make a profit from it!

Families could be broken up and sold.

Understanding What You Have Read

I. USING WORDS

Place each of the words below the paragraphs in the space where it has been left out.

    A. The —————— knew it was against the law for him to bring slaves in from Africa. Yet he knew that his crop, which he called ——————, had to have more —————— working on it. His friend, who owned the machine called a ——————, told him about a slave trader who was going to —————— a shipload of slaves into port that night.

        smuggle   planter   cotton gin   labor   King Cotton

    B. Work on the plantation was hard, and the —————— knew his job would be lost unless he brought in enough cotton. The short —————— of this crop made him decide to use the task ——————, for the slaves were often —————— when they worked in gangs. He knew they had to obey him, for the slave —————— would punish them if they did not do what they were told.

        fibers   overseer   system   code   troublesome

II. KNOWING WHY

Choose the answer that best completes each statement.

    1. Men like Jefferson and Washington freed their slaves because they:
        a. Thought this was a good way to end slavery.
        b. Feared the slaves would revolt.
        c. Wanted the slaves to return to Africa.
    2. Before the cotton gin was invented, little cotton was grown because:
        a. It would not grow in the poor soil of the South.

  b. There was no need for cotton, since wool clothing cost little.

  c. It was too hard to clean the cotton to prepare it for sale.

3. Slaveowners said slavery was a good thing because they:

  a. Knew no slave was ever treated badly.

  b. Were making money from slavery.

  c. Had taught all slaves to read and write.

4. Slaveowners wanted to see the United States grow toward the west because they:

  a. Wanted freed slaves to find free land there.

  b. Hoped to build new plantations there.

  c. Wanted to drive the Indians into the mountains.

5. We speak of "slavedrivers" today because we remember how:

  a. Slaves used to drive wagons.

  b. Leaders of slave gangs used to force slaves to work hard.

  c. Slave families were driven apart.

6. Most slaves could not read or write because:

  a. The schools they attended were very poor.

  b. Their masters wanted them to read only the Bible.

  c. Their masters refused to allow them to be educated.

7. The slave codes were written to:

  a. Help slaves keep their rights.

  b. Help slaveowners control their slaves.

  c. Keep slave families together.

8. The chief reason for the growth in the number of slaves was:

  a. The slave trade became legal.

  b. Slaveowning planters sold most of their slaves.

  c. Planters wanted more slaves to work on their cotton plantations.

9. Planters wanted to grow more cotton because:

  a. Slaves were spoiling most of what they had.

  b. The clothing industry would buy as much cotton as it could get.

  c. Growing cotton was easy work for all.

10. The homes of slaves were poorly made because:
   a. Planters did not want to spend money on better housing for slaves.
   b. Slaves never knew enough about building to put up better homes.
   c. Poor housing made people depend on themselves more.

III. FACT OR OPINION?

A fact is something that has happened or is true. An opinion is what someone thinks or feels about a fact or problem. Write FACT for each statement that is a fact. Write OPINION for each statement that is an opinion.

1. The number of slaves in the South was greatest in 1860.
2. No man has the right to make another man his slave.
3. The slave codes helped white masters control their slaves.
4. Washington did the right thing when he freed his slaves.
5. Eli Whitney invented the cotton gin in 1793.
6. The clothing industry was the best friend of every person on a cotton plantation.
7. Cotton planters wanted more slave labor.
8. Slaves were allowed to marry.
9. Slaves had many ways to fight back against their masters.
10. Most of the states in the North tried to end slavery.

IV. DO YOU AGREE OR DISAGREE?

Give your reasons for agreeing or disagreeing with each of these statements.

1. Slave children lived in fear.
2. House servants were well off as slaves.
3. It made no difference to a slave whether he worked under the gang system or the task system.

4. We have little proof that slaves wanted to be free.
5. Slaves were made to obey their masters by the use of force.

V. QUESTIONS TO DISCUSS

1. Why did the invention of the cotton gin make more white people in the South want to keep slavery?
2. Why did the plantation owners need overseers?
3. Prepare a list of all the ways a slave might be troublesome during one day on a plantation.

VI. THINGS TO DO

1. The plantation life discussed in this chapter was found mostly in the parts of the South where cotton was widely grown. Find out about the following conditions in places like Maryland and Virginia, where less cotton could be grown.
   a. How large were most farms or plantations?
   b. What was meant by "selling a slave down South"?
   c. How many free Negroes lived in these states?
2. Use a tape recorder to present the life of a slave on a cotton plantation. Have a boy, a mother and a father tell of their work and life during a week of the harvesting season.
3. Find a description of Washington's plantation at Mount Vernon. Draw pictures to show all the buildings on it. Do the same for Jefferson's home, Monticello.
4. Here is an outline for Paragraph 1 of this chapter:
   1. The African slave trade ended.
      a. United States ended slave trade in 1808.
      b. United States made slave trade piracy in 1820.
      c. Slave traders turned to smuggling of slaves.
   In the same way, write the facts that can be used to outline Paragraph 2.

5. John Hope Franklin, a leading black historian, tells us in one of his books that some free Negroes also owned slaves. In many cases these "slaves" were friends or members of their own families who could be bought but not freed under some state law. Such "slaves" were never treated as slaves. However, Dr. Franklin also tells us that some free black men owned slaves to use in farming or business. Discuss your own feelings about black slaveholders. How would other free Negroes feel about such men? How would white men who wanted to end slavery treat black slaveholders?

Chapter 11 / SLAVE REVOLTS

Let's Discover

1. How slaves revolted against their masters.
2. Why some slaves were ready to die for their freedom.
3. How fear of slave revolts spread through the slave states.

Words to Know

resolve	To make up one's mind about something.
	Nat Turner resolved to plan a revolt.
betray	To tell the enemy the secret plans of your own side.
	Again and again, some slave would betray other slaves who were planning a revolt.
execute	Put to death according to law.
	The slave was executed after being found guilty at his trial.
endeavor	To try very hard.
	He endeavored to free his fellow slaves.
pardon	To free from punishment.
	He was found guilty but was then pardoned by the governor.
lottery	A kind of gambling in which a person buys a numbered ticket. He may then win a prize if his number is chosen as a winner.
	Denmark Vesey won the lottery.
uprising	A revolt.
	The uprising led by Nat Turner was planned to free many slaves.
rebel	a) A person who fights against control.
	The rebel fought for his freedom.

b) To fight against the law.

He decided to rebel against his slavery.

rebellion   An armed fight against control.

The slave rebellion frightened all slaveowners.

confession   A telling of wrong things one has done.

His confession explained his reasons for becoming a rebel.

---

1 / *More Than 250 Slave Revolts!* We have seen how slaves showed their hatred of slavery day by day. They did this by being as troublesome as they could. In any way they could, they tried to prove that all the force in the world could not make them accept the way they had to live. Many showed their anger more openly. They planned and took part in slave revolts. They knew that they would be killed if they did not succeed. Yet they were still willing to fight their masters, to kill or be killed. We have found records of more than 250 slave revolts in the colonies and later in the United States. There may have been many more of which no records were kept. Other revolts took place on the slave ships that sailed from Africa.

2 / *The First Slave Revolt in North America.* In 1526 a group of Spanish settlers and soldiers lived in what is now South Carolina. They had 100 black slaves with them. Disease hit the colony; it killed many. The leader of the colony was one of those who died. When this happened the slaves revolted. They killed many of their masters and fled to a nearby Indian village. Only about a hundred white people remained. They left, all going back to the West Indies. A slave revolt had put an end to Spanish plans to build colonies in South Carolina!

3 / *Revolts During the 1600's.* Slavery was legal in the English colonies after 1660. There were few slaves until 1680. The only crop that needed many workers at that time was tobacco. Most of it had been raised by white indentured servants. Still, we know of nine slave uprisings in Virginia, and one each in Connecticut, New York and Massachusetts before 1700. Not all of these were successful. Slaves, sometimes helped by white indentured servants, tried to take their freedom. They often failed, but they kept trying. In 1663, for example, a slaveholder named John Smith found out about a planned revolt among his black slaves and white indentured servants when one of his servants told him of it. He had some of the slaves executed, or killed. He then freed the man who had told about the others, and gave him a gift of five thousand pounds of tobacco!

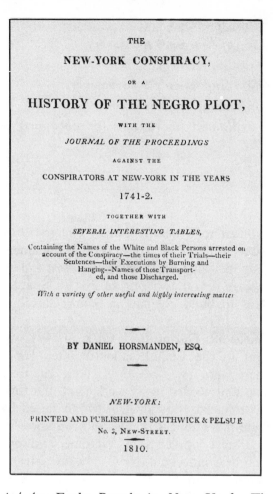

THE

NEW-YORK CONSPIRACY,

OR A

HISTORY OF THE NEGRO PLOT,

WITH THE

JOURNAL OF THE PROCEEDINGS

AGAINST THE

CONSPIRATORS AT NEW-YORK IN THE YEARS

1741-2.

TOGETHER WITH

SEVERAL INTERESTING TABLES,

Containing the Names of the White and Black Persons arrested on
account of the Conspiracy—the times of their Trials—their
Sentences—their Executions by Burning and
Hanging--Names of those Transport-
ed, and those Discharged.

With a variety of other useful and highly interesting matter

BY DANIEL HORSMANDEN, ESQ.

NEW-YORK:

PRINTED AND PUBLISHED BY SOUTHWICK & PELSUE
No. 3, New-Street.

1810.

4 / *An Early Revolt in New York*. The town of New York had a slave uprising on April 8, 1712. Slaves shot and killed nine whites. They wounded seven more. English soldiers stopped the revolt. They captured most of the slave rebels. Six of the slaves killed themselves. They had chosen to die rather than remain slaves. Twenty-one slaves were killed in cruel ways so that other slaves would learn that a revolt could only mean death. The governor of New York reported that "... some were burned, others hanged, one broken on the wheel and one hung alive on chains in the town."

5 / *A Second Uprising in New York*. What punishments could be harder? Yet slaves still tried for freedom. A second revolt took place in New York in 1741. We know that the winter had been very cold. Six feet of snow had fallen. Poor people and slaves, all poorly housed, suffered a great deal. White servants and black slaves revolted. This time 41 blacks and five whites were executed for taking part in the uprising.

6 / *Cato's Revolt*. There were revolts in the South too. We know of more than fifty of them during the 1700's. This was more than four times as many as took place in the North. One revolt was reported in Charleston, South Carolina, in 1739. It was led by a slave named Cato. He and other slaves lived on a plantation. They killed two guards and found guns. To the south, through hundreds of miles of wilderness, was Florida. Its Spanish governor had promised freedom to all English slaves. The hope for freedom moved other slaves. They joined Cato. All at once a large-scale slave revolt was on. A record from that time tells us that "Several Negroes joined them, they called out liberty, marched with colors displayed and two drums beating.... The country thereabout was full of flames."

7 / *Cato's Revolt Failed*. Cato and his followers killed about thirty white people. They did not kill every white they caught. We know from the record that one, "... a good man and kind to his slaves ...," was not killed. News of the revolt spread quickly. White settlers and soldiers caught up with the fleeing slaves. They surprised and attacked them, killing fourteen of the escaping black men. The attack went on. By the end of the third day thirty more had been killed and forty captured. Every one of these men was then executed. The report of these days of fighting tells us that the slaves "fought stoutly for some time." It is believed that ten of the slaves did escape to freedom.

"The country thereabout was full of flames."

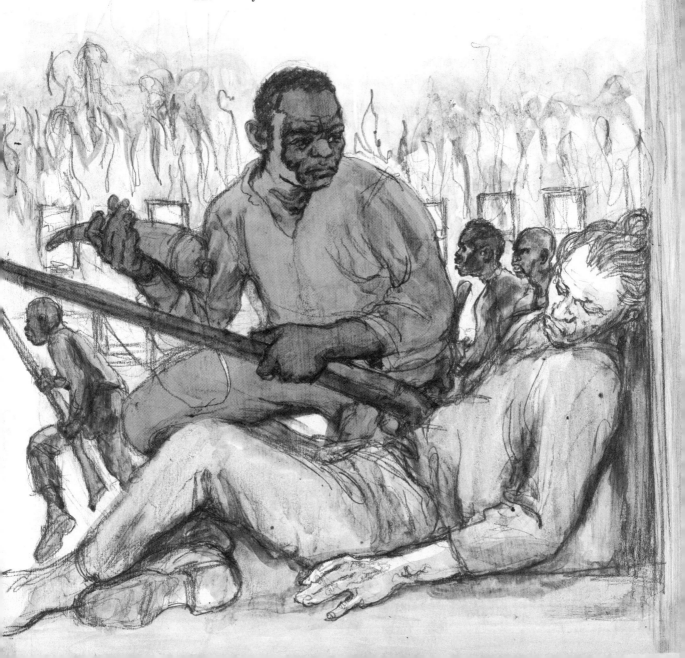

8 / *The Fear of Slave Revolts*. There were more slave revolts during the years 1800 to 1860. One writer tells us that at least a hundred took place. There may have been many more that were not reported. Slave-owners learned to sleep with pistols at their sides. They lived in daily fear that their slaves would begin to fight for their freedom. At night they patrolled their roads and checked the plantations. They told each other of the revolts that other slaveholders reported. One of the tales that made them most fearful was that of the Prosser and Bowler revolt.

9 / *The Prosser and Bowler Revolt*. It was 1800. Two slaves named Gabriel Prosser and Jack Bowler planned a revolt by thousands of slaves in the lands near Richmond, Virginia. The day they set was Saturday, August 30. Word spread. This had to be the day. Then, as one report tells us, ". . . upon that very evening, just about sunset, there came on the most terrible thunder, . . . with the most enormous rain that I ever witnessed. . . ." The storm flooded rivers. Bridges were washed away. Still, more than a thousand slaves gathered outside Richmond. They were armed with clubs and swords. It was their plan to destroy the city. But the storm went on. The group of slaves broke up. Then someone told the slave-holders which slaves had planned the revolt. The next day many of them were arrested. Four got away. One killed himself. Gabriel Prosser was caught a month later and Jack Bowler two months afterward.

10 / *Rebels on Trial*. James Monroe, later President of the United States, was the

More than a thousand slaves gathered outside Richmond.

governor of Virginia in 1800. He spoke to Gabriel Prosser. Monroe reported that, "From what he said to me, he (Prosser) had made up his mind to die, and to have resolved to say but little on the subject. . . ." All the records show that the rebels had agreed that it was "death or liberty." None of them would tell the names or plans of others in the revolt. They had been betrayed, but they would not betray one another. At the trial one slave said, "I have nothing more to offer than what General Washington would have had to offer, had he been taken by the British officers and put to trial by them. I have ventured my life in endeavoring to obtain the liberty of my countrymen and am a willing sacrifice to their cause. . . ." Prosser, Bowler and thirty-three others were executed. They all met their deaths bravely. Because of the efforts of Thomas Jefferson, ten slaves were pardoned.

11 / *Denmark Vesey*. The biggest plan for a slave revolt was made in Charleston, South Carolina, in 1822. It was led by a free Negro named Denmark Vesey. He had been a slave once. In 1800, while still a young man, he had won $1,500 in a lottery! He had bought his freedom for $600 and had gone into business in Charleston as a carpenter. For the next 22 years Denmark Vesey worked and studied. He began to make plans for a great rebellion. He would do as the slaves of Haiti, the island in the West Indies, had done. They had carried through the only really successful slave revolt in the New World. Vesey planned that he and his rebels would capture the city of

These bells were to make it harder for a slave to run away.

Charleston on the second Sunday of July, 1822. But once again a slave revolt was betrayed. One of the men who had planned to join the revolt instead told his master about the plan.

12 / *The Trial of Denmark Vesey*. The planters moved quickly. More than 130 black men were arrested. A trial followed. A few men were let go before the trial. A few others were found not guilty. Several were pardoned and sent out of the state. Four white men were fined and put into prison for helping in the planned revolt. Vesey spoke up at the trial. He said that even though he was free, he had planned the revolt to help his fellow blacks gain freedom. He and 34 others were found guilty and hanged.

Nat Turner.

13 / *Nat Turner*. The slave revolt that most frightened the people of the South was led by Nat Turner in 1831. It happened in Southampton, Virginia. Nat Turner was a very religious man. He believed that God had chosen him to lead his people to freedom. He later said that his fellow slaves ". . . believed and said my wisdom came from God." He waited for a sign that the time had come. On the evening of Sunday, August 21, 1831, Nat Turner and five other slaves began their revolt. First they killed the Travis family, the owners of Nat Turner. During the next twenty-four hours other slaves joined the group, until there were about 70 in all. They had guns and horses. They moved from farm to farm, killing the white people they met. Only one poor white family was let go, "because they thought no better of themselves than they did of the Negroes."

14 / *The Failure of Nat Turner's Revolt*. The rebellion lasted two days. The rebels fought well, but they were no match for the hundreds of armed men who were soon after them. Among these were state troops and United States soldiers and sailors. More than a hundred slaves were killed. Most of these people had nothing to do with the Turner revolt! Nat Turner escaped. He hid in a cave and then in the woods for almost two months. He was not caught until October 30, 1831. A quick trial was held. Before it had ended Nat Turner told the story of his life to a white man named Thomas R. Gray. These "Confessions" were printed the next year and were read by people all over the world. They are still being read. Nat

Turner failed, but his reasons for leading the revolt are remembered.

15 / *Memories of Nat Turner*. The slave-owners who ruled the South could not forget Nat Turner. The slaves who had joined him had said "that they were going happy . . . that God had a hand in what they had been doing." Thirteen slaves and three free Negroes were hanged after their trial. Nat Turner's hanging took place less than a week after his capture. He said he was not guilty because he did not feel guilty. But guilty or not, his revolt threw the whole South into a state of fear. If Nat Turner could cause so much trouble, couldn't other slaves do the same? During the next winter, slaves all over the South were arrested. Many were beaten or even executed because their masters feared they were ready to rebel. Slave revolts like that of Nat Turner had brought their clear meaning to the South. Slaves were willing to die if there was no other way to end their slavery!

Understanding What You Have Read

I. CHECKING YOUR VOCABULARY

Write the letter of the choice that best completes each statement.

1. If you confess to a crime, then you (a) admit that you did it, (b) tell the police that someone else did it, (c) refuse to talk about it.
2. You cannot have a rebellion without (a) slaves, (b) slaveowners, (c) rebels.
3. You might rebel against something you (a) liked, (b) disliked, (c) neither liked nor disliked.
4. When you draw lots, you (a) choose one of many slips of paper, (b) prepare a painting, (c) free a slave.
5. An uprising is (a) any meeting at which people stand; (b) a fight against a stronger person, (c) a revolt.
6. A person who is pardoned has usually (a) won a prize, (b) been found guilty, (c) been found not guilty.
7. A man who endeavors to do something is (a) refusing to do it, (b) failing to do it, (c) trying to do it.

8. A person who has been executed is (a) ready to complain, (b) given another chance, (c) dead.

9. A person who has been betrayed (a) is more easily caught, (b) would never know about it, (c) is always rewarded.

10. A person who has resolved to do something (a) always changes his mind, (b) has made up his mind, (c) has refused to make up his mind.

II. BUILDING WORD POWER

Each of these words is related to one of the new words in this chapter. Use a dictionary to find the meaning of the words. Then use each new word in a sentence.

1. resolution
2. betrayal
3. execution
4. confess
5. confessor

III. CHECKING THE MEANING

Here are some ideas found in *The Confessions of Nat Turner*. His language is different from what we use today. Use a dictionary to help you. Then write each of these thoughts in your own words.

1. "I was intended for some great purpose."
2. "(I had) uncommon intelligence."
3. "I was reflecting on many things."
4. ". . . if I had the means."
5. "I . . . wrapped myself in mystery."
6. "I had arrived at man's estate."
7. "I . . . prayed daily for light."
8. ". . . the Spirit appeared to me."
9. ". . . it was my object to carry terror and devastation wherever we went."
10. "I am here loaded with chains . . . willing to suffer the fate that awaits me."

IV. PLACES AND EVENTS

For each of the slave revolts listed, write the name of the state in which it happened.

1. The 1526 revolt against the Spanish slaveholders (See Paragraph 2.)
2. Cato's Revolt (See Paragraph 6.)
3. The Prosser and Bowler Revolt (See Paragraph 9.)
4. Denmark Vesey's planned revolt (See Paragraph 11.)
5. Nat Turner's Revolt (See Paragraph 13.)

V. REVIEWING FACTS

Write the letter of the choice that best completes each statement.

1. The revolt of Negro slaves against the whites in a Spanish colony in 1526 happened in (a) Florida, (b) the West Indies, (c) South Carolina.
2. The number of slave revolts can never be known because (a) records of slave revolts were never kept, (b) records of slave revolts were not always kept, (c) the records of all slave revolts were false.
3. The stories of the slave revolts in this chapter tell you that whites (a) always helped slave revolts, (b) sometimes helped slave revolts, (c) never helped slave revolts.
4. The story of Cato's revolt tells us that (a) Spain and England were not friendly, (b) Spain had given up slavery, (c) it was easy for slaves to escape to Spanish colonies.
5. Slaveowners patrolled the roads at night because they (a) feared bandits, (b) had no police or soldiers, (c) feared slave revolts.
6. Gabriel Prosser planned a revolt with the aid of (a) Nat Turner, (b) Denmark Vesey, (c) Jack Bowler.
7. James Monroe was at one time governor of (a) Virginia, (b) South Carolina, (c) New York.

8. The last of these three revolts was the one led by (a) Nat Turner, (b) Cato, (c) Denmark Vesey.
9. The free Negro who planned a slave revolt was (a) Jack Bowler, (b) Nat Turner, (c) Denmark Vesey.
10. Most slave revolts failed because (a) no slaves joined them, (b) they were betrayed, (c) the rebels would not use force.

VI. WORKING THINGS OUT

Each of these questions asks you to think about something discussed in this chapter. Answer each question in one or two sentences. Then discuss your answers in class.

1. Why did the Spanish give up their colony in South Carolina?
2. Why were there only twelve recorded slave revolts in the colonies during the 1600's?
3. How do you know that the slaves in New York wanted to be free?
4. How did slaveowners reward slaves who betrayed other slaves?
5. What does it mean to be "broken on the wheel"?
6. Why were rebel slaves punished so harshly?
7. Why did Denmark Vesey want to capture Charleston, South Carolina?
8. Nat Turner later described Mr. Travis as "a kind master." Why, then, was the Travis family killed?
9. A *panic* is a great fear that hits many people at once. Why do we say that Nat Turner's revolt caused a panic in the South?
10. Why did many rebel slaves kill themselves rather than be caught?

VII. THINGS TO DO

1. The slave revolts described in this chapter were an important part of the history of the United States. Use a history of the

United States to help you find the answers to each of these questions.

a) What great change in American politics took place in the year of the Prosser and Bowler revolt?

b) What agreement about free and slave states had been made in Congress two years before the Denmark Vesey revolt?

c) What had happened about 1822 in the Spanish colonies in the New World? What new laws about slavery were then made there?

d) The Nat Turner revolt took place in 1831. Who was President of the United States in that year? How did he feel about slavery?

2. Prepare a list of all the things that a group of slaves planning a revolt would have to do before they began their rebellion.

3. Take sides in class to discuss whether or not it was right for slaves to revolt, to kill and to be killed in their revolts.

4. Use an outline map of the United States. On it write the dates of the slave revolts discussed in this chapter, in the places where they happened.

5. Denmark Vesey had bought his own freedom. He was not able to buy the freedom of his children. Write a paragraph to explain how this fact helps us understand why he planned a slave revolt.

6. The number of Negroes executed with Denmark Vesey has been reported as 34, 36 and 46. Explain how the excitement of a slave revolt might have affected the way records were kept.

Chapter 12 / THE RUNAWAY SLAVE

Let's Discover

1. How slaves found freedom by running away from their masters.
2. How the Underground Railroad helped them.
3. What people like Harriet Tubman did to make the Underground Railroad succeed.

Words to Know

fugitive	Someone running away from danger or capture. *Runaway slaves were called fugitives.*
Federal	Having to do with the government of the whole country (the United States). *The Federal government helped slaveowners catch runaway slaves.*
enforce	To make people obey a rule or law. *The states could not enforce their personal liberty laws.*
underground	Done secretly. *The Underground Railroad was a secret organization trying to help fugitive slaves.*
penalty	The fine or other punishment for breaking a law. *The penalty for helping a runaway slave might be six months in jail.*
conductor	The person in charge of a train. *The Underground Railroad had its conductors too.*
depot	A railroad station. *Each home at which runaway slaves on the Underground Railroad stopped was called a depot.*

mob
: A large crowd of people out of control.
The mob attacked the building.

supreme
: Highest, biggest or most important.
The Supreme Court of the United States is the highest court in the land.

gourd
: The fruit of a vine, often dried and then used as a cup or bowl.
Runaway slaves called the Big Dipper "the drinking gourd."

1 / *More and More Slaves.* The number of slaves in the slave states grew larger each year. In 1800 there were less than a million. In thirty years there were more than twice as many. By 1860 there were almost four million black slaves—boys and girls, men and women. At that time there were also almost half a million free Negroes, most of them in the free states. For each slave the dream was the same. How can I be free? What can I do to join others who have left slavery forever?

2 / *Escape to Freedom.* Each year thousands of slaves made the same decision. They would run away. Somehow they would get to a place where they could be free. It had grown harder to buy freedom after Nat Turner's revolt. The slaveholders seemed to have reached an agreement. They would keep every slave they had. What was a slave to do? Some killed themselves when they felt that life had become hopeless. Others attacked their masters and were punished with death. But for most Afro-Americans

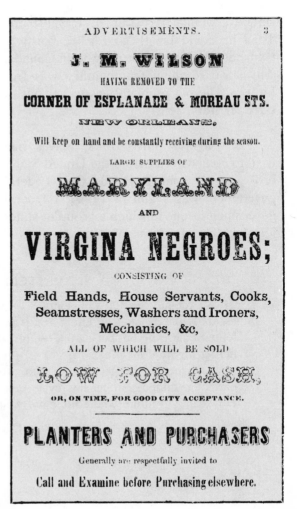

starving for freedom in the slave states, the only answer was—run away!

3 / *Routes to Freedom.* Once a slave had made up his mind to run away, he had to decide where he would try to go. If he lived near Mexico, he could cross into that country. One of the changes Mexico had made after winning its freedom from Spain was to end slavery. But few slaves lived close enough to Mexico. He could try to join an Indian tribe—but most of these were too far west. The real way to freedom was to go north until he reached a free state. It would be easier to travel there. Then he could try to go farther north to Canada. Slavery was not allowed in Canada. Any slave reaching that country was free forever. The big problem was to get out of slave territory.

4 / *The Fugitive Slave Laws.* Slaves had tried to escape even before the United States broke away from England. Our Federal government was begun in 1789. A federal government is one in which a group of states join together. Its laws must be obeyed by the people of all the states. One of the early laws passed by the new government was the Fugitive Slave Act of 1793. A fugitive is a person who is running away. This law said that a slave who had run away and was later found had to be returned to his master. Anyone helping a fugitive slave could be fined. The penalty was as much as five hundred dollars. In those days a person had to work a year or more to earn that much. A second Fugitive Slave Law in 1850 doubled the fines and added the threat of six months in jail. The power of the government of the United States was being used to help the slaveowners.

5 / *Slave-Catchers.* The Fugitive Slave Laws allowed a slaveowner or someone working for him to catch a runaway slave. The slave was then brought before a judge. If the judge agreed that the person caught was the slave being hunted, then the "fugitive" could be taken "home." This was not a trial. In most cases, the judges agreed with the slaveowner. A strange and terrible business appeared. It was called slave-catching. Slave-catchers moved through the free states

A SLAVE TELLS OF HIS FEARS

"No tongue can tell the doubt . . . a slave feels when making up his mind (to escape). If he makes an effort and is not successful, he must be laughed at by his fellows, he will be beaten . . . by his master, and then watched and used the harder for it all his life.

"And then, if he gets away, who, what, will he (then) find? . . . All the white part of mankind that he has ever seen are enemies to him and all his kindred. How can he venture where *none but* white faces shall greet him?"

Lewis Clarke, a slave who escaped from Kentucky

Fighting off slave-catchers.

looking for black people. Sometimes they caught a runaway. Just as often they grabbed someone else—a free Negro or a runaway who had been in the free state for years—and claimed he or she was the slave they were hunting. It was kidnaping! White people all over the North were shocked by it. They began to take steps against the hunting of fugitives.

6 / *Personal Liberty Laws.* A runaway slave was caught in Boston in 1843. Soon a mob of white people had gathered. This time they would not allow a black man to be returned to slavery. They rescued him. Later they raised the money to buy his freedom. The poet Whittier had this to say: "No slave-hunt in our borders . . . no slave upon our land." Many states in the North had passed laws to stop the slave-catchers. These were called personal liberty laws. They prevented the taking of any Afro-American from the state. In 1842 the Supreme Court of the United States, the highest court in the land, ruled that such state laws could not halt the enforcing of a Federal law—the Fugitive Slave Law. If the personal liberty laws could not help

escaping Negroes, then some other way had to be found. White people and free blacks all over the North joined whites and free blacks in the South. They built a new kind of road to freedom. It was called the Underground Railroad.

7 / The Underground Railroad. We do not know the story of the first slave who was helped to freedom by people along the way north. We do know that by 1830 thousands of people—black and white—were at work helping runaway slaves reach freedom. In the next thirty years at least 50,000 slaves escaped to the free states or to Canada. This was thousands every year! The routes they followed, and the way they traveled, are well known today. They used many railroad terms. The escaping slaves were called "passengers," "freight" or "packages." The homes, churches, barns, cellars, attics and secret rooms where they were hidden were called "stations" or "depots." People who helped the escaping slaves were called "conductors."

8 / The Route North. The fugitive slave first had to get some distance away from his master. It was best to start late on a Saturday, for you would not be looked for until Monday. You headed for the first "station" and hid there. As soon as your "conductor" had arranged for the next station, you would be sent on. It was best to sleep during the day and travel at night. Free Negroes and white people who wanted an end to slavery scouted for you and helped you along from place to place. You headed north. The North Star was often your only guide. You looked up at the group of stars called the Big Dipper. Following the line of two of its stars, you could see the North Star. The North Star always shows the direction north. The Big Dipper became known among slaves as "the Drinking Gourd." Their song about it is still sung today.

Follow, follow, follow the Drinkin' Gourd,
Follow, follow, follow the Drinkin' Gourd,
For the Old Man is a-waitin'
For to carry you to freedom;
Follow the Drinkin' Gourd.

A "station" on the Underground Railroad.

9 / *Harriet Tubman*. The best-known conductor on the Underground Railroad was a Negro woman named Harriet Tubman. She had been born a slave, one of eleven children. Her whole family lived in a small one-room slave cabin in Maryland. Many slave families had to live in such crowded conditions. Harriet began work as a cleaning girl and babysitter when she was only five.

10 / *Escape to Freedom*. Harriet Tubman was about 28 years old in 1849. In that year she ran away from her master. She fled north, through Delaware and into Pennsylvania. She spent a year in Philadelphia, always on guard against slave-catchers. Later she described her first moments of freedom. "I was free and I couldn't believe it. There was such a glory all around, and the sun was shining through the trees and on the hills. I was free!" She had been helped by white Quakers along the way and had learned much about the working of the Underground Railroad. William Still, a free Negro in Philadelphia, was a leading Underground Railroad worker. They became friends. She decided to work with him.

11 / *A "Black Moses" Leads the Way*. With the help of Still's friends, Harriet Tubman set up her first task. She would bring all of her family to freedom. She began with her sister and her sister's two children. In 1850 she led them from a quiet spot on Chesapeake Bay through Baltimore, Maryland, and up north to safety. Early the next year she brought back her brother and two other

A "Moses" leading the way to freedom.

men. Next she brought ten more people north to Philadelphia, and then another brother, his wife and nine others. She helped most of those she saved get to Canada. She learned the routes of the Underground Railroad better than any other conductor on it. William Still began to call her a "Moses." Like Moses in the Bible, she was leading her people from bondage to a promised land —free territory!

12 / *The Fame of Harriet Tubman.* In all, "Hatt" Tubman made nineteen known trips into the South. On one of these she brought her old parents back. She began taking more people each time. Perhaps 300 or more people in all came north with her. She carried a gun, and told her "passengers" she would use it if they did not follow her orders. "You'll be free or die," must have been her warning. She never lost a passenger! And, perhaps most important of all, other people tried to copy her success. She became one of the most admired people in the North.

13 / *Rewards for Harriet Tubman.* Time and again, slaveowners offered rewards for the capture of Harriet Tubman. White people in the North who were trying to end slavery called her "the greatest heroine of the age." Men in the South who wanted to continue slavery offered $40,000 in rewards for her capture! Between trips on the Railroad, Harriet lived in Auburn, New York, a town whose people loved freedom and gave this famous enemy of slavery a safe home.

14 / *Serving in the Civil War.* Harriet Tubman could not read or write. Still, she had many other skills. She was a nurse for the North during the Civil War. She became a spy, traveling deep into the South to bring back information needed by the generals of the North. She set up groups of spies among the slaves. In June, 1863, she was a scout for an army raiding party that destroyed southern bridges and supply lines. This raid also brought more than 700 slaves back to the North. She was still a Moses!

15 / *Final Days in Auburn.* Harriet Tubman went home to Auburn at the end of the war. Her people had been freed. Now she would try to help them live better lives. She became a public speaker, often raising money for Negro causes. She helped support two schools for freed people in the South. In 1908, when she was close to ninety, she opened a home for old people, black and white, in Auburn. At the end, old and weak but still proud, she had to live in a wheel chair. She died in 1913. That same year the people of Auburn placed a tablet on their county courthouse. It is still there. Its message tells an important part of the story of the runaway slaves who found freedom in the North.

In Memory of Harriet Tubman
Called the Moses of her people
. . . she truthfully said—
"On my Underground Railroad I never
ran my train off the track, and I never lost a passenger."

Harriet Tubman.

Understanding What You Have Read

I. USING WORDS

Fill in the correct word in each space in the paragraph below.

A. Harriet Tubman became a —————— on the ——————
Railroad. She led —————— slaves north from one secret
—————— to the next, following the group of stars the slaves
called the Drinking ——————.

fugitive   Underground   conductor   Gourd   depot

B. The Fugitive Slave Act was then the law of the land, and
the power of the —————— government was used to
—————— it. Any person breaking this law would face harsh
——————. The —————— Court had ordered states to
obey the law. Still, at times angry —————— of white people
in places like Boston used force to help runaway slaves.

Supreme   Federal   penalties   mobs   enforce

II. BUILD YOUR VOCABULARY

Each of these words is related to a new word in this chapter. Use a dictionary to find their meanings. Then use each of the words in a sentence.

1. federation	4. conduct
2. enforcement	5. supremacy
3. penal	

III. HARRIET TUBMAN'S LIFE

Here are five events from the story of Harriet Tubman. Arrange them in the order in which they happened.

1. She became a spy for the North during the Civil War.
2. She opened a home for old people in Auburn, New York.
3. She brought her parents to freedom.
4. She met William Still, a leader of the Underground Railroad.
5. She made the first of many trips as a "conductor."

IV. REVIEWING IMPORTANT FACTS

Write the letter of the choice that best completes each statement.

1. The country north of the United States that did not allow slavery was (a) Canada, (b) Mexico, (c) Florida.
2. The Fugitive Slave Law was passed to (a) help raise the price of slaves, (b) protect slaves from slave-catchers, (c) return runaway slaves to their masters.
3. A person calling himself a "conductor" on the Underground Railroad (a) really worked for a railroad, (b) knew he was breaking a law, (c) was also called a slave-catcher
4. Slave-catchers worked for (a) free Negroes, (b) the Underground Railroad, (c) slaveowners.
5. A person following the "Drinking Gourd" would be heading (a) south, (b) west, (c) north.
6. There was at one time a total of $40,000 in rewards for the capture of (a) William Still, (b) Harriet Tubman, (c) Moses.
7. Harriet Tubman was called "Black Moses" because she (a) used

that name to escape, (b) often dressed like a man, (c) led her people to freedom.

8. The cash penalty under the Fugitive Slave Law of 1793 was (a) $500, (b) $1,000, (c) as high as the judge decided.

9. The personal liberty laws tried to protect (a) slave-catchers, (b) mobs from police, (c) runaways from slave-catchers.

10. If you were a "package," then you were (a) on trial, (b) a free Negro in Canada, (c) a passenger on the Underground Railroad.

V. FINDING THE MAIN IDEA

Read each of these paragraphs again to find its main idea.

1. The main idea of Paragraph 1 is that:
   a. There were more free Negroes than slaves.
   b. The number of slaves grew greater each year.
   c. It was time for an end to slavery.

2. The main idea of Paragraph 3 is that:
   a. Most slaves tried to reach Mexico.
   b. Most slaves decided to join Indian tribes.
   c. Most slaves planned to escape to the North.

3. The main idea of Paragraph 6 is that:
   a. Personal liberty laws did not stop the working of the Fugitive Slave laws.
   b. The people of Boston did not want slavery.
   c. The Underground Railroad was a great success.

4. The main idea of Paragraph 8 is that:
   a. Runaway slaves sang on their way to freedom.
   b. Runaway slaves followed the North Star to freedom.
   c. Every runaway slave carried a drinking gourd.

5. The main idea of Paragraph 13 is that:
   a. Harriet Tubman spent most of the Civil War in the South.
   b. Harriet Tubman helped the North during the Civil War.
   c. Harriet Tubman was the only nurse who could not read.

VI. ANSWER EACH OF THESE QUESTIONS IN A SHORT PARAGRAPH.

1. Why was the power of the Federal government used to help catch runaway slaves?
2. Why didn't runaway slaves just move into the large towns of the South?
3. Why did escaping slaves try to reach Canada?
4. President Andrew Jackson was in favor of slavery. He forced most of the Indian tribes to move west of the Mississippi River. How did this make it harder for slaves to escape?
5. What might happen to a white man who was caught helping a slave escape after 1850?
6. Describe the childhood of Harriet Tubman.
7. Explain why many states in the North passed personal liberty laws.
8. Harriet Tubman carried sleeping medicine for children. Explain why she might have to use it.
9. How did the rest of Harriet Tubman's family escape to freedom?
10. How do we know that the people of Auburn, New York, agreed with the work done by Harriet Tubman?

VII. THINGS TO DO

1. Write a short story about a slave who runs away from his or her master. Make it as exciting as you can. Give it a happy ending.
2. Make a list of at least ten places in your neighborhood that would be good hiding places or "stations" for runaway slaves. Tell why each would be good for this purpose.
3. Read the part of the book *Four Took Freedom*, by Philip Sterling and Rayford Logan (Zenith Books, Doubleday and Co.), about Harriet Tubman. Tell the story of how she set up the John Brown Home.

4. Abraham Lincoln described slavery as "a moral, a social and a political wrong." Write a report of three paragraphs to explain what you think each of these "wrongs" were.

5. Use an outline map of the United States to trace each of these "Roads to Freedom" (follow rivers where you can):
   a. From Arkansas into Mexico.
   b. From Virginia to Pennsylvania and then toward Canada.
   c. From Virginia up the Inland Waterway (along the Atlantic Coast) to New Jersey.
   d. From Georgia through Kentucky and Tennessee into Ohio.

6. During most of the time when the Underground Railroad was busy bringing slaves to freedom, the United States was living under a law that divided the country into free and slave sections. It was called the Missouri Compromise of 1820. Read about the Missouri Compromise and prepare a one-page report to answer these questions:
   a. What is meant by a "compromise"?
   b. Why was this compromise passed?
   c. How did it divide the country into free and slave sections?

Chapter 13 / NORTHERN FREEDOM WITHOUT EQUALITY

Let's Discover

1. How Negroes in the North lived between 1800 and 1860.
2. How some Afro-Americans became successful during these years.

Words to Know

textile
: Having to do with weaving or woven cloth.
: *Thread and cloth are the products of the textile industry.*

manufacture
: The making of large amounts of goods, most often by the use of machinery.
: *He manufactured tools for carpenters.*

anti-
: A prefix meaning "against."
: *He was an anti-slavery man, for he hoped all slaves would soon be free.*

immigrant
: A person who leaves one country and comes to another country to live.
: *African slaves were forced immigrants.*

newcomer
: A person who has just come to a place to live.
: *Each new arrival in a city is a newcomer.*

profession
: A kind of work for which you need special education and training.
: *Medicine, law and teaching are important professions.*

discrimination
: Treating some people differently from others, usually because you like one group more than another.
: *Keeping black children out of white schools was a kind of discrimination.*

Most black people who came north settled in the cities.

segregation	Keeping one group apart from others.
	Forcing Negroes to live on certain streets or in certain neighborhoods is a form of segregation.
violence	Force used to cause damage or harm.
	The people of the town used violence to close Miss Crandall's school.
foreman	The man in charge of a group of workers in a factory.
	James Forten became a foreman.

1 / *A New Industry in the North*. The men who first grew rich in New England most often made their money from trade. The kind of trade that made the most money was the slave trade. This meant slaves and slave ships. It also meant rum and other products for the slave trade. Then the slave trade came to a halt. A new way to make money took its place. Men opened all kinds of textile factories in the North. *Textiles* is the word we use to describe cloth and clothing, from the making of thread to the sewing of buttons on a finished dress, shirt or suit.

2 / *New Kinds of Work in the North*. Once a large industry like textiles begins, others follow. Someone has to make the machines; men were soon working at this task. Iron and later steel were needed; people were soon at work in these fields. They made boxes and nails, wire and rails, railroads and better roads. Once one industry comes, dozens of others follow. Each of them brings new products and new uses for what it makes. By 1850 the North, chiefly New England, was one of the manufacturing centers of the world. We use the word *manufactured* to mean things made by machine in a factory. Iron, steel, clothing, machinery—these were the first great industries to change the North.

3 / *New Ideas About Workers*. The rich men of the North turned to manufacturing. There was never much need for slaves on the farms of New England. Untrained slaves could not be of much use in factories. Many white people in New England and the rest of the North had fought slavery for a long time. Great men like Benjamin Franklin, Alexander Hamilton and John Jay had

The United States in 1850

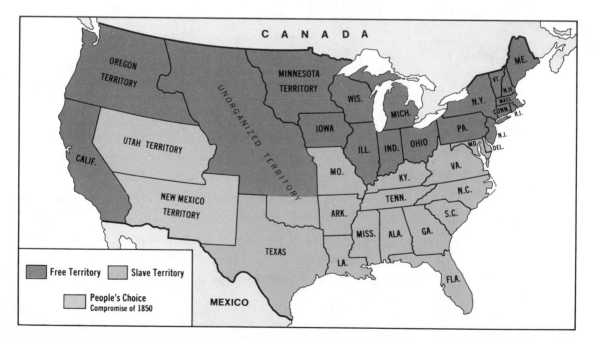

helped form societies to end slavery. There were also many of these groups in New England. A new way to handle workers came with the new industries. Businessmen in the North wanted men, women and children who would work long hours for low wages. They did not want to have to care for or own these workers. They were willing to have workers who lived freely, so long as their wages were low.

4 / *Working for Freedom.* Many people in the North worked to end slavery. Thousands of them helped the Underground Railroad. Many more joined anti-slavery groups. In 1833 an American Anti-Slavery Society was set up. It said ". . . we believe it the duty . . . of the masters immediately to (free) their slaves." It went on to call for "equality with the whites" and freedom for slaves "under the protection of the law," for "slavery is a crime." Free the slaves and make them the equal of all other citizens!

5 / *Afro-Americans in the North.* These white people in the North meant all that they said. They really wished to see all slaves freed. They gave time and money. They took dangerous chances as they broke the Fugitive Slave Laws. They did all they could to get laws passed to weaken slavery. But many of them were also businessmen. They were in business to make money. Like most people in the North they would not spend money to help build good lives for freed slaves. Afro-Americans were poor when they arrived in northern cities. They were not trained to work in the factories. They took any jobs they could get. These were the poorest jobs—sweeping and cleaning, digging and pulling—jobs in which a man could make just enough to keep alive.

6 / *Cities in the North Were Growing.* We know that most of the black people who came north settled in the cities. These cities grew and grew. New industries meant more jobs. More people were needed to hold those jobs. More people began to come to the cities. An immigrant is a person who comes to a country from another land. In the ten years before 1830 less than 150,000 immigrants came here. Four times as many came in the next ten years. Then a flood of people began to come. Between 1841 and 1850 more than one and a half million arrived. In the next ten years it was two and a half million! Most of these newcomers settled at first in the large cities of the North.

7 / *Problems in the Cities.* Each person, black or white, who moves into a city has three great problems. He must find work. He must find a place to live. He must find schools for his children. It was easier for white immigrants to solve these problems. Soon whole neighborhoods were filled by people from the same country. Members of a group would find jobs in the same industry, where businessmen were willing to have a group of workers who were friends, spoke the same language and could teach one another. Many doctors and people in other professions also came from Europe. They moved into neighborhoods where people spoke their language. The children of these immigrants were soon in public schools. There they were taught to be more like other Americans.

8 / *Special Problems for Negroes.* Imagine that you are a black man who comes to a city in the North about 1850. You find that there are not many Negroes in the city. You have the same problems that face all new-comers. Where can you get a job? You find that there are few jobs open to you. You find that the white people who helped you win freedom do not help you find work. You look for a place to live. You find that the men who own places to live do not always want to rent to a black man. The immigrant groups do not often want Negroes living among them. In the end you have to move into an old building that gives your children dirt, rats and a crowded street in which to grow up. In some towns you even find that people hate you. They may refuse to allow your children to attend public schools. You are meeting the two great problems that Afro-Americans were to know in the North: discrimination and segregation.

9 / *Discrimination and Segregation.* To discriminate is to treat a person or group differently from others. To segregate is to keep a person or group apart from others. Many white people in the North were ready to help Afro-Americans. Yet most white Northerners discriminated against them. They made Negroes sit in the back seats on a train, or in special cars. They did not allow them to enter some restaurants and stores. Some doctors would not treat black Americans. Some hospitals would not admit them. Most free Negroes were not allowed to vote. Black people were segregated. They had to stay in their own neighborhoods. They could join only with other black people in social groups. They had to form their own churches. They were free. But in the North they found that freedom was not as wonderful as they had hoped it would be.

10 / *Discrimination Could Lead to Violence.* The story of Miss Prudence Crandall's private school in Canterbury, Connecticut, shows us how feelings against Negroes led to violence, or the use of force. Miss Crandall was a white Quaker. In 1833 she admitted her first black pupil, a girl named Sarah Harris. The people of the town were angry. Most of them took their daughters out of the school. Miss Crandall then filled her school with Negro girls. The town did not like this. Miss Crandall found that no store would sell her food or supplies. She and her students were insulted in the streets. She would not close her school. She would not send away her black pupils. The town passed a law to prevent Negroes from being in such a school. Miss Crandall would not obey the law. She was put into jail. The school was attacked by a mob and wrecked. Miss Crandall was not able to re-open it. It was not until twenty years later that segregated schools were ended in much of New England.

11 / *Some Negroes Succeeded.* Life was hard for a free Negro in the North. Still, many of the success stories of the years 1800 to 1860 were stories of black Americans. We have read about Paul Cuffe, the merchant, sea captain and landowner. Catching whales was an important business in New England. A harpoon—a kind of spear with a fish-hook end—was thrown into the whale to help catch it. Lewis Temple, a Massachusetts Negro, invented a new kind of

The school was attacked and wrecked.

harpoon in 1848. Its points opened wide after it hit the whale. With it many more whales could be caught. Thomas L. Jennings, a New York tailor, invented a way to clean clothing. It made him a rich man. He used much of this wealth to fight slavery. William Whipper, a rich lumberyard owner in Pennsylvania, used much of his money to help other Afro-Americans escape to freedom. John Rock, a Boston doctor, was also a lawyer. He was made a judge. There were hundreds such success stories.

Ira Aldridge as Othello.

A MESSAGE FROM MONROVIA,
AFRICA, IN 1827

". . . Our laws are altogether our own. . . .
We have (judges), chosen from among
ourselves; we serve as jurors in the trials
of others. . . . The burden is gone from
our shoulders; we now move and breathe
freely. . . ."

(sent by freed slaves who had
returned to Africa)

12 / *The Story of Martin Delany*. We call
a man brilliant when he is much more intelligent and quick-minded than most other
people. Martin Delany was just such a man.
He studied law, science and medicine at
Harvard College. He used his talent to write
and speak for the freedom of all black people. His newspaper *The Mystery* was one of
those fighting slavery. His history of Afro-
Americans also helped turn many white people in the North against slavery. Like Paul
Cuffe, Martin Delany thought free Negroes
should move to Africa. During the Civil
War, President Lincoln made him the first
Negro major to serve in battle in the history
of the United States Army. After the war
Delany was one of the first black Americans
to become a judge in the South.

13 / *Ira Aldridge, Great Actor*. The first
world-famous Afro-American actor was Ira
Aldridge. He was born in New York City,
where he had to attend the segregated African Free Schools. He joined a Negro theater.
Anti-Negro groups forced this theater to
close. Aldridge then went to England. There
he became an actor. His best role was in

Othello, the play by William Shakespeare
about a black general of Venice. For the
next forty years he toured Europe. He was
praised and honored by kings and princes.
One writer spoke of his "magic voice." He
never came back to this country, although
he had planned to act here after the Civil
War. He died in Poland. The Society of
Polish Artists of Film and Theater still cares

PRAISE FOR IRA ALDRIDGE
FROM EUROPEAN WRITERS

"His features are capable of much ex-
pression."
"His voice (is) clear, full, resonant."
". . . a person of much study and . . . experience."
". . . captivated his audience. . . ."
". . . great applause."

for his grave. He was one of the first of many Negro artists to escape discrimination by spending most of his life in Europe.

14 / *James Forten, Inventor, Businessman and Fighter for Freedom.* James Forten was a sailor during the American Revolution. He then went to work for a sailmaker. By the time he was twenty he was a foreman. His business success began when he invented a new way to control the sails then used on all ships. He set up his own sail factory and made a fortune from its products. During the War of 1812, our second war with Eng-

land, James Forten helped raise more than 2,000 black troops to defend Philadelphia. He was one of the men who helped support the anti-slavery newspaper started by William Lloyd Garrison. You will read more about this in the next chapter. James Forten always worked to help other Afro-Americans. Men like Paul Cuffe thought free Negroes should go back to Africa to make a new life. James Forten did not agree. When he spoke and when he wrote, his thoughts were clear: This country belonged to all its people—black and white. All people had to try to make it a better home!

Understanding What You Have Read

I. MATCHING WORDS AND HEADLINES

In each group, match the headline with the numbered word it explains.

1. **manufacture**   a. FAMILY MAN MOVES HERE FROM ANOTHER CITY

2. **anti-**   b. FACTORY TO MAKE NEW PRODUCTS

3. **immigrant**   c. YOUNG MAN DECIDES TO BECOME LAWYER

4. **newcomer**   d. "I'M AGAINST IT," SAYS MAYOR

5. **profession**   e. SHIP FROM ENGLAND LANDS 250 NEW AMERICANS

6. **textile**   f. ONLY NEGROES PERMITTED TO LIVE HERE

7. **discrimination**   g. NEGROES NOT ALLOWED TO JOIN CLUB

8. **segregation**   h. JAMES FORTEN PLACED IN CHARGE OF SAIL-ROOM WORKERS

9. **violence**   i. COTTON CLOTH AND SHEETS ON SALE HERE

10. **foreman**   j. GROUP USES FORCE TO CHASE ACTORS AWAY

II. WHO AM I?

Write the name of the person who is described in each of these sentences. Look back in the chapter for help when you find it necessary.

1. I was the first great American Negro actor and became famous all over Europe.
2. I became rich in the sail-making business and used my money to help other Afro-Americans.
3. I was a famous white American who started an anti-slavery society in the North.
4. I had to close my private school in Connecticut after the people of my town objected to my taking black pupils.
5. My invention of a better kind of harpoon helped the whaling industry.
6. If you've had a suit or dress cleaned lately, then your cleaner used the method I invented.
7. I was the first black American to become a fighting major in the United States Army.
8. I'm one of the few people in Boston to have been a doctor, a lawyer and a judge.

III. UNDERSTANDING WHY

Write the letter of the choice that best completes each statement.

1. New England businessmen gave up the slave trade because (a) slave trading lost money, (b) laws were passed to end the slave trade, (c) laws were passed to end the making of rum.
2. Anti-slavery societies spread because (a) Afro-Americans hated slavery, (b) all white people wanted more slavery, (c) many white people in the North hated slavery.
3. Black men could not get good jobs in the cities of the North because (a) they were not well trained, (b) there were no jobs for anyone, (c) the cities were growing smaller and did not want more workers.
4. Negroes had to move into "black" neighborhoods because they (a) met discrimination in housing, (b) were happy to keep away from white people, (c) liked old buildings.

5. We know there was segregation in the cities because (a) there were not enough restaurants there, (b) Afro-Americans could not always get the services they needed, (c) people used to fight in the streets.

6. Miss Crandall would not keep black students out of her school because she (a) believed all children should be able to attend any school, (b) needed the money she received from Negro parents, (c) wanted to upset the people of her town.

7. Martin Delany thought black people should return to Africa because he felt (a) they would be free and equal there, (b) they would find it easy to become rich there, (c) this would make it easy for other Negroes to become free.

8. James Forten thought free Negroes should remain in America because he felt (a) all of the people of the United States loved black people, (b) they would just be sent back as slaves if they went to Africa, (c) all Americans should live and work together to improve their country.

9. Industries appear where other industries have begun because (a) all industries are alike, (b) towns with industries always grow larger, (c) each industry needs the products of other industries.

10. Immigrants from the same country settled in the same neighborhood because they (a) found better housing there, (b) would be near their jobs, (c) wanted to be with people who spoke their language.

IV. ANSWER EACH OF THESE QUESTIONS IN A COMPLETE SENTENCE.

1. How had the businessmen of New England made the money they later used to become manufacturers?

2. What is an anti-slavery society?

3. Afro-Americans lived in segregated neighborhoods. So did many white immigrant groups. How was one kind of segregation different from the other?

4. Explain what is meant by discrimination in medical care.
5. What does the story of Miss Crandall tell you about the Quaker belief in equal treatment for all?
6. How did a Negro inventor make sailing ships safer?
7. Why did free Negroes fight to defend Philadelphia during the War of 1812?
8. How did James Forten disagree with Paul Cuffe's ideas?
9. Why didn't Ira Aldridge act in American theaters?
10. Why was it harder for a black person to be successful than for a white person?

V. THINGS TO DO

1. Prepare a play called *Miss Crandall's School*. Here are some scenes you could use.
   a. Miss Crandall decides to accept her first black pupil.
   b. The white pupils in the school are taken out of school by their parents.
   c. Miss Crandall admits ten more Negro girls.
   d. The town holds a meeting against Miss Crandall.
   e. Miss Crandall refuses to dismiss her new students.
   f. Miss Crandall and three students go into town to shop.
   g. The mob attacks and breaks most of the windows in the school.
   h. Miss Crandall decides that Connecticut is not yet ready for her ideas of equal treatment in education and closes her school.
2. Some people believe that Afro-Americans would be happier in Africa. Prepare two lists. One should give the reasons favoring the move to Africa. The other should give the reasons for remaining here. Committees can combine everyone's lists and present them to the class.
3. After the slave trade ended, the price of slaves began to rise. By 1860 plantation owners were paying from $1,000 to $2,000

for a strong young slave. Use a history of the slave trade to find the answers to these questions:

(a) What price was paid for a slave in West Africa about 1800?

(b) What price was paid for the same slave when he arrived in the West Indies?

(c) Why did the price of a slave jump so much from Africa to the West Indies and then from the West Indies to the slave markets of the South?

4. Negroes suffered from discrimination and segregation. How, then, did so many of them manage to succeed in business? Explain your reasons to the class.

5. There are many books about the whaling industry. How much did it grow between 1848 and 1858? What happened to it after the Civil War? Why?

6. The defense of Philadelphia was not the only important Negro activity in the War of 1812. Find a copy of the letter General Andrew Jackson wrote to his Afro-American troops after the Battle of New Orleans. Read it to the class.

Unit Four

THE END OF SLAVERY

Introduction

This unit shows how slavery ended in the United States. It describes the work of William Lloyd Garrison and Frederick Douglass, and of the other men and women, black and white, who were called abolitionists. This group led a long fight to change the minds of all people about slavery. In the end, a war was fought between the South and the rest of the country. It decided whether black people would remain slaves.

The war went on for more than four years. It became clear that it would lead to the freeing of the slaves. Afro-Americans joined the Union armies in great numbers. They helped win the war in many other ways as well. During the years of fighting, tens of thousands of slaves gained their freedom by escaping to lands held by the armies of the North.

The war, you will see, was part of a world drive to end slavery. Freedom spread from land to land. It came to the United States too. Abraham Lincoln made freedom the country's goal with the Emancipation Proclamation. Then, after the war, a change in the Constitution freed all slaves forever.

The years following the war are known as Reconstruction. You will learn about some of the laws and changes in living at that time that gave new hope to black people. For the first time Congress tried to improve the life of Afro-Americans. For the first time, blacks joined with whites in the political life of the whole country.

Before long, however, the white people of the South again had full control of political life there. White supremacy became the South's way of life. Black people could not improve their lives. They began to lose their rights. Most of them had to become poor farmers. The hopes of Reconstruction had failed to come true.

Chapter 14 | THE ABOLITIONISTS

Let's Discover

1. How the abolitionists worked to end slavery.
2. How Frederick Douglass was a great leader of black people.

Words to Know

appeal
: To ask strongly that someone do something.
I appeal to you to help save this man's life.

abolition
: The complete end of something, particularly slavery.
William Lloyd Garrison believed in abolition.

publish
: To have something printed and then sold, like a book or newspaper.
He published the daily paper in his town.

arsenal
: A building in which guns and ammunition are made or stored.
The weapons were in the arsenal.

sojourn
: To stay in one place for a short time.
I will sojourn in this city until Monday.

proclaim
: To announce to everyone.
I proclaim my right to be free.

raid
: A sudden armed attack.
The enemy made a raid on our camp.

liberate
: To set free.
I liberate you from prison.

liberator
: A person who sets another free.
Abraham Lincoln is remembered as a liberator.

minister
: A person sent to represent his country in another country.
Frederick Douglass became the United States minister to Haiti.

150

David Walker argues for freedom.

1 / *The Abolitionists.* Again and again in this book we have spoken of "people who wanted to see an end to slavery." These people agreed on an idea. It was called abolition—the ending of slavery. The men and women who worked for it were called abolitionists. They worked hard for their goal. Some of them wrote about it. Some of them made speeches. Many of them risked their lives to bring slaves north. Some

of them were white people; some of them were black. For a while there were many abolitionists in the South too. Then, as the slaveowners gained tight control over life in the South, the fight to end slavery became chiefly a northern fight. How long could a man talk against slavery in the South when he knew that other men might shoot him or hang him for speaking out?

2 / *David Walker Fights for Freedom.* David Walker was a free Negro in Massachusetts. In 1829 he wrote a book called *Walker's Appeal.* In it he told his many readers that it was time for freedom. Slaves should use force to gain their freedom. It was right, he said, to strike down the slave masters! ". . . It is no more harm for you to kill the man who is trying to kill you, than it is for you to take a drink of water." David Walker was calling for more slave revolts. To him, a slave should kill or do anything else that would help him become free.

3 / *Danger for David Walker.* These were dangerous thoughts for an Afro-American. Friends begged Walker to go to Canada; he would be safe there. He refused to run. "I will stand my ground. Somebody must die in this cause." He was ready to be jailed, hanged or burned alive if it would help make other men free. Thousands of people bought and read *Walker's Appeal.* Men in the South are said to have offered $10,000 for his capture.

4 / *William Lloyd Garrison.* William Lloyd Garrison lived in Boston. He became one of the country's best-known white aboli-

William Lloyd Garrison, abolitionist.

tionists. On January 1, 1831, he began to publish a newspaper. He called it *The Liberator.* To liberate means to set free. Garrison raised money from his many friends. Among them was the rich James Forten. Garrison hoped to use his paper to awaken all white Americans to the evils of slavery. Then, he was certain, they would join to set all slaves free. David Walker and others were ready to find freedom through violence. William Lloyd Garrison felt reason could do the job. He would show how wrong it was for one man to own another. Once all people understood that, then laws would be passed to end slavery. He was ready to spend his life at this task. "I will not retreat an inch," he wrote. *"And I will be heard."* The newspaper was his chief work, although he also helped begin the New England Anti-Slavery Society. Two years later he was one of those who set up the American Anti-Slavery Society.

5 / *John Brown Turns to Violence*. Most of the country came to know the name of John Brown. This tall, bearded white man had helped slaves escape on the Underground Railroad. In 1855 he and his large family moved to Kansas. He felt they were needed there. Congress had just passed an important law. The people of Kansas could decide for themselves whether to become a free state or a slave state. Kansas had to have 60,000 people to become a state. These people could then vote on the question. People who believed in slavery rushed to Kansas. So did thousands of abolitionists. These two groups fought one another for more than two years. So many people were hurt or killed that the country began to speak of "Bleeding Kansas." In one of the fights, John Brown led a group that killed five of the men who hoped to make Kansas a slave state.

6 / *John Brown at Harpers Ferry*. In 1859 John Brown decided it was time to free the slaves by force. He and eighteen other men, among them his five sons, went to Virginia. They entered the little town of Harpers Ferry. There they captured the government arsenal—the building in which guns and ammunition were stored. Brown planned to spread the word to nearby slaves that the time for freedom had come. He hoped they would run to join him. With guns they could begin a slave revolt that would sweep through the South. Then the days of slavery would have to end! But John Brown was wrong. The slaves did not join him. Perhaps their fear of their masters was too great. Perhaps they did not trust this white man

The capture of
John Brown.

John Brown goes to his hanging.

who promised so much. The next day a company of United States Marines arrived. The soldiers, led by Colonel Robert E. Lee, quickly captured the arsenal. Ten of John Brown's men were killed. He was wounded. Six weeks later, after his trial, he was hanged. John Brown's Raid, as it was called, frightened the South and shocked the North. Yet it made all people face the question: What must be done to free the slaves?

7 / *Sojourner Truth—Speaker for Freedom.* A state law in 1827 freed the few slaves in New York. One of them was a young woman named Isabella. She decided to spend the rest of her life working to free other slaves. She felt her own freedom was a gift from the God she loved. It had given her a new life. "I felt so tall within . . . I felt as if the power of the nation was with me." She took a new name—Sojourner Truth. To sojourn is to stay in one place for a short time. She did just that, going on foot from place to place to tell people the truth about how wrong slavery was.

8 / *A Woman of Courage.* Sojourner Truth had not learned to read or write. But she knew how to speak. She spoke from the heart, and she found that people listened to her. Sometimes she spoke to thousands at a time. Tears would come to their eyes and a new hatred of slavery to their minds and hearts. As the years passed she became one of the best-known women in the United States. Abraham Lincoln received her at the White House. She spoke to meetings for the rights of all people. And she made many enemies. More than once she was beaten or stoned. Yet she would not stop. Across her chest she wore a banner that said: "Proclaim liberty throughout the land unto all the inhabitants thereof."

9 / *Abolitionists in Politics.* The work of people like Garrison, David Walker and Sojourner Truth was not wasted. More and more white people turned against slavery. Theodore Weld of New York became the most active white man in abolitionist politics. In 1839 he set up a new political party, the Liberty Party. It did not win many votes. Yet it did keep the subject of abolition alive. The Liberty Party later joined other anti-slavery groups. Its members went into the Free-Soil Party and then were important in the Republican Party that elected Abraham Lincoln in 1860.

10 / *Frederick Douglass*. The best-known Negro abolitionist was Frederick Douglass. His real name was Frederick Augustus Washington Bailey. He was born in 1817, son of the slave Harriet Bailey. He became the slave of Thomas Auld. Young Frederick was very bright. Mrs. Auld began to teach him to read. Then her husband found out what she was doing and made her stop. Most slaveowners felt it was dangerous to teach slaves to read and write. But Frederick had learned enough so that he was able to teach himself from then on.

11 / *Frederick Douglass Escapes*. One of the first things Douglass seems to have

Sojourner Truth visited the White House.

Frederick Douglass.

tionist meeting. People were amazed. Here was a man who had been a slave—and who could make others understand what it was like to be a slave. Douglass began to speak at more meetings. He then wrote a book, *Narrative of the Life of Frederick Douglass, an American Slave*. It boldly told the whole world what slave life did to slaves. Now his real name was known. He went to England so that he would not be caught by a slave-catcher and dragged back to Mr. Auld.

13 / *The North Star*. Frederick Douglass became a hero in England. The English people did not believe in slavery. They listened to Douglass as he spoke out for human rights. He became a leader in the fight for more rights for women. He was active in working for world peace. Yet his friends in England knew that he was needed in the United States. They raised money. For $710.96 they bought his freedom from the Auld family. They sent him home with about $2,000 to get him started again. It was 1847. Douglass settled in Rochester, New York. There he began a newspaper, which he called the *North Star*. Like the star that guided escaping slaves to freedom, his newspaper would help to make his people free. Soon its words were being read and remembered all over the North. He later changed its name to *Frederick Douglass' Paper*.

learned was that slavery was wrong. He made up his mind to run away from it. It was not easy to escape. He was caught the first time he tried. But he did get away in 1838, when he was 21 years old. He reached Massachusetts, where he changed his name to Douglass so that he would be safer from capture. He found work in a shipyard and lived quietly.

12 / *Frederick Douglass, Speaker*. Three years later he made a speech at an aboli-

14 / *Frederick Douglass, Leader of His People*. Until his death in 1895, Douglass was the most important Afro-American in the United States. He wrote and spoke, first

for freedom and then for equal rights for all. He helped escaping slaves on their way to Canada. He planned and led "sit-ins" and "freedom rides" on New England trains. During the Civil War he raised black troops for the Northern armies. His own two sons were among these soldiers. Douglass was a friend of William Lloyd Garrison and John Brown. He advised Abraham Lincoln. He became a government official in Washington, D.C. Later he was this country's minister to Haiti. Until he died, Frederick Douglass spoke to the world as a great leader of his people.

MEMORIES OF AN ESCAPED SLAVE

from

NARRATIVE OF THE LIFE OF FREDERICK DOUGLASS— AN AMERICAN SLAVE

Written by Himself

"My mother and I were separated when I was but an infant—before I knew her as my mother. It is a common custom, in the part of Maryland from which I ran away, to part children from their mothers at a very early age. . . . I never saw my mother, to know her as such, more than four or five times in my life. . . .

"(Master) . . . was a cruel man, hardened by a long life of slaveholding. He would at times seem to take great pleasure in whipping a slave.

"The men and women slaves received, as their monthly allowance of food, eight pounds of pork, or . . . fish, and one bushel of corn meal. . . . There were no beds given the slaves unless one coarse blanket be considered such, and none but the men and women had these. . . . (They slept on) the cold, damp, floor.

". . . I say this—that killing a slave . . . in Talbot County, Maryland, is not treated as a crime. . . .

". . . but for the hope of being free, I have no doubt but that I should have killed myself, or done something for which I should have been killed. . . . Every little while, I could hear something about the abolitionists. It was some time before I found what the word meant.

"White men have been known to encourage slaves to escape, and then, to get the reward, catch them and return them to their masters.

"We were worked in all weathers. It was never too hot or too cold; it could never rain, blow, hail, or snow, too hard for us to work in the field.

"I will run away. I will not stand it. Get caught, or get clear. I'll try it. . . . I have only one life to lose. I had as well be killed running as die standing. Only think of it; one hundred miles straight north, and I am free! Try it? Yes! God helping me, I will. It cannot be that I shall live and die a slave."

Understanding What You Have Read

I. CHECKING WORD MEANINGS

Write the letter of the choice that best completes each statement.

1. The great hope of the abolitionists was to (a) end slavery, (b) spread slavery, (c) forget about slavery.
2. When you appeal to someone you are (a) ordering him to stop, (b) telling him what is wrong, (c) asking him to do something.
3. A person who is liberated (a) has been set free, (b) cannot read or write, (c) becomes a newspaper owner.
4. The most dangerous happening in an arsenal would be (a) a shortage of steel, (b) a fire, (c) an open door.
5. When you proclaim that you want to abolish slavery you are (a) leading a slave revolt, (b) raiding a plantation for slaves, (c) making a speech against slavery.
6. If you are a liberator, you have (a) escaped from slavery, (b) freed slaves, (c) joined the abolitionists.
7. A person making a short sojourn in a town is (a) an abolitionist, (b) a liberator, (c) a visitor.
8. When you publish a newspaper you (a) have it written and printed, (b) fight against slavery, (c) become an abolitionist leader.
9. The citizens feared a raid because it would be (a) a terrible rain, (b) an attack, (c) a freeing of slaves.
10. The United States minister to France works for (a) the United States, (b) France, (c) the United States and France.

II. UNDERSTANDING IMPORTANT IDEAS

Answer each of these questions in a complete sentence.

1. Why were most of the abolitionists in the North? (See Paragraph 1.)
2. How did David Walker plan to end slavery? (See Paragraph 2.)

3. How did William Lloyd Garrison disagree with David Walker? (See Paragraph 4.)
4. Why did John Brown's Raid fail? (See Paragraph 6.)
5. Why did Sojourner Truth change her name? (See Paragraph 7.)
6. What did Sojourner Truth mean by "proclaim liberty"? (See Paragraph 8.)
7. Why was the Liberty Party important? (See Paragraph 9.)
8. Why did Frederick Douglass change his name? (See Paragraph 11.)
9. Why did Frederick Douglass call his newspaper the *North Star*? (See Paragraph 13.)
10. Why was Frederick Douglass called "the spokesman of his people"? (See Paragraph 14.)

III. ALWAYS, SOMETIMES OR NEVER

Write ALWAYS if the statement was *always true*. Write SOMETIMES if it was *sometimes true and sometimes false*. Write NEVER if it was *never true*.

1. Abolitionists were ready to use force to free the slaves.
2. Abolitionists changed the minds of the people who heard them.
3. Runaway slaves in the North feared slave-catchers.
4. Negro officials were in charge of Washington, D.C.
5. *Walker's Appeal* was a secret plan.

IV. WHICH HAPPENED FIRST?

Write the letter of the event that happened first in each pair. The number following each sentence is the number of the paragraph that tells about it.

1. (a) *Walker's Appeal* is published. (2)
   (b) Frederick Douglass escapes to freedom. (11)
2. (a) A reward is offered for David Walker. (3)
   (b) A New York state law gives freedom to Sojourner Truth. (7)

3. (a) John Brown fights in Kansas. (5)
   (b) Frederick Douglass begins the *North Star*. (13)
4. (a) John Brown is hanged. (6)
   (b) The Liberty Party begins. (9)
5. (a) William Lloyd Garrison begins his newspaper. (4)
   (b) Frederick Douglass joins the abolitionists. (12)

V. WHO AM I?

Write the name of the person described in each sentence.

1. I refused to escape to Canada, saying instead "I will stand my ground."
2. I was hanged in 1859 after I failed in my plan to begin a slave revolt in Virginia.
3. In my newspaper, *The Liberator,* I asked people to find peaceful ways to end slavery.
4. I could not read or write, but my speeches against slavery made people understand what it had meant for me to live as a slave.
5. After becoming a well-known abolitionist speaker, I wrote a book about my life as a slave.

VI. BUILD YOUR VOCABULARY

These words are related to words used in this chapter. Use a dictionary to find their meanings. Then write a sentence for each.

   publisher   publication   proclamation   liberation

VII. THINGS TO DO

1. Discuss these questions in class.
   a. Did the abolitionists really keep slavery alive by frightening the Southern slaveholders, who then made slavery stricter?
   b. Who was more correct, David Walker ("use force") or William Lloyd Garrison ("use reason")?

    c. John Brown was described as a hero and as a madman. In your opinion, which of these is correct? Why?

2. Copy and complete the outline below.

    A. David Walker

        1.

        2. Told slaves to fight for their freedom.

    B. William Lloyd Garrison

        1. Published *The Liberator*.

        2.

    C. John Brown

        1. Used force to fight slavery.

        2.

    D. Frederick Douglass

        1.

        2. Became the leader of his people.

3. Choose one of the people discussed in this chapter. Visit your library to find a book telling about this person. Then prepare a one-page report in which you answer these questions:

    a. How was this person important in the story of the Afro-American in United States history?

    b. How did this person change life for all people in the United States?

    c. Describe the best example of this person's work.

4. Find the answer to these questions about the law that did much to shape the history of the United States after 1820.

    a. What was the Missouri Compromise of 1820?

    b. How did the Missouri Compromise appear to "settle" the problem of free and slave states?

    c. How were black Americans affected by the Missouri Compromise?

5. Look in an encyclopedia or a textbook in American history to find the story of Harriet Beecher Stowe and her book and play *Uncle Tom's Cabin*. How were they important in the abolitionist struggle?

Chapter 15 | AFRO-AMERICANS AND THE CIVIL WAR

Let's Discover

1. How Afro-Americans helped bring victory to the Union.
2. How large numbers of slaves gained their freedom during the Civil War.

Words to Know

Republican	One of the two largest political parties in the United States.
	The Republican Party began in 1854.
decision	A statement of what has been decided.
	A court's decision should be obeyed by all citizens.
majority	More than half.
	When five of the nine judges in the court agree, they state a majority decision.
secede	To stop being one of the states in the United States; to drop out of the federation.
	South Carolina decided to secede after Lincoln was elected President.
Confederacy	The group of eleven southern states that seceded from the United States in 1860 and 1861.
	The Confederacy was a new country.
Confederates	Those joined in a confederacy.
	All rebel soldiers were called Confederates.
Union	The United States of America during the Civil War, made up of the states that did not join the Confederacy.
	Lincoln led the Union to victory over the Confederate States of America.

Black troops enter Charleston, South Carolina.

civil   Between two parts of the same country.
The Civil War was a war between the northern and southern halves of the United States.

confiscation   The act of taking something, when done by a government.
Congress passed a law for the confiscation of some slaves from their masters.

pilot   The man who steers a ship in and out of harbors.
Robert Smalls became the pilot of the steamship Planter.

---

1 / *Growing Troubles Between North and South.* The question of slavery divided the country more and more in the years after 1820. There were three parts to this ques-

tion. How long could the South and its slaveowning leaders keep their power in the nation's government? Would the country allow slavery to spread into the new states being formed in the West? Would the abolitionists be able to get most of the white people in the North to agree that slavery was wrong and should be ended?

2 / Political Changes Weaken the South. At first the men from the South held great power in the country's government. They were the Presidents. They were the leaders of government. Until 1820 they kept the question of slavery out of sight. Then new states were formed. Would they be free states or slave states? A law in 1854 allowed the people of Kansas and Nebraska to decide this for themselves. We have read about "Bleeding Kansas." The leaders of the South began to see that there could be so many free states that they would lose their hold on the government. Their fear grew when a new political party—the Republicans—was started in the North. The Republicans did not favor the spread of slavery. They would soon control the government because there were more people in the North, and more men would be sent to Congress from that part of the country.

3 / The Dred Scott Case. Perhaps peace could be kept between the North and the South. So long as people could still talk about controlling the spread of slavery to the new lands of the West, war could be delayed. Then men of peace could try to work out some way to agree. This hope was crushed in 1857. The Supreme Court of the

Dred Scott.

United States handed down its decision in the case of a man named Dred Scott. Dred Scott was a slave whose master had taken him into free territory. Since no man could be made a slave there, Dred Scott said he should now be free. The Court did not agree. Its Southern judges were a majority. They ruled that a slave could not be a citizen. They added that Congress could not pass a law to end or limit slavery! This decision angered people all over the North. More of them became abolitionists. More of them turned to the Republican Party. In 1858 it won control of the House of Representatives. Southern leaders could see that their days of power were soon to end.

4 / *The South Secedes.* The election of 1860 tore the country apart. The men who led the South said that they would pull their states out of the United States if the Republicans won. To take a state out of the country is to secede. Lincoln, a Republican, was elected. Southern leaders took quick steps to secede. They would form a new country based on slavery. They would no longer be part of the United States. They set up a new country with a new government. Its name was the Confederate States of America. Eleven slave states joined it. They were South Carolina, Mississippi, Florida, Alabama, Georgia, Louisiana, Texas, Arkansas, North Carolina, Virginia and Tennessee. This new "country," which people called the Confederacy, challenged the United States.

President Abraham Lincoln.

5 / *The Civil War Begins.* Abraham Lincoln had been chosen President. He did not believe in slavery. He felt it was evil and should be ended. He did not want to see slaves in the new states forming in the West. He did not agree with the abolitionists that all slaves should be freed at once. An important reason for this view was Lincoln's fear of losing the border states. He believed that his chief task was to keep the country— what people called the Union—together. He tried to keep peace. The Confederacy had set up its own army. It attacked a Union fort in the harbor of Charleston, South Carolina. Lincoln had to fight back. A civil war is one between two parts of the same country. The American Civil War had begun.

6 / *Lincoln's Views on Slavery.* Lincoln had spoken out against slavery many times. He had called it "wrong." He did not want it to spread. Now he was President. He had to keep the country whole. He said this about slavery: "If I could save the Union without freeing all the slaves, I would do it; if I could save it by freeing all the slaves, I would do it; and if I could save it by freeing some and leaving others alone, I would also do it. What I do about slavery and the colored race, I do because I believe it helps save the Union."

7 / *More Runaway Slaves.* The war was a great chance for freedom for tens of thousands of slaves. Lincoln knew that many people in the North were not against slavery. He needed the help of all his people. He tried to make the real question of the war the saving of the Union, not the ending of

slavery. But as the war went on, his armies moved into the South. When they arrived, slaves ran away from their masters and came to the Union troops. The generals of these armies could not drive these men, women and children away. Many stayed with the army groups. Even though it might mean death if they were caught, the slaves kept coming to the Northern armies for freedom.

8 / *Confiscation Acts.* Some of Lincoln's generals were ready to free all the slaves they could find. He did not allow them to do this at first. Then, in 1861, he agreed to a law passed by Congress. This law was called the Confiscation Act. To confiscate means to have a government take something. The Confiscation Act freed any slave who was used by the Confederate Army and then came into the hands of the Union Army. A year later a second act freed all slaves held by masters who helped the Confederacy. For the first time the government of the United States was doing something to free slaves.

9 / *Afro-Americans Join the Union Forces.* When the war began, the Union Army was a white army. Negroes were not allowed to join it. Then, in the second year of the war some Afro-Americans did become soldiers. In 1863 the doors to army and navy service were opened. Great numbers of black Americans rushed to join the fight. Most of them were placed in units called United States Colored Troops, or U.S.C.T. Most were led by white officers, although about seventy-five black soldiers became officers by the end of the war. More than 200,000 Negroes fought for the North. Of these, more than 37,000 lost their lives. Sixteen black soldiers won the Congressional Medal of Honor. One officer explained what he thought was the reason for the fine record of his black troops: "They had more to fight for than the whites."

Runaway slaves joined the Union army.

He steered the ship past the Confederate guns.

10 / *Robert Smalls, Negro, Hero*. One of the bravest acts of the Civil War was performed by a slave, Robert Smalls. When the war started he was a wheelsman—the sailor who steers a ship—on the Confederate steamboat *Planter*. On the night of May 12, 1862, he and several other slaves took over the ship while the officers were at a party. Smalls brought his wife and children on board. He was a fine pilot. He steered the ship past the Confederate guns and out of the harbor of Charleston, South Carolina. Then he turned it over to the Union Navy. If he had been stopped and caught, he and the others would have been killed. He fooled the Confederates by wearing the large straw hat and coat usually worn by the ship's captain. They let the ship pass, thinking it was just moving to some other spot in the harbor.

11 / *Robert Smalls, Captain and Congressman*. For his brave act, Robert Smalls was given money and made a pilot in the Union Navy. He was called to Washington. There he helped get the laws changed to allow runaway slaves to fight for the Union. As pilot of the *Planter*, he had to take command

during an attack when its captain was ready to give up the ship. Smalls brought the *Planter* to safety. He was not punished; instead, he was made captain himself! He served on the ship until the end of the war. By then he was a hero known all over the United States. After the war he became active in the state government of South Carolina. For a while that state lived under a constitution giving equal rights to all its people, black and white. Robert Smalls helped write that plan of government. Later he served as a member of Congress for eight years. This man, born a slave, had become a leader of his country.

12 / *Problems of Black Soldiers.* Not many Negro fighting men had as easy a time as Robert Smalls. Most of them had to fight in segregated groups. They were led by white officers who sometimes did not want to lead black troops. It was hard for an Afro-American to become an officer. The first black troops received much lower pay than white soldiers. Soon the pay was made more equal. There were not enough doctors in the Union Army. More were sent to white troops than to black ones. This meant that more Afro-Americans died from battle wounds. When new guns or supplies arrived, black soldiers knew that they would receive the older equipment. This unfair treatment did not bother them as much as the fear of capture. Confederate troops killed Negro prisoners, or made them slaves. A man had to be brave to be a soldier. A Negro had to be even more brave. His danger was always greater.

13 / *Victory Through Hard Work.* Not all of the free Negroes and runaway slaves served as soldiers or sailors. A war cannot

Company E of the 4th U.S. Colored Infantry.

be won unless a great deal of hard work is done behind the fighting lines. Forts had to be built. Wagons and railroads had to move supplies. An army needs cooks, carpenters and nurses. It needs men who will build bridges, dig tunnels and lay new roads. We will never know how many Afro-Americans worked at such tasks. It was at least as many as were in the armed forces. Their work, joined with the work of tens of thousands of white men and women, made the success of the North possible.

14 / *Negro Spies and Guides.* Afro-Americans were among the best spies for the North. They could find out where Confederate troops were. They could move among the slaves to learn how many soldiers, wagons and guns were in an enemy camp. They would take great chances as they traveled behind enemy lines. One of the stories told is about "clothesline telegraphs." A group of Negro spies and slaves might send signals for miles by putting a certain kind of clothing on clotheslines. Each was in view of the next clothesline in the "telegraph line." Once the news had come through, runaway slaves who knew the area could guide Union soldiers. They knew where rivers were low enough to cross safely. They knew where a hill might hide enemy troops. They knew the best way through hills and mountains. They could get through lowlands and swamps. Their help saved many lives and brought many victories.

15 / *Time to Change Our View of the War.* The Civil War has long been pictured as a fight between white men in which the black man was not important. We now know that this is not a true picture. In North and South, the Afro-American was active all during the war years. United States Colored Troops fought in more than 200 battles. Their courage was never questioned. From the beginning of the war, they knew that their hopes for a free and better life had to begin with the defeat of the South. Perhaps the happiest moment of the war for groups like the 55th Massachusetts Colored Company came when they entered Charleston, South Carolina, bringing freedom with them. General Butler of the Union Army said to his Negro soldiers toward the end of the war: "... You have ... (opened) new fields of freedom, liberty and equality to yourselves and your race forever." This was the hope and dream of the hundreds of thousands of Afro-Americans who helped the North win this terrible war.

Understanding What You Have Read

I. MATCHING WORDS AND HEADLINES

Write the letter of the headline that best describes each of the numbered words.

1. **Republican**
2. **majority**
3. **Confederacy**
4. **Union**
5. **secede**

a. MORE THAN HALF OF CONGRESS WANTS TO END SLAVERY
b. ELEVEN SOUTHERN STATES FORM NEW GOVERNMENT
c. STATE OF GEORGIA LEAVES THE UNITED STATES
d. FEDERAL GOVERNMENT WORKS TO KEEP COUNTRY WHOLE
e. POLITICAL PARTY WINS ELECTION OF 1860

6. **decision**
7. **Confederate**
8. **civil**
9. **pilot**
10. **confiscation**

f. REBEL FIGHTS AGAINST UNION
g. SUPREME COURT ANNOUNCES DRED SCOTT IS STILL SLAVE
h. ROBERT SMALLS STEERS SHIP OUT OF HARBOR
i. UNION TAKES PROPERTY AWAY FROM CONFEDERATES
j. WAR IS FOUGHT BETWEEN TWO PARTS OF COUNTRY

II. FACT OR OPINION?

Write the word FACT if the statement tells something that happened. Write the word OPINION if the statement tells what someone might think about something that happened.

1. Abraham Lincoln did not act to end slavery when the war began.
2. Lincoln should have ended slavery as soon as he became President.
3. Dred Scott went to court to get his freedom.
4. The Supreme Court was wrong to keep any man in slavery.
5. Any state should be allowed to leave the Union.
6. United States Colored Troops did not always receive fair treatment.
7. Robert Smalls, born a slave, became a member of Congress.
8. Negroes were among the spies of the Union armies.
9. Black soldiers were the best fighters in every battle.
10. Congress was wise in passing the Confiscation Acts.

III. REVIEWING IMPORTANT FACTS

Write the letter of the choice that best completes each statement.

1. Thousands of slaves gained freedom during the war by (a) running away to the Union armies, (b) revolting against their masters, (c) forming their own army.

2. The South lost control of Congress because (a) the people of the South had turned against slavery, (b) Lincoln was an abolitionist, (c) the number of people in the North became greater than the number of people in the South.

3. At the time of the Dred Scott decision, the majority of the Supreme Court agreed with the (a) North, (b) South, (c) slaves seeking freedom.

4. The Civil War began when (a) Lincoln was elected, (b) the Confederacy was organized, (c) Confederate armies attacked a Union fort.

5. Lincoln believed he had to (a) keep the Union together, (b) protect slavery, (c) end slavery at once.

6. The number of black soldiers fighting for the North was about (a) 200,000, (b) 37,000, (c) 4,000,000.

7. At the time Robert Smalls sailed the *Planter* out of the harbor of Charleston, South Carolina, that state was part of (a) the Union, (b) the Confederacy, (c) neither side.

8. The greatest of these dangers for a Negro soldier was to be (a) wounded in battle, (b) captured by the Confederates, (c) made an officer.

9. Lincoln was elected in (a) 1860, (b) 1861, (c) 1862.

10. The "clothesline telegraph" was used to (a) dry clothes, (b) keep in touch with President Lincoln, (c) send messages to Union armies in the field.

IV. BUILDING YOUR VOCABULARY

Here are some words you should know if you are to understand the events of the Civil War. Check each in a dictionary and use it in a sentence.

1. Copperheads
2. secession
3. civilian

4. martial law
5. Rebels

V. THE VOCABULARY OF FREEDOM

You should know each of these words in the vocabulary of freedom. Check each in a dictionary. Most of them will be important in the next chapter.

1. manumit
2. manumission
3. emancipate
4. emancipation

5. Emancipator
6. ex-slave
7. freedman
8. citizenship

VI. ANSWER EACH OF THESE QUESTIONS IN A COMPLETE SENTENCE.

1. How did the South keep control of the government for so long?
2. How did the Supreme Court attack the right of Congress to limit slavery?
3. Why did eleven slave states secede?
4. Why did so many Afro-Americans join the Union forces?
5. How did Robert Smalls become a national hero?
6. What were some of the jobs, besides fighting, that needed to be done to win the war?
7. Why did so few Afro-Americans become officers?
8. Why were Negroes so successful as spies for the Union?
9. How did the Confiscation Acts help some black Americans?
10. Why were so many black soldiers killed in action during the war?

VII. THINGS TO DO

1. Find out more about Dred Scott. Who was his master in 1857? What happened to Dred Scott after the Supreme Court decision?

2. Check *The Negro Almanac* in your library. Find out what Afro-Americans won the Congressional Medal of Honor in the Civil War. Why was each given the award? Why is the Congressional Medal of Honor so important to a soldier?

3. Congress was ready to free all slaves by law. Lincoln feared the people of the North were not ready to fight a war on the question of freeing the slaves. Discuss the reasons for each position. Was Lincoln right or wrong in your opinion? Explain.

4. Prepare a short play about the time Robert Smalls took control of the *Planter* from his captain.

5. Read a life of Frederick Douglass. What was he doing during the war years? Report your findings to the class.

6. The political party that held control of the United States before the Republicans was the Democratic Party. Read a history of the United States to find out how the Democratic Party was controlled by men from the South. How was this powerful party split into two parties in 1860? How many men ran for President in 1860? Lincoln did not receive a majority of the votes in 1860, yet he became President. Explain.

7. Prepare a list of the fifteen slave states and eighteen free states in 1860. Why did four of the slave states remain in the Union? How did this affect Lincoln's decision not to try to free the slaves at once?

Chapter 16 | EMANCIPATION AND VICTORY

Let's Discover

1. How the Civil War was part of a world movement toward freedom.
2. How the Emancipation Proclamation helped free the slaves in the United States.

Words to Know

freedman	A person freed from slavery.
	Frederick Douglass had become a freedman.
manumit	To free from slavery.
	The slaveowner decided to manumit his slaves.
manumission	The act of freeing people from slavery.
	Manumission was a path to freedom.
emancipation	The act of freeing from slavery, usually done by a government.
	The Republicans wanted a law to bring about emancipation.
proclamation	An announcement by an official of a government.
	Abraham Lincoln issued the Emancipation Proclamation.
Copperheads	People in the North who favored the South during the Civil War.
	The Copperheads in Indiana did not want to join the Union Army.
contraband	A word used to describe a slave who escaped to or was brought into the Union army.
	Contraband slaves helped win the war.
draft	To order into the armed forces.
	The poor people of New York City did not want to be drafted into the Union Army.
riot	To disturb the peace violently along with many others.
	The riot began when hundreds of angry men began to fight with the police.

---

1 / *Paths to Freedom.* During the long hundreds of years of slavery in this land, there were always some paths to freedom. Let's list them.

a) A slave could run away. If he was not caught, he would be free.

b) A slave could somehow save enough money to buy his freedom from his master.

From then on, he would be called a freedman, or a free Negro.

c) A slave could be freed by his master. This was called manumission. Many slaves were freed in this way as a special reward. Men like George Washington and Thomas Jefferson decided to manumit their slaves in their wills. That is, the slaves were freed when the master died.

d) State laws freed thousands of slaves. These laws were passed in states in the North. Massachusetts began to free its slaves after it set up a new government in 1780. Like Connecticut and Rhode Island, it freed its slaves over a number of years. States like New York and New Jersey soon passed manumission laws too. We have seen how, over the years, the country was split into free and slave states. In each case the people of the state had made their decision to end or keep slavery.

e) Laws passed by Congress drew lines on the map to divide free territory from slave territory. The lands of the Northwest Territory were made free by law. The law called the Missouri Compromise of 1820 said that there would be no slavery in the northern part of the Louisiana Territory. The Supreme Court, you will remember, later said that Congress could not pass a law to stop slavery.

2 / *Freedom Given by the Nation.* Emancipation is the freeing of all the slaves in a country, or in some part of it. This had long been one of the goals of the abolitionists. They had tried to get Congress to free all slaves. We know that they failed for two reasons. First, the men who came to Con-

Toussaint L'Ouverture.

gress from the South would not give up their defense of slavery. They did not allow an emancipation law to be passed. Second, there were still many in the North who feared that a law to end slavery would tear the country apart. Their representatives in Congress often agreed with the men from the South. They did not vote for laws to weaken or end slavery. Emancipation was the dream of the slave, the free Negro and the abolitionist. Yet it seemed that the power of the South would always be great enough to prevent it.

3 / *Slavery Ends in Other Lands.* Freeing slaves was not a new idea in the 1800's. There were slaves in other parts of the world. The slaves of Haiti had broken free. Led by men like Toussaint L'Ouverture and

Henri Christophe, they had emancipated themselves when they gained freedom for their country in 1803. The colonies of Spain soon copied them. One by one they won their freedom. Their people then took quick steps to end slavery.

4 / *Freedom in the Americas.* Such news of freedom came again and again. The people of Mexico ended slavery in 1829. The people of Bolivia freed their slaves two years later. In the 1840's and 1850's Uruguay, Colombia, Argentina, Venezuela and Peru joined the march to freedom. It seemed that only the United States would keep its slaves in bondage!

5 / *England Fights the Slave Trade.* The English ruled the seas in the 1800's. They had the largest and strongest navy. They were ready to use it to help make their laws work. In 1833 they passed a law to end slavery in all the lands they ruled. Their navy then began to roam the seas, stopping slave ships of any country. English emancipation paid the owners of slaves for their freed "property." The world drive to end slavery was growing stronger each year.

6 / *Russia Frees Its Serfs.* The country with the largest number of people in a form of slavery was Russia. These people—more than twenty millions of them—were serfs. Russia was still a feudal land. The serf was more free than a slave. Still, he could be sold. He could not leave the land on which he worked. He and his children "belonged" to the man on whose land he lived. This landowner was the judge and jury of the serf's rights. Then, in 1861, the ruler of Russia freed his country's serfs. He also gave them land to farm. During the next six years feudalism came to an end in Russia.

7 / *Lincoln Needs Support in Europe.* The Civil War seemed to be the last great fight to keep slavery alive. The people of the South were trying to hold their slaves even while the rest of the world was turning to freedom. Most people in Europe did not believe in slavery. They were trying, in country after country, to gain more rights from their rulers. The great hope of the South, and Lincoln's great fear, was that the rulers of Europe would care more about cotton for their factories than about freedom. If they gave aid to the South, then the North might lose the war. Lincoln and his advisors might have wanted to free the slaves early in the war. They were afraid to do so. Such an act might turn the powerful countries of Europe against the Union.

8 / *Republicans and Copperheads.* The Republicans ruled Congress. The men who led the party had come to agree with the abolitionists. They were ready to pass a law to free all slaves. Yet Lincoln made them wait. He felt he could not push for freedom yet. His armies were not winning the war. There were many people in the North who were ready to help the South. These people were called Copperheads, like the deadly snake that strikes and kills without warning. Lincoln felt torn. Four of the slave states had stayed with the North. If he freed the slaves, the white people of these states might join the South. So he did noth-

ing. In fact, early in the war, he asked his generals to return runaways to their masters.

9 / *Contraband Slaves*. Lincoln could not make up his mind. The slaves had no such trouble. They knew they wanted to be free. We have seen how thousands of them—men, women and children—ran away from their masters. They came to the Union armies. *Contraband* is a word that means captured war supplies. The word also came to mean slaves who had come to or been captured by the Union armies. Some of the generals, like Ben Butler, did not return these slaves to their masters. He could use captured guns and supplies. He could also use this new kind of "contraband." The runaway slaves were soon an important part of his army.

10 / *Waiting for a Victory*. In 1862 Congress pushed hard for the freeing of the slaves. Its leaders were clear. They thought Lincoln should use his power as the leader of a country at war. It would help end the war if he made a statement that he was freeing all slaves. Then the people of Europe, friends of freedom, would be more friendly to the United States. They would not allow their governments to aid the South. Then the abolitionists of the North would fight even harder to win the war. The slaves all over the South would rise up against their masters. The war would have to end. All this seemed plain. There was only one problem. The armies of the North were not winning. What would be the use of a statement of emancipation if the world saw it just as a move to weaken the South? Lincoln needed a victory. He would take steps to free all the slaves in the South as soon as his armies had won an important battle. He had to wait until September, 1862, for such a battle.

11 / *Antietam*. Robert E. Lee led the armies of the South. He won one battle after another during the first year of the war. Then, in 1862, he invaded the North. This time the Union armies held him! A great battle was fought at Antietam, Maryland. Lee could not break through the Union lines. He had to fall back to Virginia. Lincoln had his "victory" at last. A few days later he said that he would issue the proclamation of emancipation that he had been working on for months. He would, on January 1, 1863, use his power as President to order the end of slavery in the states that were still fighting the Union.

12 / *The Emancipation Proclamation*. Frederick Douglass, Republican leaders in Congress and other leading Americans had been asking Abraham Lincoln to free the slaves. When the order came—the Emancipation Proclamation—they were only partly pleased. Lincoln had freed "all persons held as slaves" in the rebel states. The slaves in the states still in the Union, or in areas held by its armies, were not yet free. Lincoln hoped that Congress would buy the freedom of these slaves. He felt he could not order their freedom. He was freeing the slaves in the South as part of his aim to win the war. He did not think he had the power to free slaves outside of the rebel states.

13 / *Freedom for Many Slaves*. The slaves in the South were not freed at once by the Proclamation. They were still under the

Many freedmen joined the Union troops.

rule of their masters. But, in the next year, the armies of the North swept into the South. As they moved ahead they freed the slaves they found. Each Union officer knew this was his duty. As part of the Proclamation, Lincoln had ordered his troops to see that these slaves were freed. He had also ordered that freed slaves be allowed to join the Union Army and Navy. More Negro groups were set up in the Army. More Afro-Americans served in the Navy. Some states gave more rights to black citizens. Congress voted to allow them to take part in Federal court cases. The Dred Scott days were soon to end. Negroes began to carry the mail. They were given other government jobs. States like Illinois and California changed their laws to give black Americans equal rights.

14 / *Trouble for Negroes in the North.* Most people in the North cheered the Proclamation. Many of them formed groups to help the freed slaves. Black freedmen came into cities in the North looking for jobs, places to live and schools for their children. But in some cities they found that poor white peo-

ple were not ready to accept them. In New York City there were four days of riots against the draft laws. These were the laws under which men were chosen for the armed forces of the United States. Mobs roamed the streets; they turned their anger against the city's black people. They broke into stores, burned homes and attacked Negroes wildly, even hanging some. Hundreds of lives were lost during the four days of the riots before soldiers were brought to the city to keep peace.

15 / *The War Ends.* The Civil War lasted for four years. It ended in 1865. The South had lost; the Union had been saved. Along the way the Union had set free most of the slaves in the country. The other slaves would soon be free too. Some people thought this was the end of the fight for freedom. They were wrong. Freedmen could do little so long as they had freedom without equality. They were to suffer for many more years. The story of their suffering would be the shame of America for the next hundred years and more.

Understanding What You Have Read

I. MATCHING WORDS AND HEADLINES

Write the letter of the headline that best explains the meaning of each numbered word.

1. **freedman**
2. **emancipation**
3. **manumit**
4. **contraband**
5. **proclamation**

a. JEFFERSON'S WILL FREES HIS SLAVES

b. MAN BORN A SLAVE NOW FREE

c. ORDER BY GOVERNMENT FREES ALL SLAVES

d. PRESIDENT LINCOLN ISSUES PUBLIC ANNOUNCEMENT

e. RUNAWAY SLAVES REACH UNION ARMY LINES

---

6. **draft**
7. **riot**
8. **manumission**
9. **Copperheads**

f. GROUP OF NORTHERNERS HELP REBEL ARMY

g. ABOLITIONIST CALLS FOR FREEDOM NOW

h. MOB WRECKS BUILDING IN WILD ATTACK

i. 500 MEN TAKEN FOR THE NAVY

Gen. Robert E. Lee surrenders to Gen. Ulysses S. Grant. The Civil War is over!

II. KNOWING WHY

Write the letter of the choice that best completes each statement.

1. Abolitionists favored emancipation because they (a) knew it would end slavery, (b) believed it would help slaves find homes in other lands, (c) were certain the South would approve of it.

2. Four slave states did not join the Confederacy because (a) their people had decided to give up slavery, (b) their armies were too weak, (c) their people loved the Union.

3. Afro-Americans praised the people of Haiti because that country (a) helped the South during the Civil War, (b) had ended slavery, (c) fought against the South during the Civil War.

4. English ships carrying slaves after 1833 could be attacked by English warships because (a) only English warships were allowed to carry slaves, (b) England had ended slavery in its empire, (c) only the United States allowed the slave trade.

5. Slaveholders were not welcome in Mexico after 1829 because (a) Mexico did not want cotton grown on its territory, (b) Mexico had ended slavery, (c) slaveholders took too much land for their plantations.

6. Lincoln did not free the slaves at the beginning of the Civil War because he (a) believed he could never control the freedmen, (b) was afraid countries in Europe would then aid the South, (c) thought the Dred Scott decision was correct.

7. Copperheads were given that name because they (a) could not be trusted by their country, (b) wore copper-colored hats, (c) used copper coins as a sign of membership.

8. Ben Butler kept his contraband slaves with his army because (a) Lincoln had given him permission to do so, (b) their masters no longer wanted these slaves, (c) he believed slaves were property he could properly take from rebels.

9. The Emancipation Proclamation was delayed because (a) Lincoln was waiting for a Union victory, (b) Lincoln had no time to

write the message earlier, (c) the Republican Party would not support the proclamation earlier.

10. The riots in New York began because (a) most people there did not like Negroes, (b) there were no police in the city, (c) many men did not want to be drafted into the armed forces.

III. FACT OR OPINION?

Which of these are statements of fact and which are someone's opinion? Write FACT or OPINION for each.

1. Manumission and emancipation have the same result for the slave who is freed.
2. Slavery had ended in much of the rest of the world before it ended in the United States.
3. The wisest act of the ruler of Russia was his freeing of the serfs.
4. Ben Butler was Lincoln's best general.
5. Afro-Americans began to receive government jobs after the Emancipation Proclamation.

IV. DO YOU AGREE OR DISAGREE?

For each of these statements, write a complete sentence giving a reason for agreeing or disagreeing with it.

1. The Emancipation Proclamation should have been issued sooner.
2. Freeing the slaves helped win the Civil War for the Union.
3. The slaves in the South should have revolted during the Civil War.
4. The Union armies had the right to keep contraband slaves.
5. England forced the slave trade to end.

V. ANSWER EACH OF THESE QUESTIONS IN A COMPLETE SENTENCE.

1. What were three ways in which a slave could gain his freedom?

2. Why was there no slavery in the states made from the Northwest Territory?

3. Why didn't the other countries in the Americas end slavery before the 1800's?

4. Why didn't Lincoln free the slaves in the four slave states that remained in the Union?

5. How did Ben Butler help escaping slaves?

6. How did the freeing of the serfs in Russia show Lincoln that it was time to free America's slaves?

7. Carrying the mail was the first Federal job Afro-Americans were allowed to hold. Why was this important?

8. Why did some people in New York City riot in 1863?

9. Why were freedmen so happy with the Emancipation Proclamation?

10. Why did Lincoln wait until after the Battle of Antietam to announce his Emancipation Proclamation?

VI. THINGS TO DO

1. In the library, find out what each of these people did to help the Union during the Civil War.

Walt Whitman	Horace Greeley
Harriet Tubman	Charles Sumner
Thaddeus Stevens	Thomas W. Higginson
Martin Delany	Frederick Douglass
Ulysses S. Grant	Hannibal Hamlin

2. Write a one-page report on how slavery was ended in the District of Columbia in 1862. What problems followed for the new freedmen?

3. How did the black Americans of the North celebrate the Emancipation Proclamation? See *The Great Proclamation* by Henry Steele Commager, published by the Bobbs-Merrill Co., Inc.

Chapter 17 | THE HOPE OF RECONSTRUCTION

Let's Discover

1. How Congress planned to rebuild the South after the Civil War.
2. How the laws passed by Congress improved the life of Afro-Americans.
3. How freedmen joined in the political life of the nation.

Words to Know

reconstruct	To build up again or make over.
	They had to reconstruct the wrecked farmhouse.
Reconstruction	The years 1865 to 1877 in United States history, when the Southern states were brought back into the Union.
	Laws were passed during Reconstruction to improve the rights of ex-slaves.
representative	A person who acts or speaks for others, such as an elected member of the House of Representatives.
	The Republican leaders of Congress would not admit the representatives of Louisiana.
loyal	Faithful to your country.
	The loyal people of the South set up new state governments.
assassination	A murder, especially the murder of a government leader.
	The assassination of Abraham Lincoln shocked the world.
radical	A person who wants to make great changes quickly.
	The Radicals in Congress hoped to change com-

184

The assassination of President
Lincoln at Ford's Theater.

pletely the way Afro-Americans were treated in the South.

amendment	A change in or an addition to the Constitution. *The Thirteenth Amendment outlawed slavery in the United States.*
contract	A business agreement in writing that will be enforced by a court. *Black Americans gained the right to make legal contracts during Reconstruction.*
legislature	The part of a government that makes the laws. *Congress is our country's legislature.*
spokesman	A person who speaks for another person or for a group of people. *Blanche K. Bruce became the spokesman for the black people of America.*

1 / *The South in 1865.* Most of the war had been fought in the South. Farms had been ruined. Cities and towns had been destroyed. Roads and railroads had been wrecked. Business was left without workers or raw materials. The men who had fought for the South saw little hope when they came home. The four million slaves who were now free had much greater worries. What work were they to do? Where would they now live? How would they educate their children? Tens of thousands of freed slaves moved through the South. Many of them feared that they would have nothing but their freedom.

2 / *The Meaning of Reconstruction.* To reconstruct is to rebuild. The South had to be rebuilt in many ways. We call the twelve years after the Civil War the years of Reconstruction. There was so much to be done. The people of the South, black and white, had to be helped to make a living. New governments had to be set up for each state, city, town and village. The new states had to be brought back into the Union; their representatives had to be sent to Congress again. Most important, the rights of four million men, women and children—the newly freed slaves—had to be made clear, protected by law and made to work in their daily lives.

3 / *Lincoln's Plan.* Abraham Lincoln had said that the states of the South never had the right to leave the Union. He planned to pardon most of the men who had fought for the South if they swore to be loyal to the United States. One-tenth of the white people of a state had to take this oath. Their state had to agree that slaves would remain free. Lincoln would then give that state back its rights in the country's government. Two

states, Louisiana and Arkansas, had tried to come back under Lincoln's plan. Congress would not admit the men sent to Washington by these states. Then, on April 14, 1865, Abraham Lincoln was shot and killed by John Wilkes Booth. This assassination made Vice-President Andrew Johnson the new President. He was soon in a great battle with Congress.

4 / *The New Leaders.* A radical is someone who wants to make great changes quickly. The men who held power in Congress hoped for many changes in the South. They have become known in history as the Radical Republicans. They were led at first by Charles Sumner in the Senate and Thaddeus Stevens in the House of Representatives. They believed that the best way to change the South was to give full rights to the freedmen. Sumner said, "If all whites vote, then must all blacks. . . . Without them the old enemy will . . . put us all in peril again." Stevens believed that no southern state should have a voice in the country's government until it had taken steps to make each black American a full and equal citizen. Such men were not going to see the war's great suffering go for nothing.

5 / *Andrew Johnson's Plan.* Many of the Radicals were certain that Johnson would let them decide on the plans for Reconstruction. One of them even said to him: "Johnson, we have faith in you . . . there will be no trouble now in running the government." But Johnson had a mind of his own. He was going to follow Lincoln's plan to get the country back together again as soon as possible. He quickly allowed the states of the

Charles Sumner.

Thaddeus Stevens.

President Andrew Johnson.

South to set up new governments. He did not first make them give full and equal rights to Negroes! He made these new governments agree that they could not secede, would end all slavery and would refuse to pay the debts made by the Confederacy or its state governments. The Radicals could not accept such a plan. It would leave the freedmen with no rights. When Congress met, they were ready to take control of Reconstruction away from Johnson.

6 / *Radical Reconstruction.* Thaddeus Stevens spoke for the men who now made plans to change the South. His party would not allow men who had led the rebels to become members of Congress. In much of the South the old slave codes were law again. This time they were called Black Codes. The freedmen saw their rights vanish before they had even won them. A black person could not work at a profession. He could not own a business or buy land in a city. His civil rights—the things any person should be allowed to do—were taken away. The Republicans had fought for freedom and equal rights for the black people of this country. They could not allow such unfair treatment to take hold again.

7 / *Changing the Constitution.* The freedmen had to be protected. Three amendments, or changes, were put into our Constitution. The Thirteenth Amendment ended slavery for all time. The Fourteenth Amendment made Negroes citizens of the United States and of their own states. It also said that no state could make or try to enforce any law that took away the rights of any citizen. Each person had to have the full protection of the law. The Fifteenth Amendment told all states that all citizens could vote, even those who had once been slaves. By 1870 all three of these changes had been approved. Meanwhile the men in Congress worked to pass laws to help freedmen in other ways.

8 / *Laws to Help the Freedman.* Many important laws were passed to help the freed slaves. Such laws promised all people in the South equal rights. If we look at three of these laws, we can see what the Radicals were trying to do.
a) *The Reconstruction Act of 1867.* This law ended the power of the governments set up under the Lincoln and Johnson plans. There were still ten states out of the Union.

SOUTH CAROLINA NEGRO SPOKESMEN ASK FOR LAND
FOR THEIR PEOPLE IN 1865

"We will never have true freedom until we abolish the system of agriculture which existed in the Southern states."

.   .   .   .

"How are we to get homesteads, to get lands? . . . Give these men a place to work . . . what we need is a system of small farms."

Black people served on juries during Reconstruction.

Stevens and his followers cut the South into five parts. They had an Army general run each of them, with his soldiers to help enforce the law. As part of the Fourteenth Amendment, the men who had led the South could not vote or hold office in the new state governments. Each of the ten states had to write a new constitution. White men and black had to have equal rights to vote. Each state had to agree to the Fourteenth Amendment. Now the promise that all people would have equal rights could be kept. It was 1870 before all of the ten states had changed their governments under the new rules.

b) *The Freedmen's Bureau.* The men who led Congress had worked out a way to help ex-slaves in March, 1865. They had passed a law to set up a Freedmen's Bureau. The white man who ran it was ex-General Oliver O. Howard. He gave years to his task of helping the Afro-Americans of the South. His first task was to teach the freedmen how to vote. He was later given the power to use the army to help keep the rights of Negroes

alive. There was much more for him and his many helpers to do. They fed black and white people who had no jobs or food. They found places for them to live. Whites and blacks all over the South were helped in the many hospitals set up by the Bureau. For the first time, schools were opened for black Americans in the South. In such ways the Radicals were trying to keep their promise. They were using the power of the government to improve the lives of four million new citizens.

c) *The Civil Rights Act.* Congress passed a Civil Rights Act in 1866. It listed the rights that freedmen, like all citizens, had to have. They could make a contract. They could buy or own land in any part of a state. They could have all the rights that white citizens of their states had. Any white person who tried to take away the rights given to freedmen could be fined or jailed. Federal courts, rather than state courts, would decide cases under this law. The President would enforce the law and in this way make the lives of the freedmen richer and better.

A CASE COMES BEFORE A FREEDMAN'S BUREAU COURT

"Here is a boy, who was formerly a slave, to whom his father, a free man, willed a sum of money, which the boy's owner borrowed, giving his note for it, but never repaid, for did not the boy and all that he had belong to his master? The worn and soiled bit of paper is produced; and now the owner will have that money to restore, with interest. Lucky for the boy he kept that torn and dirty scrap carefully hidden all these years!"

9 / *Negroes in Government.* By 1868 the new voters of the South—mostly Negroes and poor white people—had voted for new state constitutions. They had given equal rights to all. For the first time state governments in the South tried to help the poor and to give education to all. Afro-Americans, able to vote and citizens at last, were important in these new governments. Many became leaders. Two black Americans were sent to the United States Senate from Mississippi. Fourteen black men, some of whom had been born slaves, spoke for the black people of the South as members of the House of Representatives. Afro-Americans won high office in state after state. They were sheriffs and town clerks. One was mayor of a large city. Many held other city and state jobs. They served in state legislatures—the part of a state government that makes laws. From 1868 to 1876 the Negro in the South was part of government at all levels.

10 / *The Story of Blanche K. Bruce.* The only Afro-American to serve a full six-year term as a United States Senator was Blanche K. Bruce. He had been a runaway slave during the Civil War. He came back to the South after the war and settled in Missis-

sippi. When freedmen began to vote, men like Blanche K. Bruce rose to power. The governor at that time was a white man who had once owned slaves—James Alcorn. He said that his aim was to make "the colored man the equal before the law of any other man." And he and other white men in Mississippi's Republican Party really tried to do just that. Afro-Americans won office all over the state. Hiram Revels became the first Negro in the United States Senate, but he served for only one year. Blanche K. Bruce won election after election, and in 1875 he was sent to the Senate.

11 / *Blanche K. Bruce in the Senate.* Bruce quickly won the respect of other members of the Senate. Roscoe Conkling of New York, one of the leaders, became his friend. Blanche Bruce became a spokesman for the rights of all men. Again and again he rose to defend people who seemed to have no other friends. He tried to keep the rights the freedmen had just won. He tried to get better treatment for the Indians. He tried to help the millions of immigrants coming from Europe and Asia. Bruce was a rich man, but his days were filled with work to help his country's poor. After he left the Senate he held several jobs for the Federal govern-

ment. Until he died in 1898 he remained one of the most honored men in the United States.

12 / *Better Schools in the South.* Slavery had kept the black man away from schooling. Is it any wonder, then, that schools were one of the great demands of the freedmen. The Freedmen's Bureau built more than 4,000 schools! In them, boys and girls, parents and grandparents tried to fill their great gaps of learning. The Bureau also set up schools to train teachers. It started the Hampton Institute. It opened Howard and Fisk Universities. Other Negro colleges were opened during the years of Reconstruction. Among them were Atlanta University, Talladega College, Tuskegee Institute and Morgan College. These schools are still important centers of learning. One black teacher who came South to work in a new school had this to say: "I never before saw children so eager to learn." Afro-Americans were trying to make up for lost time.

Blanche K. Bruce defended the rights of all men.

The Freedmen's Bureau built more than 4,000 schools.

13 / *Hopes and Dreams.* It really seemed that the end of the Civil War would be followed by great improvement in the life of the four million who had just been freed. Laws were passed to help them. The Federal government had the power to carry out these laws. The leaders of the nation were ready to bring equal rights to all. This was the dream. It is one of the saddest truths of our country's history that the dream failed. The next chapter will show us how and why this happened.

FREDERICK DOUGLASS ASKS FOR THE RIGHT TO VOTE IN 1865

". . . You have called upon us to turn our backs upon our masters . . . to turn against the South . . . in favor of the North. . . . And now, what do you propose to do when you come to make peace? To reward your enemies, and trample in the dust your friends? . . . Do you mean to give your enemies the right to vote, and take it away from your friends? . . . I do not believe you will do it. I think you will see to it that we have the right to vote."

Understanding What You Have Read

I. MATCHING WORDS AND HEADLINES

Write the letter of the headline that best explains the meaning of each numbered word.

1. **reconstruct** (a) BETTER HOME BUILT. (b) NEW HOME BUILT. (c) HOME COMPLETELY REBUILT.

2. **representative** (a) HIRAM REVELS GOES TO SENATE. (b) PRESIDENT LINCOLN ISSUES PROCLAMATION. (c) GENERAL HOWARD MADE HEAD OF FREEDMEN'S BUREAU.

3. **assassination** (a) SOLDIER DIES IN BATTLE. (b) HEAD OF GOVERNMENT IS MURDERED. (c) SIX MEN KILLED IN ACCIDENT.

4. **amendment** (a) NEW LAW PASSED. (b) CONSTITUTION CHANGED. (c) REPORT MADE TO CONGRESS.

5. **legislature** (a) NEW LAW PASSED. (b) PRESIDENT ENFORCES LAW. (c) SUPREME COURT MAKES IMPORTANT DECISION.

6. **spokesman** (a) SENATOR MAKES SPEECH. (b) SENATOR SPEAKS FOR ALL NEGROES. (c) SENATOR ASKS FOR NEW LAW TO HELP NEGROES.

7. **Reconstruction** (a) NEW LAWS CHANGE LIFE IN THE UNITED STATES. (b) BETTER WAY TO SET UP BUILDINGS IS FOUND. (c) CITY WRECKED BY THE WAR.

8. **loyal** (a) CITIZENS GAIN RIGHT TO VOTE. (b) GOVERNMENT LEADER ASKS ALL TO BE FAITHFUL TO OUR COUNTRY. (c) LAWYER ASKS FOR END TO UNFAIR LAWS.

9. **radical** (a) REPUBLICANS REFUSE TO ALLOW CHANGES. (b) REPUBLICANS DECIDE TO MAKE SLOW CHANGES. (c) REPUBLICANS DEMAND GREAT CHANGES AT ONCE.

10. **contract** (a) BUSINESS AGREEMENT MADE. (b) PROMISE MADE TO PAY NEW TAXES. (c) MANY NEW HOMES BOUGHT.

II. WHAT WAS RECONSTRUCTION?

Write *Congress* if the statement is one that might have been made by the Radical Republicans. Write *Johnson* if the statement might have been made by President Andrew Johnson.

1. No state in the South should be allowed to return to the Union until it gives full rights to all freedmen.
2. A law is needed to protect Afro-Americans in the South from the new Black Codes.
3. A Southern state may return to the Union if it promises never to secede again, ends slavery and refuses to pay Confederate debts.
4. A Freedmen's Bureau should have the power to improve the rights of all freedmen.
5. A state should be ready to return to the Union when one-tenth of its people are loyal.

III. UNDERSTANDING IMPORTANT FACTS

Write a sentence to explain why each of these events since the Civil War was important.

1. The Freedmen's Bureau was set up to help the freedmen of the South.
2. The Radical Republicans gained control of Congress.
3. Black Codes took away the rights of Negroes in the South.
4. The Thirteenth Amendment was added to the Constitution.
5. The Fourteenth Amendment was added to the Constitution.
6. The Fifteenth Amendment was added to the Constitution.
7. The Reconstruction Act set up a way to rule the South.
8. The Civil Rights Act listed the rights all Americans of all races should have.
9. Blanche K. Bruce became an elected member of the United States Senate.
10. Afro-Americans gained the right to vote in the South during Reconstruction.

IV. ANSWER EACH OF THESE QUESTIONS WITH A SHORT PARAGRAPH.

1. How did President Lincoln want to bring the Union together? (See Paragraph 3.)
2. How did the "Civil War Amendments" prepare the way for Negro rights? (See Paragraph 7.)
3. How were President Johnson's ideas different from those in the Reconstruction Act of 1867? (See Paragraph 8.)
4. For what reasons was the Freedman's Bureau set up? (See Paragraph 8.)
5. How were Afro-Americans important in the governments of the Southern states during Reconstruction? (See Paragraph 9.)

V. QUESTIONS TO DISCUSS

1. The war had ended in the defeat of the South. All slaves had been freed. Why were Afro-Americans still treated badly in the South?
2. What plan would you have used to help ex-slaves?
3. Read the Fourteenth Amendment in class. Why was each of its ideas placed in it?
4. Why was the Army placed in control of the South?
5. Why do you think Charles Sumner was buried in a Negro cemetery? What did he mean by these words on his gravestone? "I repose in this quiet . . . spot . . . that I might illustrate in my death . . . Equality of Man before His Creator."
6. Discuss these two statements made in 1866.

By a Southern planter: "They've always been our owned servants, and we've been used to having them mind us . . . we can't bear anything else from them now."

By a Northerner who visited the South: ". . . the whites seem wholly unable to comprehend that freedom for the Negro means the same thing as freedom for them."

Chapter 18 / THE FAILURE OF RECONSTRUCTION

Let's Discover

1. How the promises of Reconstruction were not kept.
2. How white supremacy became the way of life in the South.
3. How most black people of the South became poor farmers.

Words to Know

corrupt	Dishonest.
	The corrupt man tried to cheat the farmer.
corruption	Dishonesty, as in government.
	The governor was charged with corruption when he stole money from his state government.
supremacy	Having the highest power or position.
	White supremacy in the South meant keeping Negroes in the worst jobs.
Black Codes	Laws passed in Southern states after the Civil War to limit the rights of black people.
	The Black Codes made many Afro-Americans feel that they were almost slaves again.
vagrant	A person without money or a job who wanders from place to place.
	The judge said that the freedman who had come to town looking for work was a vagrant.
vagrancy	Being a vagrant, considered a crime in some parts of this country.
	Freedmen found guilty of vagrancy were forced to work for some white man until they paid off their fines.

Ku Klux Klan (KKK)	A secret terror group set up in 1865 to fight for white supremacy. *The Ku Klux Klan is against Negroes, Catholics and Jews.*
lynching	Murder by a mob, without a legal trial. *Lynching became one of the ways in which white supremacy gripped the South.*
sharecropper	A person who farms land owned by another person and gets part of the crop in return for his work. *Most black farmers in the South had to become sharecroppers.*

1 / *The South by 1890*. Twenty-five years after the Civil War, the South was again becoming the kind of world it had been under slavery. White men ruled; they were often the same men who had led the South during the war. The power of the country's government, men had hoped, would bring equal rights for all. It did for a while. But then that power was taken away. The Freedmen's Bureau was ended. The soldiers who had come to the South to protect the rights of all citizens were gone. In one part of the South after another, black Americans grew poor and afraid. They began to lose their right to vote. Few of them dared to vote even where they could. They farmed the land owned by white men and received a small share of what they grew. Any black man who tried to improve his life, or tried to work for better lives for other Negroes, might be murdered. The men who killed him would not be punished. What had happened to the dream of Reconstruction? How had these millions of people lost so much?

2 / *Failures by the Government*. The Republicans had planned a better life for all black people. They had changed the Constitution. They had passed new laws. They had voted to spend Federal money. In some parts of the South ex-slaves had been given farms and farm animals. They had gone into business with the help of the Freedmen's Bureau. Schools had been opened. Hospitals had been built. Laws to enforce rights had been passed. But laws are not enough. A law must be made to work. It was the job of the President to see that the laws passed by Congress were carried out.

Andrew Johnson did not always do his part of the job. For example, he pardoned men who had been leaders of the South during the war. They then took back their old lands. Often this land had been given to ex-slaves. Suddenly these black farmers found they had lost the work of years! More than once Johnson tried to prevent reconstruction laws from being passed. When they were passed he did not do all he could to enforce them.

3 / *Corruption*. Congress saw to it that new state governments were set up. The freed slaves gained the right to vote. Many of them became leaders in their state governments. Pinckney B. Pinchback was the governor of Louisiana for a short time. Francis L. Cardozo became treasurer of South Carolina. Jonathan C. Gibbs was in charge of the public schools of Florida. Men like Robert Smalls, Hiram Revels and Blanche Bruce were sent to Washington. But much went wrong in most of the state governments. A man in public office who is not honest is called corrupt. The dishonest things he does are called corruption. There was great corruption in the new Southern governments. White men from the North, white men in the South, army officers and some Afro-Americans used their power in the new state governments to make money for themselves and their friends. Most men in these state governments were honest. They tried to help the people of their state. Yet there were enough crooked men in politics so that many of the fine laws that were passed could not be enforced. This was as true in the North as it was in the South. The years after

the Civil War were a time of great corruption.

4 / *White Supremacy.* The word *supreme,* as we have seen, means "highest." White people in most of the South were not ready to allow their ex-slaves to be their equals. These white people wanted some higher position in life than Afro-Americans could have. We call their desire to have more and be treated better than the Negro "white supremacy." It is the key to what has happened in the South since the Civil War. It has been the one idea on which almost all white Southerners have agreed. Slowly it spread through the nation. By the end of Reconstruction it explained why black Americans met discrimination and segregation wherever they went.

5 / *The Black Codes.* "Keep the black man in his place!" was the feeling of most white people in the South. As soon as white leaders gained control of a local or state government, they passed laws to set limits on Negro rights. All the states of the South except Tennessee wrote these Black Codes. In states like South Carolina, Mississippi and Louisiana, where there were more black people than white, the codes were harsh. In Mississippi no Negro could even rent land. A black man who held a job could not leave it. If he

tried to do so he could be arrested and brought back to his job. An ex-slave without a job could be forced to go to work for the man who had once owned him. The "master" could whip or otherwise punish the black people working for him. A Negro without a job or money—called a vagrant under the law—received a heavy fine for vagrancy and then had to work it off. Again he was in the hands of a white "master." In Louisiana the law made Negroes work ten hours a day. They were paid little. The white people they worked for could take away part of their pay for "tools," "lost time" or "bad work." This was not much better than slavery. Laws like these made white supremacy work. They were passed whenever white people gained power over a state or local government.

6 / *The Ku Klux Klan.* Black Americans were not going to let themselves be made slaves again. They went to the courts for help. They asked the army to protect them. They voted for men who would try to stop such laws as the Black Codes. Then they met a new danger—terror and murder. In 1865 Confederate General Nathan B. Forrest formed a new group that he hoped would help bring about white supremacy. It

A black Senator and Representatives were elected.

was soon called the Ku Klux Klan. Forrest had been a slave trader before the war. His secret circle, or Klan, and other groups like it quickly spread through the South. Their aim was to make black people give up all they were gaining under Reconstruction. The Ku Klux Klan became known as the KKK. Its members worked in secret. They wore white robes with hoods that covered their faces. They struck at night. They beat up black men trying to build better lives for themselves, their families and their people. They burned homes and churches.

7 / *The Use of Violence.* The weapon of the KKK was fear. As it grew in power, the Klan began to murder blacks who would not follow its orders. Thousands of its members were arrested between 1865 and 1900. Still they would not end their use of terror. They are still using it in some parts of the South! Over the years they had great success. They kept Afro-Americans from voting for almost 100 years. They wrecked many black schools. Again and again the police of Southern towns proved to be Klan members. For this reason, perhaps, few men in the Klan were punished for what they did. They turned to lynching as one of the ways to rule black people. Lynching is the murder of a person by a mob, often by hanging or burning. When such murder was not punished, it left the black people of the South afraid. In 1871 Congress gave the President power to crush the Klan. It was weakened for awhile but later came back.

8 / *The Changing Republican Party.* The Reconstruction years passed, and changes came to the country. Men like Thaddeus Stevens and Charles Sumner died. Their hopes for equal treatment for all seemed to die too. New men led the Republican Party. The party still ruled Congress. Its new leaders cared less about the rights of citizens than they did about money. Many of them were corrupt. Many of them were in the pay of business leaders who were trying to build great new industries. The West was being opened. New settlers were moving there. New railroads were needed there. By 1876 leaders of government seemed to have lost interest in the needs of the Negro. White supremacy had taken hold in the South. The Freedmen's Bureau was no more. The Supreme Court—which black men had hoped would help save their rights—would soon decide that the civil rights laws were not allowed by the Constitution!

9 / *Back on the Land.* A new kind of bondage seemed to grip millions in the South. They were no longer slaves. Each man might have some bit of land to farm. But this land did not belong to him. He was allowed to farm it by the white man who owned it. Black farmers had little or no money. How were they to get seed? How were they to feed their families while a crop was growing? The men whose land they farmed worked out a way. The farmer was loaned the seed and food he needed. When his crop was ready he paid back the loan. He gave a large share of what he had grown as this payment. He had become a sharecropper—a farmer who kept only a small share of what he grew. He remained poor. Each year his share might be less. In the

few cases where a black farmer owned the land he farmed, he still had to borrow to get through each year. Most of his crop still went to pay the loans. In most of the South, poor white farmers also had to become sharecroppers.

10 / The End of Reconstruction. The Republicans still held control of Congress and the government in 1876. Slowly the states of the South had come into the hands of white-supremacy leaders. The white people of the South voted for the Democratic Party. Black Southerners voted for the Republicans. Then in 1876 a new problem appeared. There were two sets of election returns from some Southern states! Were these states to be counted as Republican or Democrat? The leaders of Congress met. They reached a compromise in 1877. It was to mean the end of Reconstruction. It was also to mean the end of the dream of real freedom for Afro-Americans. The Republicans kept control of the Federal government. In exchange

they gave up their work to improve the lives of black people. The white Democratic leaders of the South kept control of their states. The last groups of soldiers were taken out of the South.

11 / The One-Party South. The South, it seemed, had won in peace what it had lost in the war. Much of the South became a new kind of slave world in the years 1880 to 1905. Violent white men ruled. They kept the black people in their states under tight control. The Republican Party became weak there. Only the Democrats, the party of white supremacy, ruled in the South. The men sent to Congress from the South— almost all of them white Democrats—rose to positions of power. Black Southerners lost their right to vote, sometimes by the terror of a Klan, sometimes because laws were passed to stop them from voting or holding office. We will see in the next chapter how life grew worse and worse for the South's black "citizens."

A typical sharecropper's cabin.

Understanding What You Have Read

I. REVIEWING WORD MEANINGS
Write the letter of the choice that best completes each statement.

1. A member of the KKK would believe in (a) equal treatment for all, (b) poorer treatment for Negroes, Catholics and Jews, (c) better treatment for farmers.
2. A Klan is (a) a bell, (b) a secret society, (c) an army group.
3. A person who takes money that does not belong to him is (a) borrowing, (b) corrupt, (c) vagrant.
4. One of the things a vagrant does not have is (a) a job, (b) clothing, (c) friends.
5. Black Codes were laws found in the (a) South, (b) North, (c) West.
6. A person found guilty of vagrancy has no (a) education, (b) training, (c) money.
7. Corruption in government means dishonest (a) voters, (b) officials, (c) people in jail.
8. The headline that shows white supremacy at work is (a) NEW BLACK CHURCH OPENED, (b) AFRO-AMERICAN ELECTED TO OFFICE, (c) NEGROES LOSE RIGHT TO VOTE.
9. Lynching is a kind of (a) election, (b) reward, (c) murder.
10. A sharecropper receives (a) the full value of his crop, (b) part of the value of his crop, (c) none of the value of his crop.

II. UNDERSTANDING MAIN IDEAS

Answer each of these questions in a complete sentence.

1. What does Paragraph 1 tell about the dream of Reconstruction?
2. What does Paragraph 2 tell about President Andrew Johnson's treatment of the freedmen?
3. As Paragraph 3 explains it, how can corruption weaken a good law?
4. From the discussion in Paragraph 4, write your own explanation of the meaning of *white supremacy*.

5. Why was the KKK, discussed in Paragraphs 6 and 7, a secret society?
6. According to Paragraph 8, why didn't the Republican Party continue to help the country's black citizens?
7. Review Paragraph 9 and then explain why any man was willing to become a sharecropper.
8. What reason does Paragraph 10 give for the ending of Reconstruction?

III. BUILDING YOUR WORD KNOWLEDGE

Use a dictionary to help you answer each of these questions.

1. What is the difference between a vagrant and a beggar?
2. Who was Charles Lynch, from whose name "lynching" comes?
3. What is a tenant farmer?
4. What is a crop lien?
5. Why is it an honor to be called incorruptible?

IV. USE AN ENCYCLOPEDIA TO ANSWER ONE OF THESE QUESTIONS. PRESENT YOUR ANSWER TO THE CLASS.

1. Describe the organization called the Knights of the White Camelia. Compare it to the Ku Klux Klan.
2. The Compromise of 1877, which ended Reconstruction, also resulted in a railroad through the South. How was this railroad important?
3. What kind of President was Rutherford B. Hayes, who became President as a result of the Compromise of 1877? What kinds of laws did he want?

V. THINGS TO DO

1. This is from a speech in 1871 by Jefferson Long, an Afro-American from Georgia who served in the House of Representatives.

Discuss the events Mr. Long was describing, and explain what he was objecting to.

"Why, Mr. Speaker, in my state since emancipation there have been over five hundred loyal men shot down by the disloyal men there, and not one who took part in committing those outrages has ever been brought to justice. . . . Loyal men are constantly being cruelly beaten. When we take the men who commit these outrages before judges and juries we find that they are in the hands of the very Ku Klux . . . themselves, who protect them."

2. This is from a report in 1871 of the power of the Ku Klux Klan in North Carolina. How does it explain why black farmers were never able to get out of debt once they became sharecroppers?

"They know very well . . . that they will be cleared, and it just makes it that much worse for the loyal people . . . Colored men cannot get justice, cannot get their hard earned money. They agree to give them part of the crop, and about the time of the harvest they charge them with something and run them off. They dare not say a word."

3. This is from a letter written in Mississippi in 1875, after black voters had lost most of their rights. What does it tell you about white supremacy in that state?

"When we hold church meetings, they break that up; our lives are not safe in our houses. Now we ask you who shall we look to for protection? . . . We are in the hands of murderers."

4. **Three *IF* Questions** Discuss each of these questions in class.
   a) IF Federal troops had been kept in the South after 1877, how might the lives of Negroes there been different?
   b) IF the Federal government had really broken up the Ku Klux Klan, how would life in the South have been better for all?
   c) IF black Americans had not lost the right to vote in the South, how would their economic conditions have been better? (Remember: *economic* has to do with making a living.)

5. *People to Know* Use the library to help you find the answers to these questions. Report your findings to the class.

   a) What was the Negro National Labor Union? Among its leaders was John Mercer Langston, who held many posts of honor, including membership in Congress.

   b) How was Congressman Richard H. Cain important in the growth of the Methodist Church in South Carolina?

   c) In 1869 Ebenezer Bassett became the first Afro-American to serve as a minister to another country. Describe his years of service.

   d) In 1870 Jonathan J. Wright became one of the judges in the State Supreme Court of South Carolina. Why did he have to resign in 1877?

   e) Tell the story of P.B.S. Pinchback's failure to become a member of the United States Senate, even though he had been elected.

6. *Do You Agree or Disagree?* Find out who the *carpetbaggers* were. Then find out who the *scalawags* were. Then explain why you agree or disagree with each of these statements.

   1. Carpetbaggers did more good than harm during Reconstruction.

   2. The scalawags were the men in the South who really understood that a time for change in treatment of Negroes had come.

   3. The carpetbaggers and scalawags robbed the new governments.

   4. In some parts of the South, the conditions of Negroes became better and remained better.

Unit Five

EARLY BLACK FREEDOM WITHOUT EQUALITY

Introduction

Unit 5 deals with the forty years after the end of Reconstruction. These were difficult years for Afro-Americans. Most of them lived in the South. This part of the country became the center of a strange world. We call it the Jim Crow world. In the South, and in some parts of the country outside the South, laws and customs separated blacks and whites. In every part of the country, white men kept a tight grip on local and state governments. Millions of black people lost the rights they had won under the Constitution and the laws of Congress. Some of these rights are still lost in some states.

A new kind of "justice" took the place of the equal rights men had hoped for. It was called "separate but equal." It meant that Congress and the courts would allow each state to keep blacks and whites separate. Some black leaders said that the greatest needs of Negroes were to go to school and to learn to make a better living. The best-known Afro-American after 1895 was Booker T. Washington. He led those who thought that education was the best hope for black people.

World War I brought great changes in the lives of black Americans. Many left the South to find jobs in the large cities of the North. Black soldiers were important in the fighting during the war.

After 1900 the growth of hate groups and the use of force against Negroes in the South and the North led to the most terrible practice of all—lynching. Black Americans had to take steps to fight for their rights. They set up organizations to carry on the long battle that lay ahead. Men like W.E.B. Du Bois, James Weldon Johnson and A. Philip Randolph became well known as their leaders. You will learn about the work of such men, and of the groups they led.

Chapter 19 | THE JIM CROW WORLD

Let's Discover

1. How Jim Crow laws separated blacks and whites all over the South.
2. How white men in the South kept control of local and state governments.

Words to Know

custom	The way people do things in a certain place.
	It became the custom in restaurants not to serve Negroes.
Populist	Member of a political party formed in 1891 that spoke for poor people, farmers and Negroes.
	The Populist Party worked for equal rights for all.

union
: An organization of workers that tries to get its members higher pay, shorter hours and better working conditions.

: *The Knights of Labor was a strong union for several years.*

Knights of Labor
: A national labor union in the United States between 1869 and 1886.

: *The Knights of Labor tried to help Afro-Americans in the South.*

clause
: One of the parts of a law.

: *A clause was added to the law to take away the right of black people to vote.*

poll tax
: A tax that must be paid before a person can vote, no longer allowed in the United States.

: *The poll tax kept most poor whites and poor Negroes from voting.*

literate
: Able to read and write.

: *Each voter had to take a test to show he was literate.*

register
: An official list of voters.

: *When a man qualifies to vote, his name is added to the register of voters.*

eliminate
: To remove or get rid of.

: *The men who ruled the South wanted to eliminate all black voters.*

colored
: Of a race other than white, usually used to describe Afro-Americans.

: *Signs in the South told Negroes that they had to use "colored" water fountains.*

---

1 / *The Victory of White Supremacy.* The white men who had won back control of the South made plans to keep this control forever. The Thirteenth Amendment had made all Americans free; these men could not bring back slavery. The Fourteenth Amend-

ment had made Negroes citizens. They decided to make them second-class citizens. The Fifteenth Amendment had given all citizens the right to vote. White supremacy depended on taking the right to vote *away* from black people. Instead of the better world promised by Reconstruction, a world of segregation and discrimination was forced on Afro-Americans by the white men who came to power in the South. From the day a black child was born, the life around him repeated the messages of white supremacy. The life black people had to live—the life many still have to live today—is best understood when we look at the meaning of "Jim Crow."

2 / *What "Jim Crow" Means.* We do not really know how the term "Jim Crow" began. We do know that a song by that name, written by Thomas Rice, became well known in the 1830's. The song was about a black man. "Jim Crow" later gained a special meaning. It meant the laws and customs in the South, and in some parts of the North, that kept Negroes from improving their lives. Through Jim Crow white people kept black people from gaining or keeping the rights all Americans should have. Through Jim Crow Afro-Americans lost the rights they had won.

3 / *Separate—Separate—Separate!* For about 25 years after the Civil War, whites and blacks in most of the South seemed to be working out the problems of living together. But by 1890 most of the South came under the control of white men who kept their power by making other white men act together to take away Negro rights. The Jim Crow world they built cannot be given a date. The first laws to take away Negro rights came as early as 1870. The last one has not yet been passed, for some parts of the South still refuse to give equal rights to all. Most Jim Crow laws came in the 25 years after 1890. Some are still alive. All of them seemed to have two goals: Do not let black people have the same rights white people have! Keep black people separate from white people!

4 / *Some White Men Opposed Jim Crow.* Not all white people in the South wanted to hurt black people in this way. In Louisiana, the writer George Washington Cable wrote again and again in favor of equal rights for all. Lewis Blair of Virginia told other whites that life in the South could improve only when the lives of Afro-Americans improved. In the 1890's the Populist Party became important in the South and West. Its leaders called for fair laws for all. There were white men all over the South who were ready to follow such ideas. Often, with black votes to help them, they gained power. Then laws would be passed for better schools, equal rights and better treatment for workers and farmers. But in the years after 1890, this party and every other move by white men to make life better for all Americans lost ground to the growing wave of Jim Crow laws.

5 / *The Knights of Labor.* One of the white groups that tried to help black workers was the Knights of Labor. It was a labor union with members all over the country. Afro-

The Knights of Labor tried to help black workers.

Americans like Frank Farrell were among its leaders. In 1875 it had 60,000 black members. Only ten years later the Knights of Labor had grown weak. It soon died. The United States was not yet ready for strong labor unions. Business leaders, and sometimes the Federal government, fought against them. The small unions that remained after the Knights of Labor did not always try to help Afro-Americans. Most of them did not even admit black workers! In the South, unions became part of the Jim Crow world. They kept black men out.

6 / *The Mind of the South.* Remember that the men who gained power in Southern local and state governments could do much as they pleased. The power of the Federal government was not used to protect rights. That left each town, county or state its own master. The KKK and groups like it could attack a black person without fear of real punishment. The men who owned news-

papers in the South began to work with the political leaders and KKK groups. They filled white minds with Jim Crow ideas. Terror silenced all men, white and black, who would not agree with them. They forced all of the South to accept Jim Crow.

7 / *Losing the Right to Vote*. The first right to be taken away from black Southerners was the right to vote. This was done in many ways. KKK groups used fear to keep black voters from elections. Laws were passed to make it impossible for them to vote if they did try. A clause is a part of a law. New clauses were added to voting laws in state after state in the South. One of these was the "grandfather clause." No man could vote unless his grandfather had been able to vote. Since no black man had voted in the South before the Civil War, this law meant that no Afro-American could ever vote in the South! A tax on voters called the poll tax was added. It was more than a poor farmer could afford to pay. It could keep poor white men as well as poor black men from voting. However in many places it was collected only from black voters.

8 / *Tests for Voters*. Courts held that grandfather clauses were not legal. But black people were kept from voting in other ways. One of these was the literacy test. A literate person is one who can read and write. White officials in charge of keeping a list of voters —the register of voters—would not let any black names get on this list. They made the test so hard that no one could pass it. But they did pass whites. A story was told about a Negro teacher who had graduated from

Harvard College. He was one of the best educated people in the United States. Still he was failed when he took the literacy test in a Southern town.

9 / *No Black Votes*. The drive to keep black men from voting succeeded. One white leader from South Carolina was able to say: "We have done our level best. We have scratched our heads to find out how to eliminate the last one of them (Negroes). We stuffed ballot boxes. We shot them. We are not ashamed of it." Such words could have been repeated in every state of the South for more than fifty years. In Louisiana, as an example, the number of black voters dropped from 130,000 to 5,000 in four years. The job of taking away the right to vote had been done well!

10 / *The Invisible Wall*. Once Afro-Americans lost the right to vote, they lost their hopes for fair treatment. Federal courts did little to help. In 1883 the United States Supreme Court decided that the country's civil rights law could not be used to protect black citizens. White men in the South built a wall between themselves and all blacks. They did this by laws and customs that pushed black people lower and lower. Rich and poor whites worked together to make this wall higher and higher. Rich men did it so they could keep their wealth and power. Poor whites did it to feel better than someone— in their case the Afro-American.

11 / *Jim Crow Travel*. All railroads and other ways to travel in the South were segregated. Only in the last few years has Jim

Crow travel been weakened. Laws were passed to keep white and black passengers from riding together. One railroad even named the car set aside for blacks the Jim Crow car! A black man on a bus or street car had to sit in seats set aside for Negroes. In the South the words "Colored" and "White Only" began to appear in public places. A sign would tell a black person that he had to use separate rest rooms, water fountains or waiting rooms. Railroads and bus lines in the North did not have such Jim Crow rules. When a black American crossed from the North into the South, he had to change his seat to one in a Jim Crow car or section. If he did not do so he could be arrested. Jim Crow travel rules seemed to be designed to make every Negro feel that he was of less worth than the lowest white man.

12 / *Jim Crow Schools*. All public schools in the South became segregated. Black people had their schools; whites had theirs. Black teachers taught black children; white teachers taught white children. Laws were passed to keep any white person from teaching in a black public school. State governments gave less money to black schools than to white ones. Many of these schools could do little for their pupils because there was not enough money for teachers' salaries, new books, chalk or even paper. Even the books used in Negro schools were different. In Florida these books had to be stored in separate warehouses before the children received them! Jim Crow laws even kept schools for children with handicaps separate. There were white and Negro schools for the deaf or the blind. In all possible ways, black children were made to feel the wall that Jim Crow had built between whites and blacks.

13 / *Jim Crow in Hotels and Restaurants*. Jim Crow life aimed at making all Negroes feel they were not the social equals of white people. Most restaurants were for whites only. They would not serve a black person. As late as 1960 Afro-Americans could not

Jim Crow meant separate rest rooms, water fountains and waiting rooms.

be served at a "white" lunch counter. No hotel would admit both black and white people. Instead separate sets of hotels were built all over the South. A black person seeking food or a place to sleep had to go to a segregated part of town. For more than fifty years Jim Crow ideas like this—custom rather than law—were also found in much of the North. New laws had to be passed before some hotels and restaurants there would agree to admit black Americans as well as whites.

14 / *Jim Crow Laws Went On and On.* Some of the Jim Crow laws seem silly to anyone who has not had to live under them. One law tried to stop black and white cotton-mill workers from looking out the same window! Another, in Birmingham, Alabama, said blacks and whites could not play checkers or dominoes together. In Mobile, Alabama, Negroes had to be off the streets by ten o'clock each evening. Atlanta, Georgia, did not allow Afro-Americans to swear on the same Bible used by whites in the courts! White taxi drivers could not carry black passengers; Negro drivers could not accept white passengers. There were Jim Crow elevators in office buildings. A black child could not buy an ice-cream cone at a white stand. A black college professor—or any other black American—could not use a public library. Jim Crow was the way of life; its touch soiled each day of a Negro's life.

15 / *Jim Crow from Birth to Death.* All parts of life were segregated. Laws were passed to prevent marriage between whites and blacks. There were separate hospitals for the two races. White nurses could not treat black men. Even a dying Negro would not be admitted to a "white" hospital. Southern states ran separate orphan homes for black and white children. Some states had separate prisons. If an Afro-American wanted to attend a theater or a movie, he had to buy his ticket at a separate booth. He had to enter by a separate entrance. He had to sit in the balcony, well apart from any white people. Each black person all his life was kept apart from white people. Then, when he died, he had to be buried from a black funeral home in a black cemetery. This was Jim Crow from birth to death.

16 / *Was There Any Hope?* By 1900 Afro-Americans were being forced behind the wall of Jim Crow in every state of the South and in some parts of the North. They were poor because they could not get an equal education. They were poor because they

Even state parks were segregated.

could not get jobs that paid well. The white leaders of the South had decided to keep black citizens down. One of them had said that the only way to treat a black man "is to whip him when he does not obey without it," and "never to pay him more wages than is . . . necessary to buy food and clothing." The Federal government did nothing to stop Jim Crow. There was no hope unless black and white Americans who saw its evil took action. The next chapters will show what they did try to do.

EXAMPLES OF JIM CROW LAWS IN THE UNITED STATES

Date	Place	What the Law Tried to Do
1870	Georgia	Set up first Jim Crow school systems
1891	Georgia	Jim Crow railroad seating
1900	South Carolina	Jim Crow railroad cars
1905	Georgia	Separate parks for whites and blacks
1906	Alabama	Jim Crow street cars
1910	Baltimore, Maryland	Blacks and whites not allowed to live on the same blocks
1914	Louisiana	Separate entrances and seating at circuses
1915	South Carolina	Separate entrances, working rooms, pay windows, water glasses, etc., for workers in the same factory.
	Oklahoma	Separate phone booths for whites and blacks
	South Carolina	Amount voted to educate each white child was twelve times amount voted to educate each black child
1922	Mississippi	Jim Crow taxicabs
1926	Atlanta, Georgia	Negro barbers could not cut the hair of white women
1932	Atlanta, Georgia	White and Negro baseball clubs could not play within two blocks of each other
1933	Texas	Blacks and whites could not wrestle together
1935	Oklahoma	Blacks and whites could not boat or fish together
1937	Arkansas	Segregation at race tracks
1944	Virginia	Jim Crow waiting rooms at airports
1965	Louisiana	State money could not be spent on schools attended by both white and black students

Understanding What You Have Read

I. REVIEWING WORD MEANINGS

Write the letter of the choice that best explains the meaning of each word.

1. **custom** (a) Way of speaking. (b) Way of doing things. (c) Way to travel.
2. **Populist** (a) Well-liked person. (b) Contest winner. (c) Political party.
3. **poll tax** (a) Tax on barbers. (b) Tax on voters. (c) Tax on business.
4. **literate** (a) Able to vote. (b) Able to use electricity. (c) Able to read and write.
5. **clause** (a) Part of a law. (b) Boy's name. (c) Taking away a right.
6. **union** (a) Workers' group. (b) Business group. (c) Government group.
7. **labor** (a) Work. (b) Organization. (c) Member.
8. **colored** (a) Segregated. (b) Not white. (c) Poor.
9. **register** (a) Vote. (b) Be literate. (c) Be listed as a voter.
10. **eliminate** (a) Refuse. (b) Remove. (c) Clean.

II. UNDERSTANDING JIM CROW

Five of the statements below are examples of Jim Crow rules. Five are examples of fair treatment. Write JIM CROW or FAIR for each statement.

1. Any person can be admitted into this theater.
2. Negroes have the right to eat in all restaurants in this town.
3. Only black people are allowed in this railroad car.
4. White and black people were kept separate in every way.
5. Negroes and whites played together in the chess tournament.
6. KKK members frightened many black voters away.

7. Literacy tests were used against black voters.
8. The South didn't want blacks and whites to be friends.
9. The Knights of Labor was open to all workers.
10. All people had the same rights in that judge's court.

III. FACT OR OPINION?

Write FACT for each statement that is a fact. Write OPINION for each statement that is someone's opinion.

1. The government of the United States should have tried to end Jim Crow laws.
2. The Afro-American in the South had few rights as citizen.
3. The white people of the South had the right to separate themselves from black people.
4. The KKK had much to do with who voted in the South.
5. Literacy tests show how well a person can read and write.

IV. ANSWER EACH OF THESE QUESTIONS IN A COMPLETE SENTENCE.

1. What is a Jim Crow law?
2. Why were Jim Crow laws passed?
3. Why didn't the Federal government stop Jim Crow laws?
4. How did the white men of the South use literacy tests against black citizens?
5. What is a segregated school?
6. How did the "grandfather clause" try to keep Afro-Americans from voting?
7. How did the Populist Party try to help black Americans?
8. Why didn't political leaders in the South try to help Negroes?
9. What is meant by "the invisible wall between blacks and whites"?
10. How did railroad companies join in Jim Crow rules?

V. THINGS TO DO

1. Prepare a two-column list. Head the first column WHAT THE JIM CROW LAW SAID. Head the second column HOW THIS LAW WAS UNFAIR. Fill in at least five of the Jim Crow laws discussed in this chapter. Compare your lists in class.

2. Prepare a play about a group of black men in a Southern town who decide they want to vote. They go to register. They take a literacy test. What can you put into this play to help explain Jim Crow?

3. Jim Crow meant being a second-class citizen. Discuss in class the meaning of "second-class citizen." Discuss the reasons why courts could not or would not help black Americans gain their proper rights as citizens.

4. Richard Wright, a Negro writer of our own time, wrote these words to describe what he felt Jim Crow life had done to him: "I now knew what being a Negro meant. I could [stand] the hunger. I had learned to live with hate. . . . A million times I asked myself what I could do to save myself, and there were no answers. I seemed forever . . . ringed by walls." Discuss what Richard Wright meant by these words.

5. Discuss in class or write a paragraph to answer each of these questions: How did Jim Crow mean an end to any dream of social equality in the South? How did it mean that economic equality could not be reached? How did it mean that political equality had ended?

Chapter 20 | "SEPARATE BUT EQUAL"

Let's Discover

1. How Booker T. Washington became the first head of Tuskegee Institute.
2. How Booker T. Washington thought black people should progress.
3. How "separate but equal" became legal.

Words to Know

adjust
: To change yourself so you can manage better.
People tried to adjust to the unfair laws.

leadership
: The position of leading others.
Frederick Douglass rose to leadership among Afro-Americans.

institute
: A school for some special kind of study.
Hampton Institute taught students to become teachers.

dignity
: Pride and self-respect.
The way he walks and talks shows that he has true dignity.

industrial
: Having to do with trades or factories, or the people who work in them.
A carpenter working in a furniture factory is an industrial worker.

prejudice
: Dislike of people just because they are of a certain race, nationality or religion.
There has been much prejudice against Negroes, Catholics, Jews, Puerto Ricans, Orientals and Mexican-Americans.

compromise
: A settlement of a disagreement in which each side gives up part of what it wants.
Washington's speech was called the Atlanta Compromise.

prosper
: To have economic success, such as by making a better living.
Booker T. Washington wanted black Americans to prosper.

essential
: Most needed or most necessary.
It is essential that people work together.

mutual
: Shared together.
Booker T. Washington believed that black men and white men could find mutual gain by working together.

1 / *Adjusting to a Jim Crow World.* When you do the best you can to make a bad life work out, you are trying to adjust. In the years after 1881—when Jim Crow laws began to appear in the South—many Afro-Americans looked for a way to adjust to the return of white control over their lives. Black leaders looked for ways to make life a little better. A few never stopped working for equal rights. But, the leaders said, black people needed education most of all. They had to gain enough skill so that they could earn a good living! Get a better home! Put some money in the bank! White people always said that a man should try to make money and live in comfort. Why shouldn't black people try to do the same?

2 / *A Separate Life.* White people tried to keep whites and blacks separate. Many black leaders felt they couldn't do much to stop this from happening. Perhaps when more Afro-Americans had gained skills and better jobs, blacks and whites could be equal. But if schools had to be separate, then let black schools be as good as possible. If housing had to be segregated, then let Negro homes be as good as black men could make them. Most men who rose to leadership among the black people of the South—where most of the country's Afro-Americans lived—were ready to live by adjusting. They hoped to show white men that black men were needed for the work that had to be done. They were ready to be "separate but equal." From 1895 to 1915, Booker T. Washington was the most important Negro in the country. He led those who tried to adjust rather than fight for equal rights.

3 / *Booker T. Washington's Early Life.* Booker Taliaferro Washington, called "Booker T." for most of his life, had been born a slave in 1856 in Virginia. After emancipation his family moved to West Virginia. There he was put to work in a salt mine. His mother found a spelling book for him. With it he taught himself to read. A teacher was found for the Negro children, but Booker had to work and could not attend school. Later the teacher taught him in the evenings. Booker had tasted the joy of learning. It grew to mean more and more to him.

4 / *Higher Education.* Booker T. Washington was about sixteen when he made plans to seek more learning. He wanted to go to the Hampton Institute, 500 miles away in Hampton, Virginia. This was one of the schools set up during Reconstruction. Neighbors and friends gave him some money. It got him part way. He had to walk most of the distance across two states. Once there, he was admitted. He later wrote the story of his life in the book *Up from Slavery.* From it we learn that he had to work his way through school. He held all kinds of jobs to make the money he needed. But he was a good student. His reading, writing, arithmetic and grammar improved. He read many books. He became a fine speaker. The chief lesson he learned at Hampton would remain with him all his life. A man had to learn how to work with his hands. It helped you be more honest. It gave your life more meaning. It built skills with which you could earn a living.

5 / *A Call to Tuskegee.* Booker T. Washington went back to West Virginia to teach.

Washington returned to teach at Hampton.

Then he returned to teach at Hampton. He taught the Indians who had been admitted to the school. General Samuel C. Armstrong, principal of Hampton, was a white man who thought highly of Washington. In 1881 Armstrong was asked for a principal for a new school to be begun in the town of Tuskegee, Alabama. The state of Alabama had voted $2,000 a year to pay the salaries of those who would teach in a school for black teachers in Tuskegee. Both white and black Americans gave money to help start the school. Booker T. Washington became the principal. His school became known as the Tuskegee Institute.

6 / *Problems at Tuskegee.* The state of Alabama had passed a law to pay salaries at Tuskegee. It had done nothing to put up a school. When Washington arrived, he learned that there were no buildings and no supplies. He found an unused Negro church, with an extra small building next to it, that he could use for a start. He then went around the state to get students. He opened the school on July 4, 1881. In a letter to his friends at Hampton he said, "I opened school last week. . . . The school is taught, at present, in one of the colored churches, which they kindly let us have for that purpose. This building is not very well suited to school purposes, and we hope to be able to move . . . in a short time. . . . As soon as possible I hope to get the school on a labor basis, so that . . . students can help themselves and at the same time learn the true dignity of labor . . . ."

7 / Goals for Tuskegee. Washington was twenty-five years old when he opened his school. This young man set two chief goals for the years ahead. First, he had to find the money to build a larger school. He did not want to remain with only thirty or forty students for long. Second, he had to prove to the many white people who did not like his school that it was a good thing. Raising money was first. He went around the country asking for money for Tuskegee. To get this money he said what white people wanted to hear about his school. He would train black students to do the kind of work white people needed. They would learn to read and write and do arithmetic. They would also be trained as carpenters, cooks, farmers and mechanics. They would become construction workers. Washington felt that they could build better lives if they learned the skills that white people needed and wanted. Most of the money he raised came from white people. This was the kind of school they wanted black Americans to have.

8 / Industrial Education. A school that teaches trades is offering industrial education. Washington made his school a center for this kind of learning. He also taught farming. He knew that other kinds of learning were important too. But he didn't think his people would be able to use those skills. He once said in a talk to his students: "Art and music to people who live in rented houses and with no bank account are not the most important things to which attention should be given. Such education creates wants without . . . ability to supply those wants." He believed that his students would

have to work for white people. They would be of great service. Then the white people of the South would see how black people could be helpful to them. Washington was ready to see parts of Negro life segregated. He thought making a living came before fighting for equal rights. Prejudice—the feelings and actions by one group against others —would end some day. Until then, let more black people gain skills. Booker T. Washington became one of the country's best-known Afro-Americans. He was asked to speak all over the country. As he moved about, he spread his plans for improvement through trade training.

9 / A Speech in Atlanta. In a compromise, one side or both sides give up part of what they want. The name of Booker T. Washington became known for a compromise that would affect all black people in this country. In 1895 the city of Atlanta, Georgia, had a large fair. It was planned to show the world how the states of the South had improved since the Civil War. There was a Negro exhibit at the fair. Washington was asked to speak. It was not often that an Afro-American leader spoke at a white meeting in the South. The eyes of the whole country were on him that day. What would he say about the way black Americans were treated in the South? The speech he made that day is called the Atlanta Compromise. In it he told the world that the black people of the South were ready to accept the way they were being treated!

10 / The Atlanta Compromise. First Washington told the group that one-third of the people in the South were black. He spoke about how important it was to the South that this large part of its people be successful. This would help make all of the South better. Then he spoke of what he had always believed: "No race can prosper till it learns that there is as much dignity in tilling a field as there is in writing a poem. It is at the bottom of life that we must begin and not the top. . . . To those of the white race . . . I would repeat what I say to my own race. 'Cast down your bucket where you are.' " He was saying that black people should try to adjust to life in the South. "The interests of both races" should be the same. "Negroes whose habits you know . . . have without strikes and labor wars, tilled your fields, cleared your forests, built your railroads and cities . . . and helped make possible . . . the progress of the South." Then he spoke the thought that was reported all over the world. Jim Crow laws were making the social life of black people less and less equal. Washington had this to say: "In all the things that are purely social we can be as separate as the fingers, yet one as the hand in all things essential to mutual progress."

11 / *The Country's Negro Leader*. What did the Atlanta Compromise mean? Washington had said that it was foolish for Afro-Americans to try to gain social equality at that time. An equal life would come only after black people had shown that they were good workers. A long, hard struggle for equal rights lay ahead. Until then, "the opportunity to earn a dollar in a factory now is worth more than the opportunity to spend a dollar in an opera house." To some black Americans this was giving in to Jim Crow. It would mean that the white men who ruled the South could do as they pleased. Many were shocked. But white leaders hailed the speech. They called Washington the "Moses of the Negro race." People all over the country wrote to tell him that they agreed with him. Among these was President Grover Cleveland.

12 / *The Secret Side of Booker T. Washington*. Washington became the most powerful Afro-American in the country. The richest men in the land became his friends. He raised millions for schools in the South. No black man was placed in an important Federal job for almost twenty years unless he approved. He was the voice of the Negro who would not fight back. Yet there was a second side to him that he never showed the white South. In secret he worked to make the separate life of black people better. He did not speak against Jim Crow in public. Secretly he tried to get more Afro-Americans to register and vote. Some black leaders accused him of telling Negroes not to bother with politics. Yet he held more political power than people knew. Frederick Douglass, the voice of freedom and the fighter for equal rights, died in 1895. Booker T. Washington, who would be honored by Harvard and Dartmouth colleges, soon took his place as the best known of all black leaders.

13 / *Separate but Equal*. How could Jim Crow be allowed? Hadn't the Civil War amendments given equal rights to all? In

Homer Plessy sat in a "white" seat.

1896 the United States Supreme Court heard a very important case. It was the case of Plessy against Ferguson (*Plessy versus Ferguson*). Homer Plessy, a black man, had been arrested when he tried to sit in a "white" seat on a train. He sued. The court had to decide if state laws to keep the races apart on trains were allowed by the Constitution. It ruled, by a vote of seven to one, that if the train for blacks was as good as the train for whites, it was legal to segregate the two races. It was from this case that the governments of the South from then on found legal reasons for their Jim Crow laws.

They said that they were making life "separate but equal." Booker T. Washington did not fight this kind of law. It was 1954 before the Supreme Court changed its mind and said that things that are separate cannot be equal.

Understanding What You Have Read

I. MATCHING WORDS AND HEADLINES

Write the letter of the headline that best explains each numbered word.

1. **adjust**
2. **dignity**
3. **prejudice**
4. **compromise**
5. **mutual**

a. GRADUATES OF TUSKEGEE SHOW GREAT PRIDE AND SELF-RESPECT

b. EACH ONE HELPS THE OTHER

c. MEN LEARN TO LIVE UNDER HARSH CONDITIONS

d. ONE GROUP SHOWS IT HATES OTHER GROUPS

e. EACH SIDE GIVES UP PART OF WHAT IT WANTS

6. **leadership**
7. **institute**
8. **industrial**
9. **prosper**
10. **essential**

f. FARMER SAYS HE CANNOT GET ALONG WITHOUT NEW PLOWS

g. BOOKER T. WASHINGTON HEADS GROUP OF PRINCIPALS

h. PEOPLE ARE MAKING MORE MONEY THIS YEAR

i. NEW STUDY DEALS WITH FACTORIES AND WORKERS

j. SCHOOL SET UP TO DO SPECIAL JOB

II. COMPROMISE OR STRUGGLE?

Write STRUGGLE if the statement describes part of the struggle against Jim Crow. Write COMPROMISE if it shows a way in which men like Booker T. Washington thought black people could live better under Jim Crow.

1. Every man should try to keep the right to vote.
2. Homer Plessy tried to ride where he wished in a railroad train.
3. Afro-Americans in the South gave up the desire to vote.
4. The message from Tuskegee Institute's principal was that people should remain in the South and try to make a good living.
5. The students of Tuskegee built their own buildings instead of asking the state of Alabama to build them.

6. "It is at the bottom of life that we must begin and not the top. . . ."
7. Thousands of Negroes in Mississippi tried to register, even offering to pay their poll taxes.
8. Black workers did not demand higher wages.

III. FACT OR OPINION?

Write FACT for each statement that is a fact. Write OPINION for each statement that is someone's opinion.

1. Booker T. Washington became the most important Negro leader in the United States.
2. People like Booker T. Washington should not have given up the struggle for equal rights.
3. Some people called Booker T. Washington the "Moses of the Negro race."
4. No Afro-American with dignity should have helped Booker T. Washington.
5. Booker T. Washington's compromise was probably the best way for black Americans to keep out of trouble.

IV. ANSWER EACH OF THESE QUESTIONS IN A COMPLETE SENTENCE.

1. How did Booker T. Washington show that he wanted a higher education?
2. What did Booker T. Washington learn at Hampton Institute?
3. What is industrial or vocational education?
4. How did Washington get enough money and a place to begin Tuskegee Institute?
5. What were some of the subjects taught at Tuskegee Institute?
6. What was the chief idea presented by Washington in his speech at the Atlanta Fair?
7. Why did white people in the South praise Washington's speech?

8. How did Booker T. Washington help his people?

9. In what ways was Booker T. Washington honored?

10. What did the Supreme Court mean by "separate and equal"?

V. QUESTIONS TO DISCUSS

1. How do you feel about the idea of "separate but equal"?

2. The Supreme Court is the highest court in the land. What it says about a law becomes the law of the land. Was it correct in its decision in the *Plessy versus Ferguson* case?

3. Was an industrial education best for Southern Negroes?

VI. THINGS TO DO

1. The life of Booker T. Washington is told in the book *Lift Every Voice,* by Dorothy Sterling and Benjamin Quarles (Doubleday Zenith Books). Read the part of the book about Washington and report to the class on his childhood.

2. Justice Harlan was the one member of the Supreme Court to vote against the majority in the *Plessy versus Ferguson* case. Find out what he said. How did he differ with the majority? Discuss both points of view.

3. A young man named W. E. B. Du Bois disagreed with Booker T. Washington. Who was Du Bois? What ideas did he offer instead? He too is discussed in the book *Lift Every Voice.*

4. Use an encyclopedia to find out more about Tuskegee Institute. How many students did it have when Booker T. Washington died? How many does it have today? How many buildings does it have now? What is taught there?

5. Some Negroes at the Atlanta Fair cried after Washington's speech. Why?

6. What did the National Negro Business League, organized by Booker T. Washington in 1900, try to do? Did it succeed?

Chapter 21 | A NEW CENTURY

Let's Discover

1. Why black Americans left their homes in the South to move to large cities in the North.
2. How World War I affected Afro-Americans, and how many served in it.
3. How blacks fought against lynching.
4. How Negroes were important in many fields about 1900.

Words to Know

menial
: Of or fit for servants.
Sweeping floors is a menial job.

combat
: Actual fighting during a war.
Black American soldiers went into combat in France.

protest
: To speak out against something.
Black groups held meetings to protest segregation.

racist
: Believing that one race is better than another.
Jim Crow is an example of racist thinking.

slum
: A part of a city that is very crowded, poor and dirty.
People from the South had to move into slums in Northern cities.

ghetto
: The part of some cities in Europe where Jews were once forced to live; today, the part or parts of a city where any special group of people live or are forced to live.
Negroes in the Northern cities had to move into ghettos.

229

commander	An officer in the navy, just below the rank of captain. *Commander Peary led the group that reached the North Pole.*
traitor	*Some people called Booker T. Washington a traitor to Negroes' hopes for equal rights.*
scholar	A person who has studied and learned more than most others. *W. E. B. Du Bois was one of the leading scholars in the United States.*
movement	A group of people working together for some cause. *The Niagara Movement hoped to end the Jim Crow laws.*

1 / *From Farms to Cities.* By 1900 Jim Crow held full control of the South. Booker T. Washington had offered a hope that white and black people could live together in peace and understanding. His way had failed. White people had made Jim Crow a way of life. Black people lost hope. They were never able to feel equal. Even those who had training could not find good jobs. Crops were bad for several years after 1900. Black farm workers became poorer than before. At the same time factories in both the North and the South kept growing. Maybe a man could find a better job and a home for his family in one of the big cities. At first Negroes moved to the large cities of the South. There they found Jim Crow in charge. Louisville, Baltimore, Richmond and Atlanta even passed laws to force black people to live in segregated neighborhoods. If the cities of the South were so bad, then all a man could do was move to a "promised land"—the North.

2 / *Into the Big Cities.* This was a time of great growth for the cities. Industry always seemed to need more workers. Millions came from Europe. Hundreds of thousands of black Americans also moved to the cities of the North. Soon more people had come to the cities than were needed! There were not enough jobs for all of them. Those with the most skills were hired first. Few Afro-Americans who came to these cities had the kind of skills factory owners wanted. But a man had to eat. He had to care for his family. Black people had to take the menial jobs—those lowest in pay and lowest in dignity. Jim Crow was found in the North too. Blacks were the last hired and the first fired. Yet life was somehow a little freer; this made it a little better.

3 / *Fighting in World War I.* The long record of black success in our country's wars was made longer in World War I. More than four million men were in our armed

forces during that war. About 370,000 of these were Negroes. Of this group, 100,000, were in combat. When we entered the war, about 20,000 black men were in the Army and Navy. They were placed in all-Negro units. Most were in the Army. Those in the Navy could hold only menial jobs—as cooks and in other work of that kind. The Marines and Coast Guard would not accept black Americans. No black man could become an officer at first. Many meetings and protests by black groups were held; Congress then voted to set up an officers training camp for Afro-Americans. It was opened at Fort Des Moines, Iowa. On October 15, 1917, the first group became army officers. By the end of the war, about 1,400 black men had won this honor.

Black workers were last hired and first fired.

4 / *Helping to Win the War.* Henry Johnson and Needham Roberts were the first Americans to be decorated for bravery in World War I. They, like most other Afro-Americans, were following the kind of advice given by W. E. B. Du Bois: "Let us while this war lasts . . . close our ranks shoulder to shoulder with our white fellow citizens." Yet during the war Jim Crow did not weaken. Racist problems—those in which one race hurts another—did not end. President Wilson did not fight Jim Crow. Instead he seemed to become part of it when he segregated government offices in Washington. By 1915 the KKK had again grown to power. A race riot in East

St. Louis had killed at least forty people. Still, while the war lasted most black Americans made winning the war their chief goal.

5 / Growing Cities in the North. Many young men were away fighting the war. Other men had to be found to fill their jobs. Immigration almost halted in the war years. Busy factories in the North had plenty of jobs. Thousands more Afro-Americans left the South to take these jobs. The number of black people in the big cities of the North grew quickly. New York gained 91,000 between 1900 and 1920. Chicago gained 79,000. Philadelphia gained 73,000. The number of black people in other cities in the North grew in the same way. Even though some black Americans found jobs, most of them also found that life was not as good as they had hoped it would be. Housing was segregated all over the North. Slums, the oldest neighborhoods with the worst problems, became the new homes of black people. Jews in Europe had long been forced to live in a walled part of a city called a *ghetto*. Now people began to talk about Negro ghettos in the big cities.

6 / Terror in the Land. Those who had come to the North were seeking a better chance. Those who remained in the South came to know more and more fear. The KKK was busy. Lynchings came often— sometimes for no reason except that some mob of Southern white men had gathered and found a black man whom they could blame for something. Here is a list prepared by Tuskegee Institute of lynchings in the United States between 1900 and 1919.

Lynchings in the United States— 1900-1919	
1900—115	1910— 76
1901—130	1911— 67
1902— 92	1912— 63
1903— 99	1913— 52
1904— 83	1914— 55
1905— 62	1915— 69
1906— 65	1916— 54
1907— 60	1917— 38
1908— 97	1918— 64
1909— 82	1919— 83

Most of these were in the South; some were in the North!

7 / Black Leaders Fight Lynching. Ida Wells was one of those who tried to end lynching. Her newspaper in Memphis, the *Memphis Free Speech*, had been wrecked by a white mob in 1892. She then spent years speaking and working against lynching. She moved about the United States and all over the world. She asked in a book

Ida Wells spoke out against lynching.

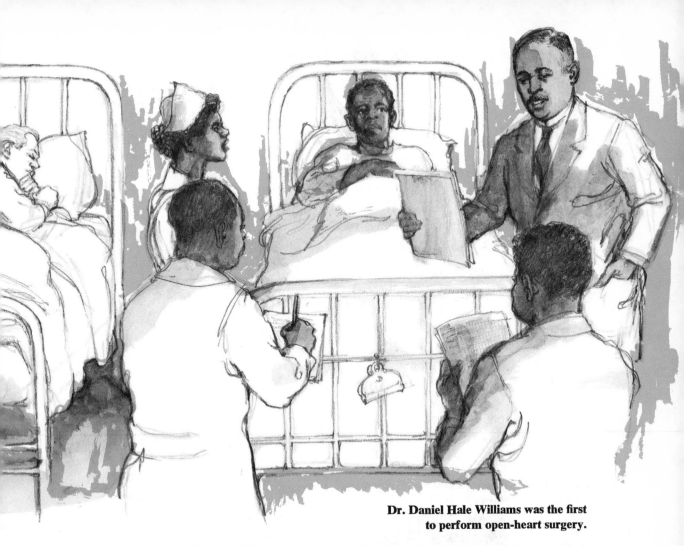

Dr. Daniel Hale Williams was the first to perform open-heart surgery.

she wrote about the problem: "Can you remain silent . . . when such things are done in our own community and country?" One of those who did not remain silent was George White, one of the few Afro-Americans in Congress during these Jim Crow years. In 1900 he asked for "a bill for the protection of all citizens of the United States against mob violence." This would have been the first Federal law to punish lynch mobs. But Congress did not listen. The law was not passed. Many years would have to pass before lynching became a crime that could be punished by the Federal government.

8 / *Firsts in Medicine.* Black Americans faced great problems in the years around 1900. Yet some gained world fame for helping improve the lives of all people. In 1893 Dr. Daniel Hale Williams was the first doctor to perform open-heart surgery. Another black scientist, Dr. Charles Richard Drew, showed how blood plasma could be kept till needed. In 1940 he set up the first blood

bank. During World War II, he directed the blood program of the American Red Cross.

9 / *A Black Poet.* Paul Lawrence Dunbar became a great poet of his people. He was one of this country's best-known writers. His poems were read and are still read all over the world. In one of them was found these lines, which pictured the problems then faced by all Afro-Americans.

We wear the mask that grins and lies,

* * *

We smile, but, O great Christ, our cries
to Thee from tortured souls arise.

10 / *A Man of Many Talents.* James Weldon Johnson had many careers. He was first of all a poet. He was a teacher and school principal. He was the first Negro lawyer in Florida. He was a leader of black organizations. He was a member of the for-

Paul Lawrence Dunbar and James Weldon Johnson were famous poets.

eign service and served in three countries. He was well known for his songs. Some of them went around the world, praised by all. One of these was "Lift Every Voice." The song became so well known that Negro meetings all over the United States were opened with it.

Lift every voice and sing
Till earth and heaven ring,
Ring with the harmonies of Liberty;
Let our rejoicing rise
High as the listening skies,
Let it resound loud as the rolling sea.

Sing a song full of the faith that the
dark past has taught us,
Sing a song full of the hope that the
present has brought us,
Facing the rising sun of our new day
begun
Let us march until victory is won.

His poem "Fifty Years," which he wrote fifty years after the Emancipation Proclamation, reminded his country that:

This land is ours by right of birth,
This land is ours by right of toil.

The work of James Weldon Johnson paved the way for other black writers. It made them see that they too could speak out and have a chance to be heard.

11 / *A Black Explorer.* Matthew A. Henson was another black man who helped the United States. On April 6, 1909, he helped discover the North Pole. A large group of

men started out on this journey. Only Commander Robert E. Peary, four Eskimos and Henson made the last dash of 140 miles to the Pole. Henson was the first to reach it. He and the others also proved that Greenland was an island in a great sea of ice. Matthew Henson told the story of this great discovery in the book *A Negro Explorer at the North Pole.* He later spoke about how hard the trip had been. Still, ". . . the glory at the end is worth while."

12 / Second-Class Citizenship Is Not Enough! In the last chapter we read about Booker T. Washington. He had done much to help his people get a better education. Some said he was ready to accept the Jim Crow world in exchange. Most white people and some black people agreed with him. Schools came first. But not all of them were ready to allow one-tenth of the country to be second-class citizens. White and black leaders of thought began to ask for full rights for all. William Monroe Trotter, black editor of the newspaper *Boston Guardian,* said that Washington was "a traitor to his race." Trotter had studied at Harvard, was a fine writer and became a strong leader. He helped change the thinking of many blacks who had agreed with Booker T. Washington.

13 / The Niagara Movement. In 1905 Trotter and Dr. William Edward Burghardt Du Bois, the country's best-known Negro scholar, took steps to fight the "Tuskegee Idea." They, with other blacks and whites, set up a new group to speak out against segregation. They called their group the

W. E. B. Du Bois

Niagara Movement. Its first meeting was held in Niagara Falls, Canada. (Those who came to it had not been able to get rooms on the New York side of the Falls!) They met and issued a call for action. Its words were clear: "We will not be satisfied to take one jot . . . less than our full manhood rights. . . . We claim for ourselves every single right that belongs to a freeborn American, political, civil and social; and until we get these rights we will never cease to protest. . . ." The next year they met again in Harpers Ferry, Virginia, where John Brown had tried and failed to free the slaves. They had begun the modern civil-rights movement.

Understanding What You Have Read

I. REVIEWING WORD MEANINGS

Write the letter of the choice that best completes each statement.

1. A good example of a menial job is (a) being a bus driver, (b) washing dishes in a restaurant, (c) being a nurse.

2. When troops are in combat, they are (a) fighting, (b) training, (c) resting.

3. A person who protests is (a) asking that things remain the same, (b) asking that things change, (c) saying that he does not care about things.

4. A person who is a racist would favor (a) equal treatment for all, (b) laws to improve the life of all races, (c) laws like the Jim Crow laws in the South about 1900.

5. Most people who live in a slum are (a) poor, (b) newcomers to a city, (c) old.

6. A segregated slum is called a ghetto because (a) all the people in it live in old buildings, (b) most of the people in it are of the same race, nationality or religious group, (c) none of the people in it are able to leave.

7. A commander would be (a) a follower, (b) a leader, (c) one who doesn't care.

8. A traitor is often hated because he (a) does nothing about problems, (b) has betrayed some idea or group, (c) agrees with everyone.

9. A scholar receives respect from others because he (a) has learned so much, (b) believes in equal rights for all, (c) will not agree to unfair laws.

10. People organize movements because they (a) hope to make money, (b) want to change the world in some way, (c) like the world as it is.

II.   UNDERSTANDING WHY

Write the letter in Column B that explains why each of the events in
Column A happened.

A

1. Tens of thousands moved to the big cities of the North.
2. By the end of World War I, 1,400 black men had become army officers.
3. Black ghettos developed in the cities.
4. A bill to make lynching a crime was introduced in Congress.
5. The lives of many soldiers were saved during World War II.

B

a. Protest meetings led to the opening of a training camp in Iowa.
b. Dr. Charles Richard Drew discovered a way to keep blood plasma till it was needed for use.
c. Farm workers in the South grew poorer and poorer.
d. Discrimination led to segregation.
e. Many hundreds of Negroes were killed by white mobs and KKK groups in both North and South.

III.   WHO AM I?

Write the name of the person described by each statement. The names
appear below the statements.

1. Needham Roberts and I were the first American soldiers to be decorated for bravery in World War I.
2. I lost my newspaper, the *Memphis Free Speech,* when a white mob wrecked it after I had written against lynchings.
3. I failed when I tried to get Congress to pass a law to punish those who took part in lynchings.
4. I was the first doctor to perform open-heart surgery.
5. My song, "Lift Every Voice," is still sung by choral groups.
6. My great moment came when I was the first to reach the North Pole.

7. In my newspaper, the *Boston Guardian,* I attacked the ideas of Booker T. Washington.

8. I joined with William Monroe Trotter and others to begin the Niagara Movement.

W. E. B. Du Bois	William Monroe Trotter
Matthew Henson	Ida Wells
Henry Johnson	George White
James Weldon Johnson	Daniel Hale Williams

IV. REVIEWING IMPORTANT FACTS

Write the letter of the choice that best completes each statement.

1. Negro families moved North to (a) make a better living, (b) find churches that would admit black people, (c) join the armed forces.

2. The actions of President Wilson showed that he (a) believed strongly that all people should receive equal treatment, (b) would not fight Jim Crow, (c) would not allow Jim Crow in the Navy.

3. People hate to live in a ghetto because they (a) have to travel to get to work, (b) are never allowed to leave the ghetto, (c) understand that they are not being allowed to live outside the ghetto.

4. Between 1900 and 1919, lynchings (a) ended in the United States, (b) continued in the United States, (c) increased in number each year.

5. When a bill was introduced in Congress to make lynching a crime, it was (a) passed but never became a law, (b) not passed, (c) never discussed.

6. Paul Lawrence Dunbar is best remembered as a (a) poet, (b) doctor, (c) member of the United States foreign service.

7. The poem "Fifty Years" was written by (a) Paul Lawrence Dunbar, (b) Ida Wells, (c) James Weldon Johnson.

8. The book *A Negro Explorer at the North Pole* was written by (a) W. E. B. Du Bois, (b) Matthew Henson, (c) William Monroe Trotter.

9. The Niagara Movement was joined by people who did not agree with (a) James Weldon Johnson, (b) Booker T. Washington, (c) John Brown.

10. Lynchings did not end because (a) laws in the South allowed them, (b) there was no protest against them, (c) those who lynched others were not punished by the courts.

V. ANSWER EACH OF THESE QUESTIONS WITH ONE OR TWO COMPLETE SENTENCES.

1. Why did many black people leave the South to settle in large Northern cities?

2. Why was it harder for a black person to find a job than for most European immigrants?

3. How did the Navy discriminate against Afro-Americans?

4. Why did the number of black people in Northern cities increase during World War I?

5. Why was the Ku Klux Klan able to continue its activities?

6. How did Ida Wells fight lynching?

7. How did Congressman George White try to end lynching?

8. How did James Weldon Johnson help other Negro writers?

9. How did William Monroe Trotter disagree with Booker T. Washington?

10. Why did a group of black and white Americans begin what was later called the Niagara Movement?

VI. THINGS TO DO

1. Get a book of poems by Paul Lawrence Dunbar from the library. Choose a favorite and read it to the class. Be ready to explain why you liked it.

The Niagara Movement, beginning of the modern civil-rights struggle.

2. Read the book *A Negro Explorer at the North Pole*. Report to the class about a favorite part of it.

3. Get the music to James Weldon Johnson's song "Lift Every Voice and Sing." Have a group prepare to sing it to the class.

4. Find out more about the goals of the Niagara Movement. Prepare a set of posters asking for the things black people needed in 1905.

5. Read the section about James Weldon Johnson in the book *Lift Every Voice*. Report to the class about his success on Broadway.

6. Use an encyclopedia to find the answer to this question about lynchings: How many of the people lynched were white?

7. What is a filibuster? How did members of the Senate from the South use filibusters to prevent the passage of a law to end lynchings?

Chapter 22 / THE CIVIL-RIGHTS MOVEMENT BEGINS

Let's Discover

1. How the Niagara Movement set up goals for improved civil rights for black Americans.
2. How other organizations were then begun to carry on the fight for equality.
3. How men like W. E. B. Du Bois, James Weldon Johnson and A. Philip Randolph led the fight for equal rights.

Words to Know

justice	Fair treatment under law.
	Each person should receive justice in a free country.
due process	The following of fair rules by a court or any part of a government, so that each person's rights are protected at all times.
	Jim Crow laws punished black Americans without due process.
scholarship	A gift of money to help a student continue his studies.
	W. E. B. Du Bois received scholarships for his college education.
denial	A taking away or holding back of rights.
	The denial of due process made courts in the South a chief cause of Jim Crow treatment of Negroes.
compulsory	Ordered by law.
	The education of all children is compulsory today.
association	A group of people working together for certain agreed goals.
	The National Association for the Advancement of

	Colored People works to improve the life of all Americans.
crisis	A time of great danger or trouble.
	The National Association for the Advancement of Colored People called its monthly magazine The Crisis.
urban	Having to do with life in cities.
	The Urban League tries to improve the life of black citizens in the cities.
porter	A man who waits on passengers in a railroad sleeping car or parlor car.
	The job of railroad porter became one held by black men only.
Brotherhood	A group of men joined together in some special organization.
	A. Philip Randolph formed the Brotherhood of Sleeping Car Porters.

---

1 / *"Liberty and Justice for All."* Chapter 19 told what Jim Crow did to the black people of the South. We saw how some parts of Jim Crow had come to the North too. Who could defend or allow such bad treatment? Yet in 1896 the Supreme Court had said that "separate but equal" was legal. We know how separate black life then became. We also know that it was not equal. Each day children all over the country heard that they lived in a nation of "liberty and justice for all." Black boys and girls, like their parents, knew that "liberty and justice" were not theirs. More and more people, black and white, made up their minds to try to get equal rights for all.

2 / *The Meaning of Equal Rights.* The United States was set up as a democracy. The chief aim of its government was to better the lives of all its people. There are three kinds of rights that people can have. First are the rights having to do with government. Each qualified person should be able to vote. He should be able to hold office. He should have the right to speak to the officials of his government. He should be able to work for changes in that government. Second are the social rights. Each person should know that he will be treated fairly in his daily life. We have seen how Jim Crow laws took this right away from black people in much of the country. The third

group of rights are called civil rights. All citizens should have these. One way to explain them is to look at one part of the Fourteenth Amendment. It says each of us should have "the equal protection of the laws."

3 / *"Due Process" and "Equal Protection."* The Constitution of the United States lists many rights that all people should have. It does this by saying that no government can pass laws to take away these rights. Each state constitution also has its list of rights. But what is a person to do when he feels that one of his rights has been taken away? The Constitution promises that he will receive "due process." This means that no government can punish him except through ways stated in laws. These laws must be the same for all. When laws are carried out fairly, then each person receives the "equal protection of the laws." Due process and equal protection were promises not kept in a Jim Crow world.

4 / *Using the Courts.* In our country, the legal way to correct a wrong is to go to court. A case is brought before a judge, or before a judge and jury. The judge can then order whoever is doing wrong to stop. It might be a person, a local government, a state government or even the national government. When the court makes its ruling, the power of the government must be used to carry it out.

5 / *Unfair Courts.* We know that the courts in the South were not fair to black Americans. Judges and juries were made up of white men. Often Negroes did not even have lawyers. Fair court rules were not followed

when a black man was on trial. Such courts were part of the Jim Crow world of the South. Federal courts would not step in to protect civil rights. The Supreme Court said that it did not have the power to tell a state what to do. Then, after 1900, new judges came to the Court. There began to be some hope that it would do what state courts had failed to do—keep the promise of "equal protection."

6 / *"Freedom Now!"* It was William Monroe Trotter who first made the demand for "Freedom Now!" We still hear these words. In 1890 black citizens from 21 states and the District of Columbia met in Chicago. They formed the Afro-American League. They asked for four changes in American life. (1) Black children should receive an equal share of the money being spent for schools. (2) Each person should receive a fair trial. (3) Laws should be passed to end lynchings. (4) Most important, all men should have the right to vote. We know that the Jim Crow laws took away such rights. No wonder Trotter and others, black and white, cried out for "Freedom Now!"

7 / *The Niagara Movement.* Think back to the key words of the statement by the Niagara Movement: "We claim for ourselves every single right that belongs to a freeborn American." Five demands were made by this group: (1) All people should have the right to vote. (2) The kind of life caused by Jim Crow laws had to end. (3) All should have the right "to walk, talk, and be with them that wish to be with us." (4) Equal protection of the laws had to begin at once. (5)

There must be better schools for black children all over the country. W. E. B. Du Bois, who wrote most of the statement, had given this advice to a young Afro-American girl: "Get the very best training possible and the doors of opportunity will fly open before you." But first the rights asked for by the Niagara Movement had to be won in some way.

8 / *W. E. B. Du Bois—Leader for Freedom.* Who was this man who led the fight to end the Jim Crow world? He had been born in Massachusetts in 1868. His father had died when the boy was still young; he and his mother were very poor. He was the only black student in his public school classes. He did so well that he earned college scholarships. He went to Fisk University in Tennessee. This was his first taste of life in a Jim Crow state. He later went to Harvard for more study. There he earned its highest degree—Doctor of Philosophy. He then won a new scholarship. This one was for more study in Germany's University of Berlin. His first book was a study of the African slave trade. He became a student of Afro-American history.

9 / *Teacher and Writer.* Du Bois was soon teaching at Atlanta University, one of the best-known Negro colleges. He wrote a long series of studies. One was the first book on Afro-American life in a large city. He showed in book after book that most of the troubles of black people came from the things done to them by white people. One of his studies showed how tax money for black schools in the South was taken away and used for white students. This was part of his proof that the schooling of black children was not equal. In 1903 he wrote his best-known book. It was called *The Souls of Black Folk.* In it he showed that he did not agree with Booker T. Washington. Dr. Du Bois called upon black people to be proud of their color. They should fight for equal rights, he said. They should not accept the Jim Crow world.

10 / *Aims of the Niagara Movement.* The group that set up the Niagara Movement turned to Dr. Du Bois to write their statement of goals. Let us look at some of the words he used. All people should "have the right to equal treatment in places of public entertainment," he wrote. "We especially complain against the denial of equal opportunity to us in economic life; . . . prejudice . . . is making it more difficult for Negro-Americans to earn a decent living. . . . School education should be free to all American children and compulsory." His words were clear. Dr. Du Bois was asking his country to give up its Jim Crow treatment of one-tenth of its people. "We plead for health . . . for an opportunity for decent houses. . . . So long as America is unjust . . . [we will be] the voice of protest of ten million Americans." There was much more. He wrote a list of needs. He made a cry for justice. Until it came, what should black Americans do? They should try to "vote, respect the rights of others, work, obey the laws, be clean and orderly, send our children to school, and respect ourselves."

11 / *Spreading the Truth.* The Niagara Movement was only a first step. It could do little. It was a group of people, not an organization. Yet its attack on Jim Crow began to

be heard. Ray Stannard Baker, a white news-
paperman, wrote a group of magazine articles. He called them *Following the Color
Line*. Baker told of what he saw as he moved
about the South. All that had been said about
Jim Crow was true. And the country's government did nothing to help end Jim Crow.
President William Howard Taft even made
speeches that showed he believed black people were not as good as white people. In
1906 a riot against Negroes swept across
Atlanta, Georgia. There were more riots.
One of the worst came in Springfield, Illinois,
two years later. This was the city in which
the "Great Emancipator," Abraham Lincoln,
had lived!

12 / *Beginning the N.A.A.C.P.* W. E. B. Du
Bois had warned all blacks after the trouble
in Atlanta: ". . . get out of the South as soon
as possible!" Yet nine out of every ten
Negroes in the country remained in the
South. A governor of Mississippi had warned
too: "If it is necessary every Negro in the
state will be lynched; it will be done to maintain white supremacy." On February 12,
1909, 100 years after Lincoln was born, a
call went forth for a meeting. It would set up
a lasting group to protect the rights of all
black people.

13 / *A Great Meeting.* The call for the meeting was written by the grandson of William
Lloyd Garrison. The group that met were
important white and black leaders. Among
the white leaders were Ray Stannard Baker
and Lincoln Steffens, who had written about
corruption in government. William Dean
Howells, the novelist, joined in. Lillian Wald
and Jane Addams, who had set up the first
settlement houses, came too. Rabbi Stephen

Wise, the Jewish leader from New York, was
present. William English Walling, who had
been writing against Jim Crow, came to the
meeting. Black leaders came in their search
for justice. Mary Church Terrell, wife of a
judge and a leader in improving schools;
Mary McLeod Bethune, who would later be
the first Negro woman to hold an important
job in Washington; Ida Wells, who had led
the fight to end lynching; Dr. Du Bois; Archi-

THE CRISIS

A RECORD OF THE DARKER RACES

Volume One   NOVEMBER, 1910   Number One

Edited by W. E. BURGHARDT DU BOIS, with the co-operation of Oswald Garrison Villard,
J. Max Barber, Charles Edward Russell, Kelly Miller, W. S. Braithwaite and M. D. Maclean.

CONTENTS

Along the Color Line   3

Opinion   7

Editorial   10

The N. A. A. C. P.   12

Athens and Browns-
ville   13
By MOORFIELD STOREY

The Burden . . .   14

What to Read . .   15

PUBLISHED MONTHLY BY THE
National Association for the Advancement of Colored People
AT TWENTY VESEY STREET   NEW YORK CITY

ONE DOLLAR A YEAR   TEN CENTS A COPY

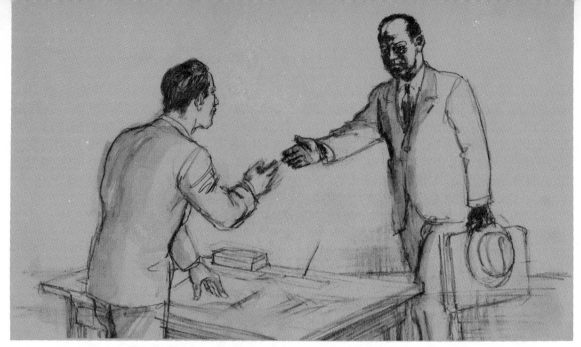

The Urban League helped Afro-Americans find jobs and homes.

bald H. Grimké, church leader—these and others came to the meeting. They were among the most respected people in the land.

14 / *Setting Up the N.A.A.C.P.* The new group was begun in 1910—the work of black and white leaders who saw that it was time to do something. It was called the National Association for the Advancement of Colored People. W. E. B. Du Bois became its best-known leader. He was in charge of news and research. He headed its magazine, *The Crisis*. All of the other officers were white at first. Moorfield Storey, a Boston lawyer, was the first president. As the years passed, black Americans became more interested in the work of the N.A.A.C.P. Today most of its leaders are black.

15 / *Fighting for Equal Rights*. How was this new group to bring about justice? It would study race problems. It would use the laws to end the wrongs it found. It would get new laws passed to protect black Americans. At all times, it would use the courts to get the rights all people should have. Local groups were set up all over the country. Hundreds of these "branches" were soon busy. James Weldon Johnson became Secretary. Lawyers were quick to help. A way had been found to fight for equal rights.

16 / *Using the Courts*. Jim Crow laws had to be ended. Negro schools had to be improved. Black men had to win back their right to vote in the South. The country's government was not doing its part to give all citizens their full rights. The courts would have to order this job done.

17 / *A Good Start*. In 1915 came the first great victory. The Supreme Court agreed that the grandfather clauses were wrong. No state could use this way to keep Afro-Americans from voting. Two years later a second case came to the Court. Could a law make black people live in only one part of a town? The Court ruled that it could not. No city or state could tell people where to live. In 1923 came the case of a black man who had been found guilty of murder by an all-white jury. The Court ruled that the trial had not been fair, for Afro-Americans had been kept off the jury. As it won such cases, the N.A.A.C.P. gained more support from blacks and whites. Ten years after it began it had more than 400 branches.

18 / *The Urban League*. In 1911 a second group was formed. It became known as the National Urban League. *Urban* means something that has to do with cities. The League was set up to help Afro-Americans new to the cities find jobs and places to live. It too

had black and white members. It sent people to visit companies to find out what jobs were open. They helped place black workers in these jobs. The League was very successful. It could not do all that should have been done, for most unions still did not admit Negroes. Yet the branches of the Urban League kept trying to open new doors to black workers.

19 / *The Brotherhood of Sleeping Car Porters*. There was one field of work in which the black man had less trouble finding a job. In fact, this work had become something done by black men only. It was the work of sleeping car porters on railroads. In 1925 an Afro-

A. Philip Randolph began the Brotherhood of Sleeping Car Porters.

American named A. Philip Randolph began a union of these workers. It was called the Brotherhood of Sleeping Car Porters. This was the first black labor group to grow strong. Both the N.A.A.C.P. and the Urban League helped it. Twelve years passed before it won the legal right to bargain for its members. Randolph, the best-known Negro labor leader, gained many honors. He spoke for Negro rights everywhere. This "elder statesman" of black leaders retired in 1970. The A. Philip Randolph Institute is headed by Bayard Rustin. It tries to improve working conditions for all.

Understanding What You Have Read

I. REVIEWING WORD MEANINGS

Write the letter of the choice that best completes each statement.

1. A person who receives justice knows he is getting (a) a trial, (b) fair treatment, (c) punishment.

2. When you receive due process, your (a) bills are paid, (b) rights are taken away, (c) rights are protected.

3. A person who is given a scholarship (a) can go to any school in the country; (b) gets a job on a ship, (c) receives money to help in his education.

4. When you suffer from a denial of rights you (a) have your rights taken away, (b) get new rights in exchange for old ones, (c) go to jail as proper punishment for a crime.

5. When education is compulsory, (a) the government makes all children attend school, (b) only white children are allowed to attend school, (c) parents must educate their own children.

6. Every association is a (a) group working for civil rights, (b) group working for some agreed set of goals, (c) a part of the government that gives all people equal protection of the laws.

7. W. E. B. Du Bois called his magazine *The Crisis* to show (a) it was dangerous for him to tell the truth in it, (b) black Americans were living in danger, (c) the magazine was in trouble because the N.A.A.C.P. was so poor.

8. An urban problem exists (a) in cities, (b) outside of cities, (c) either in or outside of cities.
9. A railroad porter helps railroad (a) passengers, (b) ticket offices, (c) repairmen.
10. The Brotherhood of Sleeping Car Porters is a (a) social organization, (b) labor union, (c) political group.

II. PLACING EVENTS IN PROPER ORDER

Place the names of the organizations listed below in the order in which they were begun.

1. The Brotherhood of Sleeping Car Porters
2. The Niagara Movement
3. The Urban League
4. The National Association for the Advancement of Colored People
5. The Afro-American League

III. JIM CROW OR EQUAL PROTECTION?

Arrange the statements below in two lists. If the statement is an example of Jim Crow, place it under the heading JIM CROW. If the statement is an example of fair treatment under law, place it under the heading EQUAL PROTECTION.

1. Election officials in the South made certain that black voters failed literacy tests.
2. Black students were excused from school in some states during harvest time on the farms.
3. All children, black or white, had to attend school.
4. Only white men served on juries in the South.
5. All persons charged with crimes were given lawyers and fair trials.
6. Each person, black or white, gained the right to vote.
7. Black workers were not admitted to most unions in the South.

8. Tax money for Negro schools in the South was used instead for white schools.
9. All persons receive the same treatment in theaters.
10. The Supreme Court decided that grandfather clauses were not allowed by the Constitution.

IV. UNDERSTANDING IMPORTANT FACTS

Write the letter of the choice that best completes each statement.

1. One of the rights a citizen should have is the right to (a) serve on a jury, (b) refuse to serve a black person in a restaurant, (c) keep his children out of school when he wishes.
2. When a court makes a decision (a) people have the right to refuse to obey it, (b) the power of the government should be used to carry out that decision, (c) no person can say that the court was wrong.
3. The leader of the Niagara Movement and later of the N.A.A.C.P. was (a) Ray Stannard Baker, (b) W. E. B. Du Bois, (c) A. Philip Randolph.
4. The Niagara Movement was chiefly an attack on (a) due process, (b) equal protection, (c) Jim Crow.
5. The first Negro woman to hold an important job in the national government was (a) Ida Wells, (b) Mary Church Terrell, (c) Mary McLeod Bethune.
6. The N.A.A.C.P. won its first successes (a) through strikes, (b) by setting up labor unions, (c) in the Supreme Court.
7. The best-known black labor leader was (a) W. E. B. Du Bois, (b) A. Philip Randolph, (c) James Weldon Johnson.
8. The cry for "Freedom Now!" was first made by (a) W. E. B. Du Bois, (b) the N.A.A.C.P., (c) William Monroe Trotter.
9. *The Souls of Black Folk* was written by (a) James Weldon Johnson, (b) William Howard Taft, (c) W. E. B. Du Bois.
10. The N.A.A.C.P. is an organization of (a) black and white Americans, (b) black Americans only, (c) white Americans only.

V. WRITE A SHORT PARAGRAPH TO ANSWER EACH OF THESE QUESTIONS.

1. Was Dr. W. E. B. Du Bois correct in his idea about the rights needed by Negroes?
2. Why wasn't the Niagara Movement able to get the changes in American life that it wanted?
3. What were the goals of the N.A.A.C.P.?
4. Why did the N.A.A.C.P. decide to use the courts to gain equal rights for black Americans?
5. How are the goals of the National Urban League different from those of the N.A.A.C.P., and how are they the same?
6. Why did A. Philip Randolph begin the Brotherhood of Sleeping Car Porters?
7. Explain one way you think your own civil rights could be improved.
8. Describe a civil-rights problem important today in your own community.

VI. THINGS TO DO

1. Prepare a class listing of THE RIGHTS OF CITIZENS. Students will have to read the Constitution of the United States, especially its Amendments, as they work on this listing. Divide your list into two parts, *Rights Already Won* and *Rights Still to Be Won*. Discuss in your class the differences between social, political and civil rights. Include the new class of rights called economic rights. Your final listing may have fifty or more rights in it!
2. Use your library to find out what rights are listed in the United Nations Declaration of Human Rights. Compare this listing to the one developed in class.
3. Lawyers speak of the differences between the *rights* of citizens, the *privileges* of citizens and the *duties* of citizens. Discuss how these are different. Give examples of each.

THE BLACK MAN IS HEARD

Introduction

This unit carries the story of the Afro-American to about 1950. These were years of trouble and change for the whole country. Negro music and writing began to be important. Yet black people did not gain equal rights. The United States remained a Jim Crow land.

The Great Depression struck the country and the world. People everywhere were out of work. Black people knew even more trouble than whites. Often the last hired, they were the first to be fired. The Federal government did not act to improve conditions. Black people were part of the great wave of voters who elected Franklin D. Roosevelt in 1932.

Unit 6 tells about the New Deal, Roosevelt's attack on the Depression. New laws were passed. They changed the lives of many Afro-Americans. A group of black people became important in government. More than a million black workers were able to join labor unions. Yet they could not end the practice of Jim Crow in the hiring of workers. Organized black groups then joined together to make the government act against Jim Crow hiring.

The coming of World War II led to more changes in the lives of black Americans. They did much to help win the war. They fought in the Army and Navy. Millions of them worked on farms and in factories to produce the goods needed by the country and its fighting men. Black people moved from the South to the North in a steady stream.

Jim Crow had continued during the war. It was found in the armed forces. It spoiled the daily life of the whole country. When the war ended, more and more Americans, black and white, called for equal rights for all. President Truman took some important steps. He ended segregation in the armed forces. He asked for laws for equal rights in all states. States like New York passed laws to work for such goals. Jim Crow began to weaken. People began to hope that one day soon it might end!

Chapter 23 / BLACK AMERICANS IN THE TWENTIES

Let's Discover

1. How Afro-American music and literature developed in the 1920's.
2. What kind of progress black Americans were able to make during these years.

Words to Know

conservative	Wanting to keep things as they are. *Most white Americans became very conservative after World War I.*
universal	For all the people. *Marcus Garvey set up The Universal Negro Improvement Association.*
anti-Semitism	Prejudice or discrimination against Jews. *Anti-Semitism spread during the 1920's.*
jazz	A kind of popular music developed by Southern Negroes. It uses a strong beat marked by syncopation (placing the accent where it would not be expected). In it, musicians may improvise—play the melody in their own way, changing its speed, rhythm or notes. *Jazz became the favorite American music during the 1920's.*
cartoon	A funny drawing, or one that shows how the artist feels about a person or happening in the news. *E. Simms Campbell, the cartoonist, drew cartoons that Americans thought very funny.*
spirituals	The best known of all American folk music, telling

the experiences of black people under slavery. They were a form of communication as well as expressions of religious feeling.

Spirituals often told stories from the Bible.

chariot   An open wagon with two wheels.

"Swing Low, Sweet Chariot," is one of the best-known Negro spirituals.

Dixieland   The South, or a kind of music that first appeared in New Orleans and other parts of the South.

Dixieland jazz bands were most popular during the 1920's.

miracle   Something so amazing that it could hardly have been done by any person on earth.

Marian Anderson's voice was called a "miracle."

artist   A person who paints, does sculpture, draws, sings, writes well or does anything else that adds to our culture.

Black poets, musicians and other artists gathered in Harlem during the 1920's.

---

1 / *Changes Caused by World War I.* After 1910 black people began to hope for a change in their lives. The N.A.A.C.P. and the Urban League were beginning their work. New jobs of all kinds were given to black workers in 1917 and 1918, most of them in the big cities of the North. During World War I, black officers in the armed forces led men who won many honors in Europe. The 369th Regiment from New York saw more fighting than most of the rest of the United States Army—and had more success! Hundreds of thousands of black people left the Jim Crow world of the South and moved to cities in the North. The first court victories against Jim Crow laws were won. When the troops came home, black Americans hoped for an end to discrimination and segregation.

2 / *Moving Backward.* After the war the whole country seemed to grow more conservative. It turned against change, and people tried to keep life as it had been. The KKK again spread through the land; it grew until it had perhaps five million members! KKK groups gained power in the South and in some parts of the North as well. Negro groups had hoped that white unions would

WAITING ROOM

WHITE ONLY

COLORED
ENTER AT REAR

now help in the fight for equal rights. Instead, hard times followed the war years. The unions grew weaker; more and more people were out of work. Negroes were fired first. White union members often seemed to become the enemies of black workers, who they feared were ready to work for very low wages. At this time, black soldiers who had been in Europe, where there were no Jim Crow laws, came back to their own home towns and cities. Many of them now refused to go back to a life of segregation.

3 / *Trouble in the Cities.* By the end of the war the United States was one of the world's great manufacturing countries. The factories, and the jobs in them, were in the cities. Black and white people moved from the farms to the cities in a steady stream. By 1920 more than half of all Americans lived in cities. But they found that their new lives were not always happy. There were not enough jobs for all. There was not enough housing. People grew angry as they struggled for jobs and places to live. New slums appeared. Whites tried to keep Afro-Americans out of some neighborhoods. In 1919 a wave of riots shocked the country. In city after city whites and blacks fought in the streets. The worst of these riots was in Chicago. In the South, lynchings went on as in the past. It began to appear that there was no hope for a black person in the United States.

4 / *Marcus Garvey and "Back to Africa."* It was during these troubles that a new black leader became known. His name was Marcus Garvey. He was a Negro from Jamaica, then an English colony in the West Indies. Garvey

**Black soldiers returned
to a Jim Crow world.**

offered a plan to end Jim Crow. Let all black people in the United States move to Africa! He felt that no other way could ever be found to live in peace with whites. Garvey set up an organization to carry out his plan. He called it the Universal Negro Improvement Association. It would buy ships on which Afro-Americans could sail "home" to Africa. Garvey's newspaper, *The Negro World,* went all over the country. We do not know how many black people joined him. The number may have been as high as four million! Many sent money to buy shares in his "Black Star Line." He had filled them with hope for a better life.

5 / *The End of Marcus Garvey's Dream.* Black people were being made proud of their color and their history. Yet not one of them was to go to Africa under Garvey's plan. The dream ended when he was arrested. He was charged with using the mails to steal money. He would not use a lawyer in his trial, but tried to defend himself. His defense was not a good one, and he was found guilty. In 1925 he went to jail. Two years later President Coolidge pardoned him and had him sent back to Jamaica. The "Back to Africa" plan died.

6 / *New York—Center of Culture.* New York had become the most important city in the country. It had the most people. Its theaters and concert halls were busy. More black people lived there than in any other city. Most large publishers had their offices in New York. If Afro-American writers and artists were to become well known, they would have to find success in New York.

Marcus Garvey's dream failed.

Such success began to come during the 1920's for a small number of black Americans. At the same time, there was for a few years a great interest in Negro art and music among white leaders of culture and white businessmen in the field of entertainment.

7 / *The Jazz Age.* In the 1920's the leaders of government, like most white people, did not favor change. Hate groups appeared. Anti-Semitism—the hatred of Jews—grew. Anti-Catholic feeling spread. White hate groups, it seemed, would use Klan thinking to hurt all minority groups. Yet large numbers of young people, white and black, were ready to turn against the old ideas. They looked for a new kind of freedom—freedom to do as they pleased. They drank, even though a Federal law had made it a crime to sell liquor. They danced a great deal. They turned to the kind of music we call jazz. The automobile, new then, gave them more freedom. People called these years the "Jazz Age." One of its best known recorders was the black cartoonist E. Simms Campbell. Most of his cartoons were about the young people of America. They made him a leading popular artist of his time.

8 / *Afro-American Music Across the Land.* It was in the 1920's that the kind of music long played and sung by black Americans spread all over the country. Spirituals came first. These were the songs that had been sung by slaves and freedmen for hundreds of years. Some held meanings that only a slave would have known. A "chariot" might have meant a wagon on the Underground Railroad. The "glory road" might have been the route to freedom. "Joshua" might, to some slaves, have been Nat Turner and his fight for freedom. In 1871 the Fisk Jubilee Singers had sung such songs all over the country. In the 1920's white people seemed to discover these songs again. They are still being sung. Other music played by black people also spread over the land. From the South came the quick beat of Dixieland music. From the sad life of Afro-Americans came the blues. These songs told of troubles that all people could understand. American music changed as Afro-American music and musicians gave the beat to the Jazz Age.

9 / *Jazz Leaders.* Music, the new language of young people, was best spoken by the

jazz artists of the day. Ethel Waters, Florence Mills and Bessie Smith sang as the world listened. Eubie Blake and Noble Sissle wrote hit shows for Broadway. Louis Armstrong's trumpet and "Duke" Ellington's piano brought thousands to Harlem. All people seemed to know the blues songs by W. C. Handy and Jelly Roll Morton. Jim Europe and his Negro band toured Europe, and brought with them the new dance called the fox trot.

10 / *In the Concert Halls.* For those who loved more serious music, there were three great voices. Roland Hayes was one of the world's most famous tenors. This black artist was certain to fill any concert hall. He toured Europe, where crowds cheered him and kings planned special concerts by him in their palaces. Paul Robeson, scholar, actor, lawyer and singer, was one of the great

Duke Ellington played for thousands.

**Everyone loved the new jazz
of Louis Armstrong
and Bessie Smith.**

talents of the country. Marian Anderson
sang her first successful concert in 1925.
Her voice has been called one of the miracles
of our time. The recordings made by these
three artists sold millions of copies all over
the world. Music in the 1920's owed much
to them and to other black artists.

11 / *Harlem, Center of Jazz.* Many of the
great jazz musicians came to New York's
Harlem, the growing Negro neighborhood.
There such white musicians as Paul White-
man, George Gershwin and Benny Goodman came to listen and learn. They then
played the kind of music they heard in
Harlem. This made it ever more popular.
Chicago was also a jazz center. Louis Armstrong had joined the band there led by
Joe "King" Oliver. Armstrong, known as
"Satchmo," was the best known of all jazz
trumpet players. He had played and been
cheered all over the world until his death
in 1971. Bessie Smith brought the blues
with her when she left the poor life she had
known in the South. She was loved wherever
she sang. She died after an automobile acci-

dent in Mississippi in 1937. She was not
allowed to get the care she needed at a
nearby white hospital in that Jim Crow
state. Even as the whole country was singing and dancing to Afro-American music,
only a few of its white people were working
to bring equal rights to all.

12 / *Black Culture and White America.* The
United States in the 1920's was still a Jim
Crow land. Black artists did not have an
easy life. Some worked in white-owned night

clubs in Harlem, where no black customer would be admitted! An artist like Aaron Douglas might sell some of his paintings, but he never received the full praise he would have earned today. Charles Gilpin, a leading actor, was a "hit" in a Broadway play, but he found it hard to get other parts. Paul Robeson, with all his talent, often went for long periods without a job. Some black artists were accepted; most were still finding it hard to get work. This problem has remained with us. Steps to solve it have been taken only during the last few years.

13 / *To Pay the Rent.* Black artists of all kinds, in Harlem and in other cities, did not give up. It was not easy for an Afro-American writer to have his poems or stories published. *The Crisis,* the N.A.A.C.P. magazine, did present black writers to the world. *Opportunity,* the magazine of the Urban League, also printed the work of Afro-American authors. But it was hard to break into the great publishing world. This world was not yet ready to accept the work of black Americans. In the late 1920's poor artists in Harlem turned to the rent party. Their friends came to visit. They listened to poems, music or a new short story and left money on the way out. This money paid the costs of the party. If some was left, it helped pay the rent. At these parties, black people were able to hear and enjoy the work of black artists.

14 / *The Poets Sing Out.* Three Afro-American poets of these years won world praise. All three lived in Harlem. The most famous

Harlem's best-known poet was Langston Hughes.

Countee Cullen was a teacher and poet.

was Langston Hughes. He is best known as a poet. He also wrote novels, plays, songs, histories and newspaper columns. He was to become one of the country's most honored authors. A second fine poet of the Jazz Age was Countee Cullen. His first book of poems, *Color,* appeared when he was still a student at New York University. He was later a public-school teacher in New York, but he did not stop writing. A third poet and writer of these years was Claude McKay. He had come to the United States from the island of Jamaica—one of tens of thousands from the West Indies who have enriched American life. In 1922 he finished a book of poems, *Harlem Shadows.* One of his best-known novels, six years later, was *Home to Harlem.* McKay, like Paul Robeson and many other black artists and writers, spent a large part of his life in Europe. But in his years in Harlem he set the tone for the work of dozens of young black writers. Like Langston Hughes and Countee Cullen, Claude McKay wrote poems of protest— strong attacks on the Jim Crow world.

15 / *The Twenties, a Time of Trouble.* The life of most black people did not improve much in the 1920's. It was a time of change for hundreds of thousands who moved from the South to cities in the North. Jim Crow lived on. The N.A.A.C.P. chipped away at it as it won some court cases. The Urban League hit at it as it found jobs for black workers. But the nation as a whole did not move ahead. One writer told the country that the South still believed "a Negro has no rights which a white man is bound to respect." Some Afro-Americans were finding success. Oscar DePriest of Chicago was elected to Congress in 1928, the only Afro-American then in the country's legislature. A few musicians, writers and artists were becoming known. W. E. B. Du Bois was hopeful. He reviewed the work of the past twenty years and saw a better future. At last, he could report, black Americans were at the door, ready to open it. A new and better life was on the other side. We know that the door would remain shut for many more years.

Understanding *What You Have Read*

I. REVIEWING WORD MEANINGS

Write the letter of the choice that best completes each statement.

1. A person who is conservative wants (a) quick changes, (b) as little change as possible, (c) any change that will improve the way people live.

2. An idea is called universal if it (a) is true for all people, (b) cannot be believed, (c) uses lies to fool people.

3. Anti-Semitism is prejudice against (a) Afro-Americans, (b) Jews, (c) all minorities.

4. Jazz is a kind of (a) language, (b) clothing, (c) music.

5. A cartoonist makes his living by (a) writing, (b) singing, (c) drawing.

6. The ideas in spiritual music are most often (a) religious, (b) social, (c) political.

7. A chariot is a kind of (a) song, (b) wagon, (c) religion.

8. A man who comes from Dixieland comes from the (a) West, (b) West Indies, (c) South.

9. A miracle is something (a) so amazing it can hardly be believed, (b) so easy anyone can do it, (c) anything you cannot understand.

10. An artist is most important to his country's (a) social life, (b) culture, (c) army.

II. WHO AM I?

From the list below each group, choose the person described by each statement.

1. My tenor voice was considered one of the best in the world, and people in one country after another rushed to hear me.

2. I wrote poems and novels about life in Harlem and helped many young black writers get their start.

3. I brought new hope to black Americans during the early 1920's with my "Back to Africa" movement.

4. My cartoons appeared in magazines and were popular with young people during the 1920's.

5. I spent my life learning and singing the blues; I died after an automobile accident in Mississippi.

| Claude McKay | Jim Crow | E. Simms Campbell |
| Bessie Smith | Roland Hayes | Marcus Garvey |

6. They call me "Satchmo" and really cheer me on when I play my trumpet.

7. My greatest success came after I began to write songs called "blues."

8. I was well known as a singer and actor, but found that there were not many jobs open for a Negro artist in the 1920's.

9. I wanted to be remembered for my poems, but I also wrote novels, plays, histories and newspaper columns.

10. When I was elected in 1928, I became the only Afro-American then a member of Congress.

Langston Hughes	Louis Armstrong	Paul Robeson
Oscar DePriest	W. C. Handy	W. E. B. Du Bois

11. It was during the 1920's that Americans began to praise my voice, and applauded my work in concert halls.

12. I was truly New York's poet, and later taught in the city's public schools.

13. People today agree that my paintings were among the best of the 1920's.

14. My best-known work was the Broadway shows I wrote with my friend, Noble Sissle.

15. I was called one of the country's best actors, but found it hard to find roles to play.

George Gershwin	Countee Cullen	Marian Anderson
Aaron Douglas	Eubie Blake	Charles Gilpin

III. UNDERSTANDING THE 1920's

Write the name of the place described by each statement.

1. The worst of many riots in 1919 took place in this city.

2. This part of New York City became the center for the work of many fine Afro-American artists.

3. Marcus Garvey came to the United States from this island and later had to return to it.

4. This was the place to which Marcus Garvey said all black Americans should move to escape Jim Crow.

5. Claude McKay, Paul Robeson and others crossed the ocean to spend many years in this part of the world.

IV. CHECKING SOME IMPORTANT IDEAS

Write the letter of the choice that best completes each statement.

1. Paragraph 2 tells you that (a) people began to walk backward during the 1920's, (b) the United States grew more conservative after World War I, (c) Jim Crow ended in the 1920's.

2. Paragraph 5 explains why (a) Marcus Garvey wanted to bring people back to Africa, (b) Marcus Garvey's plans failed, (c) Marcus Garvey became the friend of a President.

3. The Jazz Age described in Paragraph 7 meant (a) the way young people lived and thought in the 1920's, (b) the way music was more important than anything else in the 1920's, (c) the new freedom for black people after 1920.

4. Paragraph 11 tells us that jazz was played by (a) only black musicians, (b) only white musicians, (c) black and white musicians.

5. The rent parties described in Paragraph 13 were a way to (a) raise enough money to continue working as a writer, poet or musician, (b) have fun at no cost to anyone, (c) interest white publishers in the work of black writers.

V. ANSWER EACH QUESTION WITH A COMPLETE SENTENCE.

1. What did hate groups try to do in the 1920's?

2. Why didn't labor unions admit new Negro members in the years right after World War I?

3. Why did so many people follow the ideas of Marcus Garvey?

4. Why was New York City the center of American culture?

5. Why did "blues" become a popular kind of music?

6. Why did white America learn to love jazz?

7. Why did only a few black artists find success?

8. How did the N.A.A.C.P. and the Urban League help black writers?

9. What is meant by "a poem of protest"?

10. Why did the success of Oscar DePriest mean so much to all black Americans?

VI. QUESTIONS TO DISCUSS IN CLASS

1. The 1920's were called the time of the "Harlem Renaissance." What does the word *renaissance* mean? Was this word a good description of what was happening in Harlem? Why?

2. Why did the United States become so conservative in the years after World War I? How did this affect Afro-Americans and other minority groups?

3. Why did W. E. B. Du Bois believe that life would become better after 1930? How did the success of some black artists seem to show that he was right? What kind of national problems might have then come to change his hopes to disappointments?

4. Since 1920 more and more Americans have moved to the cities. How has this meant a great change in the life of black people? How much better or worse was life in the cities for them compared to the life they had known in farm areas? Why?

5. Remember the three big problems that face any newcomer to a city—jobs, housing, schools. Why didn't these problems become smaller during the 1920's? (Your discussion of Question 4 should help you to answer this question.)

6. Play examples of jazz, spirituals and blues in class. Use music of the 1920's if possible. What made such music so popular in the 1920's? Why is some of it still so popular today?

7. Spend a class period listening to poetry by Langston Hughes, Countee Cullen and Claude McKay. Each student can pick a favorite, read it to the class and explain what the poem means. Then discuss the way in which all the poems heard helped you understand how black Americans lived, and what they hoped for, during the 1920's.

Chapter 24

THE COMING OF THE DEPRESSION

Let's Discover

1. How the Great Depression came in the years after 1929.
2. How Afro-Americans were hurt by the Depression.
3. How relief programs were begun to aid people in need.

Words to Know

poverty	Being so poor that you do not have enough food, shelter and clothing.
	Negro farmers in the South often lived in poverty.
production	The making of goods by a factory or business.
	When production is high, more people have jobs.
depression	A time when there is less business and many people are out of work.
	People suffer in many ways during a depression.
stocks	Shares of ownership in a business.
	People buy stocks in the hope that their value will go up.
stock exchange	A place where stocks are bought and sold.
	The New York Stock Exchange is the most important in the United States.
unemployed	Out of work.
	When the factory closed, its workers became unemployed.
unemployment	The condition of being unemployed.
	Unemployment became a national problem in the 1930's.
relief	Aid given to people who cannot support them-

selves, usually because they are unemployed.

People who went "on relief" received aid so that they could care for their families.

candidate   A person who runs for public office.

Franklin D. Roosevelt was the Democratic Party's candidate for President in 1932.

trickle   To move little by little.

President Hoover thought aid given to big businesses would trickle down to poor people.

---

1 / *Problems of Negro Workers.* By 1930 black workers in the cities and on the farms had many problems. Most farmers in the South were tenant farmers. The owners of the land they farmed were beginning to buy farm machinery. This meant fewer farmers were needed. Machines could do more work than any man. Black farmers and their families moved from the South to the North in a steady flow. Once in the cities, they found that their farming skills did not mean much. They had to begin again. This meant the lowest-paying jobs in factories. It meant they had to work as servants, or take menial jobs in stores and restaurants. Low pay brought no real improvement in the way a family could live. Worst of all was the old Jim Crow fear. The black worker was the last to be hired. He would be the first to be fired.

2 / *What Is Poverty?* You cannot understand the troubles described in this chapter unless you first understand what poverty means. To begin with, it means being poor. It means not having enough to eat or wear, or a good place to live. It means not having the money to take care of the problems that come in every family's life. Real poverty often means being hungry. This in turn can mean that people become ill or even die.

Poverty can mean a home like this.

Without money they cannot have a doctor when someone is sick, or buy the medicine to make him better. Some Americans have only a few dollars in cash a year! This has been most true of the black and white tenant farmers in the South. It has meant that a father and mother, and their children as well, have all had to work. Such children do not always go to school. They grow up without education, and therefore remain as poor as their parents were. Poverty is one of the great enemies of human improvement. In the 1930's it spread across the whole world.

3 / *What Is a Depression?* There have been times in the history of the United States when great business troubles spread over the nation. Prices and wages go down at such times. Many businesses fail. The people who have been working in them lose their jobs. Farm prices go down, and many farmers lose their farms. As more and more people are out of work, they have less money to spend. This means that factories cannot sell as many products. The amount of their production must be lowered. With less work to be done, they must fire some of their workers. It becomes harder for a person to make a living. A thing is depressed when it is less or worse than it was. A country with business troubles such as those described here is suffering from a depression. The worst depression in this country's history began in 1929 and lasted for about ten years. It has been called the Great Depression.

4 / *Poor People During a Depression.* It is the poor people who suffer most at such a time. They have no savings to use. This means that once they lose their jobs they have no money with which to live. They then lose their homes because they cannot pay rent or the cost of owning them. They sell whatever they have to buy food. Sometimes they starve. Sometimes they get help from other people or from their government. In the Great Depression there was more suffering by more people than ever before in United States history.

5 / *The Coming of the Great Depression.* Trouble had been on its way for several years. Farmers had not been making a good living. Businesses were turning out more goods with new machinery, but wages were not rising. This meant that people did not have enough money to buy these goods. They had to borrow to buy. If they lost their jobs, they were in debt at once with no hope of paying their bills. There were few rules to keep banks from making unwise decisions. More than 5,000 of them failed during the 1920's. Each time this happened many people and businesses lost their money. Some of those who did have money bought stocks—shares of businesses. If the price of their stocks went up, they could sell them at a profit. Most stocks were bought and sold on the New York Stock Exchange. Then, in October, 1929, all the economic troubles in the country seemed to come together at once. The prices of stocks crashed down. In the next few months other things crashed too. Factories began to close. Farmers lost their land. Millions were thrown out of work. Banks failed. Trade with Europe almost ended. The Great Depression had

come to the United States and the rest of the world.

6 / *The Rise in Unemployment.* A person is unemployed when he does not have a job. Unemployment hit black workers first. It hit them hardest. In 1932 thirteen million people did not have jobs! A large part of all Negro workers were among these millions.

The thousands of small black-owned businesses in the cities—most of them in black neighborhoods—also suffered. Many of them had to close. Men who had no jobs still had to find ways to feed their families. They did anything to earn a dollar. In cities like New York and Chicago thousands of men stayed on the streets. They shined shoes. They sold apples for a nickel apiece. They went from business to business asking for work. In one city a mob of unemployed men went into a grocery and took all the food they could carry. In city after city, men without jobs or homes built shacks out of scraps of tin and board on empty city lots. Some even moved into the parks, for they had no other place to live. The number of poor people grew and grew. Many feared that a revolution would sweep the land if something were not done to help the unemployed and their families.

Many poor families lost their homes during the Depression.

7 / *The Government Did Little.* Herbert Hoover, a Republican, was President of the United States when the Depression began. He and his followers did not believe that the government should help people who did not have homes, jobs and food. Let private groups help those in need, they said. Unemployed people turned to friends and relatives for help. Often they could not get the aid they needed. Negro churches, like other religious groups, did all they could to help. They gave bread and food to those who were starving. Some of them set up soup kitchens. Soup costs less to make than most other foods. In New York City the Abyssinian Baptist Church, the largest black Protestant church in the world, fed thousands every day. Dr. Adam Clayton Powell, Sr., its minister, found that he and his church were the only help for great numbers of Afro-Americans. Millions of people had to turn to "bread lines" and soup kitchens if they were to have any food at all! Jim Crow appeared in some of these lines, in the South and in some parts of the North too. Even in such times as these, Afro-Americans were not served. The Depression went on. It became clear that city and state governments would have to help the people. There was no other way, for the President would not agree to any plan for direct aid from the Federal government.

8 / *"Going on Relief."* Something had to be done. Cities and towns began to help the families of the unemployed. They gave them food, clothing and sometimes money. Such aid is called "relief." Millions of families had to go on relief. How else could they stay

A "bread line" in New York City.

alive? Business did not improve. In 1933 some cities had as many as four out of every ten Negro families on relief. A year later half the black workers in the large northern cities were on relief. This was almost four times the rate of unemployment among white workers! In Norfolk, Virginia, in 1935, eight out of every ten black families had to have relief. "Last hired and first fired" was being proven true in the worst possible way.

9 / *The Search for Work.* There were few jobs. It grew harder and harder to find them. It was hardest for a black worker. Even those jobs that white people had never wanted to do—sweeping floors, carrying heavy loads, cleaning cellars—were now taken by whites. In some places white workers tried to drive blacks out of jobs. In 1932 the white workers of the Illinois Central Railroad fought with black workers over jobs. Ten Afro-Americans were killed in the fighting. Many families broke up under such terrible pressures. Fathers and mothers moved around the country looking for work. Children went to live with relatives.

10 / *Voting for Democrats.* Most black Americans had voted for the Republicans since the days of Abraham Lincoln. Now, when it seemed that the Republican President would not do much to end the Depression, they began to turn toward the Democrats. They knew this was the party of white supremacy and Jim Crow in the South. But a man had to seek some change when he was

In 1932 black and white railroad workers fought over jobs.

left with nothing. At least the Democrats in the North were talking about Federal action to end the Depression. Afro-Americans in the cities began to vote Democratic in national elections. They have never really returned to the Republicans. In 1932 Franklin Delano Roosevelt, candidate of the Democrats, was elected President. Black voters helped him win in many important states.

11 / *The Promises of the Democrats*. Roosevelt and the men from his party in Congress had promised to use the power of the national government to fight the Depression. They would offer direct relief. They would build roads and public buildings, and put people to work on these jobs. They would find ways to help poor farmers. Herbert

Hoover and his party had helped banks and businesses. They had hoped such help would "trickle down" to the poor people of the country. Roosevelt promised to help people rather than businesses. One of his promises would prove to be most important to black workers. Unions would be helped to organize and get new members. In the dozen years after Roosevelt became President, over a million more black workers would gain the job safety that comes from being a union member. The return of the Democrats to Washington would be the beginning of the end of the Depression. This was the hope of the millions, white and black, who voted for Franklin D. Roosevelt.

12 / *The Shock of the Depression.* Hard times hurt people all over the country. Negroes had been poorer than most other Americans even before the Depression began. Now their poverty grew even greater. They had been hoping above all else for an end to Jim Crow. Now they had a greater need. How would they be able to feed themselves tomorrow? Then, in 1932, a new President was chosen. He promised to bring an end to the Depression. Would he really help black people in a Jim Crow land? A number of black leaders decided to work with the new President. They would do all they could to make certain that blacks as well as whites were helped by the laws to be passed by Roosevelt's new government.

DEPRESSION NEWS STORIES

These are just a few of the things that happened across the United States during the Depression. The people described here were both whites and blacks, drawn together by their shared problems—poverty.

1931	Arkansas	500 farmers marched into a town and demanded food for their hungry families.
	Indiana	1,500 unemployed men were driven away from a town's largest business after they marched to it to ask for jobs.
	Michigan	2,000 men and women met in a city park to demand work; they were driven out by the police.
1932	Illinois	500 school children whose parents were unemployed marched to their city's Board of Education to ask for food.
	Pennsylvania	Police broke up a march on a city hall by thousands of unemployed.
	Ohio	6,000 people rioted at a food market that had offered some free food.
	Michigan	1,000 people rioted when a landlord tried to put out a family that had not been able to pay its rent.
1933	New York	Hundreds of unemployed gathered at a restaurant and later attacked its manager when he refused to feed them without payment.
	Washington	5,000 unemployed people stayed at a city's official building for two days asking for help.
	Louisiana	Crowds of unemployed demonstrated at a city hall and were driven away by police on horseback.
	Oklahoma	Thousands of tenant farm families, driven off their land, set off for California, where they hoped to find work.
1933-1936	Mississippi	Newspapermen from the North found that cotton-growing tenant farmers could make only ten dollars a month for food.
March 4, 1933	Washington, D.C.	Franklin D. Roosevelt, in his first speech as President, said: "This nation asks for action, and action now. . . . We must act, and act quickly."

Understanding What You Have Read

I. REVIEWING WORD MEANINGS

Write the letter of the choice that best explains the meaning of each word.

1. **poverty** (a) Being weak. (b) Being old. (c) Being poor.
2. **production** (a) Making goods. (b) Selling goods. (c) Buying goods.
3. **depression** (a) "Good times." (b) "Bad times." (c) "Old times."
4. **stocks** (a) Parts of a building. (b) Shares in a business. (c) A place for selling.
5. **stock exchange** (a) Place to buy and sell stocks. (b) Place to exchange one kind of money for another. (c) Place to store a supply of goods.
6. **unemployed** (a) Beginning a job. (b) Losing a job. (c) Changing a job.
7. **unemployment** (a) People at work. (b) People refusing to work. (c) People out of work.
8. **relief** (a) Punishment. (b) Help. (c) Unemployment.
9. **candidate** (a) Wants to be elected. (b) Owns a candy factory. (c) Special time of the year.
10. **trickle** (a) All at once. (b) Not at all. (c) Little by little.

II. UNDERSTANDING WHY

Write the letter of the choice that best explains why each statement is true.

1. Poor people are often sick.
    a. They do not have enough money to see a doctor regularly.
    b. They do not eat anything.
    c. They never go to school.
2. People built houses out of tin and boards during the Depression.
    a. Tin and wood make a house warmer.
    b. They had no other places to live.
    c. Tin companies sold scraps at special prices.

A shantytown in Oregon.

3. Men sold apples on the streets of big cities.
   a. They made a good living in this way.
   b. They had no other way to make money.
   c. They needed more money than they made on their regular jobs.
4. Eight out of every ten Negro families in Norfolk, Virginia, had to have relief.
   a. There was more unemployment among black workers than among white workers.
   b. Eight out of each ten families in Norfolk were black.
   c. Black workers were the first hired and the last fired.
5. In 1932 black voters in the cities began to turn to the Democrats.
   a. All Democrats had given up Jim Crow ideas.
   b. Franklin D. Roosevelt promised to help Negro banks first.
   c. The Republicans had not done enough to end the Depression.

III. REVIEWING ECONOMIC UNDERSTANDINGS

Answer each of these questions in a short paragraph, or discuss them in class.

1. Suppose that a town has only one large factory in it. That

factory is forced to close. How does this affect the lives of the workers in that factory? How does it affect other businesses in the town?

2. A share of stock is simply a piece of paper that tells someone he owns part of a company. Why do people buy stocks? Why do the prices of stocks go up or down in a stock market?

3. Describe some of the ways in which men who were unemployed tried to take care of their families. Why is a steady job better than these other ways of making a living?

IV. POINTS OF VIEW

Decide what you would do in each of these situations. Then explain why. Compare your answers with those of other students in your class.

1. You are a banker. You learn that farmers to whom your bank has made loans cannot pay back these loans. What will you do about it?

2. You are a tenant farmer in the South. You have very little savings. You learn that the man whose land you farm is buying machinery, and that he wants you to leave his land. What will you do?

3. You are a voter who has always favored the Republicans because you know that the Democrats in your state are under KKK control. You are out of work during the Depression. The Democratic candidate for President, Franklin D. Roosevelt, promises to help find a job for you. You know that the KKK Democrats favor Roosevelt. How should you vote?

4. You are a tenant farmer in the South in 1934. The Depression has brought hard times to your part of the country. You learn that a union of tenant farmers has been formed to help protect people like you from landlords who think only of making money. This union is open to blacks and whites alike. You have never been in an organization open to both blacks and whites. What should you do?

AFRO-AMERICANS AND THE NEW DEAL

Let's Discover

1. How the New Deal changed the lives of many Afro-Americans.
2. How Mary McLeod Bethune and other members of the "Black Cabinet" played important parts in the New Deal.
3. How pressure from organized black groups brought about the first Federal action to weaken Jim Crow in the hiring of workers.

Words to Know

reforms — Changes in laws or customs that improve the way people live or the way their government acts toward them.
One of the New Deal reforms was a law to help workers organize in unions.

project — A plan to build or to change something, or a thing that is planned or built.
A group of new buildings or a new bridge are examples of public works projects.

social security — A group of laws that help workers by giving them such things as old-age pensions and payments when they are unemployed or sick.
Workers, their companies and the Federal government share the cost of the country's social-security programs.

pension — Money paid regularly by a company or the government to a person who no longer works, usually because he has reached a certain age.
A worker could begin to receive his old-age pension when he reached the age of 65.

federation	A group made up of a number of other groups.
	The American Federation of Labor is an organization whose members are unions.
trade union	A labor union whose members all have the same skill, such as carpenters, plumbers or electricians.
	Those who worked on women's clothing formed the trade union called the International Ladies' Garment Workers Union.
industrial union	A labor union whose members are all people working in a single industry, whatever their special skills.
	The United Mine Workers of America is an industrial union whose members include miners, mechanics, clerks and others who work for mining companies.

ROOSEVELT SPEAKS TO THE
NATION, March 4, 1933

"... So, first of all let me assert my first belief that 'the only thing we have to fear is fear itself.'. . . Our greatest primary task is to put people to work. . . . We must act and act quickly . . . the emergency at home cannot wait. . . . The people of the United States have not failed. . . . They have asked for discipline and direction under leadership."

President Franklin Delano Roosevelt.

Cabinet	A group of heads of government departments, chosen by the President to help and advise him. *The "Black Cabinet" was a group of leading Afro-Americans who helped and advised President Franklin D. Roosevelt.*
council	A group of people meeting together for special purposes, such as to work for some cause or to give advice. *The National Council of Negro Women works in each of its branches to gain fuller rights for Afro-Americans.*
picketing	Standing or walking to show protest, usually carrying signs to explain why. *A. Philip Randolph planned picketing in Washington as part of his attack on Jim Crow.*

1 / *The Country in 1933.* The people were suffering in many ways when Franklin Delano Roosevelt took office as President in March, 1933. The Depression had grown worse during each of its first three years. One out of every four workers had no job. More than half the farmers in the country could not pay back loans they had taken from banks. Many of them had lost their land. Banks were failing. Businesses were closing. The country's production was about half what it had been three years earlier. Roosevelt said that one third of the people were poorly housed, poorly clothed and poorly fed. Had he spoken of black people alone, he might have said two thirds or more. Yet he had promised the people a "New Deal." They watched to see what it would be.

2 / *Goals of the New Deal.* Roosevelt and his party had won control of Congress. He was a strong leader. The Democrats were ready to follow him. They voted for the new laws he planned. Through these laws they tried to bring relief to the people. They tried to help businesses recover. They brought their country a long list of reforms. These were changes in the way the people would live and the way the government would help them. Most of the changes were planned to help all people, black and white. The New Deal was to mean a better life for a country that had almost lost hope.

3 / *Back to Work.* Many Afro-Americans were poorer than they had ever been before. New Deal laws were passed quickly to put men back to work. The government set up

Many Afro-Americans were poorer than ever before.

camps in which hundreds of thousands of men and boys, many of them black, worked to save forests and improve farmland. A great program of public works was begun. Millions worked to build schools, post offices, parks, hospitals, playgrounds and roads. Black workers found many jobs in these projects. Money went to cities and states to build public housing. The buildings would be owned by the city or state; they would be lived in by poor people. For poor Afro-Americans, public housing was a new step in the escape from poverty. There was also direct relief—food for the hungry. The number of people out of work slowly moved down.

4 / *Feeling Safe.* The New Deal passed other laws to help workers and their families. We call them social-security laws. You are "secure" when you feel safe. Through these laws, workers could get some money for a number of weeks if they lost their jobs. When they grew too old to work, they could get monthly payments called pensions. People were helped if they became sick, crippled or blind. If a worker died there was aid for his wife and children. Many Afro-Americans were not helped by these laws at first. Servants and farm workers were not included until years later. A person out of work was paid part of what he had been earning. Black workers had been getting low pay. This meant that they now received less help than whites. The first social-security laws were passed in 1935. They did not end poverty. But they did remove some of the fear that had gripped millions of poor whites and blacks.

Few black workers had been allowed to join them. CIO unions were different. The men who led them wanted all the members they could get. These unions were for all the workers in an industry, black and white. Soon more than a million black men and women were in the new unions. Now they too could gain from being in a union. Their jobs would be safer; their pay would be higher. Workers sang a song whose last words told the story: "For the Union makes us strong." These black workers could now move a little further away from poverty.

FROM THE SOCIAL SECURITY ACT, 1935

Section 202. "Every qualified individual shall be entitled to receive . . . beginning on the date he attains the age of sixty-five . . . and ending on the date of his death, an old-age benefit. . . ."

Section 203. "If any individual dies before the age of sixty-five, there shall be paid to his estate. . . ."

Section 521. ". . . protection and care of homeless, dependent and neglected children. . . ."

5 / *Unions Stand Still*. Until 1935, most unions were in the American Federation of Labor (AFL). It was made up of the unions of skilled workers. For years they had tried to win more pay, shorter hours of work and better working conditions. But the AFL would not admit all workers. John L. Lewis, leader of the United Mine Workers, said the AFL was "standing still, with its face toward the dead past." Laws passed by the New Deal Congress gave help to those who tried to set up new unions. John L. Lewis, Philip Murray, Sidney Hillman and other men and women joined to set up a new labor group. It became known as the Congress of Industrial Organizations (CIO).

THE NEW DEAL HELPS UNIONS

Section 7 of the National Labor Relations Act, 1935

"Employees shall have the right of self-organization, to form, join, or assist labor organizations, to bargain collectively through representatives of their own choosing and to engage in concerted activities for the purpose of collective bargaining or other mutual aid or protection."

6 / *Black Workers Join the CIO*. Many of the AFL unions were Jim Crow groups.

7 / *The Black Cabinet*. The President heads the executive branch of our government. It

is his job to carry out the laws. He is in charge of the departments that do this work for him. Each of them is headed by a person called a Secretary. These men and women help the President. They are called the Cabinet. Each of them reports to the President and takes orders from him. Franklin D. Roosevelt had a second "cabinet." He called a group of Afro-Americans to meetings with him. He knew that black people had great needs. He knew that part of his job was to help improve the way all people lived. The group who worked to help him in this task has been called the Black Cabinet.

with the government. Robert C. Weaver was in the Department of the Interior. He worked under Harold Ickes, the white man who had headed the Chicago N.A.A.C.P. Frank S. Horne worked to plan better housing. Ralph Bunche came to the State Department. He would later help plan the United Nations. Robert L. Vann tried to have civil-rights laws used to help all black citizens. Ira Reid worked on social-security needs. Eugene Jones tried to help black businessmen.

9 / *Goals of the Black Cabinet.* Experts such as these at last had the chance to help use the power of the government to aid all

MARIAN ANDERSON SINGS AT THE LINCOLN MEMORIAL

Constitution Hall in Washington, D.C., is the best-known concert hall in that city. It is owned by the Daughters of the American Revolution. In 1939 a concert by Marian Anderson was planned. The D.A.R. refused to allow a Negro artist to use its hall. Harold Ickes, Secretary of the Interior and for years a leader of the N.A.A.C.P., invited Miss Anderson to sing at the Lincoln Memorial. Mrs. Eleanor Roosevelt and dozens of government officials joined about 75,000 people, black and white, to hear one of their country's great artists.

The NRA (National Recovery Administration) found jobs for thousands of people.

8 / *Work of the Black Cabinet.* The people in the Black Cabinet had just taken jobs

N.A.A.C.P. head Walter White, Mary McCleod Bethune and Channing Tobias leave the White House after meeting with President Roosevelt.

people, black and white. Their goal was clear. What could they do to give more rights to all? One of their answers was to get more jobs for Afro-Americans in government. In 1933 about 50,000 Negroes worked for the United States. Thirteen years later there were four times as many! Among them were thousands of men and women in important posts. The Black Cabinet had brought a real change. A woman, Mary McLeod Bethune, was the best known of this group.

10 / *Mary McLeod.* Mary McLeod was born in South Carolina in 1875. She was one of seventeen children. Her family was poor and lived in a small farm cabin. Young Mary went to a church school. It was a five-mile walk from her home! She then received a scholarship to another religious school in North Carolina. In 1894 she won a scholarship to Moody Bible Institute in Chicago. She was the only black student at the school. After graduation she returned

to the South to teach. First she went to Georgia. Then she went back to South Carolina. In 1898 she married Albertus Bethune.

11 / *Building a School.* Six years later her husband had died. Mrs. Bethune moved to Daytona, Florida. This was a Jim Crow state in which black children had poor schools, and sometimes no schools at all. She made plans to set up a school for poor Negro girls. It opened in October, 1904, with five girls and her son as its students. Each student paid fifty cents a week. Mary McLeod Bethune had almost no money when she rented the shack in which she began her school. The story has been told that she had only a dollar and a half, and lots of faith! She soon made friends among the rich white people who spent their winters in Daytona Beach. Among those who helped her were John D. Rockefeller and Andrew Carnegie, two of the richest men in the country. She raised the money she needed. In 1905 a large building program

She was building more than a school.

began for her school—the Daytona Normal and Industrial Institute for Negro Scholars. New buildings went up. Mrs. Bethune made the school a center for black and white citizens. She held evening classes for them. She opened her school for meetings. She was building more than a school; she was showing how people could work together.

12 / *Success.* Soon Mrs. Bethune's school was a full high school. By 1923 she had made it a junior college. In that year it joined with the Cookman Institute for Boys. The new school was called the Bethune-Cookman College. By 1941 it was a four-year college with a large campus and two million dollars worth of buildings. There were 1,300 students in this college. It had begun as one woman's dream of a school for poor black children in a Jim Crow state.

13 / *A Leader in Many Fields.* Mary McLeod Bethune spent her life helping others. She set up the McLeod Hospital in Daytona. This was at a time when Negroes in the South could not get the medical care they needed. Black and white doctors worked as a team in this hospital, helped by student nurses from the college. Mrs. Bethune began and was the first president of the National Council of Negro Women. Its aim was to get women in social groups to work for equality. The Council grew to become the largest black organization in the country. Presidents Coolidge and Hoover each asked Mrs. Bethune to serve on a government study group that made plans to help children. Eleven times she was given honorary degrees by colleges. Mary McLeod Bethune was a true leader of the country's black and white citizens.

14 / *In the Black Cabinet.* Mrs. Bethune was one of the group who helped President Roosevelt. He made her the Director of Negro Affairs in the National Youth Administration. In this job she helped students who needed money so that they could stay in school. She and Mrs. Eleanor Roosevelt were good friends. Mrs. Bethune was often at the White House. She was soon the leading member of the Black Cabinet. Some of the men who worked with her won important posts. Dr. Robert C. Weaver, the first black Cabinet member, became Secretary of Housing and Urban Development. Dr. Ralph J. Bunche was later Under-Secretary of the United Nations. It was he who helped bring peace for a while to Israel and the Arab countries. For this he won the Nobel Peace Prize. This is the highest honor in the world to those who work for peace. He was the first Afro-American to win it. Carl Rowan also served in the Black Cabinet. He was later head of the United States Information Agency. Dr. William H. Hastie, a great lawyer who had worked with the N.A.A.-C.P., was the first Afro-American to be a Federal judge. Dr. James C. Evans worked for better race relations. It was he who was later to carry out a great task—the end of Jim Crow in the armed forces. These black Americans used their talent to do important jobs for the whole country. With their success came more jobs for others.

15 / *An Attack on Jim Crow.* Why didn't the President use his power to end Jim Crow? He felt that his first task was to end the Depression for all Americans. He had to change the country's laws in many ways. Men from the South were important in Congress. He needed their help to pass his laws. For this reason he did not begin a direct attack on Jim Crow. He had laws passed that would help all people make a better living. But men like A. Philip Randolph felt that much more could be done. In 1941 he planned a great "March on

Washington." There the whole world would see how deeply black people felt about Jim Crow. He made plans for marches and picketing. In this way he hoped to show the government that it was time to end Jim Crow. Even "the little man on the street" would then see how wrong Jim Crow was. It would not end until the whole country was "shocked and awakened."

16 / *Fair Employment.* Roosevelt did not want such a march against his government, which was trying to do so much. He asked Randolph and other black leaders to talk with him. What had to be done to stop the march? Randolph asked for an order to force fair treatment of black workers in government service and in industries that did work for the government. Roosevelt agreed. A week later he issued Executive Order 8802. It was to mean the start of a government attack on Jim Crow. The President next set up a Fair Employment Practices Committee. Its task was to work for equal treatment of blacks and whites in all fields of work. It was also to make certain that the new rules were followed. The March on Washington was called off. Black people waited to see how much the government would now do to end their Jim Crow world.

FROM A. PHILIP RANDOLPH'S CALL FOR A MARCH ON WASHINGTON, May, 1941

"An 'all-out' thundering March on Washington, ending in a monster and huge demonstration at Lincoln's Monument, will shake up white America. . . . It will gain respect for the Negro people. . . . (It) can cause President Roosevelt to issue an executive order abolishing discrimination in all government departments . . . and national defense jobs."

Understanding What You Have Read

I. REVIEWING WORD MEANINGS

Write the letter of the choice that best explains the meaning of each word.

1. The best example of a reform would be (a) changing a law so that new rights are given to the people, (b) correcting a law so that the government gains more tax money for the armed forces, (c) keeping a law without any changes.

2. The best example of a project would be (a) a group of private houses built by a company that then sells them to private owners, (b) some new automobiles and trucks bought by a city, (c) a group of new buildings built and owned by a city to house citizens who need places to live.

3. Our Social Security laws were passed to help all (a) workers, (b) owners of companies, (c) government officials.

4. A pension is paid to a person who (a) continues on his job, (b) no longer works, (c) works only when he wants to work.

5. A federation is made up of (a) any group of people, (b) people who represent groups of people, (c) people who want equal rights for all.

6. The group that is most probably a trade union is the (a) Cigar Makers Union, (b) United Steel Workers, (c) United Automobile Workers.

7. The group that is most probably an industrial union is the (a) Carpenters Union, (b) Textile Workers, (c) Plumbers Union.

8. The person who is a member of the President's Cabinet is the (a) Secretary of the Urban League, (b) Secretary of Housing and Urban Development, (c) Chairman of the Democratic Party.

9. A council of organizations is most like (a) a legislature, (b) a federation, (c) an industrial union.

10. People who are picketing are taking part in a (a) rebellion, (b) union meeting, (c) protest.

II. WHO AM I?

Write the name of the person described by each statement.

1. I was the President who signed the order that was the first attack on Jim Crow in industry by the Federal government.

2. I was the leader of the United Mine Workers who led in the fight to get millions of white and black workers into industrial unions.

3. I was Secretary of the Interior during the New Deal and brought Robert C. Weaver to Washington as one of my assistants.

4. Even though I was a woman, my great success in building a college in Florida, organizing the National Council of Negro Women and helping Presidents made me the leader of President Roosevelt's Black Cabinet.

5. I planned a March on Washington in 1941, but called it off after the President issued an order for fair employment.

III. PLACING EVENTS IN PROPER ORDER

Organize the five events from the life of Mary McLeod Bethune listed below in the order in which they happened.

a. She became an advisor to President Hoover.
b. She combined her school with the Cookman Institute for Boys.
c. She became the leader of the Black Cabinet.
d. She moved to Daytona, Florida.
e. By 1941 Bethune-Cookman College had 1,300 students.

IV. REVIEWING IMPORTANT FACTS

Write the letter of the choice that best completes each statement.

1. Ralph Bunche has been important in (a) the growth of social-security laws, (b) the work of the Department of Labor, (c) planning and helping the United Nations.

2. The Negro leader who, like John L. Lewis, had worked to organize workers into a union was (a) A. Philip Randolph, (b) Mary McLeod Bethune, (c) Robert Weaver.

3. The New Deal was a (a) group of black leaders, (b) group of reforms and the people who worked to bring them about, (c) Jim Crow plan to take control of the government.

4. Social-security laws were first passed by Congress in (a) 1933, (b) 1935, (c) 1940.

5. Black workers found that there was room for them in (a) the CIO, (b) the AFL, (c) any trade or industrial union.

6. The three chief goals of a union are higher wages, shorter hours of work and (a) control of the company, (b) better working conditions, (c) the right to vote.

7. Frank S. Horne, Robert L. Vann and Eugene Jones were all part of the (a) March on Washington, (b) Bethune-Cookman College, (c) New Deal.

8. One way in which the New Deal helped Afro-Americans was by (a) ending Jim Crow in the United States, (b) opening government service to more black citizens, (c) building public housing for all poor Negroes in the United States.

9. Chicago's Moody Bible Institute helped train (a) Mary McLeod, (b) A. Philip Randolph, (c) Ralph J. Bunche.

10. Dr. William H. Hastie gained fame in the field of (a) social security, (b) labor organization, (c) law.

V. ANSWER EACH QUESTION IN TWO OR THREE COMPLETE SENTENCES.

1. Why did the New Deal give hope to many Americans?
2. How did the New Deal help Afro-Americans?
3. How did social security change the life of those workers who were covered by it?
4. How was the Black Cabinet different from President Roosevelt's "real" Cabinet?
5. In what ways did Mary McLeod Bethune help Afro-Americans?
6. Why did Dr. Ralph J. Bunche win the Nobel Peace Prize?
7. Why was the appointment of Robert C. Weaver as Secretary of Housing and Urban Development important to all Americans?
8. How did A. Philip Randolph and those who worked with him change the Federal government's rules about the hiring of Negroes?
9. What was the task of the Fair Employment Practices Committee?
10. How did John L. Lewis prove to be a friend to black workers?

VI. DO YOU AGREE OR DISAGREE?

Write a sentence to explain why you agree or disagree with each of these statements.

1. The New Deal was a failure because it did not end Jim Crow laws in the states.
2. All workers should be covered by social-security laws.
3. Having a Black Cabinet was another example of Jim Crow under the New Deal.
4. Mary McLeod Bethune was as important to education as Booker T. Washington had been.
5. A. Philip Randolph, the N.A.A.C.P. and the National Urban League should not have called off their March on Washington in 1941.

VII. THINGS TO DO

1. One of the great books about life in the United States in the early years of the New Deal is *The Grapes of Wrath* by John Steinbeck. It tells of a family of white tenant farmers who had to leave their land in the South and move west looking for work. Read Chapter Five of this book. Tell your class the story it contains. How true was this story for black tenant farmers?
2. Set up a class committee to work out the needs of your own community for fair employment practices. Imagine that your committee will be meeting with the mayor. Explain the problems you will present to him.
3. Use the library to prepare a one-page report about one of these members of the Black Cabinet.

Mary McLeod Bethune	Dr. Robert C. Weaver
Dr. Ralph J. Bunche	Carl Rowan
Judge William H. Hastie	Dr. James C. Evans
Frank S. Horne	Robert L. Vann

4. The Tennessee Valley Authority was one of the great reforms of the New Deal. Read about the TVA in your library. How did it try to help the people in the area? How much were black farmers helped by it?

Chapter 26 / WORLD WAR II AND THE TRUMAN YEARS

Let's Discover

1. How black Americans joined the fight against Fascism during World War II.
2. How Afro-Americans helped the war effort at home.
3. How the Federal government under President Truman helped civil rights.

Words to Know

primary	An election to choose candidates for office. *A case brought to the Supreme Court by the N.A.A.C.P. ended "white only" primary elections in the South.*
dictator	A ruler who has complete power in his country. *Adolf Hitler was the dictator of Germany.*
Fascism	A type of government, ruled by a dictator, in which the rights of the people are taken away, war is often a national goal and a small group

Dorie Miller was our first war hero.

hold power and wealth with the dictator.

Fascism gained power in Germany, Italy and Japan.

merchant marine The ships of a country that carry goods to other parts of the world.

Black and white sailors worked together in the crews of the United States merchant marine.

distinguished Famous or outstanding.

The Distinguished Service Cross is given to war heroes like George Watson.

survey A careful study.

The Committee on Civil Rights made a survey of how Americans were treated.

flaw A fault that spoils something.

There were many flaws in the record of the United States on civil rights.

integration Doing away with segregation.

The integration of the Navy meant that any man could hold any post on a ship.

progress Moving forward toward a goal.

President Truman believed that not enough progress had been made in giving equal rights to all Americans.

entitled Having a right.

All people are entitled to equal protection of the law.

---

1 / *Keeping Up the Fight*. The N.A.A.C.P. and other groups did not stop trying to improve the life of black citizens in the 1930's. They used the courts most of all. They won some cases; they lost others. Each day more white people began to see that it was wrong to continue Jim Crow laws. The poll tax was attacked. Today it has been ended. Primary elections—those in which the members of a party choose their candidates—had kept out black voters. Today they are open to all. White people had clauses in their

contracts when they bought or sold homes. These clauses said they could not sell their homes to Negroes. The N.A.A.C.P. fought such clauses in the courts. Today they are not allowed. One of the most important cases came in 1938. The Supreme Court ruled that black students had the right to enter state colleges. The country was working out ways to help people make a living through the New Deal. Afro-Americans joined in this. They tried to gain fuller rights at the same time.

2 / *The Coming of World War II*. A second world war began in Europe in 1939. It had been coming for years. Three countries— Germany, Italy and Japan—had turned to an old kind of government. It was the tight rule of a country by a dictator. It had a new name—Fascism. In each of these three countries the rights of the people were destroyed while their rulers prepared for war. These men hoped to conquer the whole world.

Other countries did little as China, Ethiopia, Austria and Czechoslovakia were taken over. Then, in 1939, the Germans moved into Poland. England and France went to war on the side of Poland. World War II had begun.

3 / *The War Spreads*. The United States took steps to help England and France. Laws were passed to build up this country's defenses. Millions of men were drafted. France was soon conquered by the Germans. England fought on alone, with much aid from the United States. Then, on December 7, 1941, the Japanese attacked Pearl Harbor in Hawaii. We were at war. In a few days we were also at war with Germany and Italy.

4 / *The Four Freedoms*. President Roosevelt spoke of the "Four Freedoms" for which his country would fight. These were freedom of speech, freedom of worship, freedom from

FROM A LETTER IN *THE CRISIS* TO PRESIDENT ROOSEVELT IN 1943

"Your administrative officers have taken Negroes into government offices to aid in the further integration of Negro citizens into the war effort and into the life of the country. Your good wife has gone the length and breadth of this land, and over the seas, never neglecting our (part) of the population in her travels and comments. . . . However . . . in their own army they find themselves set apart from their fellow fighters for freedom . . . in too many communities your Executive Order 8802 is being defied. . . . In too many instances menial tasks and unskilled labor are all that we may secure . . . we are still lynched. . . . Six million white Americans and four million of us are barred from (voting) by the poll tax alone. We still suffer . . . discrimination in public places, in travel, and in housing. We, who are willing and anxious to fight for the Four Freedoms, are not free."

want and freedom from fear. Afro-Americans knew what these freedoms meant. They were still trying to get them in their own country. When the war came they saw that little would be done for a while to improve their rights. "Win the war" was the chief goal of most white people. Black citizens did all they could to help reach this goal. They also kept up their work to end Jim Crow.

5 / *Jim Crow in the Armed Forces.* Afro-Americans have always fought bravely in this country's wars. When we entered World War II, the armed forces were still segregated. Black soldiers were in separate groups in the Army. Afro-Americans were not allowed to join the Marines and the Coast Guard. They held only menial jobs in the Navy. Black soldiers in the Air Force were trained apart from white men. Even their officers training schools were separate until 1940. One million black men and women served in World War II. The only place where they found fair and equal treatment was in the merchant marine. In the many government-owned ships, blacks and whites worked in the same crews. Eighteen of these ships were named for great Afro-Americans.

6 / *Brave Fighters.* Again and again Negro groups won awards for their bravery. Black men in all parts of the armed forces were honored. When the Japanese attacked Pearl Harbor, a black sailor named Dorie Miller was our first war hero. He had been trained to work in his ship's kitchen. While the Japanese were attacking his ship, he took over a gun from a dying white sailor. He then shot down four enemy planes! He was

Black troops fought bravely in World War II.

Dorie Miller received the Navy Cross.

CIO unions even set up Jim Crow local groups in the South. Walter White, the Secretary of the N.A.A.C.P., had for years gathered proof of what Jim Crow did to black people in the South. He asked all Afro-Americans, in North and South, to go into all programs that could improve their lives. Men and women were needed in factories that made war goods. Federal job training was open to all. Hundreds of thousands of blacks learned new skills. It was still harder for them to find jobs than it was for whites. But more were hired each year. The government had promised profits to all companies making war goods. Most businessmen hired any worker who could help them turn out their products. Blacks worked side by side with whites all over the country. They were doing jobs that until then had been closed to them.

8 / *Helping the Country.* Mrs. Roosevelt had said, "The nation cannot expect colored

given the Navy Cross, one of the country's highest honors. George Watson, a private in the Army, was another Afro-American hero. His ship was sunk in 1943. Private Watson could swim well. He helped many men to reach a raft, with no thought of his own safety. In the end he grew so tired that he could not get back to the raft himself. He drowned. He had given his life to help others. His family received his award, the Distinguished Service Cross.

7 / *Jim Crow Goes On.* Jim Crow did not end during the war years. White people who had favored Jim Crow still favored it. Some

Walter White fought against Jim Crow.

people to feel that the United States is worth defending if the Negro continues to be treated as he is now." Black people did feel that the country was worth defending. But they did not stop trying to improve their rights. Little could be done while the war went on. When it ended in 1945, the drive for equal rights gained strength again.

9 / *New Moves for Civil Rights.* Harry S Truman became President just before the end of the war. Afro-Americans were still asking for the rights white people had. They knew that they would not get them unless the power of the Federal government was used. Congress had to pass new civil-rights laws. These laws then had to be tested in the courts. Truman agreed. He took some first steps. He set up a Committee on Civil Rights. Both blacks and whites served in this group. Their job was to show the ways in which Afro-Americans were not treated fairly. Their report came in 1947. Its title

President Truman set up a Committee on Civil Rights.

explained its message—*To Secure These Rights.* It told what the group had learned. "We have surveyed the flaws in the nation's record and have found them to be serious. We have considered what government's role should be in securing our rights and have concluded that it must assume greater leadership."

10 / *The South Refuses.* The report was hailed. The President asked for new laws to help black citizens gain equal rights. He had the planned laws made part of the program of the Democratic Party in the 1948 election. Democrats in the South would not accept such laws. They formed a new party in the South. It became known as the Dixiecrats. Its leader, J. Strom Thurmond, would for the next twenty years lead those who were against equal rights.

A SOUTHERN SENATOR WARNS THAT THE SOUTH WILL NOT CHANGE (1945)

". . . We know what is best for the white people and the colored people. We are going to treat the Negro fairly, but in so doing we do not intend for him to take over our election system or attend our white schools.

"Regardless of any Supreme Court decisions and any laws that may be passed by Congress, we of the South will maintain our political and social institutions."

Even though Thurmond won four states in the South, Truman won the election. He remained firm about civil rights. It was also clear that the whites who held power in the South would remain firm in their stand. In the years ahead these two stands were to clash and bring violence.

FROM THE NEW YORK
ANTI-DISCRIMINATION LAW, 1945

"The opportunity to obtain employment without discrimination because of race, creed, color, or national origin is hereby recognized as and declared to be a civil right. . . . It shall be an unlawful employment practice for an employer, because of the race, creed, color or national origin of any individual, to refuse to hire or employ . . . such individual."

Benjamin O. Davis, Jr., became a general
like his father.

11 / *Equal Rights in the Armed Forces.* In July, 1948, President Truman ordered "equality of treatment and opportunity for all persons in the armed services without regard to race, color, religion or national origin." A special report, "Freedom to Serve," spelled out the steps that would have to be taken. The armed forces would be integrated. Such integration was a goal of the civil-rights movement. The courts would accept it. Congress would begin to favor it. The President ordered that blacks and whites were to be treated the same in all ways. Any man or woman in the services could hold any job. The Army, Navy and Air Force would all have to follow the new orders. During World War II Negro fighters had not known equality. In 1940 the naming of Benjamin O. Davis, Sr., as the first Afro-American to be a general had made news headlines. Five years later his son, Colonel Benjamin O. Davis, Jr., became the officer in charge of an important airfield. He too was later made a general. The armed forces had been so filled with Jim Crow customs that such events were important news. Now they are less so, for the Truman plan has been carried out. The President wanted the Bill of Rights to be carried out in other ways too. "We have been trying to do this for one hundred fifty years. We are making progress but we are not making progress fast enough."

12 / *The Move to the North.* World War II had opened new jobs for Afro-Americans in the North. States like New York had passed

laws to fight job discrimination. Life in the South did not improve. White Southerners would not change their Jim Crow laws and customs. KKK groups still held power. No wonder, then, that millions more black people left the South. They came to the cities of the North. There they could look for better jobs. There they hoped to find better homes. There their children might go to better schools. Life had to be a little better in the North. Black political leaders had gained some power in the cities. It would be good to feel that you could vote, and that your vote would mean something. A black man in the South could not be sure of justice, due process or equal protection of the laws. These were promised in the North. The flow of people to the North went on and on.

13 / *Changes in the Cities.* What did people from the South find when they came to the big cities of the North? It was hard to find a place to live, for new buildings had not been put up during the war years. The housing they found was most often segregated. This was true even of public housing in some cities. In most cities, blacks and whites lived in different neighborhoods. When black people moved into "white" neighborhoods, the whites often moved away. Jim Crow would not die. But it was easier to find a job. Teaching and government service were also open to all those who had the training. The growing number of black voters in the cities meant that Afro-Americans could be elected to public office. There they could work to improve life for all black citizens. In New York, Chicago,

The number of black voters was growing.

Detroit, Cleveland and other cities, changes were taking place. The center of Afro-American life had moved from farms in the South to the big cities of the North.

14 / *The U.N. Shows the Way*. The United Nations was formed in 1945. Its chief goal was to be to keep peace in the world. It could also be the center for a world drive for greater human rights. A number of Afro-Americans helped plan the new world organ-

Ralph Bunche, Mrs. Bethune and Eleanor Roosevelt helped plan the new U.N.

ization. Among them were Mary McLeod Bethune, leader of Negro women, and Dr. Mordecai Johnson of Howard University. The N.A.A.C.P. sent Dr. W. E. B. Du Bois and Walter White. Dr. Ralph Bunche went as a member of the State Department.

15 / *A Plan for Human Rights*. Mrs. Eleanor Roosevelt, ever busy in the fight for civil rights, was one of the United States delegates. She headed the group who in 1948 completed the United Nations Declaration of Human Rights. No country voted against it. Its aims were the same as those of Afro-Americans. If the United Nations could get all countries to live up to these high aims, then life would surely improve in the United States.

Mrs. Roosevelt and a passage from the Declaration on which
she worked so hard.

Understanding What You Have Read

I.   REVIEWING WORD MEANINGS

Fill in the word that belongs in each blank space in following paragraphs. Choose from the words below each paragraph.

In the ——————— election, voters chose between the ———————
scholar and the old-fashioned politician. A court decision had brought
——————— to what had for years been a "whites only" election.
Now black citizens as well as white were ——————— to vote. This

improvement in the rights of black voters was cheered as an example of real ——————.

distinguished   integration   progress   primary   entitled

George Smith, a sailor in the ——————, visited many parts of the world in the 1930's. He made a —————— of how different governments were run. He was disturbed by ——————, the kind of government he saw in Italy, Germany and Japan. Each of these lands was being ruled by a —————— who promised great victories to his people. The —————— was that these people had lost their rights.

dictator   Fascism   merchant marine   flaw   survey

II.   UNDERSTANDING IMPORTANT FACTS

Write the letter of the choice that best completes each statement.

1. The President who set the Four Freedoms as war aims was (a) Harry S Truman, (b) Franklin D. Roosevelt, (c) Lyndon B. Johnson.
2. Dorie Miller became a hero when his ship was attacked by the (a) Japanese, (b) Germans, (c) Italians.
3. The Secretary of the N.A.A.C.P. during World War II was (a) James Weldon Johnson, (b) W. E. B. Du Bois, (c) Walter White.
4. The Committee on Civil Rights was set up (a) before the war, (b) during the war, (c) after the war.
5. The report *To Secure These Rights* told the country that greater civil rights had to come from (a) the Federal government, local governments, (c) the people themselves.
6. The first Afro-American to become a general was (a) Benjamin Davis, Jr., (b) Benjamin Davis, Sr., (c) Ossie Davis.
7. After the war black Americans began to move from the (a) North to the South, (b) South to the North, (c) East to the West.
8. The first improvement after the war was in (a) housing, (b) the ending of Jim Crow laws in the South, (c) less job discrimination.

9. Black voters gained the right to vote in primary elections in the South as the result of (a) a change in the Constitution, (b) a court decision, (c) the end of the KKK.

10. President Truman ordered an end to Jim Crow in all (a) industries in the United States, (b) the armed forces, (c) sales of property.

III. WHICH CAME FIRST?

Write the letter of the event which came first in each pair.

1. (a) The Supreme Court ruled that black students had a right to enter state colleges.
   (b) The United States entered World War II.

2. (a) The United Nations began in 1945.
   (b) President Truman ended segregation in the armed forces.

3. (a) The United Nations Declaration of Human Rights was approved.
   (b) George Watson won the Distinguished Service Cross.

4. (a) The Japanese attacked Pearl Harbor.
   (b) Harry S Truman became President.

5. (a) The Democrats promised to fight for civil rights in 1948.
   (b) The Dixiecrats set up a new party in the South.

IV. CHECKING THE MAIN IDEA

Write the letter of the title that best states what each paragraph contains.

1. The best title for Paragraph 2 is
   (a) Fascism Led to War.
   (b) The Fall of Small Nations.
   (c) Helping Poland.

2. The best title for Paragraph 5 is
   (a) Fair Treatment in the Merchant Marine.
   (b) One Million Suffer from Jim Crow.

       (c) Heroes of the Nation.

3. The best title for Paragraph 7 is
   (a) Continuing Discrimination.
   (b) New Skills End Jim Crow.
   (c) All CIO Unions Become Unfair.

4. The best titles for Paragraph 10 is
   (a) Thurmond Wins.
   (b) Southern Whites Refuse to Vote.
   (c) Civil Rights in the 1948 Election.

5. The best title for Paragraph 13 is
   (a) Problems and Progress in the Cities.
   (b) Changing Neighborhoods.
   (c) Leaving the South.

V. ANSWER EACH OF THESE QUESTIONS IN ONE OR TWO COMPLETE SENTENCES.

1. President Roosevelt said that the United States would be an "arsenal of democracy." What did he mean?

2. How did the United States enter World War II?

3. Explain the meaning of the Four Freedoms listed in Paragraph 4.

4. Why was there little progress in civil rights during World War II?

5. Why was the Navy Cross given to Dorie Miller?

6. Why were Federal job-training programs during World War II important to Afro-Americans?

7. How did black workers help win the war?

8. How did President Truman show that he believed in improving civil rights?

9. What did President Truman mean when he said "we are not making progress fast enough"?

10. Why did the Declaration of Human Rights please Afro-Americans?

VI. LET'S DISCUSS

1. Why did Afro-Americans begin to have more opportunities after World War II?

2. When the United Nations was formed, many African delegates came to the United States to represent their countries. Some suffered from Jim Crow customs. What steps could they take to prevent such troubles?

3. Why do minority groups suffer in a dictatorship? Look up the meaning of "scapegoat" before you discuss this question.

4. How were the actions of Harry S Truman a "crack in the wall of racism"?

THE CIVIL-RIGHTS REVOLUTION

Introduction

This unit traces the story of the great attack on "separate but equal"—the rule of law that had made Jim Crow laws possible. How were men to have truly equal rights? How were black people to be treated fairly under law? The first step was to try to change the laws. This was done by bringing cases to the Supreme Court. A group of lawyers led by Thurgood Marshall finally won this battle. In 1954 the Court ruled that "separate but equal" schools were not allowed by the Constitution. The white people of the South fought back. They would not give up their kind of white control of life.

Nonviolence and civil disobedience then became the weapons of black groups and their white friends in the fight for equal rights. They turned to peaceful open meetings. They refused to obey unfair laws. They used boycotts—refusing to do business with any company that followed Jim Crow ideas. The best known of these boycotts took place in Montgomery, Alabama. It led to the rise of a new leader, the Reverend Dr. Martin Luther King, Jr.

Nonviolence took many forms. Sit-ins and freedom rides spread. In some places in the South, white people agreed to end some kinds of Jim Crow. In other places, white people used violence against the drive for equal rights. The worst troubles came in Alabama. Yet new laws passed by Congress brought the power of the national government into the South. With this help, white and black people worked to get more Afro-Americans there to become voters.

The civil-rights movement began to change after 1960. New leaders appeared. They offered new plans to improve the life of black Americans. We will see how these plans were in many ways different from the plans most often followed in the 1950's.

THE 1954 SUPREME COURT DECISION

Let's Discover

1. How N.A.A.C.P. lawyers finally ended the idea that "separate but equal" was allowed by the Constitution.
2. How Thurgood Marshall led this fight to improve the civil rights of Afro-Americans.
3. How the South fought back as it tried to keep its Jim Crow laws and customs.

Words to Know

graduate school	A school whose students have already completed college and are seeking more education. *Law school and medical school are examples of graduate school.*
counsel	The lawyer or lawyers who handle a case. *Thurgood Marshall was the counsel for Oliver Brown.*
ambassador	The official who represents his country in a foreign country, or in some world organization. *James M. Nabrit, Jr., became United States Ambassador to the United Nations.*
solicitor	A lawyer for a government. *Thurgood Marshall was made Solicitor-General of the United States.*
Justice	The title of a judge in certain courts. *Judges in the United States Supreme Court are called Justices.*
deprive	To take away something that another should have.

Jim Crow laws deprived black children of an equal education.

inferiority — Being not as good as someone else.

A poor school gives its students a feeling of inferiority.

desegregate — To end the keeping of children in separate schools.

The Supreme Court ordered all school districts to desegregate their schools.

bayonet — A long knife that can be attached to the front end of a rifle.

The soldiers were armed with bayonets when they kept black students out of the school.

National Guard — An armed force organized and partly controlled by a state, but that can be called to service with the United States armed forces.

Governor Faubus of Arkansas used the National Guard of his state to keep the Little Rock high school segregated.

---

1 / *Making Changes.* How can great changes in the way people live be made in this country? In some parts of the world the only road to change is through a revolt. In the United States most great changes have come in three ways. First of all, people can agree that some old ways of doing things are wrong. New customs take the place of old ones. For example, women can now hold most jobs in the business world. We no longer allow young boys to work for years without pay while they learn a trade. The second way to bring about change is through new laws. Once people agree that they want a change, they work to pass new laws. That is how most of the New Deal changes came. That is how new civil-rights laws have come in most states. The third way is as important as the others. It is the use of our courts. A case comes to the Supreme Court. The Court explains the meaning of the Constitution in the questions raised in the case. Once the Court has ruled, its decision is the law of the land. The groups that have worked for civil rights have known this. They have used the courts to change life in the United States.

2 / *Time for a Change.* Customs changed in much of the country after World War II.

The lives of many black Americans were better. New jobs were opened by the work of unions and some business leaders. This gave Afro-Americans, chiefly those in the North, more money to spend. State after state, mostly in the North, passed laws to end Jim Crow ways. It was easier to buy a home or rent an apartment. Job discrimination was attacked. Government jobs were opened to black citizens. But such things did not happen in the South. Laws and customs still kept black Southerners on a low level of life. The men in power said they were not doing wrong. Hadn't the Supreme Court told them that Jim Crow was allowed by the Constitution? In the Plessy case in 1896 the Court had ruled that "separate but equal" was the law of the land. Jim Crow would not die or weaken while the Supreme Court held this view. N.A.A.-C.P. lawyers knew that they had to attack the Plessy ruling. They made plans to bring case after case to the Court. In each they tried to prove that "separate but equal" was wrong. It took a long time, and many cases. In the end the Court agreed with them.

3 / *Separate Schools*. Public schools in the South followed the rule of Jim Crow. All of them were segregated. If this daily Jim Crow life for millions of boys and girls could be weakened, then so could the rest of Jim Crow. The fight for integration in the schools was at the same time the fight against all discrimination. The ideas of due process and equal protection could be used in this fight. The point of attack was clear. When students are taught in separate schools only because of their race, then their education cannot be equal. N.A.A.C.P. lawyers spent years trying to prove this point. If they succeeded, the power of the country's government could begin to be used to improve the rights of all Afro-Americans.

4 / *The Gaines Case*. There were separate schools for blacks and whites all over the South and in the border states. Suppose a black student had gone to high school and college. He had finished a Negro education. Then suppose he wished to get more education. If he wanted to be a lawyer, a doctor or some other kind of professional, he would need more training. This training after college is given in graduate schools. They are open only to men and women who have finished college. There were few such schools for black students in the South. In 1938 a case came to the Supreme Court. A black student from Missouri named Lloyd Gaines wanted to become a lawyer. He was a graduate of a Negro college run by his state. It did not have a law school. Gaines tried to enter the University of Missouri Law School. This was an all-white school. He was not allowed to enter. His marks were high enough. His record was good enough. The only reason he was refused was that he was black. The state of Missouri offered to pay his expenses if he went to a law school in some other state. His lawyers said that the Plessy rule meant that Missouri had to give him an equal chance to become a lawyer in Missouri.

5 / *The Court Decides*. If life had to be "separate but equal," then Missouri would have to build a new law school for Lloyd Gaines and other black students who might

Lloyd Gaines (above) and H. Marion Sweatt (below) won the right to attend white universities.

want to study law. The Supreme Court was still agreeing with the Plessy rule—"separate but equal." But equal in this case had to mean equal protection of the law. The Court ruled that Gaines had the right to attend the University of Missouri Law School.

6 / *The Attack on "Separate but Equal."* A new road had been opened. In state after state in the South black students tried to enter graduate schools. Each state now had to admit them, or else had to build a separate school for blacks. In Texas there was such a school. It was a school of law—the State University for Negroes. A black student named H. Marion Sweatt still wanted to go to the all-white University of Texas Law School. His case came to the Supreme Court. It was decided in 1950. The Court still used the Plessy rule. It agreed in part with the N.A.A.C.P. lawyers. The black law school was not as good as the white one. It was separate but not equal. The Court ruled that Sweatt had to be allowed to attend the University of Texas. This was a new and important step toward integration.

7 / *Other Court Cases.* Two other steps were taken in 1950, the year of the Sweatt case. A black man named Elmer Henderson had been separated from other passengers in a dining car. "Separate but equal" was again weakened when the Court agreed that dining cars on railroad trains in the South had to end this Jim Crow practice. Civil-rights lawyers were showing that the Plessy rule could not work for Jim Crow any longer. But Southern governments fought back. The McLaurin case showed that they could refuse

to follow the new Court rules. G. W. McLaurin, a black student, had been admitted to the all-white graduate school of Oklahoma's state university. Once there he was made to sit apart from the white students. He had to sit alone in the classrooms, in the library and in the cafeteria. In this way he could not get an "equal" education. N.A.A.C.P. lawyers brought his case to the Supreme Court. The Court ruled that segregating black students was not permitted in classrooms or any other part of a graduate school. The word *counsel* means the lawyer in a case. Thurgood Marshall was then the General Counsel of the N.A.A.C.P. He and a group of other lawyers—men like Jawn A. Sandifer (later a justice of the New York State Supreme Court) and James M. Nabrit, Jr. (later United States Ambassador to the United Nations)—prepared, argued and won these cases. In this group also were Constance Baker Motley (later a Federal judge), Jack Greenberg (who became Counsel and Director of the N.A.A.C.P. Legal Defense and Education Fund after Thurgood Marshall was made a judge) and Robert L. Carter (later General Counsel of the N.A.A.C.P.).

8 / *Thurgood Marshall*. There have been many great lawyers in our country's history. The greatest of them seem to have been concerned with civil rights. Thurgood Marshall is one of these. He has been called "Mr. Civil Rights." As an N.A.A.C.P. lawyer he spent more than twenty years in the fight for equal rights through the courts. He became a lawyer at the age of 25. He had worked his way through college and Howard University Law School. In the next five years, many of his cases were for Negro rights. He was such a good lawyer that his fame spread.

9 / *Working for Civil Rights*. In 1938 Thurgood Marshall joined the staff of the N.A.A.C.P. He worked on cases in which the Constitution could be used to improve civil rights. He won case after case. His greatest victory came when the Supreme Court ordered an end to segregation in public schools. President John F. Kennedy later made him a Federal judge. President Lyndon Johnson chose him to be Solicitor General of the United States—the chief lawyer for the government. President Johnson later appointed him to the Supreme Court of the United States. A member of this court is called a Justice. It is the highest post any lawyer in the United States can have. Thurgood Marshall is now a Justice of the court before which he had appeared so often.

10 / *Brown versus the Board of Education —1954*. Marshall and his staff struck at the Plessy rule again. The time had come to show that any kind of Jim Crow was wrong, and not allowed by the Constitution. Five cases came to the Supreme Court. The first to be decided was that of Oliver Brown, a black citizen of Topeka, Kansas. His case set the pattern for the decisions in the other four. Brown wanted his daughter to attend the nearby white elementary school. He and his family did not want her to go to a school for blacks. Such a school could not be equal. The N.A.A.C.P., with Thurgood Marshall as its chief lawyer in the case, brought the case to the Supreme Court. In May,

As Solicitor General, Thurgood Marshall argued before the Supreme Court. In 1967, he became the first Negro to be named to that court.

1954, the new Chief Justice, Earl Warren, read the decision of the Court. All nine justices had agreed. They were ready to give up the Plessy rule!

11 / *Segregated Schools Are Not Allowed.* The case was clear. The Court had accepted Thurgood Marshall's argument. Jim Crow schools meant a taking away of "equal protection of the laws."

> . . . We come to the question presented: Does segregation of children in public schools solely on the basis of race, even though the . . . other . . . factors may be equal, deprive the children of the minority group of equal educational opportunities? We believe that it does. . . . To separate them from others of similar age . . . solely because of their race, (gives) a feeling of inferiority . . . that may affect their hearts and minds in a way unlikely ever to be undone. . . . We conclude that in the field of public education . . . "separate but equal" has no place.

12 / Next Steps. At last the Constitution was "color blind"! The Court waited a year; then it ordered that all school districts be desegregated quickly. This meant that black and white children would be together in classes. Washington, D.C., had long been a Jim Crow city. It was one of the first to integrate its schools. Other school systems, chiefly in the upper South—the old "border states"—did the same.

13 / Trouble in the South. White leaders in the states of the deep South said that they would not follow the orders of the Court. Senator James Eastland of Mississippi said that the white people of the South would never agree to the change in their schools. In March, 1956, a statement was signed by 100 members of Congress—all from the South. They said that the Court had no right to tell a state how to run its schools. They would take steps so that the new rule would not change life in their states. There were other warnings. Three Southern governors said they would close their public schools rather than allow black and white children to sit in the same classrooms. In state after state school officials used the same plan. They would not admit a black child to a white school unless a case was first brought to a Federal court and its judge ordered them to do so. About 200 school districts desegregated in 1956. The next year, with this new way to fight the decision, there were only 38 new ones. To add to the problem, more than 100 new Jim Crow laws were passed in the South. All were planned to get around the Supreme Court ruling. Southern white leaders hoped it would take years to have the Court decide that these laws were not allowed. Then they would pass new laws. During all these years, Jim Crow would live on in their schools.

14 / Little Rock, Arkansas. Governor Orval Faubus of Arkansas said that he would not obey a court order to admit black students into Central High School in Little Rock. Nine Negro boys and girls made up their minds to go to this high school. When it opened in September, the nine black students planned to enter the school. Faubus

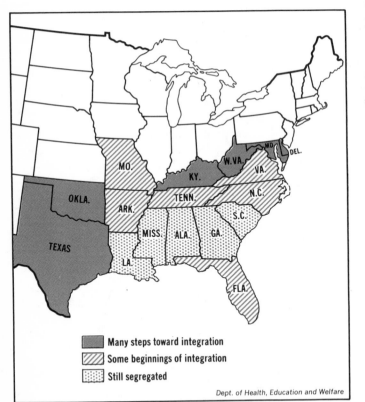

Many steps toward integration
Some beginnings of integration
Still segregated

Dept. of Health, Education and Welfare

Integration or Segregation?

**National Guard troops with bayonets kept
the nine black students out.**

had warned that blood would flow if they tried to do this. He called out the state's National Guard. He then used these soldiers to keep the black students out. Elizabeth Eckford, 15 years old, was one of the nine. She was stopped by one of the soldiers. She said, "When I tried to squeeze past him he raised his bayonet and then the other guards closed in and they raised their bayonets." People in the crowd around the school were shouting, "Lynch her!" The students could not enter the high school.

15 / *The United States Army in Little Rock.* A state had refused to obey a ruling of a Federal court. President Eisenhower saw that he had to act. He sent 1,000 soldiers to Little Rock. He explained that he could not allow mob rule to stop a court's ruling from being carried out. The Army had clear orders. The men were to protect the students. They were to make certain that they could attend Central High School. About sixty white students then left the school. The other eighteen hundred remained. Some of them became friends of the black students. One white student said that she had always been against integration. "But I know now that we're going to change our minds." Yet other students were still as racist as their parents. One of the Negro girls was treated so badly that she left the school after five months. Governor Faubus became a fighter for segregation. He closed all the schools in Little Rock. They were closed for more than a year. When they opened again few black students came to the white schools. It was hard to be a hero. Still, the country and the world had seen that justice was waiting for those ready to stand up for it. By 1968 one of every five students in Central High School was black. The "Little Rock Nine" had opened the door.

Understanding What You Have Read

I. REVIEWING WORD MEANINGS

Write the letter of the choice that best completes each statement.

1. If you are a graduate of a college you have (a) just begun college, (b) been forced to leave college, (c) completed college.
2. The counsel in a case is always a (a) lawyer, (b) judge, (c) person suing another person.
3. An ambassador is (a) an office building in a foreign country, (b) a person who represents his country in another country, (c) a lawyer who has won many cases.
4. In the United States, the Solicitor-General is (a) the Army's chief lawyer, (b) the Federal government's chief lawyer, (c) a lawyer who sues state governments.
5. A justice is always a (a) lawyer, (b) graduate student, (c) judge.
6. When you are deprived of something, (a) it is given to you, (b) you share it with someone else, (c) it is taken away from you.
7. Something that is inferior is (a) lower, (b) at the same level, (c) higher.

8. *Desegregate* is most like (a) segregate, (b) discriminate, (c) integrate.

9. A bayonet is a (a) knife-like weapon, (b) kind of gun, (c) unit of the armed forces.

10. A National Guard unit is usually under the control of the (a) mayor of a city, (b) governor of a state, (c) chief of police of a state.

II. WHO AM I?

Write the name of the person described by each statement. Use the list of names below the statements.

1. I was chief counsel for the N.A.A.C.P. and became known as "Mr. Civil Rights."

2. In 1938 the Supreme Court decided that the University of Missouri would have to admit me to its law school.

3. In 1950 the Supreme Court decided that I had a right to attend the University of Texas Law School, even though Texas had a law school for black students.

4. I was governor of Arkansas when nine black students tried to attend Little Rock's Central High School, and did all I could to keep the schools in my state segregated.

5. I was Chief Justice of the Supreme Court and wrote the decision in the case of *Brown versus Board of Education.*

Orval Faubus	Thurgood Marshall	Lloyd Gaines
Earl Warren	H. Marion Sweatt	James Eastland

III. SOME GREAT CIVIL-RIGHTS LAWYERS

Use your library to find out what each of these great lawyers did to help improve the civil rights of Americans.

1. John Quincy Adams
2. Chester A. Arthur
3. Louis D. Brandeis
4. Benjamin Cardozo

5. Robert L. Carter
6. Salmon P. Chase
7. De Witt Clinton
8. Clarence Darrow
9. Oliver Wendell Holmes
10. John Jay
11. Fiorello La Guardia
12. Thurgood Marshall
13. James M. Nabrit, Jr.
14. Wendell Phillips
15. Thaddeus Stevens
16. Moorfield Storey
17. Harry S Truman
18. Earl Warren

IV. SEGREGATION OR DESEGREGATION?

Write SEGREGATION if the statement is an example of Jim Crow education. Write DESEGREGATION if the statement shows a step toward an end of Jim Crow education.

1. The Supreme Court ruled in 1954 that Oliver Brown's daughter had the right to attend the nearby elementary school.
2. One hundred members of Congress signed a statement that they would oppose the 1954 ruling of the Supreme Court.
3. President Eisenhower sent troops to Little Rock, Arkansas.
4. School officials in the South would admit black children to white schools only when a Federal judge ordered them to do so.
5. Governor Faubus of Arkansas used the state's National Guard on the first day of school in September, 1957.

V. ANSWER EACH OF THE FOLLOWING QUESTIONS IN A SHORT PARAGRAPH OR IN CLASS DISCUSSION.

1. In what ways were conditions better for many black Americans after World War II? (See Paragraph 2.)
2. In the case of *Gaines versus the University of Missouri,* why did the court rule that Lloyd Gaines had the right to attend the University of Missouri Law School? (See Paragraph 4.)
3. How did the Henderson case weaken the rule of "separate but equal"? (See Paragraph 7.)
4. Why was Thurgood Marshall called "Mr. Civil Rights"? (See Paragraph 8.)

5. What important jobs has Thurgood Marshall held in the Federal government? (See Paragraph 9.)

6. Why did the Brown family sue the Board of Education of Topeka, Kansas? (See Paragraph 10.)

7. For what reasons did the Supreme Court rule that "separate but equal" had no place in public education? (See Paragraph 11.)

8. How did white leaders in the South oppose the decision of the Supreme Court in the Brown case? (See Paragraph 13.)

9. How did Governor Faubus of Arkansas try to prevent nine black students from entering Central High School in Little Rock? (See Paragraph 14.)

10. For what reasons did President Eisenhower decide to send troops to Little Rock? (See Paragraph 15.)

VI. THINGS TO DO

1. Check with your school librarian to find the meaning of de facto segregation. How is it different from the segregation that comes through Jim Crow laws in the South? Discuss de facto segregation in class. Should it continue? Should it be ended? How?

2. The Board of Education of Topeka, Kansas, used the Plessy rule as its defense in the 1954 case. The N.A.A.C.P. lawyers argued that schools could not be equal so long as they were separate. Discuss the two points of view in class. Why did all nine of the Justices agree with the N.A.A.C.P.?

3. An organization called the White Citizens Councils spread through the South after the 1954 decision. What was this organization? What were its goals? What methods did it use? Governor Marvin Griffin of Georgia believed in the ideas of the White Citizens Councils. He was active in Little Rock before Governor Faubus acted to keep the nine black students out. What did he say to the people who later formed a mob outside the high school? Check the facts by reading news magazines or newspapers of September, 1957.

Chapter 28 / NONVIOLENT PROTEST AGAINST JIM CROW

Let's Discover

1. How nonviolence and civil disobedience were accepted by black leaders in the South.
2. How the peaceful boycott became a new weapon in the struggle to end Jim Crow.
3. How the success of a bus boycott in Montgomery, Alabama, brought the country a new leader, the Reverend Dr. Martin Luther King, Jr.

Words to Know

boycott
: A joining together to refuse to buy or use something.
The bus boycott meant that people would not ride the buses in any part of the city.

civil disobedience
: The refusal to obey a law a person thinks is wrong.
People who engage in civil disobedience must be prepared for such punishment as going to jail.

nonviolence
: The refusal to use force as a weapon in getting change.
People who practice nonviolence do not strike back.

Baptist
: One of the Protestant Christian churches.
Dr. Martin Luther King, Jr., was the minister of a Baptist church in Montgomery, Alabama.

car pool
: An organized group of cars and drivers who work together to get people from one place to another.

320

	A huge car pool was set up to get people to and from work during the Montgomery bus boycott.
overcome	To find a good solution to a problem.
	The black citizens of Montgomery knew they would overcome the Jim Crow laws.
reverse	In law, to decide that another court has been wrong.
	The Supreme Court reversed the decision of the lower court.
District Court	The Federal court in each part of the country, whose decisions can be reversed only by a higher court.
	The district court decided that segregated travel was wrong.
just	Right and fair.
	A just man will treat other people fairly and honestly.
unjust	Unfair to other people.
	People who were unjust tried to keep Afro-Americans from gaining equal rights.

---

1 / *The Boycott—a "New" Weapon.* The people of Ireland owned little of the land in their own country about ninety years ago. English landlords charged them high rents. The agents of the English were often cruel men who treated the Irish badly. One such man was named Captain Boycott. The people of his part of Ireland turned against him. They would not talk to him or have anything to do with him. The story of what they did spread around the world. A new word was added to the English language. *Boycott* came to mean refusing to do business with a person or company, or even with a country. This idea was not new. People in the colonies had used it 200 years ago to make the English change certain laws. Colonial merchants had signed agreements to stop buying English goods. Today the boycott has become an important weapon in the fight for equal rights for Afro-Americans.

2 / *Jobs for Black Workers.* The Urban League used the boycott during the Depression to get more jobs for black workers. Black customers were told, "Don't Buy Where You Can't Work!" In New York City boycotts and a riot in 1935 led to

the opening of many jobs to Negroes. In city after city the doors to equal job opportunities were forced open by the use of this new weapon—the boycott. The greatest successes came in Chicago and New York. In Chicago more than a thousand people gained jobs in stores. In New York tens of thousands of new jobs opened up! It was ten years more before a state law could be passed in New York for equal treatment in hiring.

3 / *Civil Disobedience*. What could people do if they believed that a law of their country was wrong? Of course, they should try to change it. But suppose they could not? Many men in world history have asked this question. One answer was found by Henry David Thoreau. He had spent a day in jail for refusing to pay a tax during the Mexican War. He later explained that he had had no choice. He truly believed that no man should obey an evil law. The war with Mexico, he felt, was fought to get more land for slavery. He would not support the

Nonviolence was first used by Gandhi.

war in any way. He called his action *civil disobedience*. He believed that a person faced with a bad law should refuse to obey that law. He should then take whatever punishment came. Thoreau's ideas were followed by the tens of thousands who would not obey the Fugitive Slave Law. Instead they had worked for the Underground Railroad.

4 / *Nonviolence*. It was in India that the use of civil disobedience first brought great changes. There it was planned by Mohandas K. (Mahatma) Gandhi. Gandhi led his country's long fight for freedom from England. He was certain that he could force the English to leave. He taught the men and women who followed him to use civil disobedience. They would not pay their taxes. They would not buy English goods. They made their own salt from sea water so that they would not have to buy salt from the English. They spun their own cloth so that they would not have to buy clothing made in England.

5 / *Victory for Nonviolence*. The people of India were ready to go to jail. Gandhi told them that there were not enough jails to hold all those who wanted their country to be free. Gandhi was jailed again and again. Thousands of his followers were beaten, shot or put into prison. He did not let them strike back. He taught them not to use force. He and his followers said they were fighting evil when they disobeyed English laws. Their defense was their "soul force," which Gandhi called the strength "born of truth and love or nonviolence." For thirty years he led his people in this peaceful way. In

1947 the English gave India its freedom. Eight years later, in the United States, a young minister named Dr. Martin Luther King, Jr., used the teachings of Thoreau, Gandhi and Jesus to attack the evils of Jim Crow.

6 / *A Bus Boycott in the South.* On December 1, 1955, a black woman named Rosa

Mrs. Parks refused to move.

Parks refused to move to the rear of a bus in Montgomery, Alabama, when the driver told her to do so. Alabama has long been one of the worst Jim Crow states. A city law in Montgomery gave bus drivers the power to order black passengers to move back—or stand—to make room for whites. But this time the black passenger would not move. The bus was crowded. There were no seats in the rear, and Mrs. Parks was tired after a hard day's work. She was arrested and later fined. The next day Dr. Martin Luther King, Jr., a 27-year-old Baptist minister, met with other church leaders and black community leaders. The group agreed to boycott the city's buses as a protest against the arrest of Mrs. Parks. They would do this on the next Monday, the day of her trial. Their action was a success—the buses were empty. The 50,000 black people in the city decided to keep up their boycott. They would do so until all people had the right to take any empty seat in any bus, and remain in that seat.

7 / *The Boycott Goes On.* Here was a new way to attack a Jim Crow law! The group that had planned the first day's boycott set up the Montgomery Improvement Association. They chose Dr. King as their president. They made plans for a long struggle. Black people would stay off the buses. They added a second demand to their call for an end to segregated seating. They asked that black bus drivers be hired for routes that passed through black neighborhoods. Two kinds of Jim Crow practices were being attacked at the same time. Until these two

The Montgomery bus boycott was a success.

demands were met, no black passenger would ride a bus in the city of Montgomery.

8 / *Car Pools.* Yet people did have to get to work. Car pools were set up. Each car went back and forth as many times as possible. Money was needed to get more cars, and to pay the cost of running them. Dr. King asked the rest of the country for help. Soon $250,000 was raised. It was used to keep a car pool of 300 automobiles and station wagons going. Those who could not get a ride walked to work. A great spirit, one that was new in the South, filled the black people of the city. In this battle, they said, they would overcome.

9 / *The Boycott Hurts Business.* About three-fourths of the people who used buses in Montgomery were blacks. Most of them stopped using the buses. The bus company lost almost two-thirds of its business. It had to take many buses out of service. It did not need all of its drivers. This meant that many of them were put out of work. Downtown stores lost much of their business, for black customers could not get to them to do their shopping. These stores also had to fire some of their help. The boycott was felt by the whole city.

10 / *The City Fought the Boycott.* The Montgomery boycott went on successfully for almost three months. The city then made use of a state law that it said made such a boycott a crime. Dr. King and a hundred other leaders were arrested. This did not stop the boycott. Even earlier the homes of

Dr. King and Reverend Ralph Abernathy had been bombed. This had not stopped the boycott either. Dr. King had made his thinking clear to all. He asked those who followed him not to answer force with force: "We want to love our enemies. Love them and let them know you love them. Do not get your weapons. Put them away." When he was found guilty, he said, "We are not bitter. . . . I feel confident, as this case moves up through the higher courts, somewhere along the way the decision will be reversed." Martin Luther King was using nonviolent civil disobedience much as Gandhi had. He was also using the courts. A Federal district court ruled that the Jim Crow seating rules in the buses were not allowed by the Constitution. In November, 1956, the Supreme Court agreed. The city had to end its Jim Crow travel laws. The next month, 381 days after it had begun, the bus boycott came to an end. The first black bus drivers were hired. Dr. King and a white minister rode side by side on one of the buses.

11 / *Peaceful Change*. Dr. King had explained that he did not want his followers to hate those who were against them. After his arrest he had said: "If we are arrested every day . . . if we are trampled over every day, don't ever let anyone pull you so low as to hate them. . . . We must realize so many people are taught to hate us that they are not totally responsible for their hate." And, by going to jail, Martin Luther King showed that he agreed with Henry David Thoreau. Thoreau had said: "Under a government which imprisons any unjustly, the true place for a just man is also a prison." Yet Dr. King felt no anger himself. When the bus boycott's goals had been won, he again reminded his followers that nonviolence was

the best rule to follow. He said, "We must act in such a way as to make possible a coming together of white people and colored people on the basis of a real understanding. We seek an integration based upon mutual respect." He kept this goal in mind: "We are out to defeat injustice and not white persons who may be unjust."

12 / *Lessons Learned*. The bus boycott had been watched by the whole country. Black Americans in one city had changed the life of all black Americans. They had learned that much could be gained without fighting and bloodshed. They had learned to use their economic power. The way they spent or didn't spend their money could change the world around them. A boycott could lead to the gaining of rights. A black community could gain much from working together. Being well-organized was most important. It could mean success when there were leaders like Martin Luther King, Jr.

13 / *The S.C.L.C.* The work done by Dr. King and Reverend Ralph Abernathy made these church leaders well known. The story of their bus boycott had meaning for the whole world. Dr. King became most famous. In 1957 he and other church leaders formed a new organization. It would work in the South to gain further civil rights for Afro-Americans. It was called the Southern Christian Leadership Conference, or S.C.L.C. We will learn more about this group and its president, Dr. King, in later chapters.

Rev. Ralph Abernathy, Dr. Martin Luther King and Rev. Glenn Smiley of New York on a Montgomery bus after the boycott.

Understanding What You Have Read

I. REVIEWING WORD MEANINGS

Write the letter of the choice that best explains the meaning of each word.

1. **boycott** (a) Buy more! (b) Buy less! (c) Don't buy at all!
2. **civil disobedience** (a) Obey the law! (b) Do not obey the law! (c) Study the law!
3. **nonviolence** (a) Hit those who attack you! (b) Use peaceful methods only! (c) Ask people to attack you!
4. **Baptist** (a) A Christian church. (b) Another word for "minister." (c) A plan for a boycott.
5. **car pool** (a) An automobile laundry. (b) A movable pool. (c) An organized group of cars and drivers.
6. **overcome** (a) Work it out. (b) Reach the top. (c) Arrive.
7. **reverse** (a) Your decision was correct. (b) Your decision was wrong. (c) Your decision was not obeyed.
8. **district** (a) Part of a city, state or country. (b) Office of the head of a government. (c) Building in which a judge works.
9. **just** (a) He is a fair man! (b) He cares only about himself! (c) He is very poor!
10. **unjust** (a) The law tries to hurt black people. (b) The law is the same for all people. (c) There is no law on this subject.

II. VIOLENT OR NONVIOLENT

If the statement describes a violent way to act, write VIOLENT. If the statement describes a nonviolent way to act, write NONVIOLENT.

1. The home of Dr. Martin Luther King, Jr., was bombed.
2. Dr. King told his followers to put away their weapons.
3. Henry David Thoreau refused to pay the tax.
4. The English troops shot at the marching Indians.
5. The city of Montgomery was forced to end its Jim Crow travel laws by a Supreme Court decision.
6. He hit the boy who had called him a name.

7. He told his friends that he was going to pray for his enemies.
8. The boycott wrecked the company's business.
9. Police used their clubs to break up the meeting.
10. Mrs. Parks refused to change her seat.

III. PLACING EVENTS IN CORRECT ORDER

Arrange each group of events in the order in which they happened.

A. 1. Henry David Thoreau refused to pay a tax.
   2. Dr. King was willing to go to jail.
   3. Mohandas Gandhi succeeded in gaining freedom for India.
B. 1. The Urban League organized boycotts to get jobs for black workers.
   2. The black citizens of Montgomery organized a boycott.
   3. Captain Boycott found that no one would talk to him.
C. 1. The Supreme Court ruled that segregated travel was unconstitutional.
   2. The Montgomery Improvement Association was organized.
   3. The first day of the bus boycott was a success.

IV. DO YOU AGREE OR DISAGREE?

Explain your reasons for agreeing or disagreeing with each of these statements. Remember that other students have the right to disagree with you. Can you defend your position against theirs?

1. The best way to improve civil rights is to follow the idea of nonviolence.
2. Nonviolent ways of working for civil rights are too slow.
3. If we allow civil disobedience against one law, just or unjust, then people will disobey all laws.
4. Each person should have the right to decide for himself what laws he will obey or will disobey.
5. A government whose laws are disobeyed should not punish those who give good reasons for disobeying the laws.
6. The Montgomery bus boycott was one of the most important events in the history of civil rights.

7. Boycotts should be used whenever people want to see a law changed.

8. Sending Dr. Martin Luther King to jail helped the cause of black people more than it hurt it.

9. The Montgomery Improvement Association should have demanded the end of *all* Jim Crow laws at the same time.

10. No person should hate those who wrong him because they don't know any better.

V.   THINGS TO DO

1. Give a short play on the events of December 1, 1955, when Mrs. Rosa Parks was told to give up her seat on the bus. Act out her arrest. Then show her explaining the reasons for her action to a group of reporters after she has been released from jail.

2. Have a group of students prepare a panel discussion. Each of them should first read books by and about Dr. Martin Luther King. The topic for their discussion should be: *Violence or Non-violence?* The members of the panel should be ready to answer questions from other members of the class.

3. Write a one-page report to answer this question: How was the Southern Christian Leadership Conference different from such older groups as the N.A.A.C.P. and the National Urban League?

4. For class discussion: Why have ministers been so important in the civil-rights movement? How have ministers like Dr. Adam Clayton Powell, Jr., been important in both religion and politics? Should ministers become active in civil rights or other political matters? Why or why not?

5. From this point on, the events described in this book can be found illustrated in the news magazines found in your library. Set up a class committee to check the library for each chapter. The committees can then bring in magazines containing pictures taken at the time an event took place. If your school or town has a microfilm library, then it will also have newspapers on film.

Chapter 29 / SIT-INS, FREEDOM RIDES AND VOTER REGISTRATION

Let's Discover

1. How nonviolent sit-ins and freedom rides helped end segregation in many places in the South.
2. How the Federal government became more active in protecting civil rights in the South.
3. How peaceful demonstrations in Birmingham were met by violence.
4. How whites and blacks worked together to get more Afro-Americans in the South to become voters.

Words to Know

conscience	The feeling that tells a person to do what he knows is right rather than what he knows is wrong. *Nonviolence by blacks was aimed at the conscience of whites.*
abuse	To hurt someone or someone's feelings by bad treatment. *Angry Southerners abused the black and white students during the sit-ins.*
marshal	An officer of a United States Federal court who has the powers of a police officer and takes his orders from that court or the President. *President Kennedy used United States marshals to protect freedom riders.*
demonstration	A meeting or march by a large group of people to show others how they feel about some problem. *Dr. King planned demonstrations against Jim Crow in Birmingham, Alabama.*

331

dynamite   A powerful explosive most used in mining.
Racists used dynamite to blow up buildings used by black leaders in Birmingham.

hoodlum   A person who attacks others and does not respect the law.
KKK hoodlums have lynched Afro-Americans in many parts of this country.

credit   The willingness of a bank to lend money to a person or a business.
The White Citizens Councils tried to get banks to refuse credit to those who favored integration.

sheriff   The chief law officer in a county.
Many sheriffs in the South agreed with the KKK.

---

1 / *A New Nonviolent Weapon*. The bus boycott had shown the world that a Jim Crow law or custom could be defeated when large numbers of people joined to fight it. White racists in the South did not want to give up Jim Crow. Yet not all of them were willing to use force to keep it alive. The sit-in was a test for these whites as well as for blacks. Suppose that a group of black people were to sit down somewhere and ask for a right that Jim Crow had taken away. Suppose as well that these blacks were nonviolent. No matter what was done to them, they would not strike back. What would be the result? There had been sit-ins before. But it was not until 1960 that tens of thousands of people, white and black, used the sit-in as a way to fight Jim Crow all over the South.

2 / *Four College Boys Sit Down*. It was February 1, 1960. Four black students from a college in Greensboro, North Carolina, walked into a Woolworth store. They went to the lunch counter. They knew this was a counter that served whites only. They sat down and asked for coffee. They would not leave until they had been served. The boys, Joseph McNeil, Ezell Blair, Jr., Franklin McLain and David Richmond, felt that they could no longer accept the Jim Crow custom that would not let them be served in a restaurant. The manager of the Woolworth's did not use force to make the boys leave. "They can just sit there," he said. They were not served. A news broadcast told about the four boys. More black students came in and sat down with them. None of them would leave until they were served. Each day they came back to sit on their stools and ask to be served. Soon the whole country was waiting to see what would happen. Many blacks and whites came to Greensboro to help. Martin Luther King

The first lunch-counter sit-in.

came, as did men from the N.A.A.C.P. and CORE (the Congress of Racial Equality).

3 / *CORE Gives Lessons.* The lunch counter sit-ins spread quickly. The N.A.A.C.P. had used sit-ins before. So had CORE. CORE was an organization of blacks and some whites that had begun in 1942. In 1961 its head was James Farmer. CORE began to train sit-in students to protest in a peaceful way. They would show that Dr. Martin Luther King was right when he had said: "We will soon wear you down by our capacity to suffer, and in winning our freedom we will so appeal to your heart and con-

science that we will win you in the process." Each person trained by CORE was given a card that told him or her how to behave during a sit-in:

Don't strike back or curse if abused—
Don't laugh out—
Don't hold conversations with floor workers—
Show yourself courteous and friendly at all times—
Sit straight and always face the counter—
Remember love and non-violence—
May God bless you.

James Farmer was head of CORE.

more than a hundred cities in the South were serving whites and blacks. Congress later passed a Civil Rights Act. One part of the law said that no public business could be segregated. The sit-ins had led to this great defeat for an important part of Jim Crow.

6 / *Freedom's Costs.* The victory won by the sit-ins had not been easy. There had been more than 800 sit-ins. More than 70,000 blacks and whites had taken part. These men, women and children had been cursed, beaten and arrested. More than 4,000 had been sent to jail. In most cases they were judged by racist courts in Jim Crow states that found them guilty no matter what defense they offered. This was as true for the whites who had come to help as it was for the Negroes. Yet the new freedom that was gained seemed well worth the cost.

4 / *CORE Grows.* The sit-ins were well planned. They spread. There were hundreds in cities across the South, most of them by students. There were also "wade-ins" at some beaches. Some young men and women tried "read-ins" at public libraries. Others tried "walk-ins" at theaters and parks. There were even "kneel-ins" at churches. CORE was one of the groups that planned these actions. It had been a small civil-rights group, but now it grew quickly. Its national director, James Farmer, was soon one of the country's best-known Afro-Americans.

7 / *The "Freedom Rides."* The sit-ins had weakened one part of Jim Crow. There were still other parts to be fought. James Farmer and the members of CORE made plans to end Jim Crow travel. Most bus and train stations in the South still segregated whites and blacks. The courts had said this was not allowed. But it was still being done, even when buses or trains crossed state lines. The CORE plan was to send buses filled with whites and blacks from the North to the South. There they would test food counters, waiting rooms and rest rooms. In a few places there was no trouble. In others mobs of angry whites attacked buses while police watched and did nothing. Many of the riders were beaten. One man needed more than

5 / *Gains Through the Sit-Ins.* At last there was a full attack on Jim Crow. Blacks and whites all over the country took part in sit-ins. By September, 1961, restaurants in

This bus carrying freedom riders was set afire in Anniston, Alabama.

fifty stitches for his head wounds. A second almost died after a beating in Birmingham, Alabama. One bus in Anniston, Alabama, was set afire, and twelve freedom riders had to be sent to a hospital. Yet the goal of the freedom rides was reached. The Federal government had to act. It sent marshals to protect the freedom riders. More than 1,000 black and white people risked their lives in the freedom rides. In city after city in the South, they had helped end Jim Crow in bus and train stations.

8 / *A Jim Crow State.* Mississippi has used Jim Crow rules more than any other state. More whites there have been ready to use force to keep segregation than in any other state. In the 1950's, when lynchings had almost ended in the rest of the country, black people were still being murdered in Mississippi. Police chiefs in town after town were members of or close to the KKK.

9 / *The Oxford Riot.* In September, 1962, Federal judges ordered the state university at Oxford, Mississippi, to admit James Meredith, an Afro-American. This led to a great change. The college had no black students. Thousands of whites poured into the town. They came to keep Meredith out of the all-white school. President Kennedy saw that there would be trouble. He sent more than 300 marshals to Oxford to keep the peace. He spoke to the country on television, saying to the people of Mississippi that "the honor of your university and the

state are in the balance." Still the marshals had to fight off the attack of about 2,500 people who had gathered to make this one black student leave. Two men died in the rioting. More than half of the marshals were hurt; 29 of them were shot. For the rest of the school year hundreds of soldiers stayed on the college grounds to keep peace. Yet when Meredith finished his studies the next year, he said that the teachers and most of the students had been friendly.

10 / *Marches for Equal Rights*. Many people felt that the most segregated city in the country was Birmingham, Alabama. If Jim Crow could be weakened there, it would be weaker everywhere. Black and white leaders in the city met. They talked about integrating schools, stores and other places. The talks failed. Dr. King and the S.C.L.C. made plans to use nonviolent demonstrations to win an end to Jim Crow. A demonstration is a large gathering of people in a public place for a meeting, a march, picketing or some other planned act. On April 3, 1963, sit-ins and picketers carrying signs appeared at a number of stores. About 150 of them were arrested. More people, many of them young boys and girls, joined the protest. Governor George Wallace of Alabama had told the people of his state that he would never give up segregation. Eugene "Bull" Connor, who headed the police in Birmingham, was ready to use force to help keep the governor's promise.

11 / *Police Violence*. The police soon had an order from a judge to end the demonstrations. Until this time the S.C.L.C. had

obeyed court orders. This time they felt that the order was wrong, and that a higher court would reverse the decision. All people had the right to meet peacefully. Dr. King and other church leaders were arrested when they refused to stop the marches. But the marches went on. On May 2 the police took 500 people to jail. The next day they used fire hoses to knock down marching students. They used police dogs to attack them. A news picture of a large dog leaping at a young boy who was held by a policeman went around the world. President Kennedy saw it. He knew that he had to step in. He had already asked the city to treat its prisoners well. Now he sent in his Assistant Attorney General. The city then promised to end some kinds of segregation. The marches stopped. A few days later the home of Dr. King's brother was bombed, and then the building used by the leaders of the protest. A riot followed as thousands of Afro-Americans went into the streets and fought back against attacking police. Fifty people went to hospitals that night. The city, it seemed, would have to obey the laws of the land. Yet its racists would not stop hating and hurting black people.

12 / *Birmingham Sunday*. Two more terrible attacks took place before the South seemed to quiet down for a while. In June Medgar Evers, the state secretary of the N.A.A.C.P. in Mississippi, was murdered. In September President Kennedy used Federal power to make Birmingham admit black students to white schools. An event that shocked the whole world then took place. Dynamite wrecked the Sixteenth

Federal marshals guarded James Meredith.

Street Baptist Church in that city. Four Negro girls who had been studying in a Bible class were killed. Thousands of angry blacks rushed out of their homes when they heard the news. The police fired "over their heads"—and killed two boys. Fights between whites and blacks spread through the South.

13 / *The White Citizens Councils.* Who were the people who had acted with such terrible force? White racists had set up groups in each state of the South. They were called White Citizens Councils. Leading businessmen and KKK hoodlums had joined to fight for Jim Crow. They fought hard. By 1960 they had banned books in many states. They had control of newspapers. They kept magazines that favored equal rights from newsstands. They blocked television programs that gave a fair picture of events in the South. They even kept out motion pictures that showed black actors in important roles. Any white man who spoke out against them might lose his job or be forced out of business. Black businessmen who worked with civil-rights groups found that they could not get gasoline, supplies or bank credit. Governors and mayors all over the South were part of these Councils. Working with them were the KKK groups, always ready to use force. They felt

**The Mississippi Summer Project signed up
thousands of voters.**

safe, for most local judges were as racist as
the Klan.

14 / *What to Do?* It seemed that all the
rules of the Supreme Court and all the laws
of the country would not end Jim Crow.
The millions of Afro-Americans in the
South would have to do the job themselves.
They would have to become voters and
then use the power of their votes to change
life in their part of the country.

Birmingham Sunday **by Judy Binder.**

15 / *Voter Registrations.* It was clear that
the right to vote was important. White men
who needed black votes to keep power
would have to be less racist. Negro groups
joined in 1964 to set up the "Mississippi
Summer Project." This was a drive to register black voters in that deeply Jim Crow
state. More than a thousand whites came
from the North to help thousands of black
citizens in this great task. Most Afro-Americans in Mississippi had never been able to

vote. They had to be taught how to register and then how to vote. "Freedom schools" were set up by the young black and white civil-rights workers. All summer the enemies of equal rights struck at these young people. About 1,000 of them were arrested; shots were fired at them 35 times; eighty of them were beaten; 35 Negro churches were burned; six people were murdered. The white racists of Mississippi were not going to let the black people in their state vote. They were ready to kill to prevent it. In June two white students from the North, Andrew Goodman and Michael Schwerner, and a young Afro-American, James Chaney, were beaten and then murdered. Six months later the F.B.I. arrested 21 men—one of them the local sheriff—for this murder. Some of these men were sent to jail for their part in the murder. It was the first time a white man had been jailed for such

a murder or lynching in Mississippi! Black voters in the state set up the Freedom Democratic Party. In four years it would become the official Democratic party of the state. What had happened in Mississippi had cracked the walls of Jim Crow. More attacks, it was hoped, would bring these walls crashing down.

16 / *Nonviolence Weakens.* By 1964 the nonviolence movement had been struck by white racist attacks and murders many times. Some young black people began to wonder: Could nonviolence work any more? Some of them turned to new leaders and new groups who said force should be used to meet force. We will read about these groups in later chapters. Ten years of peaceful methods had weakened Jim Crow. Other problems still remained as black citizens asked for equality in fact as well as in law.

**Michael Schwerner, James Chaney and Andrew Goodman
were beaten and then murdered.**

Understanding What You Have Read

I. REVIEWING WORD MEANINGS

Write the letter of the choice that best completes each statement.

1. Your conscience tells you to do (a) whatever you want to do, (b) things you know are right, (c) things you know are wrong.

2. A person who seems to act without a conscience (a) does not show that he understands the difference between right and wrong, (b) defends the rights of others, (c) never uses violence.

3. When a person is abused he is (a) treated fairly, (b) punished according to law, (c) treated unfairly.

4. When your rights are abused they are (a) made greater, (b) taken away, (c) protected by law.

5. The marshals discussed in this chapter worked for (a) cities in the South, (b) state governments, (c) the Federal government.

6. One example of a demonstration is a (a) sit-in, (b) meeting in someone's home, (c) fire drill in a school.

7. When you demonstrate you are (a) voting for freedom in an election, (b) carrying on a boycott, (c) protesting in public together with others.

8. Dynamite is dangerous because it (a) causes fires, (b) explodes with great force, (c) burns the skin.

9. A hoodlum is most likely to use (a) peaceful methods, (b) demonstrations, (c) violence.

10. The actions of hoodlums described in this chapter were (a) according to law, (b) against the law, (c) peaceful protests.

11. When you have credit you can get (a) a bank loan, (b) higher pay, (c) a better job.

12. When you lose your credit you suffer (a) in a social way, (b) in a political way, (c) in an economic way.

13. A sheriff works for (a) a county, (b) a state, (c) the United States.

14. A sheriff is chiefly (a) a county's chief lawyer, (b) the head of a police force, (c) the assistant to a governor.

15. When a Federal law must be enforced, the job is given to (a) a sheriff, (b) a marshal, (c) marshals and sheriffs together.

II. PROTEST AND ITS GOAL

Complete each of these statements, using one of the words or phrases in the list below the statements.

1. The sit-in was first used to get service at ——————.
2. The kneel-in was used to show that any person should be allowed into ——————.
3. When you walk around a building in a group, carrying signs to show why you are marching, you are ——————.
4. A group of white and black passengers on a bus going from Chicago to Birmingham in 1961 might have been part of a ——————.
5. A read-in would be an action to integrate ——————.
6. The first "freedom schools" were used to teach Afro-Americans in Mississippi about ——————.
7. The most important group fighting *for* segregation in the South has been the ——————.
8. Sit-ins and freedom rides were used with success by the ——————.
9. The organization headed by Dr. Martin Luther King, Jr., was the ——————.
10. Racists believe in ——————.

churches	segregation
libraries	lunch counters
voting	White Citizens Councils
Congress of Racial Equality	picketing
Southern Christian Leadership Conference	freedom ride

III. WHO AM I?

Write the name of the person described by each statement.

1. When I was governor of Alabama, I said that I would try to keep segregation forever.
2. I was the first black student admitted to the University of Mississippi.
3. I was the President of the United States who first used Federal marshals to protect the freedom riders.
4. As head of CORE, I planned many freedom rides and sit-ins.
5. I led the group that planned the demonstrations against Jim Crow in Birmingham, Alabama.

IV. ANSWER EACH OF THESE QUESTIONS IN ONE OR TWO SENTENCES.

1. Why was Birmingham chosen for the demonstrations against Jim Crow?
2. How did the sit-ins help end many Jim Crow customs?
3. How was religion an important part of the nonviolent movement?
4. How did television help make Americans agree that Jim Crow was wrong?
5. Why did President Kennedy use Federal marshals in Oxford, Mississippi, a town that had its own police force?
6. Why didn't the jailing of demonstrators end the marches in Birmingham?
7. Why have Mississippi and Alabama fought hardest to keep Jim Crow?
8. How did the White Citizens Councils use boycotts to keep segregation?
9. Why were "freedom schools" needed in Mississippi?
10. Explain the chief successes of the nonviolent movement.

V. THINGS TO DO

1. Three men were President during the events described in Chapters 28 and 29. They were Dwight D. Eisenhower, John F.

Kennedy and Lyndon B. Johnson. Many books have been written about each of them. Set up three class committees. Each should choose one of these Presidents. Then each should use the library to find the answers to these questions and report their findings to the class.

a) What were his views on civil rights?

b) How did he help improve civil rights?

2. Use a news magazine of the early 1960's to find the information you need to describe a sit-in or freedom ride reported in it. Write a one-page report that tells how this sit-in or freedom ride was organized and what happened to it. Compare your report with those prepared by other students. How were all the sit-ins or freedom rides alike? How was each different?

3. Prepare a chart based on Chapters 27, 28 and 29. Its title should be *Gaining Equal Rights*. Head four columns as shown below. Fill in the information needed for each column. The class can then set up a committee to prepare a large bulletin-board display based on this chart.

DATE(s)	METHOD USED TO GAIN RIGHTS	GROUPS WHO USED IT	EXAMPLE OF WHAT WAS GAINED

VI. QUESTIONS TO DISCUSS

1. What does nonviolence mean to you? When would you favor it? When would you refuse to use it? Why?

2. Why did Negroes in Mississippi have to set up a new political party? Why didn't they work within the Democratic Party?

3. How did the use of police dogs in Birmingham shake "the conscience of mankind"?

4. Afro-Americans used economic pressure, such as boycotts, to improve their rights. The White Citizens Councils used economic pressure too. Why did people who favor equal rights cheer the first group but not the second one?

5. Was it right to allow young boys and girls to take part in demonstrations? Why or why not?

Chapter 30 / THE CHANGING CIVIL-RIGHTS MOVEMENT

Let's Discover

1. How new leaders rose within the civil-rights movement after 1960.
2. How these new leaders planned to improve the life of black Americans.

Words to Know

standard   Something set up as a model for measuring other things like it.
People in the slums do not live in standard housing.

director   The person in charge of the work of an organization.
Roy Wilkins became Executive Director of the N.A.A.C.P. after the death of Walter White.

coordinating   Making several groups work together well.
James Forman's new group coordinated the work of student protest groups.

militant   Ready to take strong action for a cause.
Militant groups gave up nonviolence.

reactionary   Wanting to return to some earlier or more backward condition.
Many blacks and whites feel that any return to segregation would be reactionary.

moderate   A person who favors reform and progress through changes in laws and customs rather than through violent action.
Moderates have refused to follow the ideas and methods of the militants.

Muslims   Believers in the religion of Islam.

Elijah Muhammad leads the group known as the Black Muslims.

nationalist   One who believes that his country or people is better than others.

Black nationalists have tried to break away from white groups.

Puritans   The early settlers of New England, or those like them, who followed stricter rules of personal conduct than most other people.

Puritans did not permit drinking or smoking.

unity   Many brought together and acting as one.

Malcolm X set up the Organization of Afro-American Unity, which he hoped all black Americans would join and follow.

---

1 / *A Share of the Good Life.* What progress had black people made in the hundred years since the Civil War? They had suffered in many ways. They had lived with Jim Crow. They had known discrimination and segregation. But, with the days of the New Deal, they had begun to gain fuller rights. They now entered many parts of the country's life. They held jobs in government. Some Afro-Americans became members of the middle class. They had better homes and cars. They had money for travel and education. They could hope for an even better life in the years ahead. For some people, real gains had been made by the middle of the 1960's.

2 / *Toward a Better Life.* Studies made by the United States government showed what these gains were. Two out of every five black families had moved out of poverty. There were Afro-American doctors, lawyers, businessmen, engineers, teachers and craftsmen —in ever greater numbers. More than half the country's black citizens had moved to cities in the North. There new kinds of work were being opened to them—jobs at all levels in offices, stores and factories. More than half of all Negro boys and girls were finishing high school. Tens of thousands were going on to finish college. The government calls a building that is in good condition a "standard housing unit." Three out of every five black families in the cities lived in such "good" homes. More Afro-Americans were voting. In the South more than three million had been registered. A study of twenty cities showed that one out of every ten men and women in public office was black. There had even been a great growth in the number of black policemen. In Washington, D.C., one of every five was black. Even in Atlanta, Georgia, deep in the South, one of every ten policemen was black. Life had changed in many ways. Blacks and whites who for years had tried to build a better life for all could say that many steps had been taken toward this goal.

3 / *Rising Hopes.* These steps were welcomed. Yet millions of blacks had not yet improved their lives. Some unions still kept out black workers. More black students than white dropped out of school or did not go on to college. Most black families earned less than white families. More black people in the large cities lived in homes that were below standard. They watched television programs that showed white middle class life and asked why they and their friends could not share in their country's great wealth. They knew their lives were a little better than their parents' lives had been. But they wanted much more. Their hopes and their demands rose.

4 / *Black Organizations at Work.* The older civil-rights groups had helped bring many of the changes in the lives of Afro-Americans. They had worked for equal rights for more than fifty years. There were 500,000 members in the N.A.A.C.P. They had learned to use the courts and had won case after case. Their victories in these cases had ended Jim Crow laws in much of the country. They had worked for better laws. In state after state they had tried to get fair employment, fair housing and other rights. They had worked with white groups

Roy Wilkins, N.A.A.C.P.

Whitney Young, Urban League.

that had the same goals. The Urban League carried on its search for jobs. It made plans to train young black workers in many new fields. It worked closely with white business leaders to get jobs in these new fields. Roy Wilkins, Executive Director of the N.A.A.C.P., became well known to all Americans through his appearances on television. So did Whitney Young, Jr., head of the Urban League until his death in 1971.

5 / *In the Labor Movement.* Black workers had become leaders in many unions. A. Philip Randolph remained the best-known figure. Men like Bayard Rustin worked with him and became well known in the struggle for better rights for all people, black and white. Each union in which black workers entered in large numbers soon had some Negro officers. This was true of the musicians, the laundry workers, the clothing workers, the sailors, the hospital workers, the department store workers, the truck drivers and others. Roosevelt Watts became a vice-president of the union of truck drivers, a giant union that had long been under complete white control. He and men like him worked for the rights of all workers. They helped such organizations as the Workers Defense League to protect these rights. They felt that black workers would gain through being part of the labor movement.

6 / *Changes in CORE.* CORE had been active in planning sit-ins and freedom rides. The group had been set up in 1942 by James Farmer and a group of young people in Chicago. It had done much during World War II. Its members had helped bring fair employment to many factories. CORE had remained small. James Farmer led it, but was a leader of the N.A.A.C.P. at the same time. From 1961 to 1966 he gave all his time to CORE. Then he left it to lead a new group, the National Center for Community Action and Organization. His job in CORE was taken for the next two years by a North Carolina lawyer named Floyd McKissick. In 1968 Mr. McKissick's job was given to Roy Innis. CORE had always had black and white members. After James Farmer left it, its new leaders took steps to make the group more "black." Most of the white members left, many of them because they felt CORE's black members did not want them.

7 / *SNCC—A Student Group.* Much of the success of the sit-ins and freedom rides came from the work of young people. Remember that four black students had begun the sit-ins. Hundreds of students went on the freedom rides. Thousands more black and white students were ready to work for civil rights. The older civil-rights groups helped young people plan their protests. But the students felt they wanted a group of their own. In 1960 Dr. King helped them set up the Student Non-violent Coordinating Committee (SNCC). Most people call it "SNICK." The small groups that had been set up in colleges all over the country joined it. The young men who first led SNCC agreed with Dr. King. They used peaceful methods. The two best known were James Forman and John Lewis. Five years later the members of SNCC seemed ready to give up nonviolence. Stokely Carmichael

became their leader. He spoke openly about the use of force to improve the rights of black people. This move away from nonviolence went further with SNCC's next leader, H. Rap Brown. The number of members and their activities grew less. Yet H. Rap Brown's militant speeches gained great attention in newspapers and on television.

8 / *What Is a Militant?* The changes that came to some of the civil-rights groups can best be understood when we look at some new words that are used today. The key question was: How closely should black civil-rights groups work with whites who shared the same goals? People began to call names as they reached different answers to this question. A man who worked closely with whites might find himself called an "Uncle Tom," one who was like a slave to the whites. He might in his turn call someone else a reactionary, one who wanted to go back to some kind of segregated life. The leaders of the N.A.A.C.P. and the Urban League, who had made great gains by working with whites, became known as moderates. Those who said they were no longer nonviolent, and who were ready to challenge whites in many ways—even by using force—were called militants. They began to say that blacks should work alone to gain the rights they had not yet been given by the white world. They felt they would make faster gains if they worked with blacks only. Whites, they said, could never know the true feelings of black people. CORE and SNCC now have few white members. They have become more and more militant.

9 / *Much to Be Done.* The same studies that showed how much better the life of black people had become also showed how much more still had to be done. Let us compare averages for Afro-Americans with those for whites. Twice as many black people are out of work. Not as many black students go on to college. Some Negro workers earn less than whites doing the same kind of work. More black people live in real poverty; fewer have full-time jobs. In most

James Farmer became Assistant Secretary of the Department of Health, Education and Welfare in 1969—the first important post held by a black leader under President Nixon.

large cities, more black people live in slums. They have little hope that they will be able to leave them. The great dreams that began with the New Deal had not all come true more than twenty years later. Some Afro-Americans began to fear that the work of the older black organizations could not bring them full equality. They turned to militant groups who promised the better life that had not yet come.

10 / *The Muslims.* Islam is the religion taught by Mohammed that spread from Arabia in the years after 622. Those who follow its teachings are called Moslems or Muslims. They believe that there is one God, whom they call Allah. Today Islam is a leading religion in North Africa and in parts of Asia. In 1930 a Negro in Detroit, Michigan, named Wallace D. Fard began a group of black Muslims. They called themselves "the Nation of Islam in the wilderness of North America." Three years later a new leader, Elijah Muhammad, became the head of this group. It was soon known as the Black Muslims. We do not know how many thousands are in this movement. However, temples of Islam have been set up in city after city. Muslim groups have been very active.

Elijah Muhammad addresses a group of Black Muslims.

11 / *"Black Is Better."* A nationalist thinks and says that his people or his country is better than others. The Black Muslims are nationalists in this sense. They say black people are better than white people. Blacks, they say, should not mix with whites. Integration has long been the goal of most civil-rights groups. It is not a goal of black nationalists. Groups like the Black Muslims have asked that a part of the United States be given to black people so that a new black country can be formed. This kind of black nationalism is different from that of Marcus Garvey. Garvey hoped to return to Africa. However, Afro-Americans do not have their own country. How do they feel they should act toward white Americans? The Muslims tell them to have little to do with whites. They have set up their own businesses. They have begun private schools for Muslim children. They have taught that black people should learn to protect themselves—even if this means using guns. Members of Islam are told to follow strict rules. They must not smoke, drink or use drugs. They must remain very close to their families. They must work hard and save money. In many of their rules the Black Muslims are like the Puritans who first settled New England.

12 / *Malcolm X.* One of the best-known Muslims was a man called Malcolm X. His name had been Malcolm Little. Like many of those who joined the Muslims, he gave up his "slave name" and chose a new last name. Malcolm X believed in black nationalism. He spoke about moving to Africa. In 1964 he left the Muslims. He made trips to Moslem countries. When he returned he had become a different kind of leader. He set up a new group, the Organization of Afro-American Unity. He did not believe in nonviolence. "I'm for brotherhood for everybody," he said, but he believed that white people did not really want to help blacks. He said that "the blacks must take the lead in their own fight." For a few months he worked to build his new group. Then, in February, 1965, he was shot and killed by three men, two of them Black Muslims. Malcolm X had been moving toward some new paths in the search for a better life for his people. He died before he could do much. In the years since his death, Malcolm X has become a hero to large numbers of young black people.

13 / *Equal Rights for All.* Most of the black people in our country now live in the large cities. Their lives improve slowly. Full equality has not yet arrived. Much must still be done. In the South laws have been changed, but black Southerners are still poor people with few rights. The civil-rights groups we have read about in this chapter agree that black people must keep up the fight for equal rights. No one is certain that any one group has all the answers. How can the lives of more than twenty million Afro-Americans be improved? Black and white organizations, students, workers, the government and others—all try to find the answer. Millions of whites are still racists and fight equal rights. Millions more whites agree that black people have waited too long already. They work with black men and women to spread the rights and freedoms that should belong to all Americans.

The Honorable Elijah Muhammad

Malcolm X.

Understanding What You Have Read

I. REVIEWING WORD MEANINGS

Write the letter of the choice that best completes each statement.

1. A standard housing unit is one that is (a) much better than people need, (b) as good as people need, (c) worse than people need.

2. The director of an organization is (a) in charge of its activities, (b) the secret owner of the organization, (c) the person who takes orders from all other officials in the organization.

3. When you coordinate the work of two groups you (a) keep them apart, (b) make them fight one another, (c) get them to work together.

4. A militant is most ready to (a) take stronger action, (b) use only nonviolent methods, (c) accept whatever is happening.

5. A reactionary would be most interested in (a) going forward, (b) keeping things as they are, (c) going back to some older way of doing things.

6. A person who is a moderate hopes to make changes through (a) violence, (b) revolution, (c) changing laws and customs.

7. Muslims in the Afro-American world have followed the leadership of (a) Roy Innis, (b) Roy Wilkins, (c) Elijah Muhammad.

8. A black nationalist in the United States wants to (a) work closely with white reform groups, (b) keep blacks apart from whites, (c) bring all blacks back to the South.

9. A person with Puritan ideas (a) has nothing to do with other people, (b) tries to act like everyone else, (c) follows very strict rules of personal conduct.

10. If Afro-American groups reached unity, they would (a) be further apart, (b) work closely together, (c) remain separate.

II. CHECKING IMPORTANT FACTS

Write the answer to each of these questions. The number following each question tells you which paragraph contains the answer.

1. Where do most Afro-Americans live today? (2)
2. Of every hundred policemen in Washington, D.C., about how many are black? (2)
3. Who became the Executive Director of the N.A.A.C.P.? (4)
4. In what field of activity was A. Philip Randolph the best-known black American? (5)
5. What group was headed by James Farmer? (6)
6. What is the full name of the organization called SNICK? (7)
7. What group was begun by Wallace D. Fard? (10)
8. Why did Malcolm Little change his name to Malcolm X? (12)
9. How did Malcolm X die? (12)

10. How much has the life of black people in the South improved? (13)

III. FACT OR OPINION?

Write FACT if the sentence states a fact. Write OPINION if the sentence tells you what someone believes about some fact or problem.

1. By 1965 black workers had become secretaries and salespeople.
2. Atlanta, Georgia, began to hire black policemen.
3. Whitney Young, Jr., didn't work hard enough for black unity.
4. CORE was a better organization than SNCC.
5. Black labor leaders grew more important in the 1960's.
6. No civil-rights group should admit white members.
7. Stokely Carmichael said he did not believe in nonviolence.
8. Malcolm X was too militant.
9. Some groups have said that blacks are better than whites.
10. No man is truly free so long as anyone hates him.

IV. QUESTIONS TO DISCUSS

1. Malcolm X, in the months before his death, said he was ready to work with some white people. First, he said, they would have to give up their "whiteness." He meant by this that they would have to agree that all white people were really racists. Why did very few whites then join Malcolm X? Was he asking for more than white civil-rights workers should be expected to give? Why or why not?
2. Militants often call themselves revolutionaries. What can they mean by this? What great changes do they seek? How do they expect to make these changes?
3. With all these changes in the civil-rights movement, what organizations in your community are the most active and the most supported by black Americans? Why?

4. It has been said that the militants have received great publicity on television because their statements are so extreme. What does the word *extreme* mean? Is this the only reason for the public interest in militants?

V.   THINGS TO DO

1. Write a two-page report on the Black Muslims in America. The library may have books about them. Speak to your librarian about news-magazine articles on the Black Muslims during the 1960's.

2. The class can dramatize a meeting of a civil-rights organization. The group has black and white members. It is election time. The members discuss whether or not white members should be allowed to run for office. Try to express all points of view on this question. One student can act as chairman. Another should list the arguments of each side on the chalkboard.

TOWARD A BETTER LIFE

Introduction

This unit tells two stories at the same time. First it explains how some black Americans have become part of the country's cultural and sports life. Then it tells about the lasting problem that remains for most black people—poverty.

American culture, you will see, has been the work of many people. It has come from many lands. Afro-Americans have played an important part in its development. They brought new life to music and art. They became leading performers. They wrote plays and books of all kinds. At all times they had to fight a bitter and lasting Jim Crow. Slowly they won against it. They became leaders in the field of popular music. They wrote and played the best in jazz. They turned the ears of the country to folk music. They began to find better roles in motion pictures.

Great records were made in the world of sports. Slowly Jim Crow began to end there. You will learn how black boxers from Jack Johnson to Mohammed Ali have been most important in that sport. You will see how Jackie Robinson opened the door to Negro players in baseball. These players have been among the leaders of the game ever since. You will see that Afro-Americans have shown skill in every sport. They have risen to the highest ranks in such fields as chess, basketball, football, tennis and the Olympics.

In such ways, a few thousand black Americans were able to make good livings. But most black people still knew poverty. New laws gave more rights to all. These were civil rights, not economic rights. Such meetings as the March on Washington, and such drives as the one to gain voting rights in Selma, Alabama, did bring new laws for equal rights. Other laws were needed to attack poverty. This was still the great enemy. Housing was still a great need. Unit 8 explains some of the ways in which all levels of government are trying to end poverty.

Gwendolyn Brooks won
the Pulitzer Prize.

Chapter 31 | THE AFRO-AMERICAN IN OUR COUNTRY'S CULTURE

Let's Discover

1. How American culture is a mixture of many cultures from many lands.

2. What special contributions Afro-Americans have made to American culture.

358

Words to Know

literature All the writings of a country or of a certain time.
Black writers have added much to American literature.

background The events that came before.
The slaves had known much music in their African background.

xylophone A musical instrument made of wooden bars on a frame, played by striking it with wooden hammers.
Africans used a form of the xylophone hundreds of years ago.

complex Difficult to do or understand because it is very complicated.
Complex African music sometimes uses five different beats at the same time.

rhythm The pattern of beats followed in a piece of music.
Most of the early music of the Beatles used a four-beat rhythm.

sculptor An artist who cuts stone or wood, casts metal or uses materials like clay to form statues or other figures.
African sculptors showed man in different forms than European sculptors did.

tapestry A heavy cloth with designs or pictures woven into it.
The tapestry from Africa hung on the wall of the museum.

playwright A person who writes plays.
The novelist James Baldwin is also a playwright.

native A person born in a certain country.
Richard Wright was a native of the United States.

contribution Something added to the culture of a country.
Henry O. Tanner made great contributions to American painting.

1 / *What Do We Mean by "American Culture"?* Many peoples from other parts of the world have settled in the United States. Each group has come with its own art and music. First came the Europeans. The cultures of many groups and countries had been mixed in Europe to make what we call "Western culture." The people from each country brought ideas that were a little different. They were also much alike. They mixed here to form American culture. The English were most important. They ruled. Their ways were most followed. Americans spoke English. The kinds of art, literature and music that developed among white Americans were closest to those of the English settlers.

2 / *The African Background.* The slaves who were brought to the New World came from a part of the world that had its own forms of culture. They were different from Western forms. Western art copied life; that of Africa had other aims. African music used instruments and rhythms that were not used in Europe. Western poetry had become set in its form. That of Africa was closer to music. If the Africans had been able to develop their arts freely in the New World, they too would have entered into the mixture that became early American culture. Instead, they were slaves. They did not have their old instruments. They did not have their old tools. In time most of them lost the memory of their old culture. In much of what they did they had to copy the ideas and forms used by their masters. Their African past remained, but much of it was hidden; some of it was lost.

3 / *Music in Africa.* Most of the slaves had come from West Africa. We know that music was important there. Men used many instruments. They used groups of drums whose sounds were much like the xylophone. They had stringed instruments and wind instruments. They had long made music. They did not write this music, but played it and passed it on. Songs were most important. They might be sung with instruments or without them. Some were simple lullabies. Others, with complex rhythms, were hard to learn. This kind of music is still heard in Africa today. New instruments have been

African musicians play for a young dancer.

developed there. Many kinds of drums are used, often to provide the beat for dancers. There are new wind instruments. The music of Africa is still alive with feeling. Even African church music has its own forms.

4 / *Music—Friend of the Slave.* The slave ships had no room for musical instruments. They were left behind. Yet the kind of music the slaves had known remained in their minds. They sang and hummed it as they worked in the fields. White people thought little of this music at first. It was something the slaves did. They could not believe that these strange rhythms were part of an important culture. Their music was one of the few things the slaves could keep. They filled their bits of free time with it. When they could get an instrument of any kind, they cared for it and learned how to play it. They were self-taught musicians. They had no help from music teachers. As the years passed, the words and melodies of their old African music became less known. Afro-Americans began to build new forms. They took the music they heard the whites play and changed it. They used their experiences and feelings to build a new kind of American music. It has many names today, and it keeps growing. We speak of jazz, blues songs, spirituals, bop, rock and roll and soul rock. We hear Afro-Cuban, gospel, folk rock and other forms. White composers heard this music and made use of it. Anton Dvorak, Maurice Ravel, George Gershwin, Aaron Copland, Igor Stravinsky, Leonard Bernstein, Darius Milhaud—a long list of men in many lands used the Afro-American's rhythm and style as they wrote their music.

BEGINNING LINES OF SOME WORK SONGS

"Here comes the captain—Stand right steady.
Walking like Samson—Stand right steady."

. . . .

"Take this hammer—huh!
Take it to the captain—huh!
Tell him that I'm gone—huh!
Tell him that I'm gone—huh!"

. . . .

"Well she asked me—huh!
In the parlor—huh!
And she cooled me—huh!
With her new fan—huh!
And she whispered—huh!
To her mother—huh!
'Mama, how I love—huh!
That dark-eyed man'—huh!"

. . . .

"Jump down, turn around, pick a bale of cotton.
Jump down, turn around, pick a bale a day."

5 / *Religious and Work Songs.* The slaves soon became Christians. Most of the churches made use of music. This music changed when it was played and sung by blacks. Spirituals, with their many meanings, spread all over the world. These were often used in place of hymns. They began to sing work songs—much as groups in other parts of the world did when they had to work hard. These songs were made to fit the movement of a group of workers as they swung axes, pulled boats, used hoes

BEGINNING LINES OF SOME FAMOUS SPIRITUALS

"Sometimes I feel like a motherless child,
Sometimes I feel like a motherless child,
Sometimes I feel like a motherless child,
A long way from home."

. . . .

"No more auction block for me,
No more, no more,
No more auction block for me,
Many thousand gone."

. . . .

"Oh, nobody knows the troubles I've seen,
Nobody knows but Jesus."

. . . .

"Deep river, my home is over Jordan,
Deep river, Lord—I want to cross over
into camp ground."

. . . .

"Sit down, sinner!"
"I can't sit down!"

. . . .

'Cause I just got to heaven
An' I can't sit down!"

. . . .

"When the saints go marching in—
When the saints go marching in—
I want to be in that number—
When the saints go marching in."

or dug holes. The singing made the work seem a little easier. It made the day go a little faster. It might help a man forget how hard he had to work.

Beautifully decorated gourds and basket tray from Africa.

6 / African Art. Some parts of Africa had advanced forms of carving and sculpture. Men used wood, stone and ivory. The work they did was different from that done in Europe. With great skill they shaped works of art that followed their own forms. Craftsmen could be artists too. They worked with gold, silver, glass and clay. Today their work is found in museums all over the world. Slowly, people of the Western world have come to understand that the African art forms have great meaning and beauty. They have seen how other cultures show the human body. They have seen different ways of using the materials of art. Some white artists have learned from African forms. Pablo Picasso, Paul Klee and Henri Matisse were three of those who used both African and Western ideas in great works of art. Other artists are learning from beautifully carved African spoons and knives, carefully made pottery, woven mats, cloth and tapestries.

7 / Black Artists. For many years most whites could not accept the idea that black

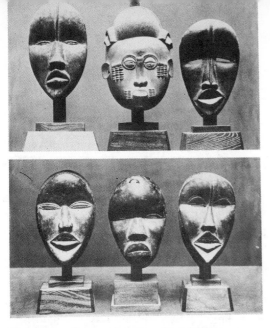

Carved wooden masks of ancient Africa.

men and women could produce works of art. Yet a few Afro-Americans did break through. Henry O. Tanner, who did much of his work in Paris, was one of the world's great artists in the 1890's. After he gained fame in Europe, his paintings were bought by many museums in this country. Many of them were on religious subjects. Tanner was not the first important black artist. In the 1830's Edmonia Lewis was well known as a sculptor. Her most famous work was a statue called *Forever Free*. She was later matched in fame by Meta Fuller, who studied in Paris at the same time as Tanner. Her greatest sculpture, *The Wretches,* showed how she cared for all suffering people.

8 / *More Leading Artists.* Other black artists have been leaders in their fields of work. Among them are Horace Pippin, Richmond Barthé, Jacob Lawrence, Charles White, Romare Bearden and Charles Alston. Pippin was one of the word's greatest self-taught painters. One of his best-known works is *John Brown Goes to His Hanging.* Richmond Barthé was the first black sculptor to be made a member of the

AFRO-AMERICAN INVENTORS HELPED MAKE LIFE BETTER FOR ALL

Inventors have done much to improve the way Americans live. Some of the most important improvements have been the work of black Americans. Elijah McCoy's invention of the lubricating cup meant that machines could be oiled while they were working. Lewis H. Latimer helped Alexander Graham Bell in his work on the telephone. He also worked with Thomas A. Edison on the electric light and other projects. Granville T. Woods invented a way for trains to send telegraph messages while they were moving. He sold some of his inventions to other men, among them Bell, Edison and Westinghouse. One of his important inventions was an air brake for trains that made railroads safer.

Jan Matzeliger, who died a poor man at the age of 36, sold his greatest invention for very little. It was a machine that made most of a shoe in one operation. The company that bought it became worth millions of dollars. Newspapers made Garret A. Morgan a hero when he rescued some men trapped in a tunnel below Lake Erie in 1916. He did it with the help of his new invention, a gas mask! Seven years later, when automobiles were becoming a problem in the cities, he invented the traffic light.

These and other Afro-American inventors have helped bring about our modern world.

artists. One of his best-known paintings is at Hampton Institute today. It tells the story of the Negro's part in American life. Romare Bearden's paintings were loved by President and Mrs. John F. Kennedy. They hung them in the White House. His work is also found in many museums. Charles Alston is an artist of many talents. His paintings have become well known. He has also designed public buildings. One of the best known of these is the Harriet Tubman Elementary School in New York City. These and many other black artists have made our life richer in two main ways. They have produced works of art that all can see and enjoy. They have also brought Afro-American history and daily life into their work so that all may understand them better.

9 / *Afro-Americans in the Theater*. No black man or woman appeared in the American theater until the 1800's. At that time a new kind of program became popular. It was called the minstrel show. White actors blackened their faces and sang and danced the way they thought black people did. These shows made use of the many prejudices of the time. They showed black men as foolish. It was not until the 1920's that plays were written in which black people were real men and women with real problems and real lives. The white playwright who was first to write about Afro-Americans was Eugene O'Neill. In 1924 his play *All God's Chillun Got Wings* opened with Paul Robeson, the great actor and singer, as its star. In 1930 Marc Connelly's play *The Green Pastures* opened with an all-black cast. It was a telling of the Bible story as seen by a group of Negroes. Its star,

Jacob Lawrence and Charles White, artists.

National Academy of Arts and Letters, the organization of the most honored artists in the United States. Jacob Lawrence, one of the best-known Afro-American painters, has painted many works that show life in the black slums. Charles White was one of the many artists to be aided by the Rosenwald Fund, set up by a Jewish family to aid young

The Negro Looks Ahead **by Richmond Barthé.**

Richard B. Harrison, won many awards for his role. Among other successful plays about black people were O'Neill's *Emperor Jones* and *Porgy* by DuBose Heyward. *Porgy* was later made into a "folk opera," *Porgy and Bess,* by George Gershwin. It has been one of the most loved musical works all over the world.

10 / *Plays by Black Writers.* New York City has been the center of play production in the United States. Only a few black playwrights have had their work presented there. Langston Hughes was one of the first. His plays and musical comedies were well received. Richard Wright's novel *Native Son*

**Paul Robeson as Othello,
one of his greatest roles.**

was a popular play. Perhaps the best-known play by a black writer is Lorraine Hansberry's *A Raisin in the Sun*. It is the story of a black family and its plans to move to a white neighborhood. Other black artists have also written plays. James Baldwin's *Blues for Mr. Charley* was an attack on racism. The term "Mr. Charley" is often used to mean a white man. The plays of Leroi Jones and Roi Ottley have made whites and blacks think deeply about their country's racial problems. Since 1960 a number of black theater groups have appeared. From their work may come many new plays to enrich the world's culture.

11 / *Afro-Americans in Our Literature*. We have learned about black poets and writers in the 1700's and 1800's. Their works added to American culture. The best-known books by black writers began to appear during the New Deal. One of the New Deal programs paid writers while they wrote. The first of the new Negro writers to have a large following, both black and white, was Richard Wright. His novel *Native Son* was one of the most widely read books of the 1940's. It was a tale of life in a black ghetto. It

GEORGE WASHINGTON CARVER, OUTSTANDING SCIENTIST

George Washington Carver was one of America's greatest agricultural scientists. Dr. Carver had been a slave. He became a teacher at the Negro college, Tuskegee Institute. There he tried to solve the great problem faced by southern farmers—the boll weevil. In the early 1900's this insect almost destroyed the South's cotton crop. What could a man grow besides cotton and still make a good living? Dr. Carver found new uses for peanuts, sweet potatoes and soy beans. From the peanut alone he developed paper, ink, meal, metal polish, linoleum, plastics and many more products! His experiments were so important he was asked to explain them before Congress. The Department of Agriculture published his ideas for farmers all over the world. Henry Ford, one of America's richest men, gave Dr. Carver a laboratory. Many leading world figures visited the scientist there.

George Washington Carver lived a long and productive life. When he died in 1943 he was buried next to his friend, Booker T. Washington. He left his life savings to the George Washington Carver Foundation, to continue his work of finding new products.

Carver teaching at Tuskeegee.

made him famous all over the world. The book became a play and then a motion picture in which Wright played the leading role. In a later book, *Black Boy,* Wright told of his life as a boy in Jim Crow Mississippi. Richard Wright began what can be called a "school" of black writing. Its members told what it meant to be a black person in a world run by whites. Others have been important in this kind of writing also.

Famed author Richard Wright.

Invisible Man by Ralph Ellison has been called one of the great novels of our time. It is the story of a Negro boy who comes to the North and tries to find meaning and dignity for himself. Gwendolyn Brooks, who won the Pulitzer Prize for poetry, wrote of the troubled lives of black people. One of her best-known poems tells of a young man who has died. It begins:

> He was born in Alabama,
> He was bred in Illinois,
> He was nothing but a plain black boy.

James Baldwin has lived largely in Europe. His novel *Go Tell It on the Mountain* shows the problems faced by black Americans today. One of his most important books was *The Fire Next Time*. In it he warned that blacks would grow more and more militant unless they soon gained equal rights. The evils of life in a slum were made clear in Claude Brown's *Manchild in the Promised Land*. It showed what life in Harlem could do to a person. This story was made more real by the study *Dark Ghetto* by Kenneth Clark. These and other works have shown that the problems of black people come largely from their long history of slavery and Jim Crow treatment.

12 / *The Growing Black Contribution.* We have only touched on all that black people have added to American culture. Why has so much of what they did been lost or forgotten? For more than 200 years most black people were slaves. Then, for the next 100 years, they had to fight for each new right in a Jim Crow world. They have made great contributions in that time. They will make ever greater ones as their rights and economic position improve.

James Baldwin (left), Ralph Ellison and playwright Leroi Jones.

Understanding What You Have Read

I. REVIEWING WORD MEANINGS

Write the letter of the choice that best explains the meaning of each word.

1. **literature** (a) Books and other writings. (b) Music and instruments. (c) Art and artists.
2. **background** (a) Things to come. (b) Things today. (c) Things of the past.
3. **xylophone** (a) Wood hitting wood. (b) Metal hitting metal. (c) Strings being plucked.
4. **complex** (a) Easy to understand. (b) Hard to understand. (c) Cannot be understood.
5. **rhythm** (a) Beat of the music. (b) Melody of the music. (c) Key of the music.
6. **sculptor** (a) Writes music. (b) Makes tools. (c) Makes statues.
7. **tapestry** (a) Kind of carpet. (b) Heavy cloth with designs woven into it. (c) Special cloth used in African clothing.
8. **playwright** (a) A good ball player. (b) Man who builds playgrounds. (c) One who writes plays.
9. **native** (a) I'm an immigrant! (b) I am moving to Africa! (c) I was born here!
10. **contribution** (a) An addition. (b) A subtraction. (c) A doubling.

II. PEOPLE AND CONTRIBUTIONS

Write the letter of the field in which each of the following made an important contribution. You can use the same field as many times as it is correct.

PERSON WHO CONTRIBUTED

1. Henry O. Tanner
2. Richard B. Harrison
3. Gwendolyn Brooks
4. Edmonia Lewis
5. Jacob Lawrence
6. Ralph Ellison
7. Granville T. Woods
8. Richmond Barthé
9. Lorraine Hansberry
10. George Washington Carver

FIELD OF CONTRIBUTION

a. painting
b. sculpture
c. theater

d. science and invention
e. literature

III. ANSWER EACH OF THESE QUESTIONS IN ONE OR TWO SENTENCES.

1. Why did English ideas about art, music and literature have the greatest effect on early American culture?
2. Why didn't the culture of West Africa continue to develop among the West Africans who came to the New World?
3. How was African music different from European music?
4. List and explain four kinds of music in the United States that were developed by Afro-Americans.
5. How are work songs different from other kinds of music?
6. Why have so many black American artists worked in Europe?
7. Who has been the best-known Negro painter in the United States?
8. Why have minstrel shows been given up by the American theater?
9. How have the plays of black playwrights been alike?
10. What have the books by the black authors discussed in Paragraph 11 tried to show about life in the United States?

IV. QUESTIONS TO DISCUSS

1. How did black Americans help shape American culture?
2. How has American popular music been shaped by Afro-American contributions? As part of this discussion, play examples of each kind of music discussed in Paragraphs 4 and 5.
3. How is music important in the lives of young people today?

V. THINGS TO DO

1. The people discussed in this chapter are only a sample of the
    many black artists and scientists. Here is a list of others, some
    just as important as those we have read about. Use your library
    to prepare a short report on one of the people listed below.

Painters	Sculptors	Inventors
Robert Bannister	William E. Artis	Andrew J. Beard
John Biggers	Sargent C. Johnson	Norbert Rillieux
Ernest Crichlow	Isaac Hathaway	Lewis Temple
Robert Duncanson	May Howard Jackson	
William Harper	Geraldine McCullough	
Hector Hill	Augusta Savage	
Hale Woodruff		

2. Here is a list of other Afro-Americans who have been important
    in literature. This list is not complete. It contains the names of
    men and women who have been concerned with topics impor-
    tant to the life of black America. Use your library to prepare a
    short report on one of the people listed below.

Arna Bontemps	William Melvin Kelley
William Stanley Braithwaite	John Oliver Killens
William Wells Brown	Alain Leroy Locke
Charles W. Chesnutt	J. Saunders Redding
Shirley Graham	Melvin B. Tolson
Zora Neale Hurston	Charles Wesley

3. Look in an index of magazine publishers at the public library
    to find out how many publications are devoted to Afro-Amer-
    ican studies. Try to get copies of some of these to show to the
    class.

Chapter 32 / MODERN AFRO-AMERICAN LEADERS IN THE PERFORMING ARTS

Let's Discover

1. How Afro-American performers have had to fight Jim Crow in the performing arts.
2. How black artists have been most important in popular music and are becoming important in the other performing arts.
3. How changes since the New Deal have helped open the field of entertainment.

Words to Know

composer
: A person who writes music.
William Grant Still and William L. Dawson were composers of music for orchestra.

conductor
: A person who leads an orchestra.
Dean Dixon has been an important conductor of leading symphony orchestras.

opera
: A play in which all or most of the speeches are sung, usually to music·played by an orchestra.
Leontyne Price is a famous soprano who sings opera.

metropolitan
: Of or part of a large city.
The Metropolitan Opera House is in New York City.

victorious
: Winning.
The play Purlie Victorious *is the story of how a group of black people win out against the white racist who owns the land they farm.*

clarinet
: One of the wood-wind musical instruments, using a reed in its mouthpiece to produce sound.
Jimmie Lunceford's band used the clarinet more than other bands had.

saxophone	A musical instrument similar to the clarinet, but with a larger and curved metal body and a deeper tone. *The saxophone has been most important as a jazz instrument.*
vibraphone	A musical instrument similar to the xylophone, but using electric power to keep or change the sounds it makes. *Lionel Hampton first introduced the vibraphone to large audiences.*
choral	Done by a chorus—a group of people trained to sing or speak together. *Hall Johnson arranged many songs for choral groups.*
ballet	A dance performed on a stage, usually by a group of dancers in costume, that often tells a story. *Arthur Mitchell gained fame as a ballet dancer.*

NOTE: The material in this chapter is not a complete study of Afro-American contributions to the performing arts. It can only present some selected parts of a story that could fill several books.

---

1 / *Kept Out.* We know that talent has nothing to do with skin color. Yet until recent years the arts have been part of the Jim Crow world. Afro-Americans have been kept out. Perhaps the men who ran show business feared some white people would not accept black artists outside the field of jazz. We know that groups in the South have often tried to keep blacks from performing. Remember how Marian Anderson could not sing at Constitution Hall in Washington. Roland Hayes was one of the great voices of his time. He did not become a member of an opera company. The change did not begin until the New Deal in the 1930's. Since then black artists have, one by one, broken through the Jim Crow wall. Before then few black people could make a living as performers, except in jazz.

2 / *In the World of Opera.* The most important opera group is New York's Metropolitan Opera Company. For years those who ran it would not use black artists. It was great news when Paul Robeson sang a single performance in *Emperor Jones*. Many years passed

before the first black artist was hired for regular work. Marian Anderson had been one of the country's great singers for more than twenty years. In 1955 she joined the "Met" as a star. Six years later Leontyne Price, one of the world's leading sopranos, began to sing with the same company. She had toured Europe with *Porgy and Bess*. She had also starred in concerts and on television. She was followed by other black artists, among them Shirley Verett and Martina Arroyo. The world of opera has at last accepted Negro talent.

3 / *Writing and Playing Music*. Those who write music are called composers. Those who lead the orchestras that play it are called conductors. Jim Crow lived in the concert world too. Many thousands of men and women played in orchestras; only a few were black. As late as 1965 there was only one symphony orchestra in the country in which a large number of black artists played. Yet orchestras, choral groups and concert artists did use the work of some black composers. They sang the songs written or arranged by men like Harry T. Burleigh, Hall Johnson and R. Nathaniel Dett. They played the music written by William Grant Still and William L. Dawson. In 1936 Still became the first Afro-American to conduct a leading symphony orchestra. Five years later Dean Dixon, at 26, was the first black man and the youngest man ever to lead the New York Philharmonic Orchestra. Since then a few more Negro conductors have appeared. One of them, Everett Lee, has done most of his work in Europe. Henry Lewis has gained great attention as the conductor of the New Jersey Symphony Orchestra. Many black artists have appeared with leading symphony groups. Among them have been Andre Watts and Philippa Schuyler at the piano, the singers William Warfield, Carol Brice and Dorothy Maynor and, in Europe, the American sopranos Mattiwilda Dobbs and Reri Grist.

Marian Anderson in *The Masked Ball* **at the Metropolitan Opera.**

Mahalia Jackson's gospel music is loved everywhere.

4 / *Singers.* Jazz was first made popular by black artists. The singers were well known. First there was Bessie Smith. She was followed by Billie Holiday, Lena Horne, Ella Fitzgerald and Sarah Vaughan. Each of these artists offered a style all her own. Billie Holiday, a leading blues singer, died in 1959. More than ten years later her records are still being sold. Ella Fitzgerald is the most popular woman among jazz musicians. She was discovered in 1934 by Chick Webb, master of rhythm and blues, during an amateur contest at Harlem's Apollo Theater. Lena Horne, whose beauty and talent have made her world famous, has also been a star of films and television. Sarah Vaughan first sang in a church group. She became a great star soon after she won a contest at the Apollo. Other stars have also risen to the top. Ethel Waters was a singer at first. She became one of the country's best-loved stars on Broadway and in films. Josephine Baker, a great jazz singer, went to Paris. She was soon France's favorite. Nat "King" Cole wrote popular music and sang as well. Todd Duncan, who for years played the lead role in *Porgy and Bess,* has also been a concert singer.

AN HONOR FOR WILLIAM L. DAWSON

William L. Dawson, the composer, served as director of music at Tuskegee Institute. After he retired he received an important assignment. He was sent by the United States State Department to train Spanish choral groups in the singing of Negro spirituals.

5 / *Folk Music.* The songs people have been singing for hundreds of years—songs whose composers often are not known—are called folk music. John and Alan Lomax of the Library of Congress gathered such songs in the New Deal days. One of the singers they found was Huddie Ledbetter, known as "Leadbelly." Leadbelly had spent years in jail. He knew hundreds of songs, and wrote many more. One of them, *Good Night Irene,* spread throughout the country. His singing led to a world-wide interest in American folk music. It grew with the work of a second artist, Josh White. Today folk music and music using its styles are loved by people of all ages. Mixed with it are gospel songs such as those sung by the late Mahalia Jackson. Her songs are loved in Europe as well as in this country. She has been chosen many times to sing at important national events. Her appearances on television have brought the beauty of gospel music to all people.

6 / *Dance Stars*. In the 1930's and 1940's, one of the best-known dancers in the United States was Bill Robinson. These were the years during which people loved tap dancing. All people knew the "million-dollar feet" of "Bojangles" Robinson. Once a year he danced his way along Broadway, from Times Square to Harlem, while thousands watched and cheered. Some black artists turned to other forms of dance. Katherine Dunham was one of those helped by the Rosenwald Fund. She went to the Caribbean and Brazil to study the life of their people. She then became a dancer and a writer of dances. Her dance group, with which she toured the United States and Europe, offered new rhythms based on African and other cultures. Pearl Primus also studied life in other lands. She was born in the West Indies. She studied dance in Africa and then set up a dance group that uses African dance forms. In the 1960's a new dance star appeared. His name was Arthur Mitchell. He is a star of the New York City Ballet Company. In 1968 he became a Broadway star as well.

7 / *In the Films*. Most silent films and then the "talkies" gave a false picture of life in this country. It was a world of whites, most of them middle class or rich. Black performers, when they were used, often had parts that made them seem weak or foolish. Bill Robinson appeared many times as a servant. Eddie Anderson played Jack Benny's valet. Louise Beavers, with her great talent, had to play servant roles. Rex Ingram, one of the best of all actors, played a genie, a giant or a trusted servant. Just a few times

Josephine Baker was France's favorite.

Ella Fitzgerald – America's most popular female jazz singer.

Nat "King" Cole wrote music and sang.

in his dozens of roles was he able to play a man whose part did not depend on his color. Hattie McDaniel was the first Afro-American to win the "Oscar" award. She won it for a role as a slave who loved her mistress. It seemed that the film industry was trying to keep its business in the South. It would not make many films that might attack race problems. From 1932 on, films were made that treated black Americans more fairly. Yet until after World War II such films were few and far between. In 1949 Stanley Kramer produced *Home of the Brave*. This story of a Negro soldier was a success. Other film companies began to show black people in better roles.

8 / New Stars of Theater and Films. For years the number of black artists in the theater and in films remained small. There were few roles for them. It was during the New Deal that changes began. One of the best plays of 1941, *Native Son,* starred a young man named Canada Lee. His success

pushed the door open a bit. Three years later the American Negro Theater in Harlem offered a play about a black family— the first of its kind. It was called *Anna Lucasta* and was later brought to Broadway. Its stars were Hilda Simms, Canada Lee and Frederick O'Neal. O'Neal, one of the country's best actors, was elected president of Actors Equity, which represents all actors in the American theater. He has long been a leader in the fight to end all race prejudice in the arts. Both Canada Lee and Frederick O'Neal did win a few important roles in films, some of them the kinds of parts only whites had been given before. One of Canada Lee's last roles before he died in 1951 was as the star of a film that attacked racism in South Africa. It was called *Cry, the Beloved Country,* from the book by a white South African, Alan Paton.

9 / New Cracks in the Wall. In the 1950's and 1960's some new black performers became important in films. They would only play roles that gave them proper dignity. These new stars also appeared on television and, often, in the theater. Ossie Davis and his wife Ruby Dee have visited schools many times as they try to teach young black people to have pride in themselves. Ossie Davis wrote and starred with his wife in the play *Purlie Victorious* (later a film too.) It was a humorous attack on white supremacy in the South. The best known of this new group of actors has been Sidney Poitier. Since 1950 he has played roles in which, as a black man, he fought prejudice in some form. In 1952 he played a soldier fighting in Korea.

Two years later he played a member of the Harlem Globetrotters. In another film he played a rebel leader in Africa. He gained fame in 1957 in a role as an escaped convict who learns and teaches the value of brotherhood. He played other important parts—as a doctor, as a social worker and, in 1964, as a traveling craftsman who helps a group of nuns build a chapel. For this role he won the Academy Award in 1965 as the best actor of the year. Harry Belafonte and Sammy Davis, Jr., men who can sing as well as act, have been in many films. They have also starred on television. There they have been joined by such artists as James Earl Jones, who won the award as Broadway's best actor of 1968-69, and Diahann Carroll, the first black actress to be the star of a weekly television series.

10 / *Changes on the TV Screen*. At first television had no jobs for black artists. It was an important step when the first Afro-Americans appeared "on screen." Mal Goode, Bob Teague, Joan Murray and others were seen on news and other programs. Many black comedians became well known. Godfrey Cambridge's jokes hit at race prejudice. He became a star in the theater and in films as well. Bill Cosby is known for his dry wit. He was the first black actor to star in a weekly television series. Flip Wilson, a gifted comedian, also starred on TV. Dick Gregory became well known for poking fun at race prejudice. Later he gave most of his time to civil-rights causes. Each year new black artists appear on television. Here too the old walls of Jim Crow have cracked and may in

Singer-actor Harry Belafonte.

time be destroyed completely.

11 / *Music for All*. Jazz music is one part of American culture that has been filled with black artists. In 1969 the great star was James Brown. His song "I'm Black and I'm Proud" was a great favorite. Singers and "groups" were most important by then. Young people everywhere listened to such stars as Wilson Pickett, Aretha Franklin, the Supremes and the Temptations. Yet few knew that these were part of a long list of black artists. Jazz has its history too. Let's look at some of the men who made jazz and other new kinds of music so important.

12 / *The Great Bands*. The music young

W. C. Handy, "Father of the Blues."

people love today began with the Dixieland music brought out of the South by men like the trumpet players W. C. Handy and Louis Armstrong. Handy, "Father of the Blues," wrote many songs. Armstrong sang and played the new music. Until the 1950's jazz depended on the work of big bands. The bands of men like Cab Calloway, singer, star of theater and films and a songwriter, spread jazz that involved the audience. Duke Ellington, composer and arranger, led a band that introduced many of the great names in jazz. Among them were Billy Stray-

Ray Charles sang with deep feeling.

horne, Johnny Hodges and Sy Oliver. One of his new ideas, which others soon copied, was to use the voice as an instrument. Ella Fitzgerald was one of those who sang with his band. Duke Ellington and the people who worked with him played their music around the world. There were many "big bands." Jimmie Lunceford, who could play many instruments, was one of the first to play the "smooth" sound. It made great use of clarinets and saxophones. Benny Goodman and Charlie Barnet, leading white jazz musicians, began to play in a style like Lunceford's. These two men did much to bring black artists into integrated bands. Billie Holiday became a star while singing with Benny Goodman. Lena Horne made her first records with Barnet's band. Charlie Christian, of Goodman's band, was the first star player of the electric guitar. William "Count" Basie and his band brought some important changes. His piano solos were featured, as well as those by other instruments. Rhythm was most important in his playing. People began to speak of "swing" music.

13 / *At the Piano.* New sounds began to be heard. The blind Ray Charles played the piano and sang with deep feeling. Art Tatum was for years one of the best pianists in the country. His complex music was copied by others. Both of these men followed the paths set by Thomas "Fats" Waller and Earl "Fatha" Hines. Hines had made the piano a key part of the band. Waller had shown new ways to use the piano and the organ in jazz. "Fats" Waller, who had played for Bessie Smith, also wrote some all-time "hit"

**Two of the most popular singers in America—
James Brown and Aretha Franklin.**

songs. The best known of these may be "Honeysuckle Rose." One of the piano stars, Teddy Wilson, had come from Texas. He brought the Dixieland spirit to life again. He made many recordings with small groups of black and white musicians.

14 / *New Sounds*. A number of black musicians made new instruments popular. Lionel Hampton was one of these. He and his band toured the world. He was featured playing the vibraphone. Sidney Bechet played the soprano saxophone so well it was soon used by bands and orchestras. Charlie Parker did the same with the alto saxophone and Coleman Hawkins with the tenor saxophone. Parker and Dizzy Gillespie began to write and play a new kind of music. They called it "bop." For years it was played all over the world. Then men like Miles Davis (trumpet) moved to newer sounds. They began to play what was called "cool" music. It led to the love for new sounds in music found in the 1960's.

15 / *Jazz Lives On*. Both black and white musicians play jazz today. It has become the favorite music of young people. Since 1960 new kinds of jazz have appeared. Men like John Coltrane and Ornette Coleman kept reaching for new sounds. James Brown's use of jazz and gospel music is one of the many new steps jazz may take. But the most popular music is that of the hundreds of small groups that appear each year. These groups try to build their own "sound." They are the latest stage in the long history of jazz begun by small groups of men from the South.

Understanding What You Have Read

I. REVIEWING WORD MEANINGS

Write the letter of the choice that best completes each statement.

1. A man who writes music is called (a) a conductor, (b) an arranger, (c) a composer.
2. A person who leads an orchestra is called (a) a conductor, (b) an arranger, (c) a composer.
3. An opera is (a) the music played by a symphony orchestra, (b) a play with music in which the speeches are sung, (c) a building in which musical plays are presented.
4. A metropolitan area would be a (a) small city, (b) middle-sized city, (c) large city.
5. A person is victorious when he (a) sings well, (b) wins, (c) plays an instrument.
6. A clarinet produces sound when air is blown through a (a) reed, (b) metal opening, (c) plastic slit.
7. A saxophone is most like a (a) trumpet, (b) violin, (c) clarinet.
8. The vibraphone is different from other instruments because it (a) can be used only with a band, (b) uses electricity, (c) is the largest of all wind instruments.
9. Choral music is written for (a) solo singers, (b) groups of people singing together, (c) small bands.
10. A person trained in ballet is a (a) solo musician, (b) singer, (c) dancer.

II. PEOPLE TO REMEMBER

Write the letter of the field in the performing arts in which each of the following people has been most important.

A. Opera, Concerts and Symphonic Music
B. Motion Pictures and Theater
C. Dance
D. Television
E. Folk Music and Choral Music
F. Jazz Music

1. William Grant Still
2. Billie Holiday
3. Katherine Dunham
4. Rex Ingram
5. Canada Lee
6. Cab Calloway
7. Ossie Davis
8. Leontyne Price
9. James Earl Jones
10. Sidney Bechet
11. Ella Fitzgerald
12. Arthur Mitchell
13. Mal Goode
14. Earl Hines
15. Bill Cosby
16. Charlie Parker
17. Shirley Verett
18. Hall Johnson
19. Sarah Vaughan
20. Huddie "Leadbelly" Ledbetter
21. Bill Robinson
22. Hattie McDaniel
23. Frederick O'Neal
24. Pearl Primus
25. Harry T. Burleigh
26. Sammy Davis, Jr.
27. Diahann Carroll
28. Bob Teague
29. Duke Ellington
30. William "Count" Basie
31. Thomas "Fats" Waller
32. James Brown
33. Lionel Hampton
34. Marian Anderson
35. Martina Arroyo
36. William L. Dawson
37. Josh White
38. Mahalia Jackson
39. Hilda Simms
40. W. C. Handy

III. DO YOU AGREE OR DISAGREE?

Write a sentence to explain why you agree or disagree with each of these statements. Discuss your answers in class.

1. Jazz was made popular only by black musicians.
2. Dizzy Gillespie played the same kind of music other jazz artists had been playing.
3. Opera has remained closed to Afro-American singers.
4. Ethel Waters was best known as a singer.
5. Negro dance groups have presented only African types of dance.
6. It makes little difference to other black people when a man like Sidney Poitier becomes a movie star.

7. The motion picture industry has never been willing to show Negroes as real people with real problems.

8. James Brown is the best singer of the new jazz and gospel music in the United States.

9. Black musicians still find it difficult to get jobs with symphony orchestras.

10. Folk music is sung chiefly by black artists.

IV. QUESTIONS TO DISCUSS

1. Why have black Americans been most important in the field of jazz?

2. What changes would you like to see in the direction of "equality" in the performing arts? Be specific. The class could list its suggested changes. Then discuss how these changes can be brought about.

3. The people discussed in this chapter are only a small number of those who have made important contributions. Discuss the chapter with adults you know. What people would they add to any part of the chapter? Why? Bring your findings to class. Try to reach an agreement in class on what makes a contribution important.

4. Are young people less interested in folk music than older people? Why is folk music still so popular in this modern age? Give examples to prove your point of view is correct.

5. Discuss a television play or motion picture you have seen in which black actors had important parts. Tell the story of the play or film. Do you feel the characters in it were real? Why or why not?

6. Prepare a class listing of the black people students agree are most important in the performing arts today. You should have at least three in each of these fields: Opera; Dance; Singers; Jazz Groups; Television Stars; Newscasters; Motion-Picture Stars; Folk Music; Concerts.

7. Hold a *Hall of Fame* election in class. Choose ten of the people discussed in this chapter. Students can do research in the library to find out more about their favorites. Prepare ballots after the reports have been given in class. Discuss the reasons why you want other students to vote for your candidate. Then number the ten people 1 to 10. Total the numbers for each name. The lowest total is the first in your "Top Ten."

8. This chapter has only mentioned the type of jazz called "rhythm and blues," or "R and B." When was it important? (Check in a history of jazz.) Who were some of the men who developed it? What happened to it? Why?

Joe Louis,
"The Brown Bomber."

Chapter 33 | AFRO-AMERICANS IN THE WORLD OF SPORTS

Let's Discover

1. How Jim Crow is coming to an end in most of the popular sports.
2. How black athletes have gained fame in sports.

Words to Know

organized
: In sports, the way teams are matched by some central group that sets up rules and plans contests. *Baseball is organized into leagues.*

heavyweight
: In boxing, a man who weighs more than 175 pounds. *Joe Louis was the heavyweight champion for almost twelve years.*

inferior
: Not as good as another. *Hitler said that black men were inferior to white Nazis.*

athlete
: A person who is skilled at a sport in which one needs strength, special ability and speed.
Bob Gibson is one of the best athletes in the history of baseball.

league
: A sports organization, as in baseball, basketball and football, made up of a group of teams who play each other.
The St. Louis Cardinals are in the National League.

tournament
: A series of contests in a sport in which a person or a team tries to make a better score than all others.
Arthur Ashe won the tennis tournament.

Globetrotters
: The all-Negro professional basketball team from New York City that has toured the world many times to show the skill of its players.
Wilt Chamberlain was once a member of the Harlem Globetrotters.

superstar
: In sports, a player, usually a professional, who is much better than other leading players.
Jackie Robinson was a superstar of baseball.

quarterback
: The player on a football team who usually calls the signals and receives the ball to start each play.
In 1968 only Denver among the professional football teams made use of a Negro quarterback.

Olympics
: A contest between athletes of all nations, held every four years, in which the winners in events receive medals while they and their country are honored.
Jesse Owens won four gold medals at the 1936 Olympics.

---

1 / *Organized Sports.* Most of today's sports grew popular after the Civil War. Professional baseball dates from the 1880's. The first World Series was played in 1903. Basketball was first played in 1891. The modern Olympic Games began five years after that. The first United States golf championship was held in 1900. Professional football

leagues began in 1933. These early years of sports were also the years during which Jim Crow was the custom or law in much of the country. It is no surprise that black athletes did not gain fame at that time. They were kept out of most organized sports.

2 / *Jack Johnson.* Boxing has been a popular sport for hundreds of years. In 1889 John L. Sullivan was the world champion. Since then the title has been held by the man who beat the last champion, or who won a boxing tournament when a champion retired. In 1908 Jack Johnson became the first Negro heavyweight champion. White people were amazed; many racists looked for some "great white hope"—a white man who could beat Johnson. Yet he held the title for almost seven years. He defended his title and won nine times. The story of Jack Johnson is told in the play *The Great White Hope*, in which James Earl Jones has starred on Broadway.

3 / *Joe Louis.* In 1935 a young boxer from Detroit knocked out Primo Carnera, at one time champion of the world. Joe Louis was from then on called "The Brown Bomber." Two years later he won the world title. Joe Louis was the champion for almost twelve years. He fought and won 25 more times. In all but four of these fights he knocked the other boxer out. Afro-Americans were proud of his success. One of his most-remembered fights was against the German Max Schmeling. Hitler and the Nazis then ruled Germany. They were saying that black people were an inferior race who could never do as well as Germans. Joe Louis knocked out Max Schmeling in the first round!

4 / *Other Champions.* Joe Louis had opened the door for black boxers. "Sugar" Ray Robinson was called the "sweetest fighter" of his time. He won world championships at two weights. Henry Armstrong did the same at three weights! Black boxers have again

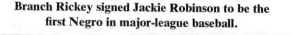

Branch Rickey signed Jackie Robinson to be the first Negro in major-league baseball.

One of the all-time best hitters – Willie Mays.

and again won the heavyweight title. Ezzard Charles, Joe Walcott, Floyd Patterson, Sonny Liston and Joe Frazier have been champions. In 1964 Cassius Clay gained the world title. As a Black Muslim he changed his name to Mohammed Ali. He was later drafted into the armed services. He refused to serve saying he was a minister of the Muslims. His case went to court and his title was taken away. In 1970 he was freed of all charges. He then fought against Joe Frazier in the world's greatest boxing match. Frazier then become champion.

5 / *First in Baseball.* The major leagues are made up of teams in all parts of the country. Those from the South, and some of those in the North, followed Jim Crow. They would not play a team that had a black ball player. None of these teams, then, had any Afro-American players. Negro leagues were set up. They had many great players. Satchel Paige was called the best pitcher in all of baseball. In one year he allowed only two runs in 93 innings! Yet until 1945 no black athlete could gain a place on a white team. In that year Branch Rickey, who ran the Brooklyn Dodgers, placed a young man named Jackie Robinson on his Montreal ball team. Two years later Rickey asked Robinson to join the Dodgers. Robinson had to make one promise. He had been chosen to prove that black ball players were good and should be on major-league teams. He promised not to strike back or to become angry, no matter what any players or fans said or did. He kept his promise. For the next nine years he was a "superstar." He was named the most valuable player; he helped his team

reach the World Series six times. Most important, he proved that baseball would be better if it gave up Jim Crow.

6 / *More Baseball Greats.* Jackie Robinson was the first to integrate baseball. Roy Campanella and Don Newcombe soon joined him on the Dodgers. Later Willie Mays, one of the best hitters of all time, was signed by the Giants. Henry (Hank) Aaron won prize after prize. This great hitter was with the Milwaukee Braves. He continued with the team when it moved to Atlanta. How great a change this was for a town that had once kept black people out of "white" elevators! Satchel Paige joined a major-league team too. One by one, others followed. Elston Howard joined the Yankees. Frank Robinson was with Cincinnati, Baltimore, and the Los Angeles Dodgers. He is the only man in baseball to win the most valuable player award in both major leagues! Team after team added black athletes. In 1968 pitcher Bob Gibson of the St. Louis Cardinals was one of the most famous names in baseball. In 1971 Vida Blue, a pitcher for the Oakland Athletics won the Cy Young award for being the best pitcher of the year.

7 / *The Sport Called Chess.* The game of chess is treated as a sport by the record books. It is played in chess clubs and at tournaments. Until the 1940's black chess players were kept by custom from most chess centers. The change began in New York City when two brothers named Dunn came from Ohio State to play in a college event. At first some schools would not play against black students. Then, with the help of those who ran the country's chess tournaments, the walls broke down. Chess clubs also accepted black players. The best chess players in the country are given the title of chess master. Walter Harris became the first Afro-American to gain this prize. Today most chess events in the United States are open to any player, black or white, who plays well enough to take part in them.

8 / *Basketball.* More people watch basketball games than any other sport. They see the games played by professionals. There they watch the superstars at work. In the 1920's and 1930's these teams did not admit black players. The first all-black team was the Renaissance club. It played with success against white professional teams during the several years it was active. Abe Saperstein set up a black team in New York City that he named the Harlem Globetrotters. Its athletes were soon known as the best in the world. But the Jim Crow walls remained. It was not until the 1950's that black players could join the professional teams. Wilt Chamberlain, who had been with the Globetrotters, became the world's leading player. In his first year he broke eight records! Ten years later he was still one of the great stars. Oscar Robertson set fourteen records while still in college. He has also been one of the game's highest scorers. Bill Russell was voted the most valuable player four times. He helped his team become world champions eight years in a row. In 1969 the best new player in the country was Lew Alcindor. The star center for the Milwaukee Bucks became a Muslim and was renamed Kareem Abdul-Jabbar.

9 / *Football.* Professional football teams have been slow to use black athletes. Perhaps this has been because most football players become well known through the games they play for their college teams. Until the last twenty years, only small numbers of Negroes went to college. Most of them were in Negro colleges. Football was important there but was not really reported in white-owned newspapers. From time to time a black football player did gain fame. Paul Robeson was one of these. But since 1950 the number of black students at the older white colleges has grown greatly. Some schools give scholarships for football. Jimmy Brown, one of the best athletes in the country, won one from Syracuse University. He later went into professional football. He won award after award. In 1966 he gave up the game to act in films. One of the black athletes who may be a football "great" in the years ahead is Gale Sayers. From 1968 on there was great pressure to make black players quarterbacks of important teams. Some college teams had already done this. Only Denver among the "pro" teams had made the breakthrough. Being a quarterback is much like being captain of a team,

A great basketball player—Kareem Abdul-Jabbar.

Arthur Ashe – one of the world's
finest tennis players.

for the quarterback makes important decisions for his team's next plays.

10 / *Tennis.* Few Afro-Americans play tennis. It is hard to find a court. Rackets and tennis balls are expensive. Most tennis events are run by private clubs. Even in the late 1960's many of these would not admit blacks. Yet a young lady from Harlem named Althea Gibson began to play "paddle tennis" on play streets. She liked it and moved on to real tennis. She was soon the champion of New York's public parks. In 1942 she joined an integrated club in New York. At that time separate tournaments were held for whites and blacks. Althea Gibson won the championship of all Negro girls. She became the star of her college team. She played more after college. In 1957 she won the world-famous tournament at Wimbledon, England. She was the best woman player in the world. Her success has led more and more young black people to play tennis.

11 / *Open Champion.* Arthur Ashe is one of the best tennis players in the world. He learned to play in a Virginia club set up by a group of Negroes who loved the game. In 1960 he won the national junior title. For the next few years he played against and beat most of the best players to be found. Then, in 1968, a new kind of event was held in New York City. It was called an "open" tournament. People thought Arthur Ashe would do well but did not think he could beat the professionals. He did, however. He became the first Open Tennis Champion of the United States! He had

gone even farther than Althea Gibson, for tennis has been a man's sport more than a woman's.

12 / *At the Olympics.* Early in the 1930's the name of a young black athlete began to appear in newspapers. It was Jesse Owens. Even while in high school he could run faster than any person of his age ever had. While at college he broke more records in one day than any man had ever done before. He made new world records in five track events! Owens was chosen to be part of the United States team at the 1936 Olympics in Germany. There he won four gold medals for first places in four events. This was more than any man had ever done before! Adolf Hitler, who ruled Germany, refused to present the medals. He could not admit that a black man could do better than a German. Since the success of Owens, more and more black athletes have been on our Olympic teams. The men who manage these teams are ending Jim Crow. Their chief goal is to build the best possible teams. A great athlete like Rafer Johnson or Milt Campbell makes all Americans proud when he wins the decathlon—a group of track and field contests that are the hardest test for any athlete. The same is true of Wilma Rudolph, who won three gold medals for her running at the Olympics in 1960. By 1968 black athletes were among the most important on the United States Olympic Team.

13 / *Playing Together.* This chapter has only touched on the work done by Afro-Americans in sports. Any young boy can name dozens more who are stars in one sport or another. Yet one point should be clear. Black athletes, playing on the same teams with whites, want to be measured by their ability. They have shown that Jim Crow makes no sense on any playing field.

THE DECATHLON

The decathlon is considered the most difficult test of the skill of any athlete. He must compete with others in ten events. They are:

1. 100-meter dash	6. discus throw
2. 400-meter run	7. shot put
3. 1,500-meter run	8. pole vault
4. 110-meter high hurdles	9. high jump
5. javelin throw	10. broad jump

Points are awarded in each event. The athlete with the highest total score is declared the winner of the decathlon. He does not have to win every event, but must make the highest score for all ten combined.

Jesse Owens won four gold medals at the 1936 Olympics.

Understanding What You Have Read

I. REVIEWING WORD MEANINGS

Write the letter of the choice that best completes each statement.

1. When something is organized it is (a) left alone, (b) planned, (c) closed.

2. A heavyweight is (a) a man weighing 175 pounds or more, (b) something too heavy for anyone to carry, (c) any weight made of lead or iron.

3. If you are inferior to someone else you are (a) just as good, (b) better, (c) not as good.
4. An athlete does well at (a) sports, (b) organizing, (c) acting.
5. A major league is made up of (a) teams of the best players, (b) teams whose players say they are good, (c) teams whose owners can build big ball parks.
6. A tournament is a kind of (a) defeat, (b) champion, (c) contest.
7. The Globetrotters are called by that name because (a) basketball is round like a globe, (b) they play all over the world, (c) they run while they play.
8. A man who is a superstar is (a) as good as other players, (b) better than other players, (c) not as good as other players.
9. The quarterback is important in (a) baseball, (b) basketball, (c) football.
10. The Olympic Games are held every (a) year, (b) two years, (c) four years.

II. SOME OF THE GREAT STARS

Write the letter of the sport in which each of these athletes has been important.

A. Tennis   D. Boxing
B. Football   E. Olympics (track and field)
C. Baseball   F. Basketball

1. Rafer Johnson
2. Jimmy Brown
3. Jack Johnson
4. Henry Aaron
5. Willie Mays
6. Arthur Ashe
7. Jesse Owens
8. Wilma Rudolph
9. Jackie Robinson
10. Mohammed Ali
11. Joe Louis
12. Frank Robinson
13. Wilt Chamberlain
14. Kareem Abdul-Jabbar
15. Althea Gibson
16. Floyd Patterson
17. Roy Campanella
18. Oscar Robertson
19. Paul Robeson
20. Milt Campbell

III. ANSWER EACH QUESTION IN ONE OR TWO SENTENCES.

1. When did most of our organized sports become popular?
2. What kind of people wanted a "great white hope" to defeat Jack Johnson?
3. Why was Joe Louis called a "knockout king"?
4. How did Cassius Clay (Mohammed Ali) lose his title?
5. Why didn't Satchel Paige, the "best pitcher in the world," play for a major league team before 1948?
6. How did Jackie Robinson help open the way for other black baseball players in the big leagues?
7. Why weren't the Harlem Globetrotters able to play in the same league with the leading white professional teams?
8. How did Althea Gibson learn tennis?
9. What made Jesse Owens so well known at the 1936 Olympics?
10. How do black athletes want to be judged in sports?

IV. QUESTIONS TO DISCUSS

1. *Be a Better Expert!* Has this chapter told about the player or players in baseball, basketball or football who you think are the best? You will need a sports record book to help you as your class discusses the superstars of today in each of these sports. Which of these are Afro-Americans?
2. *In the Boxing World.* Many black boxers have been important. Discuss some of them. You should first make clear the different weights at which men fight—flyweight, bantamweight, featherweight, lightweight, welterweight, middleweight, light heavyweight and heavyweight. Check newspapers for pictures and stories of some who are professional fighters. Why has boxing remained so popular? Why do some people want it ended?
3. Why has it been important to Afro-Americans when a black athlete became a star?
4. What sports still bar Negroes? Why are they kept from these sports? It has been said that there are some sports that are

closed to all but rich people—just because you must spend so much money to enter the sports. List some of these. How important is it that these sports be open to all?

5. What has happened to the Negro baseball leagues since the major leagues began to open the door to black athletes? Check at the library. Explain your answer. Discuss the reasons for what you have found.

6. Suppose the best black football players were all on one team. Would you favor setting up such a team? Why or why not? Would you then favor breaking up the Harlem Globetrotters and the placing of its players on major-league basketball teams? Why or why not? Discuss the same question in baseball.

Chapter 34 / NEW LAWS FOR EQUALITY

Let's Discover

1. How the rules of the United States Senate long prevented the passage of civil-rights laws by Congress.
2. How new laws between 1957 and 1965 put the power of the Federal government behind equal rights for all.
3. What changes were made in American life by the Civil Rights Act of 1964.

Words to Know

veto
: Refusing to approve something, usually in government, as when the President uses his power to keep a bill from becoming law.
The President thought the new bill was unconstitutional, so he decided to use his veto against it.

filibuster
: Keeping a bill from being passed in a legislature by making long speeches or speaking about other things.
A group of Senators could defeat a civil-rights bill through a filibuster.

conservative
: In a legislature, being against laws that will result in changes or reforms.
Conservative members of the Senate did not favor new civil-rights laws.

memorial
: Something meant to remind people of some past event or person who has died.
The Lincoln Memorial is a building in Washington that reminds us of the life and ideals of President Abraham Lincoln.

character
: The special qualities of a person by which other people judge him.

He wanted his children to be judged for their character rather than for the color of their skin.

commission
: A group of people chosen for some special activity in the government.

The Civil Rights Commission tries to help people gain the rights that every American should have.

relations
: The dealings between groups of people.

The Community Relations Service tries to help solve problems between blacks and whites in all parts of the country.

trooper
: A policeman working for a state government.

Alabama state troopers attacked the peaceful marchers who were trying to walk from Selma to Montgomery.

insure
: To make certain.

The right to vote could not be insured unless local election officials registered all voters.

denied
: Not given.

The right to vote was long denied to Afro-Americans in the South.

---

1 / *Passing a Law.* We have spoken many times in this book of the need to pass laws to give all people fair and equal treatment. But what does "passing a law" mean? What happens after a law is passed? How can it then change the way people live? To understand the meaning of "change through law" we must first know how laws are passed and then enforced.

2 / *In the Legislature.* Let us see how laws are passed by Congress. It takes time to pass a law. First it must be prepared by some member of the Congress. The new law, or bill, is sent to a committee of the house of Congress in which it has been introduced. This can be the House of Representatives or the Senate. The committee studies the bill. It may hold public hearings on the bill. There people can speak for or against it. If the committee then agrees that the bill would be a good law, they report on it to their house of Congress. Members discuss the bill. They then vote. If they vote for the

bill, it is sent to the other house. Again it is studied by a committee; more hearings may be held. Finally a vote is taken. Suppose both houses of Congress have voted for the bill. It is not a law until the President signs it. If he feels it is not a good bill, he can refuse to sign it and send it back to Congress with his reasons for doing so. This is called a veto. Then it does not become a law unless two-thirds of the members of both houses vote for it, over the President's veto.

3 / *The Filibuster.* One great problem has faced members of the Congress who have worked for civil-rights laws. In the Senate, members may talk as long as they wish on any subject. A group of them can speak on and on against some law they do not want. There are 100 members in the Senate. A group of twenty or more of them can stop all business there by talking and talking. They can take turns day and night. In the end, with other work that has to be done, the other members of the Senate may give in. They may agree not to bring up the civil-rights law. This endless talking is called a *filibuster.* It has been used many times to defeat civil-rights laws. Today, new Senate rules make it possible to stop a filibuster if two-thirds of the members agree. They have done this only a few times. They have usually felt that the right to speak is so important it should almost never be limited.

4 / *Getting Needed Laws Passed.* Once a law has been passed, it must be enforced. This is the task of the President. If he does not do this part of his job, then the law

President Eisenhower asked for a new civil-rights law.

has no real meaning. It does not change life in the country. Presidents after Reconstruction had done little to make civil-rights laws work. The change began with Franklin D. Roosevelt. It grew with Harry S Truman. New laws were needed. Truman could not get Congress to pass them. The House might be ready; the Senate, blocked by the filibuster, was not. A group of conservative Senators from the North joined with those from the South to block new civil-rights laws.

5 / *The Civil Rights Act of 1957.* In 1957 President Eisenhower asked for a new law on civil rights. This time the men who led the Senate agreed that the law had to be passed. It was called the Civil Rights Act. Under it Federal power would be used to improve the rights of all. The law attacked

Leaders of the March on Washington met with President Kennedy. Among them were lawyer, Floyd McKissick, Whitney Young (Urban League), Martin Luther King (S.C.L.C.), Rabbi Joachim Prinz (American Jewish Congress), A. Philip Randolph (AFL-CIO), Walter Reuther (United Auto Workers) and Roy Wilkins (N.A.A.C.P.).

the great problem of getting the right to vote in the South. The Federal government could bring a court case against anyone who tried to deny a person his right to vote. The law also set up a United States Commission on Civil Rights. Its job was to study all cases where a person did not receive "equal protection of the laws." A second law passed in 1960 added to the powers of the Commission. By 1962 the government had brought more than thirty cases to court to protect the right of black citizens to vote in five Southern states. For the first time since Reconstruction, Congress and the President were acting to improve civil rights! But the white racists of the South had organized. They saw to it that progress was slow.

6 / *The March on Washington.* The year 1963 may be remembered as the year of the "Negro revolt." There were peaceful demonstrations all over the country. They were held even where police used great force to try to stop them. Television was by then in tens of millions of homes. People saw what was happening. They saw that stronger laws were needed. In August, 1963, more than 200,000 people—many of them white—gathered at the Lincoln Memorial in Washington. Their meeting was the largest demonstration of its kind ever held in the United States. They called it the March on Washington. It had been planned by A. Philip Randolph, Bayard Rustin and other black and white civil-rights leaders. Randolph was

". . . make justice a reality for all of God's children."

then 75 years old. He had brought together the N.A.A.C.P., the National Urban League, the S.C.L.C., CORE, the United Auto Workers, SNCC, the American Jewish Congress and hundreds of other groups. They gathered to make a peaceful plea for equal rights and justice. Millions watched on television as speakers called for "freedom now."

7 / "I Have a Dream." The last speech was made by the Reverend Dr. Martin Luther King, Jr. In it he spoke of Negro hopes to share in the country's dream of equal rights. He said: "Now is the time to make real the promises of democracy. . . . Now is the time to make justice a reality for all of God's children." He pointed out that the road to freedom had not been easy. Yet he saw hope. He had a dream that the country would make all people equal under law. One of his closing paragraphs reached the hearts of millions: "I have a dream that my four little children will one day live in a nation where they will not be judged by the color of their skin, but by the content of their character."

8 / John F. Kennedy and Civil Rights. Even before the March on Washington, President Kennedy had asked for a new civil-rights law. He had said: "Our country . . . for all its boasts, will not be fully free until all its citizens are free. . . . Now the time has come for the nation to fulfill its promises. . . . It is a time to act in Congress, in your state and local legislative body and, above all, in all of our daily lives." The day after this speech, Medgar Evers was killed in Mississippi. In September, a few weeks after the March on Washington, "Birmingham Sunday" saw the bombing of a Negro church with the murder of four of the children in it. The racists would not give up. Then, on November 22, 1963, President Kennedy was killed. Violence seemed to rule. For many black Americans it seemed that the death of their President would mean the end of any chance for a strong civil-rights law.

Medgar Evers was killed in Mississippi.

9 / *Lyndon Johnson and Civil Rights*. Lyndon B. Johnson became President. He spoke to the country about the need for new laws. He made it clear that he wanted Congress to pass a civil-rights bill. The House passed one. In June the Senate also approved the Civil Rights Act of 1964, 73 in favor and 27 against. President Johnson signed it. He had helped change the way Afro-Americans would be treated in the whole country, and chiefly in the South.

10 / *The Civil Rights Act of 1964*. Let us look at what each part of this law said. Each part is called a Title.

Title One—Voting. The law set up rules to make it harder for officials in the South to keep black people from voting. Literacy tests had to be written. Blacks and whites had to be given the same tests. Any man or woman who had finished the sixth grade did not have to take a test.

Title Two. This part of the law was quickly challenged by people in the South. The Supreme Court ruled that Title Two was in keeping with the Constitution and would have to be obeyed. It ordered an end to discrimination in such public places as hotels, motels, restaurants and theaters. This could lead to an end to "White Only" Jim Crow customs.

Title Three. Under this part of the law black Americans had to be treated the same as whites in all public parks, swimming pools, beaches and stadiums.

Title Four—Public Schools. The government would help all school districts take steps to desegregate. As in the other parts of the law, the Attorney General could use the courts to make sure that this title was obeyed.

Title Five. The Civil Rights Commission would be continued. People who felt their civil rights were being taken away could ask this group for help.

Title Six—Aid. There are hundreds of state and local aid programs helped by Federal money. There was to be no discrimination because of race in any of them. If it was found, then the money would no longer be given.

Title Seven. Businessmen and unions could not discriminate against any race. Today this part of the law can be used when there are 25 or more workers in a business or a union group.

Title Eight. The government is to keep records of how many blacks and whites can and do vote. This means that it can act quickly when some place in the South does not allow its black citizens to vote.

Title Nine—Courts. One of the old sayings in law has been, "Justice delayed is justice denied." Most of the Federal judges in the South were Southerners. Some of them had not been making decisions in civil-rights cases. Instead, they sent them back to state or local courts to be "reviewed." This was a way to delay justice. Title Nine allowed higher Federal courts to order the lower courts to decide such cases.

Title Ten. This part of the law set up a Community Relations Service. Its job would be to try to settle racial problems at the local level. In hundreds of cases, its work has helped keep small problems from growing large.

Title Eleven—Other Rights. The law was new in so many ways that there would surely be court cases as it was enforced. This title promised a jury trial to those who were punished by judges for not obeying the law. It also promised not to upset state laws that gave the same rights that the law promised. Finally, it said that the courts would have to judge the law one title at a time. If any title was found not to be allowed by the Constitution, then only that title would end.

11 / *A Time of Testing.* President Johnson

President Johnson signs the Civil Rights Act of 1964.

spoke to the country when he signed the new Civil Rights Act. He said that "Americans of every race and color have worked to build a nation of widening opportunities. Now, (we have) been called on to continue the . . . search for justice within our own borders. . . . This Civil Rights Act is a challenge to all of us to go to work in our communities and our states, in our homes and in our hearts to (end) injustice in our beloved country . . . we have come now to a time of testing. We must not fail. . . ." In the election of 1964, Lyndon Johnson favored the Civil Rights Act and asked for more laws for equal rights. Senator Barry Goldwater, who ran against him, had voted against the Civil Rights Act. He lost. Voting records

The march to Selma, Alabama.

show that most Afro-Americans voted for Johnson.

12 / *Trying to Vote.* Many officials in the South did not obey the voting rules in the Civil Rights Act. So long as black people could not vote, the rest of the law would mean little. Selma, Alabama, was a town where black voters were still not allowed to register. In 1965 thousands of people from the North poured into Selma to join in a great protest. The sheriff jailed 2,000 of them. Dr. Martin Luther King then called for a march to Montgomery, the state capital. Governor Wallace ordered the marchers not to leave Selma. They did not obey him. On March 7, a Sunday, state troopers attacked them with whips, tear gas and clubs. The country watched on television. More people rushed to Selma to join the march. Two weeks later the march was held. Under the protection of the United States Army, 20,000 people reached Montgomery on the road from Selma. That night a white woman civil-rights worker was murdered in her car on the way back to Selma.

13 / *The Voting Rights Act of 1965.* The President then spoke to all the people. He asked for a law to make certain that all citizens would be able to vote. "I speak tonight for the dignity of man . . . should we defeat every enemy, and should we double our wealth and conquer the stars, and still be unequal to this issue, then we shall have failed as a people and as a nation. . . . There is no Negro problem. There is no Southern problem. There is no Northern problem. There is only an American problem. . . . No law that we now have on the books . . . can

insure the right to vote when local officials are determined to deny it." Under the new law, he told the country, voters could be registered by Federal officials. "What happened in Selma is part of a far larger movement which reaches into every section and state of America. It is the effort of American Negroes to secure for themselves the full blessings of American life. Their cause must be our cause too. . . . And we shall overcome. . . ." Congress then passed the law. The President signed it. What could be a killing blow had been struck at Jim Crow. It could mean the end, in the years ahead, of laws and customs directed against black Americans.

Understanding What You Have Read

I. REVIEWING WORD MEANINGS

Write the letter of the choice that best explains the meaning of each word.

1. **veto** (a) Sign the bill into law. (b) Keep the bill from becoming a law. (c) Write a new bill.
2. **filibuster** (a) Talk it to death! (b) Vote against it! (c) Vote for it!
3. **conservative** (a) Let's make changes! (b) Take away all rights! (c) Keep things as they are!
4. **memorial** (a) Let's meet to pass better laws! (b) This will help us remember how great he was! (c) Let's try to forget it!
5. **character** (a) This is the kind of person I am. (b) This is what I hope to become. (c) This is what I look like.
6. **commission** (a) We have a special job to do! (b) We try to make peaceful changes! (c) We work in secret for you!
7. **relations** (a) My group works all alone. (b) My group works with other groups. (c) My group has ended its work.
8. **trooper** (a) City police. (b) Federal police. (c) State police.
9. **insure** (a) Maybe it will happen. (b) I'm certain it will happen. (c) Maybe it will happen and maybe it won't.
10. **denied** (a) I give it to you! (b) You may lose it! (c) You can't have it!

II.   UNDERSTANDING A LAW

Write a sentence to explain the meaning of each of these phrases. The number following the phrase tells you what title of the Civil Rights Act of 1964 covers it.

1. Written literacy tests (1)
2. Public places (2)
3. Public parks and stadiums (3)
4. School district (4)
5. Civil Rights Commission (5)
6. Aid programs (6)
7. "Against any race" (7)
8. Voting records (8)
9. Justice delayed (9)
10. The local level (10)

III.   CHECKING THE MAIN IDEA

Write the letter of the title that best states what each paragraph contains.

1. The best title for Paragraph 2 is
   a. How Laws Are Changed.
   b. How Laws Are Passed.
   c. The Power of the President.
2. The best title for Paragraph 6 is
   a. Success for A. Philip Randolph.
   b. The Television Meeting.
   c. Meeting to Demand Justice.
3. The best title for Paragraph 8 is
   a. Failing Hopes in 1963.
   b. A Memorial for John F. Kennedy.
   c. Death in Mississippi and Alabama.
4. The best title for Paragraph 11 is
   a. The Election of 1964.

b. Progress in 1964.

c. Voting for Civil Rights.

5. The best title for Paragraph 13 is

a. Voting for All.

b. The Southern Problem.

c. The Blessings of American Life.

IV. ANSWER EACH OF THESE QUESTIONS IN A SHORT
SENTENCE.

1. In what part of Congress has the filibuster been a problem?

2. In what state is the town of Selma?

3. Who was governor of Alabama at the time of the march to
Montgomery?

4. Who became President in 1963?

5. In what year was the Civil Rights Commission set up?

6. Why was the March on Washington important?

7. How much education must a person have to become a voter
without taking a literacy test?

8. Why is a jury trial an important right?

9. Why did most black voters favor Johnson in 1964?

10. How did President Johnson make the Montgomery march
possible?

V. THOUGHTS TO DISCUSS

Discuss the meaning of each of these statements made by leading Americans. Check the meaning of any words or phrases new to you. Explain as well how each of these statements helps you understand the content of this chapter. Do you agree or disagree with the statement? Why?

1. "We have talked long enough in this country about equal rights.
We have talked for 100 years or more. It is time NOW to write
the next chapter—and to write it in the books of law."

Lyndon B. Johnson, 1963

2. "From the time Negro Americans leave home in the morning, en route to school or to work, to shopping or to visiting, until they return home at night, humiliation stalks them. Public transportation, eating establishments, hotels, lodging houses . . . and other places and services catering to the general public offer them differentiated service or none at all."

Roy Wilkins,

Executive Secretary of N.A.A.C.P., 1963

3. ". . . a jealous care of the right of election by the people—a mild and safe corrective of abuses. . . ."

Thomas Jefferson, 1801

4. "The struggle of today is not altogether for today—it is for a vast future also."

Abraham Lincoln, 1861

5. "I ask you to look into your hearts—not in search of charity, for the Negro neither wants nor needs condescension, but for the one plain, proud and priceless quality that unites us all as Americans: a sense of justice. In this year of the Emancipation Centennial, justice requires us to insure the blessings of liberty for all Americans and their posterity—not merely for reasons of economic efficiency, world diplomacy and domestic tranquility, but, above all, because it is right."

John F. Kennedy, 1963

6. "One aspect of the civil-rights struggle that receives little attention is the contribution it makes to the whole society. The Negro in winning rights for himself produces substantial benefits for the nation. Just as a doctor will occasionally reopen a wound because a dangerous infection hovers beneath the half-healed surface, the revolution for human rights is opening up unhealthy areas in American life and permitting a new and wholesome healing to take place. Eventually the civil-rights movement will have . . . enlarged the concept of brotherhood to a vision of total interrelatedness. . . ."

Martin Luther King, Jr., 1963

Chapter 35 / THE WAR ON POVERTY

Let's Discover

1. The problems of poverty.
2. Why housing is a special problem.
3. How local, state and Federal groups are trying to solve some of the problems of poverty.

Words to Know

urban renewal Planned rebuilding of large parts of a city, usually to end slums or improve neighborhoods.
Under urban-renewal plans, housing projects have been built and small parks added to neighborhoods.

gouging Charging too high a price.

The mule-drawn wagon, symbol of the Poor People's March.

People speak of "rent gouging" when they see landlords charging high rents for slum apartments.

environment
The conditions of living for a person, including the neighborhood in which he lives.
A slum environment limits the way a person can develop.

program
A plan for doing something.
Each city works out the aid programs its people need.

guidance
Advice or assistance to help solve a problem.
Some families need guidance in spending their money wisely.

corps
A group of people who work together in a special program.
The Job Corps is a training program to help young people develop skills.

impact
The shock of hitting at a thing or problem with great force.
The Special Impact program puts people to work at once in order to solve their economic problems, rather than trying to do a little at a time.

mainstream
The direction of life in a country that includes most people.
To join the mainstream of American life, the poor need better jobs, housing and education.

resurrection
Bringing back to life.
The War on Poverty caused a resurrection of the hopes of many poor people.

guaranteed annual income
A plan under which each family in the United States would receive every year, through earnings or government aid, enough money to make a living at a level above poverty.
The guaranteed annual income would be paid for chiefly by Federal funds.

A huge housing project in New York City.

1 / *Being Poor*. We live in the richest country in the world. Yet millions of our people live in deep poverty. They live in crowded city slums. They live in rural "pockets of poverty," their homes old and in need of repair. Poverty means a long list of "can'ts." Poor people can't buy the kind and amounts of food that will keep them healthy. They can't buy the clothing they need. They can't pay for the doctors they need. A family can't have its mother at home, for both father and mother must work to make even a poor living. Boys and girls in these families can't escape from poverty; young people often have to leave school and go to work to help their families.

2 / *Living in Slums*. A slum is the most crowded, run-down part of a town or city. There is much disease and crime. Houses are not in good repair. Rats may run through the buildings. Paint cracks and peels from the walls. Roaches move freely through rotting floors and ceilings. Plumbing and heating are often out of order. Apartments are crowded; rooms are small, yet three or four people may have to share each room. People who have to live in this way may tend to be less peaceful than others, for they are probably less happy. Children often grow up seeing violence in many forms. Some grow up with little hope for the future. They may see no way to better their lives. Most people live in slums because they are poor. Others are there because of discrimination. They could find no other place in which to live.

3 / *Better Housing*. Some cities have tried to do away with their slums. They repair or rebuild the worst housing. The improvement of housing in a city is part of "urban renewal." Public housing gets rid of many slum buildings. Yet it does not always end a slum. A slum is crowded. A large number of people must be placed in public housing. Today, with state and Federal aid, more and more people of the big-city slums are being moved into giant housing projects. This means that tall apartment houses are often built. Some of them become slums again—or new ghettos filled with poor people.

4 / *Federal Aid*. Congress has passed laws to help build public housing. Robert Weaver,

Former Secretary of HUD Robert Weaver.

an early member of the "Black Cabinet," was our first Secretary of Housing and Urban Development. He has led the work of the government in these fields. He has tried to get cities to build small units of public housing. He believes it is better to have small apartment houses in many parts of a city than many large buildings in one neighborhood. This gives the poor a chance to be part of the city as a whole instead of having to remain in a slum. He has also tried to have private homes built for the poor. They would rent these homes but pay only as much as they could afford. The government would pay the rest of the cost. Dr. Weaver has pointed out that at least thirty to forty million people live in real poverty! Perhaps twenty million of these are in the cities. At least half of the poor in the cities are black. Their need for better housing grows stronger each year.

5 / *Open Housing.* Our cities have long had discrimination in housing against Afro-Americans and other minorities. In most of the country, neighborhoods tend to be segregated. A black person has fewer choices in housing than a white person. In 1947 the Supreme Court ended racial discrimination clauses in housing contracts. Since then some states have passed "fair housing" laws. They make it illegal to discriminate when a home is sold or rented. It is not easy to enforce such laws. Civil-rights groups have worked for "open housing." This means that a person can buy or rent wherever he wishes. They have also tried to end "rent gouging." This is charging higher rent for an apartment than it is worth. Some slum apartments have high rents even though they are not kept in good repair. In 1963 black people in New York City began to hold "rent strikes." They would not pay their rent unless their apartments were kept in good repair. In 1966 the black community in Chicago began a great drive for open housing in that city. Dr. Martin Luther King, Jr., spent many months helping in this effort.

6 / *A Decent Home.* Better housing has been needed for a long time. An important law was passed in 1949—the Housing Act. It said in part:

> The Congress hereby declares that the general welfare and security of the nation and the health and living standards of its people require . . . the goal of a decent home and a suita-

sands of jobs each month. The Federal government has tried to help. It has set up training programs. These help people who are out of work to learn new skills. Then they may be able to find better jobs.

The unemployed need to learn new skills.

The Job Corps trains many for good jobs.

ble living environment for every American family.

More housing laws have been passed since then. They give aid to state and local governments. Such housing laws, and other laws to end slums and poverty, deal with one problem at a time. In 1964 President Johnson and Congress declared a War on Poverty. It would attack many parts of being poor at the same time.

7 / *Training*. Millions of black people were poor in the South and remained poor when they moved to the big cities of the North. Housing was one of their needs. They also had to find work. Few had the training they needed for jobs in factories. Those who did have skills could not always find jobs. New kinds of machines have taken away thou-

Head Start helps young children in many ways.

8 / A New Plan. The Economic Opportunity Act of 1964 began the War on Poverty. It set up the Office of Economic Opportunity to carry out the law. It faced the question: How can poverty be ended? Each city must find the best ways to help its poor people. This is called community action. The city works out the aid programs it needs. Then the Federal government gives money to the city to carry them out. Where possible, poor people themselves help to plan and run the programs.

9 / Upward Bound. Poor high-school boys and girls often drop out of school to go to work. Many may want to go to college, but

they need help. A program called Upward Bound (or College Bound) has been set up to help them. During the summer these students can spend eight weeks at a college or boarding high school. There they study. Teachers work with them, one at a time. They go on trips. During the school year they spend extra time in school. They attend some evening and Saturday classes. They also receive other kinds of aid. Doctors check their health. They get some money for their daily expenses. In 1968 this was ten dollars a week during the summer program and five dollars a week during the school year. While these boys and girls are prepared for college, their families can receive guidance on the needs of their college-bound children.

10 / *Work-Study*. The work-study program is also part of the War on Poverty. In this program college students from poor families hold part-time jobs. If they live at a college, they may work in a school cafeteria, library or office. If they live at home and go to a nearby college, they may hold jobs as tutors or youth workers or in community service groups. This kind of aid gives students meaningful work to do while they are earning money. Their salary is paid by the Federal government.

11 / *The Job Corps*. Many young men and women from 16 to 21 are out of school and out of work. The Job Corps was set up to train them for jobs. They go to live at a Job Corps Center. There they are trained in reading, mathematics and other subjects. They may learn how to run office machines. They may become clerks. Some learn how to repair automobiles or become cooks or waiters. They may be trained for hospital jobs. Some become farm workers. There is no end to the kinds of training that may be offered. Those at the center also enjoy sports, arts, crafts, music and drama.

12 / *Head Start*. One way to help children do well in school is to start their education earlier. Head Start is a program for pre-school children, some as young as three. They spend time in classes until they begin regular school. As part of Head Start they receive medical care. The whole family is helped in this and other ways. Each boy or girl in a Head Start class eats at least one

good meal a day in school. Head Start tries to improve their health. It builds their self-confidence. It teaches them new words and new ideas. They learn how to speak better and how to get along with other children in school. They learn more about the world around them. Parents take an active part in the Head Start program. Many help in the classrooms. They may also attend their own adult courses. There they can learn more about home economics and home planning. In such classes the parents decide much of what is to be taught.

13 / *Other Plans*. The War on Poverty is fought in many ways. The Neighborhood Youth Corps tries to train young people for good jobs while it keeps them in school. Special Impact gives work to young people and adults in cities. Operation Mainstream does the same in rural areas. The people in these programs try to improve their area or town. They may work to lessen air or water pollution. They may be part of programs to improve parks. They may help protect wildlife. New Careers is a plan to train adult workers. Health Service Centers have been set up in the slums. People can go to them to be treated by doctors and dentists. Men and women who live in the neighborhood work at these centers. Another new program gives the help of lawyers to people who do not have enough money to pay for them.

14 / *The Poor People's March*. Poor black people in the South have suffered more than other Afro-Americans. Poor people in the large cities have had much more aid. They have been more sure of a place to live and

of money for food. In the South white officials have often tried to keep aid from black people. Poor people there grow poorer year after year. In 1968 a Poor People's March was planned by Dr. Martin Luther King, Jr., and Reverend Ralph Abernathy. It was held after Dr. King's death. Thousands of poor people, most of them from the South, camped in Washington for weeks. They had come to try to get Congress to take steps to better their lives. They built a camp called Resurrection City. Through new laws and real aid, they said, they would "come back to life." Many members of Congress promised to work harder to help the poor. The years ahead will show how many of these promises will be kept.

15 / *The Long Road Ahead*. It will not be easy to end poverty. No one law or plan can do the job. The Economic Opportunity Act has made a beginning. In 1968 Congress voted almost two billion dollars for its programs. Much more will be needed. It also passed a law for open housing. It voted money to help build 1,700,000 new housing units in the next three years. It agreed to other laws for urban renewal, rent payments and city planning. Poverty will not end quickly. Much must be done in the areas of housing, schools, jobs and community life. Some people believe that all families should have a guaranteed annual income. This means that the government would see to it that each family, whether or not its members have jobs, would receive enough money to rise above poverty. Other people feel that the government is already doing too much to help poor people. New steps in the war on poverty will depend on which of these two points of view is followed in the years to come.

Building Resurrection City.

Understanding What You Have Read

I. REVIEWING WORD MEANINGS

Write the letter of the choice that best completes each statement.

1. Something that has been renewed has been (a) returned, (b) rebuilt, (c) reborn.
2. A person who "gouges" (a) refuses to pay, (b) pays too much, (c) charges too much.
3. One example of improving the environment is to (a) build a park, (b) borrow money, (c) pay less rent.
4. A program is a (a) special plan, (b) new direction, (c) guaranteed income.
5. Someone who gives guidance is giving (a) money, (b) job training, (c) advice or assistance.
6. A corps is a (a) group of people, (b) government office, (c) something that must be brought back to life.
7. Something that has great impact will result in (a) change, (b) low prices, (c) high costs.
8. If you are in the mainstream, you are (a) different from others, (b) more like others, (c) better than others.
9. When something is resurrected it is (a) torn down, (b) brought back to life, (c) made part of a program.
10. Something that is annual happens (a) daily, (b) yearly, (c) weekly.

II. BUILDING YOUR VOCABULARY

Use the dictionary to check the meaning of each of these words. Then use it in a sentence.

1. *pocket* as in "pocket of poverty"
2. *aid* as in "Federal aid"
3. *open* as in "open housing"
4. *strike* as in "rent strike"

5. *welfare* as in "general welfare"
6. *opportunity* as in "economic opportunity"
7. *service* as in "community service"
8. *drama* as in "drama program"
9. *head* as in "Head Start"
10. *career* as in the "New Careers Program"

III. UNDERSTANDING WHY

Answer each of these questions in one or two sentences.

1. Why is family life often difficult for poor people? (See Paragraph 1.)
2. Why do many poor people lose hope for the future? (See Paragraph 2.)
3. Why do some public housing projects become slums again? (See Paragraph 3.)
4. Why have most city neighborhoods been segregated? (See Paragraph 5.)
5. Why did Congress decide to pass housing laws? (See Paragraph 6.)
6. Why does each city work out its own anti-poverty programs? (See Paragraph 8.)
7. Why do students in College Bound programs receive medical care? (See Paragraph 9.)
8. Why do some college students enter the work-study program? (See Paragraph 10.)
9. Why are children placed in Head Start classes before they are ready for regular school? (See Paragraph 12.)
10. Why did Reverend Ralph Abernathy lead the Poor People's March on Washington? (See Paragraph 14.)

IV. PROBLEMS AND PROGRAMS

Tell what might be done or what is being done to solve each of these problems of poverty. Compare your answers in class.

1. Even though a man has a job, he cannot make enough money to meet the needs of his family.
2. Poor black people in the South receive less aid than poor people in the North.
3. Slum families cannot afford medical care.
4. Some cities want to place poor people from the slums in new neighborhoods.
5. Poor people who have moved to the cities do not have the skills they need to get good jobs.
6. Young boys and girls from poor families have talent but cannot afford to go to college.
7. A poor student in a college needs money for daily expenses.
8. A young man of 18 is out of school and out of work.
9. The parent of a child in a Head Start class has never been trained in wise buying.
10. A large number of young people in a rural area are out of work.

V.   THINGS TO DO

1. Write to your Representative or Senator. Ask for information about programs against poverty in your state or community. Then report to the class about these programs.
2. Write to the Department of Housing and Urban Development, Washington, D.C. Ask for information about the work of the Department. Then discuss what parts of the Department's programs are important in your community. Your local government may provide more information.
3. Choose one of the programs in the Economic Opportunity Act that is of interest to you. Write to the Office of Economic Opportunity, Washington, D.C. Ask for information about that program. Discuss the program in class.
4. Gather information about any Office of Economic Opportunity programs that may be in your community. Try to get one of the people active in that program to describe it to your class.

Unit Nine

NEW DIRECTIONS

Introduction

This is the last unit in our study of the Afro-American. It begins with the story of the life of one of the greatest of all Americans—Martin Luther King, Jr. You will learn how Dr. King became a leader in the drive for equal rights. You will see how he and those who worked with him forced the country to face its race questions. In 1964 Dr. King won the Nobel Peace Prize—proof of the world's understanding of his great work. Then, in 1968, he was killed while trying to help a group of black workers improve their lives.

A new term became well known after 1960. "Civil disorders" took place in many cities. They came to a peak in 1967. You will learn how they were studied by a national commission. What happened, why did it happen, what could be done—these were the questions the commission tried to answer. The commission then asked for a large number of changes in the country's life and laws so that such troubles would not come again.

New voting laws had brought black people into politics all over the country. They made use of their voting power. Black citizens registered and voted in great numbers. Adam Clayton Powell and many others became leaders in the country's government. In the 1960's black voters elected hundreds of leaders to jobs at all levels of government. It was clear that black political power was here to stay.

Unit 9 closes with a review of the different goals and methods being followed by groups of black Americans. Each of these groups has its own path to the future. All agree that the most important goal is better education for black boys and girls. They do not agree on how it can be brought about. They also agree that black people should have more real power in the United States. This promises to be the new goal of civil-rights groups in the 1970's.

419

Chapter 36 | "I HAVE A DREAM"

The Nonviolent Years—Dr. Martin Luther King, Jr.

Let's Discover

1. How Martin Luther King, Jr., became a leader of the civil-rights movement.
2. How Dr. King forced the nation to face its racial problems.
3. How he won the Nobel Peace Prize.
4. How Martin Luther King was murdered while trying to help a group of black workers improve their lives.

Words to Know

unconditional	Without any questions or limits. *Dr. King believed in unconditional love, even for your enemies.*
oppressed	Kept down by the cruel use of power. *White racists in the South have long oppressed the black citizens of their towns.*
ordained	Appointed as a minister. *The Reverend Martin Luther King, Jr., was ordained in 1947.*
theological seminary	A school for the training of ministers. *Martin Luther King studied at Crozer Theological Seminary.*
pastorate	The position of a pastor—a minister in charge of a church. *Reverend Martin Luther King, Jr., accepted the pastorate of the Dexter Avenue Baptist Church.*

420

courageously	Bravely.
	Dr. King led the marchers courageously.
passive resistance	Using peaceful methods while refusing to obey.
	Dr. King taught his followers to use passive resistance against unjust laws.
sanitation	The system of removing garbage and wastes.
	Dr. King went to Memphis to aid the sanitation workers in their strike.
majestic	Grand and dignified.
	Dr. King was a majestic leader.
philosophy	A system of thinking about a problem or way of life.
	Dr. Martin Luther King followed the philosophy of nonviolence.

"He dreamed for the black youth of his country. . . . He dreamed for the poor of his country. . . . He dreamed for the peace of his countrymen, at home and abroad."
The New York Times, April 7, 1968

Dr. Martin Luther King, his wife Coretta and their three children.

1 / *Standing Tall.* The story of the civil-rights movement in the country has its great names and its heroes. Tall among them stands the figure of Martin Luther King, Jr. For more than ten years he was the most followed and the best loved of all civil-rights leaders. He was a man who gave his life to this cause. He was the symbol of non-violence as a road to change. He has been called a "peaceful warrior." When he died—murdered—the United States held a national day of mourning for him.

"All men are created equal. Not some men. Not white men. All men. America, rise up and come home."

Martin Luther King, Jr.

2 / *Early Years.* Martin Luther King, Jr., was born in Atlanta, Georgia, on January 15, 1929. (Martin Luther, for whom he was named, had been the founder of the Protestant religion more than 300 years earlier.) Young Martin's father and grandfather were ministers. They had made the Ebenezer Baptist Church one of the best known in the South. The Kings lived in a large twelve-room house on Auburn Avenue, near the church. The church was important to the boy from his first days. The Bible was soon his friend. Hymns and church songs were part of his life. He sang in the church choir, his young voice telling the stories of faith, hope and trouble that are part of the music of all black people.

"I believe that unarmed truth and unconditional love will have the final word. . . ."

Martin Luther King, Jr.

3 / *Growing Up.* What was it like to grow up in Jim Crow Atlanta? This was the city that used law and custom to keep the Negro "in his place." Martin Luther King went to a segregated school. The family tried not to use public buses, for they were marked with such signs as "Colored Exit by Rear Door" and "Colored Seat from the Rear." After completing the sixth grade he went to the private school run by Atlanta University. Martin Luther King learned quickly. Small classes and close attention from teachers helped shape his mind. He learned as well to control his feelings. A story is told of young Martin and a bully. The bully struck him again and again. But he did not strike back. Perhaps his belief in nonviolence had already begun to form. After two years at the private school he went on to Booker T. Washington High School, a segregated public school in Atlanta. When he was fifteen he was ready to enter college!

"I do not want a kingdom, salvation, or heaven; what I want is to remove the troubles of the oppressed and the poor."

Mahatma Gandhi

4 / *Training for a Life's Work.* Martin Luther King entered Morehouse College in Atlanta in 1944. This is one of the best known and oldest of the Negro colleges. In it ideas flow and students are urged to move in new directions. Martin studied history. He learned sociology—the study of how people live in groups. He found that he had real talent as a public speaker. He learned the thoughts of men like Thoreau and Gandhi—civil disobedience, nonviolence and the duty to fight evil laws. In 1947 he was ordained a minister in his father's church. He was only eighteen! He had made the decision to spend his life leading and guiding his people. He went on to Crozer Theological Seminary in Chester, Pennsylvania, to continue his studies as a minister. There he was one of six black students

in a school of about a hundred. He became the first Afro-American to be elected class president at the school. The studies went on—of Jesus and Gandhi, of love of mankind and changing the way men live. Martin Luther King finished his studies at the top of his class and won a scholarship for further study.

> "The Negro needs the white man to free him from his fears. The white man needs the Negro to free him from his guilt."
>
> Martin Luther King, Jr.

5 / *The Years in Boston*. The highest degree one can earn for his studies is the doctor's degree. Martin Luther King used his scholarship at Boston University. While in Boston he met Coretta Scott. She had graduated from Antioch College and was studying music in Boston. They were married by Martin Luther King, Sr., in June, 1953. It was two more years before the young Reverend King received his doctor's degree. He had finished long study and research in the work of leading Protestant thinkers. But before then, he had made the decision to return to the South. He accepted the pastorate of the Dexter Avenue Baptist Church in Montgomery, Alabama, in 1954. Two years later, after the success of the bus boycott, *Time* magazine named him one of the ten "outstanding people in the world." For Martin Luther King had set himself a great goal. He would lead his people to freedom from Jim Crow, and what had become known as "second-class citizenship."

> "Don't ride the bus to work, to town, to school, or anyplace, Monday, December 5. If you work, take a cab, or share a ride, or walk."
>
> Advertisement in Montgomery, Alabama

6 / *A National Leader*. Montgomery, like all of Alabama, lived in a world of Jim Crow. Dr. King spoke out against it in his Sunday sermons. Then the bus boycott came. Dr. King was soon its leader. As president of the Montgomery Improvement Association he spoke at its first meeting. He was not yet 27 when his voice was heard by the whole world: "Love must be our . . . ideal. . . . Once again, we must hear the words of Jesus . . . Love your enemies, bless them that curse you, and pray for them that . . . use you. . . . If you will protest courageously, and yet with dignity and Christian love, when the history books are written in future . . . the historians will have to pause and say, 'There lived a great people—a black people'. . . ." With these words Martin Luther King became a leader of people all over the United States. He gave them a new hope. At the same time he taught them a new way to fight for their rights—nonviolence.

> "We are not bitter. We are . . . using the method of passive resistance."
>
> Martin Luther King, Jr.

7 / *No Hate*. Dr. King called his way of fighting injustice "nonviolent direct action." There were many laws in the Jim Crow

"We are marching to freedom."

South that he knew were wrong. Jim Crow seating in buses was one of them. Dr. King believed that more men were good than evil. If a town were forced to choose between doing right and doing wrong, then it would most often choose right. But first it had to be forced to make the choice. "We are marching to freedom," he said to thousands of fellow churchmen and millions of Afro-Americans. Freedom would come when black people had so sharply shaped the Jim Crow question "that it can no longer be ignored." This meant that unjust laws and customs would not be obeyed. White groups in the South might then use force against blacks. But those who followed Dr. King

agreed with his call for civil disobedience. "We will meet your physical force with soul force. We will not hate you, but we cannot . . . obey your unjust laws."

> "It may get me crucified. I may die. But I want it said even if I die in the struggle that 'He died to make me free.' "
> Martin Luther King, Jr.
> Speech in Albany, Georgia, 1962

8 / *Years of Danger.* Dr. King always knew that he had set forth on a dangerous road. He was jailed many times. He was struck; he was stabbed; in the end a bullet killed

him. Yet he never called for violence. Other chapters of this book have told of his part in the bus boycott and of some of his other activities. His way to fight became the way to fight for millions. Dr. King spoke all over the country. Men and women, boys and girls, black and white listened to him. They became the freedom riders. They joined in the sit-ins. They came to the March on Washington. Then, in 1964, the Civil Rights Act was passed by Congress. Long years of peaceful protest had led to a great change in the country's laws. Dr. King knew that a change in law did not always mean a quick change in the way people lived. He said at the end of a speech on the new law: "I say good night to you by quoting an old Negro slave preacher who said, 'We ain't what we ought to be, and we ain't what we want to be, and we ain't what we're going to be. But thank God, we ain't what we was.'"

"The heart of the question is whether all Americans are to be afforded equal rights and equal opportunities, whether we are going to treat our fellow Americans as we want to be treated."
John F. Kennedy, 1963

"We will reach the goal of freedom . . . all over the nation, because the goal of America is freedom."
Martin Luther King, Jr., 1963

9 / *The Nobel Peace Prize.* On December 10, 1964, Martin Luther King went to Stockholm, Sweden. He went there to receive the Nobel Peace Prize—the award that can be won each year by the person who has done the most for peace in the world. Dr. King was 35 years old, the youngest person ever to win the prize. He gave the $54,000 that came with it to the civil-rights movement. His words at that time showed that he was not going to give up his fight for equal rights. He spoke of "the long night of racial injustice." Then he said: "I accept this award in behalf of a civil-rights movement which is moving with determination and a majestic scorn for risk and danger to establish a reign of freedom and a rule of justice."

"I know you are asking today, 'How long will it take?' . . . Not long, because you will reap what you sow."
Martin Luther King, Jr., 1965

10 / *Selma to Memphis.* There was no end of places in which Dr. King was needed. He went to Selma, where he led the struggle that helped bring the Voting Act of 1965. He

Dr. King receives the Nobel Prize from the King of Norway.

went to Chicago to help in the drive to gain open housing laws in that city. While there he helped set up "Operation Breadbasket." Through it he tried to get job training and better jobs for black workers. He rested in Atlanta for a while. Yet he kept telling the whole country that it could not rest until each black person had rights equal to those of whites. Perhaps Jim Crow laws had been ended. In time black people would overcome Jim Crow customs. But these gains could not be enough. People had to make a living too. In March, 1968 Dr. King was in Memphis, Tennessee. There the sanitation workers were on strike for higher wages. Most of these men were black. The leaders of S.C.L.C. had decided to aid them. Meetings were held night after night. On the night of April 3, Martin Luther King spoke at one of them. Here are some of the thoughts in this, his last speech:

Dr. King on the balcony of his motel room the day before his assassination.

I may not get there with you, but I want you to know tonight that we as a people will get to the promised land. . . . So I'm happy tonight. I'm not worried about anything. I'm not fearing any man. . . . We've got some difficult days ahead. But it really doesn't matter with me now, because I've been to the mountaintop, and I don't mind. Like anybody, I would like to live a long life. . . . But I'm not concerned about that now. I just want to do God's will. And He's allowed me to go up to the mountain. And I've looked over, and I've seen the promised land.

"In our . . . bitterness of this awful event, we must not lose sight of the meaning of this great man's life . . . brotherly love and equal justice."
Senator Edward W. Brooke

"Nonviolence is a dead philosophy."
Floyd McKissick
The New York Times, April 5, 1968

11 / *Death in Memphis.* It was the evening of April 4, 1968. Dr. King and other black leaders were staying at the black-owned Lorraine Motel in Memphis. He stepped out to the balcony for a breath of fresh air. A shot came from a nearby building. It hit the right side of his neck, killing him. The whole country went into shock. The death of Dr. King brought back the horror of the day when John F. Kennedy was assassinated. Now a second great leader was dead. The whole world mourned Dr. Martin Luther King. Thousands of meetings and marches were held to honor his memory. Tens of

thousands of people came to Atlanta, where his funeral was held. The man who had kept open a bridge between the races was dead. In the next few days troubles between blacks and whites took place in forty cities.

> "We must learn to live together as brothers or we will perish together as fools. . . . Racial injustice is still the black man's burden and the white man's shame."
> Martin Luther King, Jr., 1968

12 / *The Work Does Not End.* Before he died Dr. King had planned a great gathering in Washington. Its goal was to get Congress to act to end poverty. It was called the Poor People's March, or the Poor People's Campaign. The Reverend Ralph Abernathy took Dr. King's place as the leader of S.C.L.C. He, and thousands all over the country, worked to carry out Dr. King's last plan. They built a huge "city" of tents and other simple "roofs over the head" in Washington. Dr. King had been brought to his final resting place on a wagon drawn by a mule. The wagon drawn by a mule became the symbol of the Poor People's March. Each day the thousands of poor people in the camp went to leaders of the government. They asked for laws to help them live a decent life. From Resurrection City they were showing that Dr. King's ideas were still alive, even though he was dead.

> "He sought not to reform a single town but to shame a nation to action."
> *The New York Times,* April 5, 1968

13 / *Another Memphis?* In 1969 Reverend Abernathy and Mrs. King came to the aid of another group of workers. Hospital workers in Charleston, South Carolina had gone on strike for higher wages and better working conditions. Most of these men and women were black. The S.C.L.C. led a national drive to help them. Again the country could only watch as Dr. Abernathy and other leaders were jailed by white officials. Yet it seemed that the question raised in Memphis demanded an answer. When would black workers in the South receive fair treatment?

"He died to make me free."

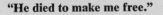

REV. MARTIN LUTHER KING JR.
1929 — 1968
"FREE AT LAST, FREE AT LAST,
THANK GOD ALMIGHTY, I'M FREE AT LAST"

Understanding What You Have Read

I. REVIEWING WORD MEANINGS

Write the letter of the choice that best completes each statement.

1. An unconditional promise is (a) always kept, (b) always made, (c) never allowed.
2. Oppressed people are (a) always happy, (b) not given their rights, (c) powerful.
3. A person who has been ordained is important in a (a) civil-rights movement, (b) school system, (c) religion.
4. A seminary is a kind of (a) school, (b) system of thinking, (c) religion.
5. A pastor is in charge of a (a) school, (b) church, (c) government.
6. A courageous person is not (a) afraid, (b) arrested, (c) allowed to speak.
7. If you do something in a passive way you are (a) using force, (b) not allowing someone else to use a right, (c) refusing to use force.
8. The chief task of sanitation workers is to (a) hold public meetings, (b) improve public housing, (c) remove garbage.
9. A majestic person has great (a) power, (b) intelligence, (c) dignity.
10. A philosophy is a way of (a) gaining power, (b) thinking and acting, (c) changing laws.

II. ANSWER EACH QUESTION IN ONE OR TWO SENTENCES.

1. Why was Martin Luther King, Jr., called a "peaceful warrior"?
2. How was religion important in Martin Luther King's boyhood?
3. Why did the King family try not to use public buses in Atlanta?
4. How did King become a minister?
5. What ideas did he learn from Thoreau and Gandhi?
6. Why was Martin Luther King honored by national magazines?

7. What did Dr. King mean by "forcing a town to face its Jim Crow issues"?
8. Why did so many young people follow Martin Luther King?
9. Why did Dr. King believe changed laws were not enough?
10. Why was the Poor People's March held?

III. DO YOU AGREE OR DISAGREE?

Write your reasons for agreeing or disagreeing with each statement.

1. Martin Luther King, Jr., was a martyr. (Look up the word *martyr* in your dictionary.)
2. Dr. King was correct to use nonviolence at all times.
3. If Martin Luther King had not been a minister, few people would have agreed with his ideas.
4. A minister's job is to work in his church; he should not take a stand on social or political problems.
5. The end of Jim Crow laws would have come soon even without the work of Dr. King.

IV. EXPLAINING IMPORTANT STATEMENTS

Each of the following statements was made by Dr. Martin Luther King, Jr. Discuss the meaning of each in class.

1. "Jailing the Negro was once as much of a threat as the loss of a job. . . . The Negro knew what going to jail meant. It meant not only confinement and isolation from his loved ones. It meant that at the jailhouse he could probably expect a severe beating, and it meant that his day in court, if he had it, would be a mockery of justice."
2. "We have waited for more than 340 years for our Constitutional and God-given rights . . . we still creep at horse-and-buggy pace toward gaining a cup of coffee at a lunch counter . . . you see the vast majority of your . . . Negro brothers smothering in an airtight cage of poverty in the midst of society; . . . you are

humiliated day in and day out by nagging signs reading 'white' and 'colored'; . . . you are forever fighting a sense of 'nobodiness'—then you will understand why we find it difficult to wait. There comes a time when the cup of endurance runs over. . . ."

3. "It was the people who moved their leaders, not the leaders who moved the people . . . the command post was in the bursting hearts of millions of Negroes. When such a people begin to move, they create their own theories, shape their own destinies and choose the leaders who share their own philosophy."

4. "The Negroes' real problem has been that they have seldom had adequate choices. Political life, as a rule, did not attract the best elements of the Negro community, and white candidates who represented their views were few and far between."

5. "Negro leaders of talent and unimpeachable character . . . must move out into political life as candidates and infuse it with their humanity, their honesty and their vision."

6. "(Man) has now reached the day when violence toward another human being must become as (hateful) as eating another's flesh. Nonviolence, the answer to the Negroes' need, may become the answer to the most desperate need of all humanity."

7. "The world is changing, and anyone who thinks he can live alone is sleeping through a revolution."

8. "We are tired of living in the dungeons of poverty, ignorance and want. We have come to the day when a piece of freedom is not enough for us as human beings. . . . We feel that we are the conscience of America."

V. THINGS TO DO

1. Draw an original cartoon to show your understanding of the importance of the Reverend Dr. Martin Luther King, Jr., in the history of the United States. A class committee can arrange a display of these cartoons.

2. Prepare a poster that tells of some important event in the civil-rights movement during the years it was led by Dr. Martin Luther King. Write the date and place at the bottom of your poster. Example: March on Washington—Washington, D.C., 1963.

3. What happened to James Earl Ray, the man charged with the murder of Dr. Martin Luther King, Jr.? Check *The New York Times* Index beginning with June, 1968, and especially for March, 1969.

Chapter 37 | CIVIL DISORDERS

Let's Discover

1. How riots took place in many large cities from 1964 to 1967.
2. What the National Advisory Commission on Civil Disorders reported on
   a) what happened,
   b) why it happened,
   c) what can be done.

Words to Know

civil disorder
: A riot or other great disturbance in a city.
In the civil disorders of 1967, many people were hurt and many others lost their property.

looting
: Stealing or robbing, such as breaking into a store during a riot.
There was much looting during the riot in Detroit.

inflict
: Causing suffering or damage.
The President asked people not to inflict harm on others.

advisory
: Able to give advice about a problem.
The Advisory Commission was set up to study the riots and tell what should be done to prevent them.

addiction
: Having a habit too strong to control.
Drug addiction has wrecked many lives.

quality
: How good something is.
We should improve the quality of each person's life.

432

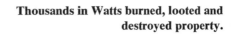
Thousands in Watts burned, looted and destroyed property.

public assistance | Aid given to people by a government.
Millions of people depend on public assistance.

destruction | Being destroyed.
The riot in 1965 resulted in the destruction of a large part of the Watts section of Los Angeles.

---

1 / Trouble in the Cities. It was July, 1964. A policeman in New York City had shot and killed a fifteen-year-old Negro boy. For the next few days there was trouble in the city. Protest meetings were held; some of them were broken up by the police. Some fighting broke out. Both officers and citizens were hurt; one person was killed. Police began to call the clashes "riots." They were the first of many troubles in many cities that summer. There was violence in Rochester (N.Y.), Chicago, Philadelphia and cities in New Jersey. In each case police used force in clashes with people in black neighborhoods. Fires were started. Bricks were thrown. The police answered with bullets. In each city large numbers of black people were arrested. The troubles seemed to end in late August. Yet they left questions all people had to face: What was happening in the big-city slums? Why were people who lived there ready to turn to violence after years of peaceful protest?

2 / Watts. The cities were quiet that winter. The next August, Watts, a part of Los Angeles, California, seemed to explode. About 90,000 black people live in this neighborhood. Trouble began when a crowd gathered around two policemen who were arresting the black driver of an automobile. The policemen called for help. The crowd grew larger. Eighty more policemen were rushed in, but they could not stop the growing anger of the crowd. Soon the crowd had grown too large to control. People began to break into food, liquor and clothing stores. Windows were broken; goods were taken. Young men threw stones at cars and buses. They fought with the police. Things were beyond control. The trouble went on for six days.

3 / After the Disorders. Police and soldiers finally brought peace to Watts. Thousands of men, women and children had looted, burned and destroyed property. President Johnson had asked them to stop. "Rights will not be won through violence. . . . No person has the right to inflict harm on the life or property of others," he said. By the end of the disorder six whites and 28 blacks were dead; 864 people had been treated in hospitals. Black leaders had not been able to end the violence. They had moved through the streets, but their efforts had been ignored. Perhaps $200,000,000 in damage had been done. More than 3,800 black people had been arrested. They had been charged with many crimes. They had burned and destroyed hundreds of stores and buildings owned by whites. They had also wrecked buildings, homes and stores owned by blacks.

Police shot at looters in Newark, New Jersey.

4 / *More Troubles.* After Watts there were riots in other cities. For three summers they came—New York City; Newark, New Jersey; Detroit, Michigan; Cleveland, Ohio; and many more places. Fire and fighting, shootings and looting, mobs, police and soldiers attacking—television screens showed a picture of trouble all over the nation. In July, 1967 President Johnson spoke to the people of the country about the riots. He told them that he understood the causes of the violence. He spoke of poor education, discrimination, slums, poverty, disease and the lack of jobs. Then he set up the National Advisory Commission on Civil Disorders. Its head was Otto Kerner, the governor of Illinois. The Commission made its report in March, 1968. It tried to answer the three questions asked by the President: What happened? Why did it happen? What can be done so that it will not happen again?

5 / *Telling What Happened.* The Commission called the troubles in the cities "civil disorders." It found that the eight largest disorders, which it called riots, were alike in some ways. Each time black people had been angry at white control of their lives. Each time they had fought the police. Each time they had tried to damage or take things that belonged to whites in black neighborhoods. Each time large numbers of people had been killed. Most of them were black people who lived in these neighborhoods. In each city millions of dollars worth of damage had been done. In 1967 there were 164 civil disorders in the country. Forty-one of these had been serious or "major" riots.

6 / *Who Rioted?* The report tried to show who had taken part in the riots. It found that young black men had been most active. They were in their teens or were young

adults. Most were high-school dropouts. They did not have good jobs; many of them had no jobs at all. In Detroit only one-tenth of the black people of the neighborhoods in which the riot began took part in it. Most of them had been brought up in that city. They had found that life in this country did not give them enough. For them, once the trouble began, "to riot and destroy appeared more and more to become ends in themselves." In each city the riot seemed to grow on itself. Young black people were "getting back" at the world that had for so long kept them down.

7 / Why Did They Riot? The report spelled out the kinds of problems that had led these young people to such actions. It reviewed the long history of racism. In most cities there

A block in Detroit during the 1967 riot.

was still much job discrimination. Housing was still segregated. The United States had grown richer from year to year. Yet most black people in the cities had not improved their lives. Whites had gained more; many of them had moved out of the cities to the suburbs. Blacks had remained poor; they were still in the crowded centers of the cities. In the black ghettos, the report told the country, Afro-Americans suffered from crime, disease, lack of jobs and broken families. People there had grown bitter against the rest of the country. Many had grown to hate all whites. The civil-rights movement had given hope to black people, but not much had been done to give them a better living. For years there had been a war in Vietnam and violence against blacks in the South. Many Afro-Americans had lost their faith in peaceful change. Some black leaders and new groups were telling them to turn to violence instead. Cries of "Black Power" were being heard.

8 / Black Power. What did this new cry for "Black Power" mean? It might mean the use of force to end police or mob violence against Negroes. In the South black self-defense groups formed. In the North groups like the Black Panthers trained in the use of guns and other weapons. Black Power might mean working to gain political power. Black leaders were running for office in every state. It might mean setting up black-owned businesses to gain economic power. CORE began to speak of "green power"—the power of money. It might mean black control of schools, police, firemen and other services in black neighborhoods. Black Power was a magic phrase. It had many meanings. It gave young Afro-Americans a new sense of pride. Some of them began to say they would no longer take orders from the whites who were in charge of most of city life. Once a riot began in their city, they might rush to join in it. Thousands of them did.

SELF-DEFENSE GROUPS

Two important groups appeared during the 1960's to help black Americans defend themselves against "white racist violence." The first was called the Deacons for Defense. In many communities in the South, black men secretly began to arm themselves. They were ready to meet KKK hoodlums with bullets! The fact that the secret Deacons group would take action has helped keep peace in many southern towns.

Another group, the Black Panthers, has been less secret. Its membership has grown steadily, moving east from California. In many places the Black Panthers are now a known revolutionary political group and even a local political party. The best-known Panther leaders, Huey Newton and Eldridge Cleaver, advise their members to arm themselves and prepare for action to overthrow the "white racist world." In some cities the Black Panthers have been treated like criminals. In others their success in gaining members has made them important voices in the black community.

9 / *Being Poor*. The report told what it was like to be poor in the slums. Here are some of the findings: "Negro men are more than three times as likely as white men to be in low-paying jobs." They were also almost nine times as likely to have no jobs or only part-time work. Two out of every five black families in the cities had to live "below the poverty level." Men who could not make a living were "often unable or unwilling to remain with their families." Children who grew up with such problems would be more ready to join in a riot. They had much to be angry about. The report told of their health problems. It spoke of the poor sanitation in the slums. It told of rat bites and infant deaths. It explained that many stores in the slums, both large and small, charged higher prices than stores in other parts of the same city.

10 / *How to Escape?* Why hadn't black people in the cities been able to escape from poverty? The report told some of the reasons. It showed that black workers who had moved to the North from the South did not have the skills they needed to get or hold jobs. There was little work for people who were not trained. Job discrimination had not

This new store is owned and run by Afro-Americans.

died. Black workers were still often the last hired. Even where black people were a large part of a city, they had not taken steps to gain political power. This meant that state or local laws were not passed to attack the causes of their poverty. Federal programs were too few and too weak. The report saw little hope. For Negroes, it said, "the future seemed to lead only to a dead end."

11 / *What Can Be Done?* The Commission asked for action. There were some things that those running city governments could do. They could try to get closer to the people. Then problems could at least be better understood. They could train their police to protect the people of the slums more than in the past, and to treat them with respect. Afro-Americans should be in the police and in other parts of city governments. Newspapers, radio and television should stop giving so much attention to violence in all its forms. But the chief goal in any plan to prevent riots is to end poverty first. The hopeless life of the slums must be changed. "Large-scale improvement in the quality of ghetto life" was the greatest need. But how could the cities do this alone? It would cost much more than any of them could afford. The whole country had to join in the attack on the problems of the cities.

12 / *National Needs.* The report explained that there was a pressing need for action soon. It spelled out the need. More should be done to end discrimination and segregation. Poor people should gain some power to improve their lives. Public and private groups should do more to solve city prob-

lems. The report told the country that the men who had joined in the riots had not had jobs that could give them real dignity. It was time to do the many things needed to build each person's pride. There should be more Head Start programs. Adults should get more training and education. Parents should have a real role in the running of schools. Poor boys and girls should be helped to finish high school and college. Much more money should be spent on city slum schools. The wealth of the whole country should be used to solve such problems. They were the whole country's problems. They grew more pressing each day. People who were not poor would have to accept the higher taxes that would be needed.

13 / *Welfare and Housing.* More and more of the people in each city could not make a living. Almost one-eighth of the people in New York City had to have help to get enough food, clothing and housing. There were great numbers of poor people in each city. The help given to them is called "welfare," or "public assistance." The report called for much more such aid. It said that a family of four had to have at least $3,335 a year. This amount has since been raised. The cost of living keeps rising. The Federal government should pay most of the welfare costs, the report said. In time this kind of guaranteed annual income would save boys and girls "from the prison of poverty that has held their parents." The Commission asked Congress to pass open-housing laws. It passed one a few months after the report was made public. In the same year the Supreme Court said it was illegal to refuse to rent or sell to anyone because of race. The report asked for more public housing outside the slums. It called for at least six million new housing units. Congress soon passed a law to build almost one-third of this number. Perhaps the country would pass the kind of laws asked for by the Commission. The problem was clear. Steps had to be taken if people wanted to avoid new riots in their cities. For, the Commission said, "It is time now to end the destruction and the violence, not only in the streets of the ghetto but in the lives of people."

"Storefront universities" are helping young people finish school.

Understanding What You Have Read

I. REVIEWING WORD MEANINGS

Write the letter of the choice that best completes each statement.

1. One of the meanings of the word *civil* is (a) having to do with riots, (b) related to a city, (c) not in the armed forces.
2. A disorder is (a) a disturbance, (b) an election, (c) a report.
3. If you inflict harm on someone you are (a) hurting him, (b) helping to cure him, (c) giving him special assistance.
4. A person who is busy looting is (a) burning something, (b) fighting the police, (c) stealing.
5. People who receive public assistance are (a) in need of help, (b) tired of working, (c) ready for a pension.
6. An advisory group tells (a) how a problem grows important, (b) when a problem is important, (c) what should be done to solve a problem.
7. To improve the quality of a person's life is to make it (a) worse, (b) the same, (c) better.
8. Destruction is most like (a) building up, (b) tearing down, (c) leaving alone.
9. Addiction is a health problem because it (a) causes diseases like measles to spread, (b) makes people depend on drugs that harm them, (c) leads to great gain in weight.
10. A serious disorder might be a (a) fire, (b) robbery, (c) riot.

II. BUILDING NEW VOCABULARY

The report of the National Advisory Commission on Civil Disorders named twelve deeply held grievances, listed below. What is a "grievance"? Set up twelve committees in your class. Each committee should find out why one of the listed grievances was important. Report to the class on its meaning and explain the facts that help to understand it. The report itself has been published by Bantam Books and by the Government Printing Office.

1. Police practices
2. Unemployment and under-employment
3. Inadequate housing
4. Inadequate education
5. Poor recreation facilities and programs
6. Ineffectiveness of the political structure and grievance mechanisms
7. Disrespectful white attitudes
8. Discriminatory administration of justice
9. Inadequate Federal programs
10. Inadequate municipal services
11. Discriminatory consumer and credit practices
12. Inadequate welfare programs

III. COMMUNITY SURVEY

Check with someone who is a member of a civil-rights organization in your community. Show that person the list of grievances in II. above. What does he or she know about the importance of these problems in your community? Report to the class. What information would you seek in addition to the report from this person? Discuss in class.

IV. JUDGING AMERICA'S PAST

Compare the following two points of view about American history. Discuss them with your parents and other adults. Then share your conclusions and the reasons for them with your class.

1. Martin Luther King was right when he said the United States is a guilty land. Its white people have built a nation's wealth on the crushed hopes of its minorities.
2. Guilt does not belong to all whites, but only to those who kept Jim Crow alive and fought equality in every way they could.

V. THINGS TO DO

1. Check one of the picture news magazines for the summer of 1964, 1965, 1966 or 1967. Report to the class in detail on one of the riots. What did the magazine tell you of how the trouble began? What then happened? With what result? How did the riot end?

2. In every riot there were people who told others to "Burn, baby, burn!" and others who told people to "Cool it!" Prepare a one-page speech that might have been used to a crowd to increase a riot or to try to end it. Read and discuss these speeches in class.

3. Try to get newspaper articles or leaflets dealing with Black Power movements in your community. Explain these to the class. What are the goals of these movements? What methods are being used to gain them?

4. What steps have been taken in your community toward school decentralization and community control of schools? With what results? Discuss the problems that developed in New York City beginning in 1968. What new steps were taken there beginning in 1969?

5. What other examples of community control movements have been important in your community, or in others that you know?

Chapter 38 / AFRO-AMERICANS IN POLITICS

Let's Discover

1. How Afro-American political power continues to grow.
2. What some important black political leaders have done.

Shirley Chisholm was the first black woman to be elected to Congress. In 1972 she became the first black woman to actively seek her party's nomination for President.

Words to Know

delegate
A person sent to speak for a large group of people, such as a local political party, or for a government. *Julian Bond was a delegate from Georgia to the Democratic Party's national convention in 1968.*

pollution
Made dirty or impure. *Pollution of air and water is a serious problem in the cities.*

deputy
A person chosen to assist another or to do his work. *Harriet Conn was made deputy attorney general of Indiana.*

borough
One of the five divisions of New York City. *Manhattan and Brooklyn are boroughs of New York City.*

agency
A group set up to do some special task within a government. *Carl Rowan headed the United States Information Agency.*

mission
A group of persons sent to a foreign government, to a conference among nations or to an organization like the United Nations. *Marian Anderson was part of the United States Mission to the United Nations.*

white collar
Having to do with work at which a man might wear a white shirt—such as a clerk, office worker or professional. It is usually compared with blue-collar jobs—those at which workers wear such clothing as overalls and work shirts. *Adam Clayton Powell, Jr., tried to get white-collar jobs for Negroes.*

minimum
The least amount allowed. *The new law raised the minimum wage to $1.50 an hour.*

investigate   To search into something so as to gather all the facts about it.

The committee investigated the charges against the official.

finance   The management of money, as for a government.

Edward Brooke served on the Boston Finance Commission.

---

1 / *A Sign of Change*. It was August, 1968. The Democrats were holding their national convention in Chicago. Millions watched it on television. They saw many proofs that black people were now part of the country's political life. They saw Dr. Aaron Henry leading the Mississippi delegates. They watched as Dr. Channing Phillips of Washington, D.C., became one of those nominated to be the party's candidate for President. They saw young Julian Bond of Georgia gain half of his state's votes at the convention for his civil-rights group. They saw the excitement when he was one of those nominated for Vice-President. Such scenes in Chicago were new signs of a great change in the country's life. Black men and women had begun to gain political power.

Julian Bond and Channing Phillips were nominated at the 1968 Democratic Convention.

2/ Black Voting Power. The Fifteenth Amendment had given all citizens the right to vote. Most black citizens then lived in the South. Jim Crow laws and customs there had taken away this right. Slowly the vote was won back. There were the many law cases. There were the marches and protests all over the South. There was the Twenty-fourth Amendment, which ended poll taxes. Then there was the Voting Rights Act, which meant more people would soon vote. Meanwhile black people in the North began to register and vote. They saw that this would give them a voice in improving their lives. Slowly they made the political life of the country a little more equal. In 1875 there had been seven Afro-Americans in the House of Representatives and one in the Senate. In 1967-1968 there were six black members of the House and one in the Senate. In city and state governments the new black voters had shown real power. They had become one of the most important groups of voters.

3/ New Mayors. Once black voters grow important, black leaders can be elected. This has happened in city after city. In most cases black and white voters have agreed that some person is the best choice for the job. Springfield, Ohio, with its 90,000 people, is one such place. About one-seventh of the people are Negroes. One of them, Robert C. Henry, became mayor in 1965. Ypsilanti, Michigan, is a small city. One-fifth of its 25,000 people are black. John Buron, an Afro-American, was elected mayor in 1967. Saginaw, Michigan, has 100,000 people. In 1967 its mayor was a Negro lawyer named Henry March. Flint, in the same state, has more than 200,000 people. One-fourth are black. Mayor Floyd McCree is one of them. Milpitas, California, grew from 500 to more than 23,000 in less than fifteen years. Its Negro mayor, Ben Gross, has lived in it all that time. And back across the country in Washington, D.C., where the people do not elect a mayor, President Johnson chose Afro-American

Former Mayor Carl B. Stokes of Cleveland, Ohio.

Walter Washington to be mayor. In 1969 President Nixon asked him to continue in that job. Also in 1969, Chapel Hill, North Carolina, elected Negro Howard Nathaniel Lee as its mayor. In 1970 Kenneth Gibson, a civil engineer, fought and won a hard battle to become the first black mayor of Newark, New Jersey.

4 / *Mayor Carl B. Stokes.* Cleveland, Ohio, is our eighth largest city. It has about 900,000 people. One-third are black. In 1967 Carl B. Stokes, the great grandson of a slave, ran for mayor against Seth B. Taft, the grandson of a President of the United States. Stokes won. He was helped by both blacks and whites who agreed he was the best man for the job. Carl Stokes had grown up in an all-Negro ghetto in Cleveland. He was a good student; he went on to college and law school and then returned to Cleveland. He was one of many black leaders in the city who turned to public service. In 1968 they were one-third of the City Council. Charles V. Carr, leader of the city's Democrats, led them in the work of improving life in their city. In this he was much like Percy Sutton, president of the borough of Manhattan in New York City, and other men and women who have gained important posts in city governments.

5 / *"Vote for Stokes!"* Carl Stokes knew that Cleveland had great problems. Housing was segregated. Schools were poor. Too many black workers were out of work or had only part-time jobs. There was a great need for better health services. Carl Stokes had run for mayor two years before. He had lost by a few thousand votes. For the 1967 election Dr. Martin Luther King, Jr., came to Cleveland to help. He spoke of "pride in our own." He got thousands of black voters to register so that they could vote for Stokes. Stokes had been a leader of the N.A.A.C.P. It too worked to get people to register. CORE joined in. These and other groups, black and white, agreed with Carl Stokes when he said: "Help me to prove something about the American dream."

6 / *Richard G. Hatcher.* The city of Gary, Indiana, is near Chicago. It has about 200,000 people. Richard Hatcher, at thirty-four, became the first Afro-American mayor in its history. He too had grown up in an all-black ghetto. He was the grandson of a slave. At fifteen he had a job washing dishes. His employer would not serve black people. Young Hatcher and some of his friends staged the city's first sit-in! Although the family was poor, Richard Hatcher had made up his mind to stay in school. He went on to the state university. By 1959 he was a lawyer. Four years later he was a member

Mayor Richard G. Hatcher of Gary, Indiana.

of Gary's City Council. The next year he was its president. He began to press for an open-housing law. In 1965 the law was passed.

7 / *Becoming Mayor*. Hatcher studied Gary's needs. He learned about air pollution, housing and taxes. When he ran for mayor in 1967 he showed the voters that he knew what his city needed. The last mayor, he told them, had kept Afro-Americans out of important posts in the police, fire and health departments. There was so much that had not been done. "I ask you," he said, "are the slums any prettier? Are our schools less crowded? Have they built one single public-housing unit? Have they torn down one single building for urban renewal? Have they desegregated the schools?" Richard Hatcher is a Democrat. The men who ran that party in Gary would not help him in his campaign. He turned to the rest of the country. Hubert Humphrey, then Vice-President, helped him. So did Robert F. Kennedy, then Senator from New York. Money came in from all over the country. Hatcher won. He then said: "When we first started in this campaign, people said that with the forces against us we didn't have a chance. But I thought that we were right. I thought that what we were trying to do was right. I never thought we would lose."

8 / *Negro Women in State Governments*. Most of our state legislatures have two houses. The upper house, with a smaller number of members, is most often called the Senate. The lower houses have a number of names. In 1968 many Afro-American women served as State Senators or as members of the lower houses of our state governments. Barbara Jordan, a Houston lawyer, served in the Texas State Senate—the youngest member and the only woman there! Verda Welcome served in the Maryland State Senate. Yvonne Braithwaite was the first black woman in California's legislature. In her first year in office she introduced thirteen bills dealing with the needs of young people. Four of those became state laws. Grace Hamilton is a member of the Georgia House of Representatives. She had spent seventeen years as director of the Atlanta Urban League. After her election she said: "I hope that no one voted for me just because I am a woman or just because I am a Negro." This was a thought many black leaders had shared with the voters. Choose the best person for each job. If that person happens to be black, then vote for him or her because of ability, not because of color.

9 / *More Women in Government*. Harriet Bailey Conn was elected to Indiana's state legislature. The next year she was named that state's deputy attorney general. Ethel Maynard became a state representative in Arizona. June Franklin, who has long worked for better housing, became a member of Iowa's House of Representatives. Soon the state had a fair housing law. Victorina Adams, of the Maryland House of Representatives, has worked to get more people to register and vote. In the same state Lena K. Lee, teacher, principal and lawyer, works for better schools as a member of the state legislature. Michigan has its urban problems.

Among those who try to help solve them are Daisy Elliot and Rosetta Ferguson of the state's House of Representatives. The first black woman in Missouri's legislature was Verne Lee Calloway, a founder of CORE. Working there with her is Elsa D. Hill. Two Afro-American women have long been members of Pennsylvania's House of Representatives. Suzie Monroe has served since 1948. Sarah A. Anderson joined her six years later. In Tennessee Dorothy L. Brown became the first Negro woman in the state legislature in 1966. Shirley Chisholm has held the same honor in New York. In 1969 she became the first black woman in American history to be elected to Congress.

10 / *Federal Judges.* The number of black men and women who are Federal judges grows each year. Some of these first gain fame in some other field. Thurgood

Federal judge Constance Baker Motley.

Marshall, of the Supreme Court, was a civil-rights lawyer. Wade McCree had been a well-known judge in Detroit. James Parsons had been a judge in Chicago. Marjorie Lawson, first Negro woman to become a Federal judge, was a leader of the National Urban League who had worked for fair employment. Joseph Waddy was an expert in family problems. Spottswood Robinson was dean of Howard Law School and then a member of the United States Commission on Civil Rights. William Benson Bryant was a well-known government lawyer. Walter A. Gordon had been Governor of the Virgin Islands. William H. Hastie had worked in the Department of Labor and was Governor of the Virgin Islands. A. Leon Higginbotham was the youngest person ever to serve on the Federal Trade Commission. Constance Baker Motley had been president of New York City's borough of Manhattan.

11 / *Positions of Trust.* An ambassador of the United States holds a high position of trust. Carl Rowan, one of the first Afro-Americans to be an officer in the Navy, later became a well-known writer. In 1963 he was made Ambassador to Finland. He has also been Director of the United States Information Agency. In this post he was in charge of sending news about this country to all parts of the world. He has not been the only black American to be an ambassador. Clifton B. Wharton held this post in Norway for three years. He had spent most of his life in the United States Foreign Service. Dr. Mercer Cook has been ambassador to three African countries. He had taught at Howard University, and had worked at

Adam Powell worked for many reforms for the black community.

the United Nations. Mrs. Patricia Harris, who has been Ambassador to Luxembourg, was the first Negro woman to hold such a position. She has also served the United States at the United Nations. Franklin H. Williams, best known as the Ambassador to Ghana, used to work with Thurgood Marshall.

12 / *At the United Nations.* Black Americans have held many positions at the United Nations. Ralph J. Bunche was there when

it began. Until his death in 1971, Bunche was its Undersecretary for Special Political Affairs. In 1950 he won the Nobel Peace Prize. Marian Anderson was a member of the United States delegation. Edith Sampson was the first black woman to be a member of the United States Mission. Channing Tobias, a civil-rights leader, also served with the Mission. The first Negro to become a permanent member of the United States delegation was Charles H. Mahoney. James M. Nabrit, Jr., well known as president of Howard University, has been a full Ambassador to the United Nations. These and other Afro-Americans have been part of the work for peace and world understanding for which the United Nations was organized.

13 / *Adam Clayton Powell, Jr.* The best-known black member of Congress has been the late Adam Clayton Powell, Jr. He was a hero to the people of Harlem in New York City. Again and again they sent him back to Washington as their Congressman. He became one of the most powerful men in our government. Adam Clayton Powell was born in 1908. He was brought up in New York City. There his father was pastor of the world's largest Protestant congregation, Harlem's Abyssinian Baptist Church. The younger Powell became a minister too.

14 / *Into Politics.* In 1937 Adam Clayton Powell, Jr., replaced his father as pastor of the Abyssinian Baptist Church. He had already taken part in reform movements in New York City. He had worked with other Negro leaders to try to get large companies in the city to hire more black workers. He helped lead the drive to get Harlem Hospital to integrate its staff of doctors and nurses. He worked to get stores in Harlem to hire black workers. He joined with A. Philip Randolph in a drive to get New York City's electric companies to hire more black workers, and to place them in white-collar jobs as well. A "blackout boycott" was planned. Each Tuesday night the people in the city's black communities were told to use candles instead of electric lights. The success of such drives led Powell into poli-

tics. In 1941 he was elected to the New York City Council.

15 / *In Washington.* Adam Clayton Powell was then elected to Congress. He has served there since 1945, speaking for a community that is chiefly black—New York's Harlem. For years he was a lonely voice crying out for civil-rights laws. The Powell Amendment became well known. He tried again and again to keep the government from spending money for any project in which there was discrimination against a minority group. Today Powell's idea is placed in many laws passed each year. He brought a number of changes to life in Washington, D.C. He made it possible for Afro-Americans to sit in the special seats for newsmen in the Senate and House chambers. He introduced bills to end Jim Crow travel in Washington. He offered the first bill to integrate the armed services. Then, in 1960, he was made chairman of the House Committee on Education and Labor.

16 / *The Powell Case.* Powell's committee prepared many important laws. One of these raised minimum wages; others gave aid to education and helped in the war on poverty. Later some members of Congress charged Powell with questionable use of public money. In his defense, others pointed out that many white committee chairmen had spent their committee funds in similar ways, but had not been charged with wrongdoing. The House investigated the charges in 1967. It voted to refuse Powell his seat and took steps to make him repay the money he had been charged with misusing. A special election for Powell's seat was held in Harlem. Powell ran and won easily. He ran and won again

Senator Edward Brooke of Massachusetts.

in 1968. But Congress refused to seat him until 1969. Later that year the U.S. Supreme Court ruled that the House had acted improperly in barring Powell in 1967. In 1971, Charles Rengel replaced Powell as Harlem's Congressman after a close election. Powell returned to his home in Bimini where he lived until his death in 1972.

17 / *Edward W. Brooke III*. In November, 1966 an Afro-American was elected to the United States Senate for the first time since Reconstruction. His name was Edward W. Brooke. He is a Republican from Massachusetts. Edward Brooke was born in 1919 in Washington, D.C. He studied at Howard University. During World War II he was a captain in the United States Army and won an award for his work. When he returned home he studied law. He became active in politics. In 1961 the governor of Massachusetts made him chairman of the Boston Finance Commission. His work in that post made him well known all over the state. The next year he was elected state attorney general. For the next four years Edward Brooke held the highest elected state office won by any Afro-American in his lifetime. Then he was elected to the Senate.

Edward Brooke, who had not been an active member of civil-rights groups, had clear ideas about the country's needs. He soon wrote about them. He said that it was up to Congress to lead the nation to changes in the way people lived. Once the people were certain that Congress was ready to pass laws to give an equal chance to all citizens, then the problems that led to civil disorders might end. In 1968 Senator Brooke became even more widely known as he toured the country to speak for his party's candidate for President.

18 / *William L. Dawson of Illinois*. William Dawson had been a member of the House of Representatives from 1943 to 1970. His long service led to his chairmanship of the important Committee on Government Operations. Congressman Dawson is the grandson of slaves. He studied at Fisk University, where he won high honors. He was one of the first Negro officers in the Army in World War I. He studied law and settled in Chicago. He was a member of the Chicago City Council, first as a Republican and then as a Democrat. Then he went to Congress. Some people say he is one of the few Afro-Americans who are really part of the political machines that hold power in most states. They charge that he should have been more concerned with civil rights. Others pointed to his long service and his good voting record. They say that his door was always open to the people. They say a telephone call from William Dawson could get more done than several protest meetings.

19 / *President Nixon's Appointments*. Since taking office in 1969, President Richard M.

Nixon has added to the list of Afro-Americans in government by making several important appointments. James Farmer, the former CORE leader, was named Assistant Secretary of Health, Education and Welfare. The position of Assistant Secretary of Labor was given to Arthur A. Fletcher. William H. Brown was appointed to the Equal Opportunities Commission and, immediately after his swearing in, was made its chairman. It is hoped that through appointments like these, President Nixon will continue—and increase—the practice of other recent Presidents of trying to give Afro-Americans an ever greater voice in the nation's government.

20 / *More Voting Power.* Power in government comes to minority groups in our country only when their members vote. Black Americans have not yet voted in the numbers they might. Where they do vote, they can help elect people they want in office. John Conyers and Charles Cole Diggs, both from Michigan, have worked to get the people in their districts to vote. So have Robert Nix of Pennsylvania and Augustus Hawkins of California. Louis Stokes of Ohio was elected after a succeessful drive to register black voters in 1970. Twelve of these Afro-American members of Congress come from large cities to which large numbers of black people have moved. Charles Evers, brother of the slain Medgar Evers, tried to gain a seat in Congress from Mississippi in 1967. He failed. Since then he has worked at the task of getting more Afro-Americans to register to vote. This resulted in his election in 1969 as mayor of Fayette, Mississippi. Evers and other black leaders understand that only in this way can they again represent the South

in all levels of government. Meanwhile, after the 1971 elections, the number of black officeholders in the South passed the 700 mark. More voting power was beginning to have its effect!

Mississippi leader Charles Evers.

President Nixon with William H. Brown, whom he appointed head of the Equal Employment Opportunities Commission.

Understanding What You Have Read

I. REVIEWING WORD MEANINGS

Write the letter of the choice that best explains the meaning of each word.

1. **delegate** (a) Speak for the group who sent you! (b) Speak for yourself! (c) Speak for me!
2. **pollution** (a) The air is changed by this machine. (b) The water is filtered every hour. (c) The air and water are dirty.
3. **deputy** (a) He helps me. (b) He fights me. (c) He is my boss.
4. **borough** (a) Part of a country. (b) Part of a state. (c) Part of a city.
5. **agency** (a) A government debt. (b) A special law. (c) A part of a government.
6. **mission** (a) A group of delegates. (b) People at a convention. (b) Members of a legislature.
7. **white collar** (a) He's a salesman. (b) He fixes radios. (c) He's a porter.
8. **minimum** (a) No more than this! (b) Exactly like this! (c) No less than this!
9. **investigate** (a) Read the report! (b) Find out everything about this matter! (c) Write a better law!
10. **finance** (a) Dealing with law. (b) Dealing with money. (c) Dealing with poverty.

II. CHECKING IMPORTANT FACTS

Write the letter of the choice that best completes each statement.

1. A leader of the fight for civil rights in Mississippi has been (a) Senator Edward Brooke, (b) Richard Hatcher, (c) Aaron Henry.
2. Julian Bond is a political leader in (a) Illinois, (b) Georgia, (c) Missouri.

3. Adam Clayton Powell was a Congressman and a (a) lawyer, (b) minister, (c) dentist.

4. A city in Michigan with a black mayor is (a) Detroit, (b) Flint, (c) Springfield.

5. The District Commissioner of Washington, D.C., is named (a) Washington, (b) Henry, (c) Stokes.

6. A one-time leader of the N.A.A.C.P. who became mayor of Cleveland was (a) Carl Stokes, (b) Richard Hatcher, (c) William Dawson.

7. Yvonne Braithwaite, member of the California legislature, has been a leader in work to improve the lives of (a) young people, (b) soldiers and sailors, (c) farm workers.

8. Franklin H. Williams has served his country as (a) a member of Congress, (b) a Senator, (c) an ambassador.

9. Carl Rowan first gained fame as a (a) businessman, (b) lawyer, (c) writer.

10. Channing Tobias, who was a member of the United States Mission to the United Nations, had earlier been known as (a) a civil-rights leader, (b) an organizer of bus boycotts, (c) mayor of a city.

11. Adam Clayton Powell, Jr., was chairman of the Committee on (a) Government Operations, (b) Education and Labor, (c) Foreign Relations.

12. William Dawson was best known as a member of the (a) Senate, (b) House of Representatives, (c) Republican Party of Illinois.

13. John Conyers, Charles Cole Diggs, Robert Nix and Augustus Hawkins all came to Congress as representatives from (a) small states, (b) cities in the South, (c) cities in the North.

14. A black leader who failed to be elected to a seat in Congress was (a) Charles Evers, (b) Adam Clayton Powell, (c) Channing Phillips.

15. Carl B. Stokes, mayor of Cleveland, was helped in his 1967 election campaign by (a) Robert F. Kennedy, (b) Martin Luther King, Jr., (c) William Dawson.

16. The truest of these statements is that (a) Afro-American women have become active and successful in politics, (b) the N.A.A.C.P. has kept out of political campaigns, (c) CORE has gained control of big-city politics.

17. Marjorie Lawson, a leader of the National Urban League, later became a (a) city mayor, (b) member of Congress, (c) Federal judge.

18. Constance Baker Motley once held the same elected position later held by (a) Adam Clayton Powell, (b) Percy Sutton, (c) William H. Hastie.

19. Mrs. Patricia Harris was the first black woman to become (a) a judge, (b) an ambassador, (c) a United States delegate to the United Nations.

20. Ralph J. Bunche has worked in the United Nations with (a) Charles H. Mahoney, (b) Edward Brooke, (c) Walter Washington.

III. ANSWER EACH OF THESE QUESTIONS IN A SINGLE SENTENCE.

1. In what year were black political leaders first considered for President and Vice-President by the Democratic Party?

2. How did the Twenty-fourth Amendment make it easier to vote?

3. How was Walter Washington made District Commissioner of Washington, D.C.?

4. Why did Carl Stokes try to get more people to register in Cleveland?

5. How did Richard Hatcher help the idea of open housing in Gary?

6. Why did Richard Hatcher need outside help in his campaign?

7. How many women were in the Texas State Senate in 1968?

8. What jobs are held in Pennsylvania by Suzie Monroe and Sarah A. Anderson?

9. What position does Thurgood Marshall hold?

10. What jobs has Spottswood Robinson held?
11. In what way was the work done by Marian Anderson like that done by Edith Sampson?
12. Why has James M. Nabrit, Jr., been called "Mr. Ambassador"?
13. What area in what city has Adam Clayton Powell represented in Congress?
14. What change did Adam Clayton Powell bring to Harlem Hospital?
15. What is a "blackout boycott"?
16. What is the Powell Amendment?
17. What is a minimum-wage law?
18. How can a minimum-wage law fight poverty?
19. How did Edward Brooke believe civil disorders might be brought to an end?
20. Why do many black political leaders still say that registering voters is their most important task?

IV. QUESTIONS TO DISCUSS

1. With which of these positions do you agree? Why?
   a) Black voters should always vote for a black candidate, no matter what party he represents.
   b) Black voters should vote for any candidate, black or white, who will act to better the position of black people.
   c) Since white people control politics in this country, black voters should vote for the white candidate who will do the most for them.
   d) It doesn't make much difference how black people vote, for the politicians will never do much to help them.
   e) Black voters should set up their own political parties.
2. For what reasons has it taken so long to get Afro-Americans to register and vote—even in those states where there is no problem in registering? What can be done about this problem?

3. What will happen to other black political leaders if men like Carl Stokes and Richard Hatcher succeed or fail in their efforts to solve urban problems? Why, then, does the rest of the country follow events in Cleveland and Gary so carefully?

4. Adam Clayton Powell, Jr., has described himself as a radical. William Dawson has been called a "regular Democrat." Which of these two approaches to politics seems most successful? Why?

5. In 1968 Eldridge Cleaver and Dick Gregory were candidates for President. Find out what they said and did as candidates. What importance was there in their being candidates when they knew they could not be elected?

V. THINGS TO DO

1. Prepare a list of the black political leaders active in your community. What offices do they hold? What changes have they tried to bring about? How?

2. How have such new ideas as school decentralization and anti-poverty programs brought more Afro-Americans into local politics? Describe one such leader in your community. Interview him or her if possible. Report in detail to your class on this person's political plans for the future.

3. How has the growth in the number of black voters in your state affected the work of your state legislature? To prove your answer is correct, explain one or more new laws that have been passed to meet the special needs of minority groups in your state, or old laws that have been changed.

4. Prepare a short speech to be given in one of these situations:
   a) You are working to get people in Mississippi to register and vote and are visiting a family whose adults have never voted.
   b) You are speaking to a white political club in a city to which thousands of Afro-Americans have moved since 1950. You want this club to try to get black people interested in politics.

Chapter 39

MOVING AHEAD—
ROADS TO FOLLOW

Let's Discover

1. How different black people and groups want Afro-Americans to gain full citizenship and equality.
2. What actions might follow from these different paths to the future.

Words to Know

separatism	The belief that one group should remain apart from other groups.
	Black Americans who believe in separatism want to have little to do with whites.
integrationist	Believing that black and white people should work together for agreed goals, and that both groups should be equal in all respects under law.
	The N.A.A.C.P. has followed integrationist ideas and has white as well as black members.
independence	Freedom from control by others.
	Many black leaders want independence for black communities.
self-image	The picture of himself that a person carries in his mind, usually as compared with other people.
	A person who has pride and dignity will have a good self-image.
structure	The way in which something is organized or put together.
	A small number of people are at the top in the structure of American society.

459

limited	Kept from passing some set point.
	Your income will be limited if you have not completed your education.

---

1 / *The Violent Path to Equal Rights.* For most of our history civil-rights groups and black Americans used peaceful means to reach their goals. Each group might work in its own ways, but all used legal methods. They marched and picketed. They ran boycotts and demonstrations. They tried to get laws passed to improve their rights. They used the courts to stop those who tried to take away these rights. For all of this, real change was slow. Some Afro-Americans came to feel that new methods were needed to bring change.

2 / *The Road of Separatism.* Some black people want to be apart from whites. They do not mean by this the separate life that was forced by Jim Crow. What they want is a new kind of "separate *and* equal." We call their plan separatism. Their goal is to work, form friendships and live chiefly with other black people. They speak of "black control of the black community." Some, like the Black Muslims, think they should have their own "country" somewhere in North America. We do not know how many of the 24,000,000 Afro-Americans in the United States believe in it. But the idea of separatism has grown since 1960.

3 / *The Integration Road.* The largest black civil-rights groups still seem to believe in the goals with which the civil-rights movement began. They want to work for equal rights and equal treatment under law. Their way is called integration. Those who believe in it review the story of this country. They show how it grew great and rich through the hard work of many groups of people from all over the world. One of these groups was the black Africans. They had been forced to come here as slaves. Because of their slave past and white racism they have never known full equality with other Americans. But integrationists feel that equality will come. They are ready to work for it as they have in the past. They will continue to use the courts. They will try to get better laws. They will fight all forms of discrimination. They are willing to work with white people who believe in equal rights for all. They feel that their way is best. The changes they can bring, they say, will make black Americans "first-class citizens."

4 / *Hope from Africa.* We know that the black American's roots are in Africa. We know that Afro-American ancestors lost their freedom and were brought here as slaves. In time almost all of the countries in Africa also lost their freedom. Since World War II most of them have won their independence. Now that they are free they are taking great steps to build and spread their culture. These new nations are treated with respect. They are an important part of the United Nations. Afro-Americans have watched this happen. Many are proud of

BLACK POWER

Stokeley Carmichael was one of the first to call for "Black Power."

the gains made in Africa. They feel that their history here has been much like that of their "African brothers." They too were long ruled by white men. They too want the respect and sense of equality that Africans have won.

5 / *"Black Is Beautiful."* Black Americans have begun to gain more of the rights for which they have waited and fought so long. At the same time, many feel a new dignity and sense of self-worth. We call this having a good "self-image," the feeling you have of what kind of person you are. As part of this changed self-image, the words "Black

is beautiful" have grown important. This is not the "Black is better" belief of some groups. Rather it is the feeling that the time has come to throw off the old sense of being inferior that was forced on Afro-Americans in the Jim Crow world. There is at the same time a desire for independence within American life. Many black people want to run their own programs for improving schools and city life. They feel that they will not have real freedom until and unless they can control more of their daily lives.

6 / *Gaining Real Power.* Who really makes the decisions that change life in a country?

The term "power structure" has been used to describe the small number of people in a country who have great power. They are the political leaders. They are the groups who control the universities. They are the heads of the great businesses. They are the directors of giant foundations who can spend millions to bring about some desired change. They are the leaders of pressure groups. Some say that there is no power structure. They say that some are leaders and that others just follow them. But Afro-Americans have begun to speak out against those who hold great power in the country's life. They say that such men have always kept black people out of positions of power. Now a change has come. With the rise of black voting strength, black leaders are seeking

Huey Newton – leader of militants in California.

more ways to use real power. This helps explain their drive for control of schools and other services. Black leaders ask for more than just better jobs. They want more than just higher pay for black people. They want more than just equal rights. They want to be part of the power structure. This is the meaning of Black Power.

7 / *The Need for Housing.* Afro-Americans still need better housing. Most of them still live crowded in "black districts." Some of these are called ghettos. Most are slums. In many cities and towns there is still a "wall" that keeps black people from moving out of such neighborhoods. Some Negroes want to live near other black people. Others would prefer to live in integrated neighborhoods. What is important to all is the right to feel that one can live where he pleases. The open-housing law passed by Congress in 1968 followed this idea. It made it illegal to refuse to rent or sell a home or an apartment to someone because of his color or religion. Once such laws are well enforced, much of the housing problem may come to an end.

8 / *The Path of Learning.* Afro-Americans disagree on many questions. Some believe in violence, some in nonviolence. Some are separatists; others are integrationists. Yet all agree on one road to the future. That road is education. Progress and power cannot come without knowledge. Machines are doing more and more of the simple jobs people once did. A person with a limited education will have a limited life. Black parents are deeply interested in education. They know that their children must stay in school. They

agree that more black students must go on to college and beyond. They are doing so in greater numbers each year. In the colleges the presence of black students brings many changes. Large numbers of white and black young people are living and learning together, working out their differences as part of a single group.

9 / *Afro-American Studies.* The colleges are seeing young black people in a new kind of struggle. Black students have begun to demand a voice in what their colleges teach. They ask for Afro-American studies and more black professors. In some cases they even asked for "black colleges" within a university. Newspapers and television bring us the almost daily story of this newest part of Black Power in action. It has raised some new questions. What will the young people of the black community do with their increased education? Will they use it to build new paths for themselves and the nation? The story of the Afro-American's long history in the United States has not ended. Its next chapters will be written by the young men and women, black and white, who will be tomorrow's leaders.

Perhaps education will be the road to true equality and justice.

Index